THE COMPLETE BOOK OF

Christian Parenting & Child Care

THE COMPLETE BOOK OF

Christian Parenting & Child Care

A Medical & Moral Guide to Raising Happy, Healthy Children

WILLIAM SEARS, M.D.

& MARTHA SEARS, R.N.

Nashville, Tennessee

© 1997
by William Sears, M. D.
All rights reserved
Printed in the United States of America

0-8054-6198-1

Published by Broadman & Holman Publishers, Nashville, Tennessee
Acquisitions and Development Editor: Janis Whipple
Page Design: Anderson Thomas Design
Typesetting: PerfecType

Dewey Decimal Classification: 649
Subject Heading: PARENTING \ CHILDREARING
Library of Congress Card Catalog Number: 97-26143

Unless otherwise stated all Scripture citation is from the Holy Bible, New International Version, copyright © 1973, 1978, 1984 by International Bible Society. Also cited is The Message, the New Testament in Contemporary English, © 1993 by Eugene H. Peterson, published by NavPress, Colorado Springs, Colorado.

Published in association with the literary agency of Alive Communications, Inc., 1465 Kelly Johnson Blvd., Suite 320, Colorado Springs, CO 80902

Library of Congress Cataloging-in-Publication Data

Sears, William, M.D.
The complete book of Christian parenting and child care : a medical and moral guide to raising children / by William Sears, Martha Sears.
p. cm.
Includes index.
Includes bibliographical references.
ISBN 0-8054-6198-1 (pbk.)
1. Family—Religious life. 2. Parenting—Religious aspects—Christianity. 3. Child rearing—Religious aspects—Christianity. I. Sears, Martha. II. Title
BV4526.2.S433 1997
248.8'45—dc21

97-26143
CIP

1 2 3 4 5 01 00 99 98 97

OVERTON MEMORIAL LIBRARY
HERITAGE CHRISTIAN UNIVERSITY
P.O. Box HCU
Florence, Alabama 35630

Dedicated to our children

James
Robert
Peter
Hayden
Erin
Matthew
Stephen
Lauren

Sons are a heritage from the Lord,
children a reward from Him.

Psalm 127:3

Table of Contents

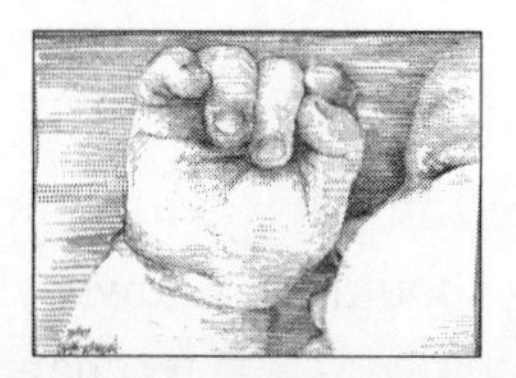

INTRODUCTION

Discerning Your **Parenting Style**

During the final months of your pregnancy or early months of parenthood, it's important to consider what parenting style you're going to adopt. Developing a parenting style means a way of caring for your baby, the mindset you're going to approach motherhood and fatherhood with, how you are going to help baby fit into the family and yourself fit into parenthood. What parenting style you choose will depend upon three main factors: your total family situation, your own basic temperament and mindset about parenthood, and the temperament of your baby. Remember, all three of these must be considered in working out the parenting style that is right for you. The important thing is it has to be right for you. This is your baby, and you are his parents. This baby does not belong to a book, the church, your doctor, your in-laws. This is your baby, and only you can work out a parenting style that works for you. We will simply give you the tools to help you work out your individual parenting style. But again, the important key is to keep working at it until it works for you.

When I (Bill) first started practice more than twenty-five years ago, it was a shock to me to realize that although I had trained in the two top pediatric hospitals in the world, I knew only about sick babies and not about parenting styles. In my early days of practice parents would come into my office and ask me questions, such as "How long should I nurse?" "Where should my baby sleep?" "How do I respond to our baby's cries?" "Will I spoil our baby?" These were not medical questions, these were parenting style questions which I was not trained to answer. What I did learn, early on in Medicine 101, was first, do no harm. So, even though I was in a position of trusted authority, I should not have been giving advice on something I knew little about, especially on such important issues as may affect the joy of a family and the outcome of the child.

I kept thinking when parents asked me these questions, *Why don't they ask an experienced mother? Why don't they pick out the mother in their church or their neighborhood who has had the most kids and whose children they like; then find out what she did? Parents are likely to get a better answer from this mother than from me.* (In fact, this is a biblical model—experienced parents teaching novices.)

I decided to follow my own advice—to learn from experienced parents in my practice. I felt like hanging a sign outside my office saying, "Dr. Bill is still in training." I would pick out the most experienced mothers and fathers in my practice, those who seemed to have a joy about their parenting, who seemed to have a handle on parenting, whose children were well disciplined, whose kids I liked. I wrote down what these parents did. They were my teachers. In fact, at the time,I was also an associate professor of pediatrics teaching residents who were about to go out into practice. I advised them: "As soon as you get out into practice, surround yourself with wise and experienced parents, and have the wisdom and humility to learn from them."

Over the next twenty-five years I wrote down what these parents (including my wife, Martha), whose children turned out well, did. Now, there was not a perfect correlation between what parents did and how their children turned out, and that's a very important point that you need to immediately learn—not to take either fully the credit or the blame for the person your child later becomes. You do your best with the talents that God has given you and with the support of the body of Christ, and the rest is up to the child and the work of the Holy Spirit. Here within these pages is what Martha and I have learned throughout twenty-five years of pediatric practice, nearly three decades of parenting eight children of our own, and in our experience counseling thousands of parents as to what works for most parents most of the time.

You will be a good parent. Many of us start our mothering and fathering careers wondering, "Will I be a good parent?" "How will my child turn out?" "Will I be able to raise a godly child?" At this point, don't immediately think of turning to books, classes, or advisors. Tune into yourself—you will realize it is comforting to know that God would not have given you a child without the built-in means to raise that child to love and serve the Lord. This would violate the concept of "Creator." God designed within every mother or father the necessary tools to parent their individual child; for example, God would not have given you a child with a temperament that you cannot handle. The key is to discover these built-in tools and use them to develop your skills according to the plan and design that God has for you and your child—it may be a different plan than your next door neighbor's or anyone else in your church. Early on in your pregnancy and your parenting realize that you must become an expert on your baby. To do so, remember to be prayerful and discerning about any advice you receive.

Let's look at how a hypothetical couple might prepare to develop their parenting style as they explore options during their first pregnancy.

A Seminar on Parenting

Barry and Susan were expecting their first child. This was one of the greatest blessings of their lives, a long wanted and long prayed for baby. They were dedicated to being godly parents and raising godly children; but, like most new parents, they weren't sure what these two commitments meant. They just knew that this was their goal. This excited couple had just finished their childbirth classes and felt they had learned so much about having a healthy pregnancy and a safe and satisfying birth that they were in the mood to take a parenting class. Fortunately, one was being offered at their church.

Now that they were thinking about parenting, not just birth, Barry and Susan began to realize there were different opinions, especially in their church, about raising godly children. Feeling a little confused, they decided to talk this idea over with their family physician, Dr. Joan, when they went for Susan's next prenatal. Dr. Joan, an experienced mother of three, was also going to be their baby's doctor.

Dr. Joan advised, "By all means, study up on parenting. I want you to become an expert on your child. Read those books I've recommended and go to as many classes as you can, but remember this is your baby and you are her parents. You must become an expert on your baby and develop your own method. No one else can have a method for your baby." *Wise counsel from someone who should know*, this couple thought.

Dr. Joan added one more piece of advice: "Remember how vulnerable you are to advice on raising a child. Because this is the most important event in your life right now, you want to do it right, and you feel God has called you to do this. This burning desire to be good parents makes you vulnerable to all kinds of advice, all promising to turn out godly parents and a godly child. No one can guarantee that. Also, remember you are vulnerable in another way, as all Christians are. Part of our belief system, our Christianity, is our submission to authority figures—and to a certain extent rightly so. We are taught from birth to obey our parents, to obey our teachers, to obey our pastors. Yet, parenting advice is often a matter of opinion. And when it comes to parenting opinions, everyone is certain that their way is the right way. Remember, nothing divides people like a difference in opinion on how to raise children. There is no one way to take care of every child. If there were, we would all be clones, children would all have the same temperaments, and this would be a dull world. There are certain basic principles of childrearing that are founded on biblical principles and supported by scientific research, experience, and plain old common sense, and I will be sure you are well grounded in these principles. Yet much of what you are going to hear in various classes is in the realm of opinion. I will help you to be discerning parents."

These expectant parents, eager to learn with open eyes and ears, attended their first class. Minutes into the class the couple realized that the class leader was more preacher than teacher. The opening statement was a powerful commentary on the sad condition of the culture in which today's parents must raise children—the permissive society, in a downward spiral, with undisciplined children who have no respect for their elders or for God. Then the point was made that God has clearly ordained that parents are to be in control of their children. The purpose of the teaching would be to show parents practical ways to do this. There was a general air of affirmation throughout the class. Most of them were thinking, *Certainly, yes, this is what we want—control. After all, it is biblical that we take charge of our children.* The leader went on to elaborate on the philosophy of how to manage a newborn. The practical point dwelt upon the most was the importance of not letting a baby get used to being picked up every time he or she cries.

The few veteran parents in the class were a bit uneasy as one said to another, "I don't know about this control parenting. Seems like it's just a way of raising babies conveniently. If only these young parents realized that it's just not that easy." One veteran raised a few objections: "But what if you have a fussy baby, a strong-willed child, or one of those babies who have high needs and a persistent personality?" The teacher had an answer for this objection: "Who's in charge, you or the baby? If you don't take control of the baby, the baby's going to take control of you." Another veteran whispered to his wife, "They're making no allowances for differences in temperament traits or personality." She agreed and added, "Nor of the different personalities of the parents." The teacher went on to add some warnings about the danger of letting the baby manipulate the parents and of not recognizing and taking into account the baby's sin nature.

Barry was beginning to like this class: "Control," "order," "being in charge," "being able to get away," "a plan," he liked that. He no longer felt lost. He had some direction, and in some ways felt empowered because now he and Susan could enter their parenting with a plan. Susan, however, was uneasy. She said to Barry, "I don't know what it is, honey, but something tells me that something's not quite right here. I honestly can't imagine letting our baby cry like that."

"Oh, you're just being emotional. That happens to all pregnant women whose hormones are running so high. Remember, honey, how the teacher warned us that mothers need to react out of logic and order, not emotion, and that I might need to insist on that as your husband?"

Susan shared her misgivings with Dr. Joan at her check-up later that week. "It's important to listen to those 'gut feelings.' You'll be having them more and more now that you're becoming a mother. Mother's intuition is a God-given way for you to develop a sense of what's right for your baby," said Dr. Joan. "It would be hard to ignore," confided Susan, "except that Barry seems so convinced that what the leader says is right. After all, he's my husband and I need to submit to his decisions." Dr. Joan reassured Susan they would talk some more after the next class and asked her to have Barry come along. Her parting comment was, "You will find some useful information in every class, but remember to be discerning."

The next class began with the teacher reiterating the control issue. "In this class you're going to learn some practical ways of how to be in control." Barry's attentiveness picked up. That's what all the new parents wanted, practical ways of taking charge of their babies. The teacher asked for a show of hands: "Do you want to control your baby, or do you want your baby to control you?" The show of hands was unanimously in favor of parents controlling baby. The teacher went on, "One of the earliest ways you learn to control your baby, and the baby learns there is a plan and you are in charge, is to decide when you will feed him. And for a newborn, you start with every three hours." Many of the first-time mothers liked this approach because they all were wondering, "How will I know when my baby is hungry?" A few others weren't comfortable with seeing how some of their friends seemed to spend their days—and nights—catering to their babies' demands. To most, this was beginning to sound like the parenting style they wanted to follow.

The veterans in the class became increasingly uneasy. One whispered to another, "I wonder how many babies they have." The other whispered back, "You'd think the baby would have some say in the matter." The novice parents seemed to be relieved, however, since they had no idea how often babies should eat. This gave them a plan, rules. It put them in charge. The idea that a tiny baby could know when he or she was hungry better than the parents doing the feeding was not even open for discussion. Barry liked the idea of having a set feeding schedule. It would be easier on them. They could plan their day. Susan wouldn't be controlled by the baby, and it would put some order in their day. This was very important to him.

Susan had the same uneasy feelings that she did about the control issue, but she couldn't quite put her finger on why this didn't feel right to her, it just didn't. They had spent a lot of time researching the feeding issue and had decided that they were going to feed their baby the milk designed by God and not by man. Susan said, "Let's bounce this off Dr. Joan; after all, she's going to be our baby's doctor, and she's fed lots of babies and advised a lot of breastfeeding mothers."

Dr. Joan sighed when they related this new information. "Barry, what do you do when you're hungry?"

"I eat."

"What's the first thing you do when you're hungry, look at your watch?"

"No," Barry responded, "I get something to eat if it's convenient for me."

"Suppose the government decided that we're going to take charge of feeding everyone in the country, and you can only feed on a schedule that we determine, that we know best how you need to be fed."

Barry laughed, "Nonsense. I wouldn't go along with that."

"Well, that's what is being advised for your baby."

"Yes, but we want to be in charge."

"But who is the hungry person, you or the baby? Do you think that the Creator of the universe would not have designed the tiniest of human beings to know when they are hungry? Don't even the sunflowers turn to the sun when they need nourishment, and isn't your baby more intricately designed than the flowers?" Dr. Joan went on, "You are going to be spending a lot of time feeding your infant during the first year, so you might as well enjoy it. Feeding is such an individual issue. We can't know until your baby is born what his or her style will be. Some babies require short, frequent feeds; others like longer feeds, spaced farther apart. The important thing is to come up with an approach to feeding a baby that fits the nutritional and comforting needs of baby without excessively draining the mother. I see, Susan, from your chart that you have chosen to breastfeed."

Barry piped up, "Yes, we are going to breastfeed."

"I'm glad you said 'we,' Barry," Dr. Joan said, "because as we will discuss later, fathers play an important role in 'feeding' the mother so she can better feed the baby. Scheduled feeding works fairly well for formula-fed babies, but for breastfed babies it is usually not a good idea. Many breastfeeding mothers have serious problems with their milk supply when a schedule is followed so closely.

"It sounds like whoever developed this system doesn't understand mothers, babies, or, quite frankly, the nature of breast milk. Breast milk, unlike formula, is digested very rapidly," Dr. Joan continued. "In fact, it can empty from the baby's stomach within twenty minutes. There are a lot of factors that determine when a baby gets hungry again. For example, babies go through periodic growth spurts where they marathon nurse—they want to eat every couple hours for a few days. They are simply doing what their God-given biology tells them they need to do to thrive. This causes the milk supply to get boosted to a higher level. So, Susan, your baby may need to nurse more often than every three hours, though some babies do fine on that schedule. We'll have to wait and see."

The next class began with another control issue—crying. The teacher warned parents against letting their baby's cries manipulate them; they needed to be in charge and teach their baby that they were not going to let his cries control them. Two veteran moms turned to each other and one said, "I can see this would really appeal to new parents." The other reminded her that these were just young, inexperienced parents trying to learn what's best for the baby.

The teacher went on to explain, "If you don't pick up your baby every time he cries, he will stop crying and will become a 'good baby.'" The veterans noticed the novices nodding with approval. After all, doesn't everyone want a good baby?

Finally, one of the veterans protested, "This is beginning to sound too harsh." The teacher backed off a bit, "Of course, you should pick your baby up if, in your judgment, baby seems to be hurting, in pain, or really upset. But if you know your baby has just been fed, is not sick, is not hurting, and seems to have no reason to be crying, you may have to harden your heart a bit initially, but you'll get used to it." The novices again nodded approvingly because they really didn't know how to handle the cries of a baby and this gave them a plan. Barry liked this approach; as before, Susan felt uneasy. "Well, looks like we'll have to run this one by Dr. Joan too."

"Let 'em cry it out; that old line again," Dr. Joan lamented. "You know, that was around thirty years ago when I began medical school. Didn't work then, doesn't work now. I thought that philosophy had died out, but I guess it's coming back again."

"Sure sounded convenient," Barry persisted.

"I don't know if I can do it," Susan revealed. "I've always had a tender heart for babies. I can't stand to let them cry."

Barry objected, "I'm not going to let that baby run our lives."

"Sounds like you both are really getting deep into this class," observed Dr. Joan. "I'm going to have you consult a friend of mine, a developmental specialist who is also a Christian, about this issue of infant cries. Dr. Johnson is a father of four himself. He is a professor of pediatrics at one of the local universities and has spent years researching the crying issue. I think you would profit from what he has to say."

Dr. Johnson had a learned yet grandfatherly demeanor, and immediately both Barry and Susan felt in the presence of someone who really knew his stuff. Dr. Johnson said, "Crying it out—there's probably more difference of opinion on this issue than any in parenting. It's bound to confuse new parents; not even all professionals agree. And certainly I'm not going to make up your mind for you. All I'm going to do is present the facts, to teach you something about the signal value of the infant's cry, and you can make up your own mind."

"Where do you get your information?" Barry, ever the inquisitive physicist, respectfully prodded.

"Actually, Barry, there are volumes written about the signal value of the infant's cry. Researchers have studied the infant cry, and even more importantly, its effects on the mother, and why an infant's cries will affect you and Susan differently."

Dr. Johnson went on to explain, "A baby's cry is a baby's language, designed for the survival of the baby and the development of a mother. It's the only way babies have of communicating their needs. Think of your baby's cries as his form of communication. The key is to learn how to listen."

"But I don't want our baby to manipulate us," Barry interjected.

"Tiny babies don't manipulate, they communicate," Dr. Johnson corrected.

"Okay, convince me!" Barry challenged.

Dr. Johnson proceeded, "Not only is a baby's cry a unique signal, your baby's cry will do something to you, Susan. Suppose we were to take you into a laboratory and wire you up with measuring devices to see what happens to your physiology when your baby cries. We would see that the blood flow to your breasts would increase, your heart rate would go up, the hormones in your system would increase, and you would have a biological urge to pick up and nurse and comfort your baby. The response of mothers to their baby's cries has been well studied. To make a long story short, Susan, you are biologically wired—and I believe God designed it that way—for you to give a nurturing response to your baby when she cries, not to restrain yourself. The restraint philosophy goes against what we scientifically know about a baby's cries."

"I don't trust behavioral science," Barry objected.

"Some Christians don't," Dr. Johnson acknowledged, "and science is not always right. But sometimes the distrust of science is simply a way of not wanting to acknowledge anything that might invalidate one's unresearched opinions. I've found this particular research to be valid." Dr. Johnson went on, "Susan, no one in the whole world should ever advise you to let your baby cry it out. No one else is biologically wired to your baby. It's easy for someone else to tell you to let your baby cry because nothing happens to their physiology when your baby cries."

"Something just dawned on me," Susan interrupted, "What does the *it* mean in the 'cry it out' advice?"

"Ah," Dr. Johnson picked up on her insight, "you've just put your finger on the weak point of this philosophy. The 'controllers,' as I call them, feel 'it' is a habit, a manipulation, a tool to get at parents. I don't believe this. That is placing adult values on tiny babies. One of the hardest decisions for new parents to make is whether a baby's cry is a need or a habit. And many times you won't know. Part of your maturity as a parent is learning to tell the difference. In the early months, to be on the safe side, consider the cry a need and give a nurturant response according to your God-given mother's instinct. In time, you will know when to pick up your baby, when to put your baby down, when to give a quick response, when to let baby handle it, and when to let baby fuss a bit. Certainly, you don't have to pick up a seven-month-old baby as quickly as you do a seven-day-old baby. That is a cue-response network that you and your baby have to work out."

"But I don't want a clingy, whiny baby," Barry protested.

"No one does," agreed Dr. Johnson. "Barry, this cry-it-out theory has been well researched. It may comfort you to know that when the babies of nurturant responders were compared with those whose mothers held back, those babies whose mothers gave an appropriate and nurturant response to their babies' cries actually learned to cry less. The babies who were insecure and didn't know whether they were going to get picked up or not, and didn't know what response they were going to get from moment to moment and from hour to hour were the ones that became clingy and whiny; or they simply shut down, clammed up, and didn't bother anyone. I don't think that's what you want."

Dr. Johnson now used a more serious, but sincere, tone, "Susan, how do babies' cries affect you now?"

"I can't stand to hear a baby cry. I just want to pick up one as soon as I hear it."

"Good," Dr. Johnson quickly added. "A cry is supposed to bother the mother. You are supposed to be sensitive to your baby's cries. In fact, when a mother says to me, 'My baby's cry doesn't bother me,' I worry that distance has developed between that mother and baby. The mother may have desensitized herself to the cries of her baby. Let me tell you a story that happened to me one day. I was counseling a mother because she wasn't getting a handle on parenting. She and her one-month-old baby were sitting in my office when baby started to cry. Baby kept crying, and the cries escalated. Mother seemed oblivious to her baby's cry. The cries were bothering me and the baby wasn't even mine. I finally said, 'Carol, it's okay, pick up your baby. We can continue our conversation later.' The mother kept looking at me instead of baby and said, 'No, it's not time.' I realized then why she was there in my office in the first place. I said, 'Carol, where did you hear that?' and she told me it was at a parenting class at her church. I believed there was a problem. This mother had become desensitized to her God-given signals, and it is insensitivity that gets a new mother in trouble. She was starting her parenting career at a distance with her baby, yet she didn't realize it. She actually thought she was doing the right thing because her baby's cries weren't getting to her. It took a few months to get her and her baby reconnected, but now she is a much more sensitive mother and person.

"Try starting your mothering career responding to your baby's cry from your heart, and in time you will work out a communication system that works for you, as you trust your response and baby trusts it too. You will learn to respond *appropriately*; you will know when to pick your baby up and when to put her down. This will require that you and baby keep working at a communication system until you find one that works for the both of you," continued Dr. Johnson. "You will also discover that you, Susan, are more closely attuned to your baby's moment-by-moment needs in his early life than Barry is. This is part of God's design in the make-up of a mother's physiology. A wise father will appreciate the unique ability mothers have to discern their babies' needs. When fathers ask me to comment on a situation involving a difference of opinion on baby care, I tell them that this is one area where mother usually knows best."

Barry and Susan both thought that Dr. Johnson made good sense. They left—Barry had a lot of thinking to do, and Susan was feeling more confident in her ability to understand what babies need.

The next class was about training babies to sleep through the night, and it seemed to be one of the most popular classes. The teacher opened with a bit of a review, "There are three areas in which you must be in control: baby's eating, baby's crying, and baby's sleeping," and he went on to remind the couples about seeing their friends drained from the nighttime feeding demands of their babies. "This is unnecessary and avoidable. You can train your eight-week-old baby to sleep through the night." Like an election-year promise, the novices embraced this night training; the veterans were skeptical, but this was a real selling point for the class. As soon as the novices heard the promise of nocturnal bliss, many of them were won over to this method. "Be sure your baby is well fed, changed, not sick, and then let him cry, perhaps checking on him occasionally. Soon he'll be sleeping through the night. Now, you new moms may have to harden your hearts a bit because you're going to want to go to your baby, but don't give in. If you do go in, your baby simply learns that if he keeps crying, he can control you and get his way. Also, don't rock or nurse your baby to sleep, otherwise he'll get used to this way of going to sleep and will need rocking or nursing to get back to sleep. He needs to learn to go to sleep on his own."

The dads particularly liked this advice. They had heard about little "nighttime tyrants" that had cranky, tired moms all day, and they were not about to let this happen to their wives and in their families.

"How are you parenting experts-to-be getting along in your class?" Dr. Joan inquired.

"Last week we learned how to train our baby to sleep through the night," Barry said happily.

"Susan and Barry," Dr. Joan said earnestly, more in her mother voice than doctor voice, "let me warn you against such easy, quick-fix methods. There is no short and easy road to parenting, though, admittedly, some babies are easier to care for than others."

Dr. Joan went on, "What's important to you? Are you in this for the short or the long haul? You may sleep easier now, but will you sleep better later? The important thing is to create a healthy sleep attitude in your baby, that your child grows up regarding sleep as a pleasant state to enter and not a fearful state to remain in. Simply letting a baby cry until he falls asleep is an effective way to teach him that no one is there for him when he needs help. Studies suggest that though a baby may be taught to sleep through the night, the deeper lesson of no one helping has serious, long-term side effects on psychological development."

"Then why is the 'let them cry themselves to sleep' and 'let them cry it out' advice so popular?" Barry asked.

"Because it's quick advice, easy to give," Dr. Joan admitted. "This philosophy can be found in several sleep-training books written for parents who want to train their babies to sleep all the way through the night. In my early years of practice, I used to give the same advice; that is, before I had children of my own and when I didn't have the time or the knowledge to give couples better advice. The let-them-cry-it-out advice for any infant behavior is unfair to the parents and unfair to baby. It assumes that baby is crying simply to be manipulative or controlling, which is not true. It also keeps you from working at finding a reason why your baby is waking up and why your baby is crying. Letting him cry it out teaches him that his cries have no value. And naturally some babies do stop crying and eventually learn to sleep. Throughout the years, I've had babies in my practice whose well-meaning parents let them cry it out, but the babies kept crying. Once we considered the cry as a signal to be evaluated rather than a problem or behavior to be broken, we discovered that there were medical reasons why these babies woke up. I would have missed these medical problems had I simply advised the parents to persist in letting them cry it out—which few parents can do anyway. What are you supposed to do, Susan, while your baby is crying off to sleep? Plug your ears? Go for a walk? You are not biologically wired to do that. I'm glad that in my early days most of the parents to whom I gave that advice didn't follow it. There are more humane and intuitive ways to help your baby sleep longer and develop healthy sleeping habits. Let's wait and see how your baby naturally sleeps. Some lucky babies and their parents are born sleepers; others do need a bit of nighttime training."

Susan had a new question. "I've read that it's good to sleep with babies, at least during the early months, but I was afraid to ask that question in our class for fear they would think I'm some sort of radical. Is sleeping with our baby okay?"

"Certainly," Dr. Joan reassured. "Most of the world sleeps with their babies. There is no right or wrong place for your baby to sleep. Whatever sleeping arrangement gets all family members the best sleep is the right arrangement for you. There is a whole chapter on sharing sleep, and a discussion of certain essentials that make the practice safe, in that book I recommended."

The next class was on what the Bible has to say about childrearing, and the teacher opened with, "This is the right way . . ." Immediately the novices perked up their ears at this term; after all, this is what they came to the class for. They truly wanted to be godly parents. The veterans, however, continued to be skeptical, as one leaned over to the other and said, "Just how can any one person know what is the right way for everyone?" The class time was devoted to examining various verses of Scripture to draw out conclusions about the right way to care for a baby. Barry and Susan were impressed that so much Scripture was studied and applied.

"What did you learn this week?" Dr. Joan asked Barry and Susan, who had by now become her most interesting parents-to-be.

"We learned what the Bible says about the right way to take care of babies," Barry triumphantly volunteered. Skeptically, Dr. Joan interjected, "Wish I knew exactly what that is. I'm not sure that God has only one way for every family. We are all different, you know, as are your children. Maybe there is a way for you, a way for me, and an individual way for everyone in the class. I want you to discover what God wants for you, and not strictly follow anyone else's method."

As usual, Dr. Joan was not being judgmental, she was instructing these parents to be cautious and to think through any advice they hear. Dr. Joan inquired, "For example, what does the Bible say when it comes to crying?"

"The teacher reminded us that we all have a sin nature, even our babies. So, God does not always give us what we ask for, because He has a greater good in mind. He even let His Son cry out on the cross and didn't rescue Him from it."

"Hmmm! I'm not a biblical scholar, but this sounds a bit questionable. I'd like you to talk to my friend, Pastor Paul, and run that by him. I'll say this though: that one time that God did not respond to Jesus was the only time, because it was for the purpose of our salvation. God's constant response to Jesus throughout His life is surely the model we are to follow."

Pastor Paul was respected by his congregation not only for his knowledge of the

Bible but also for his cautious openness to new ideas. "Dr. Joan tells me you're about to become new parents, and naturally want to be godly parents and raise godly children. How can I help you?"

"We're confused," Barry admitted. "We are hearing various opinions about what is God's design for parenting. And these differences of opinion are even dividing our friends."

"It's dividing my church too," Pastor Paul admitted. "I've been giving that some thought lately and here's what I've found. First of all, the Bible is not clear or dogmatic on many of the day-to-day issues of baby-care. Remember, in biblical teaching, like in every profession, sometimes we are guilty of manipulating God's Word to support our own bias. This is a natural human weakness that all teachers have to guard against, especially those who are teaching vulnerable new parents and new Christians about how to care for babies. What concerns you most about the advice you've been hearing?" Pastor Paul asked.

"I guess it's the let-baby-cry-it-out advice," Susan volunteered. "It seems that much of the controlling style of parenting boils down to that, and I don't think I'm going to be able to let my baby cry."

"In times of need when you cry out to God, what do you expect?" asked Pastor Paul.

"Of course, I expect Him to respond," said Barry.

Susan had more to say. "The Bible says that God will never leave me or forsake me. Even when He says 'no' or 'wait' to what I'm asking for, I know He's there for me, and that is very comforting. I know I won't give my baby everything he wants either, but I surely want to be there for him when he cries."

"And what would you think of God if He didn't seem to hear you or respond?" asked Pastor Paul.

"I wouldn't trust Him. It's not what I expect," said Susan.

"I guess it would cause me to lower my expectations," responded Barry. "It's important to me to know that God hears my prayers and responds to me."

"Do you think you're controlling God if you expect a response to your cries?" asked Pastor Paul.

"Of course not," said Barry.

"Neither is your baby controlling you when you listen to his cries," said Pastor Paul. "In fact, the Bible is clear that God hears our prayers. Psalm 34:17 says, 'The righteous cry out, and the LORD hears them; he delivers them from all their troubles.' Psalm 55:17 says, 'Evening, morning and noon I cry out in distress, and he hears my voice.' Psalm

145:18 says, 'The Lord is near to all who call on him. To all who call on him in truth.'

"I suggest that you think about your relationship with God and the biblical passages that talk about it. Think about the meaning of 'Creator.' Your heavenly Father would not have given you a child without the built-in means to care for him. It sounds like you just need to discover those means. The Bible tells us clearly to 'train up a child in the way he should go,' and this is a passage with a promise—'and when he is old he will not depart from it.' This is a good investment, but I believe, as do most biblical scholars, that each parent has to discover which way their individual child should go. Pastor Chuck Swindoll calls this discovering a child's individual bent. Pray to develop a parenting style for you and your family. Be discerning before you develop anyone else's method for taking care of your baby. I agree with Dr. Joan, I believe that God wants you to develop your own method for your baby. It's good to go to a variety of classes and talk to a lot of parents—parents who enjoy their children. Take what seems to fit your own temperament and your desire for parenting. Keep trying until you discover what that is and you will then find out how to train up *your* child in the way *he* should go."

Barry and Susan left Pastor Paul's office concluding that the last word in parenting, at least for themselves and their child, would be found not in any class, any book, or any person. It would be eventually found in themselves, through the Holy Spirit's leading. The wisest thing for them to do would be to surround themselves with wise and experienced parents and consultants, and then selectively glean and add practical tips to their own repertoire of parenting tools, which can only be developed on the job, working with their child. They realized the importance of working at a style of parenting until they find what works for them, and that they would have to be more discerning.

Susan and Barry went back to their reliable standby for parenting advice, Dr. Joan. "You've been exposed to so much conflicting advice, maybe you should consult the real experts—godly moms and dads who have successfully parented a lot of children with various personalities—and whose kids you would like. Here are some names and phone numbers for you. Talk to these parents about what they did and see what you can learn, again keeping in mind that what works for one family and one child may not work for you or for each one of your children."

So Barry and Susan made their rounds from family to family in search of the perfect parenting style. The first home they visited was the home of Jason and Sarah and their three children. They watched Sarah mother her four-month-old baby, Andrew. "I carry Andrew in a sling most of the day. This makes life easier for me and I don't feel so tied down since I can go anywhere with him."

"What do you do if he cries," inquired Barry, curiously watching how mother and her "sling baby" related.

"Oh, he doesn't cry very much; he doesn't need to. And why should he? Since he's right with me in the sling, I can read him so well. I know when he needs to nurse. I know when he needs to sleep. I know when he needs playtime. I know when he needs downtime. He doesn't have to cry to let me know what he needs."

Immediately, Susan's antennae went up. "I never thought of that before, setting the stage so baby doesn't need to cry. Now that appeals to me much more than just letting him cry."

"It's a lot easier on the ears and the nerves too," Sarah added.

"Don't you feel you're spoiling him a bit," Barry wondered.

"Not at all," Sarah responded. "I'm training him that he doesn't need to cry. I'm training him to fit into my day. And I feel it's good for him to be in my arms. You know I don't believe that babies learn much lying on their back in a crib most of the day, or sitting in a playpen. I'm a busy person, and I believe that babies learn a lot in the arms of a busy mother. I don't look upon it as control or who's in charge of whom. Obviously, I'm in charge. I'm his mother and he knows that. I can choose when to pick him up and when to put him down. Instead of spoiling, I prefer to think of it as being in harmony with each other. Because we're with each other so much, I've gotten to know his cues, and I can read them pretty well. That certainly makes life easier for me. With my first two children I adopted a more restrained style of parenting because we didn't know better then. I didn't really feel that close to my babies and felt insecure because I couldn't read their cues, even though I had a plan for their day. This really bothered me. That's when I felt I had a lot less control. I really couldn't trust myself to read my baby, nor could I trust my baby to know how to tell me what she needed. It took us many, many months to really get in sync with one another. Once I followed my own heart and listened to what the heart of my baby was needing, we both got along much better. I read something in the Bible a while back that made me feel even better about keeping my baby so close to me. It's in Isaiah 49:16. It says, 'See, I have engraved you on the palms of my hands.' That's how close God keeps me!"

"Sling babies! I've got to run that by Dr. Joan," decided Susan.

"Oh yes," Dr. Joan said excitedly, "that's called babywearing—an age-old concept in caring for babies. It's nothing new, you know. For centuries mothers have been carrying babies in slings. It's beginning to be a lot more common in our country."

"But I thought it was simply to keep babies safe from predators and other dangers in primitive cultures," Barry said.

"There are many important reasons why babies need to be near their mothers," Dr. Joan said. "But I think mothers the world over have simply learned that carried babies cry less, and a baby who fusses less is more fun to be with. In fact, new research proves what insightful mothers have long known — that babywearing is good for their babies and makes life easier for themselves."

"But won't that make the babies too dependent?" Barry wondered.

"Barry, there are several things I want you to file away as unhelpful parenting advice. Those are: fear of manipulation, fear of spoiling, fear of dependency. How many parents, once their baby is grown, have ever said they regret holding their baby too much?"

Barry and Susan also visited the home of Lisa and Matt, parents of two young children, including a newborn baby, Emily. Lisa had adopted a more restrained style of parenting and was working hard at getting Emily on a predictable schedule. She would feed her at certain times of the day, put her down to sleep at certain times, and wasn't in a hurry to pick her up when she fussed. In some ways Emily's cries bothered Susan (and even Barry), but didn't seem to bother Lisa.

Susan asked, "Don't her cries bother you?"

Lisa responded, "I know what I need for my well-being. I need some order in my life. And, I don't want to cater to her every whim. I also think it's best for her. If she really needs to be picked up and held, certainly I do it. I'm at a stage of my life right now where I need her to know that there is a daily plan for her care."

"Different," Barry wondered, "but it seems to be working for her. The mother seems happy and the baby seems none the worse for wear."

Barry and Susan reported what they had observed to Dr. Joan. She summed up for them: "The important thing is that these styles of parenting seem to be working for both mothers. One mother is not better than the other because she breastfeeds and the other bottlefeeds, or one carries her baby more than the other, or one responds to baby's cry quicker than another. In fact, you can learn a very important lesson in parenting from Lisa — every parent must work out a style of caring for their baby that works for them and takes into account their own well-being. One of the important things that I want both of you to learn is that what your baby needs most is a happy, rested mother. When you come in for your well-baby checks, the first question I'm going to ask is "How are *you* doing?" because I know if you are doing well, baby will get along just fine."

Barry picked up on this sage advice, "It seems to be a question of balance and different strokes for different folks."

"Exactly! It is a question of balance. Now, as your family doctor and your advisor, I'm not going to play the politically correct game of saying 'whatever feels good, do it' and 'whatever you want to do with baby is going to be okay,' because there are some basic principles of babycare that I feel strongly about. But in general, it is a question of balance and it is a question of different styles for different families, and even different babies in the same family."

The Rest of Your Story

Now that you've seen an example of how an expectant couple needs to be discerning in developing their own parenting style, we will devote the remainder of this book to giving you the tools to become your own expert on your own baby. You will notice that these are starter tips, a way of starting out with your baby, a way of becoming your own baby expert. After using these basic starter tools for a while, you will then branch out and develop your own style of caring in the way that works for you. But always remember: this must be your style for your family and baby, regardless of the advice from any authority figure around you, the prevailing style of the neighborhood, the prevailing style in your church, or any childbirth class. Study your baby. Read your baby. This is *your* baby, and *you* are his mother and his father.

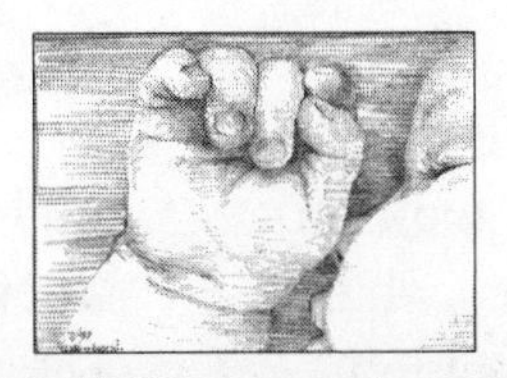

CHAPTER ONE

Laying the **Foundation**

"We are going to have a baby!" These words will change your lives forever. And this is good. Ranked right up there with your decision to be a Christian and the decision to marry, the adventure of becoming parents is equally as life changing; and it will challenge you to incredible personal growth. The commitment that mothers and fathers make to the young ones put in their care can only be termed "God inspired." Men and women become cocreators with the heavenly Father, engaging in the work of adding one healthy, loving child to society. No small task for mere humans, and we need all the help we can get. This chapter explains the three steps you must take to receive this help: (1) commitment to a God-centered life; (2) commitment to the husband-wife relationship; and (3) commitment to God's design for parents.

COMMITMENT TO A GOD-CENTERED LIFE

The first and most important step toward successful Christian parenting is to commit yourself wholeheartedly to God. The most important ingredient in any relationship is commitment. The more you are committed to a relationship, the deeper that relationship will be. The relationship between parent and child is the strongest of all human bonds. One of the joys of working over the years in pediatric practice is seeing how strongly most parents are committed to their children. Yet for many parents, commitment to God is a concept they struggle with because they have never taken the time to get to know Him. How can they know someone they have never met?

The good news is that God took on human form and lived among us, which means He was able to show Himself to us, show us how to live, and show us how to be radically committed to Him as our Lord and Savior. Knowledge of a person helps the commitment to that person. This was illustrated very simply by our daughter, Hayden, who said one day at the tender age of four, "The reason children love their mommy and daddy more than God is because they know Mommy and Daddy better than God." Our job as parents is to reflect God to our children so they will want to know and love Him.

God anticipated the difficulty parents would have making a full commitment to Him; He knew that we would need help knowing and loving Him and caring for our children according to His plan. For this reason, He has promised to help us, to hear our prayers, and to support us with His love. He has also given us specific details of what He wants and what we should do in His Word. Deuteronomy 6:5–9 sums up His plan for committed parents:

> *Love the LORD your God with all your heart and with all your soul and with all your strength. These commandments that I give you today are to be upon your hearts. Impress them on your children. Talk about them when you sit at your house and when you walk along the road, when you lie down and when you get up. Tie them as symbols on your hands and bind them on your foreheads. Write them on the doorframes of your houses and on your gates.*

The Bible is God's timeless handbook for parents. It is the inspired Word of God talking to us through the men He chose to write His book. In it God promises that He will reward our personal commitment to Jesus as Lord and Savior. "I am the Vine, you are the branches. When you're joined with me and I with you, the relation intimate and organic, the harvest is sure to be abundant. Separated, you can't produce a thing" (John 15:5, *The Message*).

Having committed yourselves to God and to your children, you must examine more specifically what He expects of you as parents. Besides the instruction to love God wholeheartedly and to diligently teach your children God's commandments, there are other specifics:

- To fear Him (Deut. 10:12): "What does the Lord your God ask of you but to fear the Lord your God. . . ."
- To walk in His ways and serve Him (Deut. 10:12): ". . . to walk in all his ways, to love him, to serve the Lord your God with all your heart and with all your soul."

- To abide by what He says (Deut. 10:13): "And to observe the Lord's commands and decrees that I am giving you today for your own good?"

God makes it clear that before you can instruct your children, you must understand His Word yourselves. You can impart these concepts to your children only if the knowledge, love, and fear of God is the first priority in your own life.

To Love God

It is significant that God's first message to parents in this passage from Deuteronomy is to love Him. This message occurs frequently in the Old and New Testaments. In any person-to-person relationship where there is genuine love, all else automatically follows.

There are three Greek words for love: *eros*, meaning sexual love; *phileo*, meaning demonstrated natural affection; and *agape*, meaning unconditional love. Most of the time when the word *love* is mentioned in the Bible's Greek text, it is the word *agape*, which is the love God expects from Christians. Agape love takes you out of your preoccupation with yourself and into a commitment toward others. The word *phileo* reminds us that love must be demonstrated and experienced in our day-to-day lives. We show our love for God in our daily lives, in praise and worship, and in our stewardship of His gifts. We experience God's love for us when we turn our hearts and minds toward Him and receive His love. We express our love to a child in ways that he or she can experience, through the things we say and do for that child every day. The best way for a child to learn agape and phileo love is to experience it from you as parents, and to see it between you as a couple and also between you and God.

Before reading any further, take a few minutes to dwell upon your commitment to God as the foundation for your parenting. Consider God's commitment to you in John 3:16: "For God so loved the world that he gave his one and only Son, that whoever believes in him shall not perish but have eternal life."

To Fear the Lord

The concepts of love and fear coexist inseparably throughout the Bible. The term *fear* in the Bible implies an awesome respect for the power and wisdom of God. In the Book of Proverbs, Solomon said, "The fear of the LORD is the beginning of knowledge" (Prov. 1:7). When we think about this concept of the fear of the Lord, we think of the awesome wonder of God's plan for us and His design for parents and children. We also consider that we are accountable to God in caring for our children according to His plan. Always keep this respect for God's plan and this concept of accountability in mind. Dwell upon

HELP!! I'M A SINGLE PARENT

Being a single parent* is difficult, but it is certainly not unusual. Approximately one out of every two children will spend some part of their childhood in a household with only one parent. Our prayers are with mothers who, by choice or by circumstance, have to rear their children without a husband. Here are some tips on how you can care for your children, while having some time left over to care for yourself.

Get support from your church. There was a time when churches did not support divorced parents as much as they did widowed parents. Yet, you will find that most churches have support groups for all single parents, whether by divorce or by the death of a spouse. The Bible contains clear instructions that churches and Christian homes should act as extended families to the single parent and the children of single-parented households: "He defends the cause of the fatherless and the widow, and loves the alien, giving him food and clothing" (Deut. 10:18); "At the end of every three years bring all the tithes of that year's produce and store it in your towns, . . . and the fatherless and the widows who live in your towns may come and eat and be satisfied. . . ." (Deut. 14:28–29); "The LORD watches over the alien . . . and sustains the fatherless and the widow" (Ps. 146:9); and "Religion that God our Father accepts as pure and faultless is this: to look after orphans and widows in their distress. . . ." (James 1:27). The church can help children from single-parent families by taking an active part in their spiritual training. How a child handles a loss or difficult circumstances depends on the support received from the community. The church family can bring a child closer to God and surround him with Christian models and persons of significance.

Get connected to your child. Since you do not have the help of a mate to give you some relief from middle-of-the-night infant feedings or for toddler discipline problems, it's helpful for you to choose the style of parenting that helps you better know your child, be able to read your child's behavior more sensitively, and respond to your child's needs more intuitively. The style of attachment parenting (discussed on p. 34) is especially valuable for single mothers. Yet, you may find you are not able to do all the elements of attachment parenting all the time. You will feel stretched as you juggle the economic realities of carrying on a job outside the home and trying to be a mother to your children inside the home, while at the same time having enough of a social life to meet your own needs. This is why the more connected you are to your infant, the easier it will be for you to make the many discipline decisions that arise when your child is a

HELP!! I'M A SINGLE PARENT (CONT.)

toddler and preschooler. Keep working at a style of parenting with one of your goals being that you do whatever you need to do to like living with your child.

Reserve time for yourself. During our years of counseling thousands of parents, we have found that the happiest families—whether single-parent or not—have mothers who nurture themselves in addition to nurturing their children. Single moms are especially prone to "martyr mothering," yet this sets you up for burn-out as a mother, and as a person. When you feel guilty wondering if you are doing enough for your child, paste up this motto on your refrigerator:

What My Child Needs Most Is a Happy Mother

Involve your child in your work. One of the most challenging juggling acts single mothers have is juggling their job outside the home (which you will need for financial and personal satisfaction) and their job as a parent. As often as possible, involve your child in your job. Occasionally, take your child to work so she has the chance to see what Mommy does when she's away from home. If possible, seek employment that allows you the flexibility of doing work within your home or involving your child in your job. (See chapter 7: "Going Back to Work?" for more suggestions.)

Discipline your child. A piece of advice we give to all parents is: develop whatever style of parenting helps you to like living with your child. Double this for single parents. It's easy for discipline and household routines to become disorganized in single-parent homes. Yet, the realistic fact of life is that you actually need more structure and more organization if you are a single parent. When parenting solo, you will need to run a tighter ship. Give your children extra responsibilities, not so much to cause them to be angry about growing up in a single-family home, but just enough jobs around the house to help the family run more smoothly.

Both of us spent most of our childhoods being raised by a single parent—Martha due to the death of her father, and Bill due to divorce. Both of our mothers were helped by their parents. We were raised in the homes of our grandparents, and our mothers were employed outside the home. What we remember most about the way we grew up is that our mothers did the best they could in a less than ideal family situation. That's all your children will ever expect of you.

*Even though there are many single-parenting family situations, we are limiting our discussion to single mothers.

PERSONS OF SIGNIFICANCE

It is important to help a child compensate for the loss of a two-parent home by surrounding her with other adult role models. This is especially important when the noncustodial parent has a very limited involvement in the child's life. These persons of significance could include a pastor, a teacher, a coach, a Scout leader—anyone who models for your child the Christian person you want her to be. In a single-parent family, the parent must choose the persons of significance very wisely because the child needs extra help to understand what values are important and which standards should be followed.

it by the day, even by the hour; think about it as you go to bed and as you get up.

To Walk in His Ways and Serve Him

In addition to telling us to love Him and fear Him, God says we should "walk in all his ways" (Deut. 10:12) and serve Him. Then He adds: "with all your heart and with all your soul." God does not want half-hearted, semi-committed men and women serving Him. Parenting is a ministry, a service to God, as well as to our children; and He asks for depth in our commitment. He wants our knowing, loving, and serving to be from our innermost being, resulting in commitment that dictates our daily living.

To Teach Your Children

In Deuteronomy, God speaks specifically to parents: "Teach them [His words] to your children. . . . impress them [His commandments] on your children" (Deut. 11:19; 6:7). These verses are compelling biblical mandates for parents to teach their children about God and His commandments.

In fact, Deuteronomy even tells parents *how* to teach. Saturate your child's environment with His words: "Talk about them when you sit at home and when you walk along the road, when you lie down and when you get up. Tie them as symbols on your hands and bind them on your foreheads. Write them on the doorframes of your houses and on your gates" (Deut. 6:7–9). In case you are a slow learner, God repeats the message in Deuteronomy 11:18–20. Christian parents should read these passages over and over again. These are verses of commitment. It is clear that God desires more than Sunday-only Christian teaching. Not only are you to know God's commandments, but you are to make them part of your daily life.

These passages in Deuteronomy also tell parents to teach by example, giving your children models to observe rather than commandments to obey. You must show your children how to walk in the way of the Lord. Parents are always on stage in front of their children—a fact that makes their accountability in Christian living an awesome responsibility.

But your witness is not limited to your children. You are told to "write them on the doorposts of your house and on your gates." It seems that God is laying down specific guidelines for Christian families; they are to be examples to all who enter their homes. There should be no doubt who is the central figure in your household. Your family life should proclaim, "As for me and my household, we will serve the LORD" (Josh. 24:15).

To Discipline Your Children

In addition to telling you to teach your children His Word, God tells you to discipline them: "Discipline your son, for in that there is hope" (Prov. 19:18). It's helpful to remember that *teach* and *discipline* are similar terms. This will help you avoid equating discipline with punishment. Punishment is only a small part of disciplining a child. Discipline means shaping behavior and modifying personal tendencies so that eventually children are guided by inner rules, not just the fear of punishment.

In the Book of Proverbs, God emphatically tells us how to discipline our children and what kind of inner rules to impart. Details of discipline will be discussed in a subsequent chapter, but consider the following important points.

In Proverbs, God repeats the message of Deuteronomy: before parents can impart wisdom and discipline to their children, they must be wise and disciplined themselves and recognize that discipline is founded on a commitment to God. "The fear of the LORD is the beginning of knowledge" (Prov. 1:7) and "of wisdom" (Prov. 9:10). To discipline children effectively, parents must first commit their own way to the Lord and commit themselves to Christ-centered living. Children need to see that those in charge, their parents, are disciplined according to God's plan. They will rebel against having something imposed on them that their parents are unwilling to accept for themselves.

Proverbs 22:6 also introduces the continuum of Christian parenting. (*Continuum* means "a series of interrelated steps, a chain of events.") Proverbs 22:6 is often called the master verse of discipline: "Train [or start] a child in the way he should go, and when he is old he will not turn from it." God's plan is that the child who is disciplined wisely will impart this same discipline to his or her own children and so on throughout the continuum of successive generations. Parents are accountable for a longstanding Christian heritage, one that extends to their grandchildren, great-grandchildren, and beyond.

COMMITMENT TO THE HUSBAND-WIFE RELATIONSHIP

In counseling parents with marital problems in our pediatric practice and in observing fulfilled Christian marriages, we firmly believe that commitment to marriage is the second step toward successful Christian parenting. Your personal commitment to God plus your commitment to your marriage forms the foundation for the third step: commitment to parenting according to God's design. And each step is related to the other steps. Two important ingredients in a Christian marriage are stability and fulfillment. Marriages can have both of these ingredients, in spite of the world's message to the contrary.

A Lifelong Commitment

Christian marriage is a lifelong commitment: "What God has joined together, let man not separate" (Matt. 19:6). The commitment to stay married means that a couple works at the marriage, yet this idea is increasingly threatened in our society. Keep this commitment a priority in your marriage, and God will help you to do this.

Acknowledge God as the head of your household. After all, it is God who joined you together, and with His presence in your marriage the relationship evolves into a triangle. In the divine plan, husband and wife are committed to each other; both are committed to God. As husband and wife each grows closer to God, they also grow closer to each other.

You may feel you can keep your marriage commitment without God's help; however, as in most things, the spirit is willing but the flesh is weak. A Christian who marries accepts a different standard of commitment to the relationship than does a non-Christian. Acknowledging God as the cornerstone of your marriage is not just a nice, pious thought or a tip that may make your marriage work better; it is an absolute necessity for a healthy marriage. Throughout many years of counseling parents, we have seen that couples who acknowledge this triangle weather the storms of marriage crises more successfully than those going at it alone.

Pray for your marriage. Each day, preferably upon awakening or upon retiring, kneel together before your Lord. Invite God into your marriage and ask Him to bless your relationship. This marriage prayer should be such an integral part of your daily living that without it your day feels incomplete.

By praying for your marriage you accomplish at least two things. First, the more you pray, the more deeply rooted becomes your faith that God will strengthen what He has joined together. Second, your communication with each other improves. During the marriage prayer, besides talking to God, you are giving your spouse the message: "I value our relationship enough to ask continually for God's blessing on our marriage. No one prays for something he doesn't want. I acknowledge God as the foundation of our marriage, and I reaffirm my commitment to you." You both emerge from the prayer feeling more secure in your relationship with each other and with your God, and the entire marriage relationship operates at a higher level. We are firmly convinced that a marriage without God as the chief Counselor is likely to succumb to the way of the world, that is, to explore other options and alternatives. Why are we so convinced of this? Very simply because marriage is between two humans.

A Fulfilling Relationship

Ideally, a three-way commitment should be enough to keep a Christian couple together for a lifetime; however, there is another quality needed. A relationship that is not fulfilling has a high risk of eventually dissolving. God intends Christian couples to be fulfilled in their marriages.

The concept of fulfillment may be more important for Christian than for non-Christian marriages because, for most Christians, divorce is not an option. As a result, they put stability and commitment first. Therefore, a Christian couple may be unfulfilled, but remain married.

The world's view of marriage puts fulfillment before, or in place of, commitment. It says that as long as both parties are fulfilled, they remain committed to their relationship. If one of the parties becomes dissatisfied, the commitment may dissolve. As a consequence, a nonbelieving couple may actually work harder to fulfill each other than would the Christian couple since remaining together depends on mutual satisfaction.

Many couples may not realize that the concept of mutual fulfillment is biblical. First Corinthians 7:3 states this beautifully: "The husband should fulfill his marital duty to his wife, and likewise the wife to the husband." Eugene Peterson puts it this way in *The Message*: "The marital bed must be a place of mutuality—the husband seeking to satisfy his wife, the wife seeking to satisfy her husband." God wants marriages to be happy and satisfying.

Ingredients for a Fulfilled Marriage

What are some of the ingredients that go into creating a fulfilled marriage? *Mutual esteem* is one ingredient. Throughout childhood, adolescence, and the adult single life a person is occupied with his or her own pursuits.

Most daily living is dedicated to one's own goals. However, when people marry, that focus needs to shift. Instead of remaining egocentric, they must direct some of their energy toward meeting the needs of their mates. The more energy you can direct into fulfilling the needs of your mate, the more fulfilled you can be in marriage. At first glance this may seem self-defeating. You may wonder if you would be unfair to yourself if you continually strive to meet your mate's needs. You have needs too! How are your needs going to be met?

When you make an unconditional commitment to another person and acknowledge your need for an outside Counselor, you have consciously come out of yourself. Perhaps for the first time in your life you have realized that someone else is as important or even more important to you than yourself. This acknowledgement is the first step toward mutual esteem.

As you direct your energies toward your mate, being more tuned in to him or her and becoming more sensitive to his or her needs, your mate feels two things: (1) his or her self-worth is boosted—he or she feels better as a person and consequently more fulfilled—and (2) he or she feels your unconditional giving. This stimulates your mate to redirect some of his or her energy toward you. You often end up getting more than you give, and the result is that you wind up feeling more fulfilled than if you had selfishly directed all your energies toward yourself in the first place.

The world's view of marriage is "What can I *get* from this relationship?" The Christian view of marriage is "What can I *give* to this relationship?" Marriages that are based on *getting* rather than *giving* fail. Once they have gotten all they can out of the relationship, partners are back to the old song "Is That All There Is?" You are more secure when you give because giving depends only on yourself, whom you can control; getting depends on other people, whom you can't control.

Couples who practice this concept of mutual esteem-building seem to develop a radar system. Each partner's system is on the alert for the other's needs and feelings, and so each partner is available and ready to respond.

Mutual love is another ingredient of a fulfilled marriage. What is healthy love in marriage? A marriage based primarily on *eros* (sexual love) will wear out just as soon as those physical attributes that stimulated the *eros* wear out. Marriage based on mutual *agape* (unconditional love) will weather all the storms because *agape* implies being able to give up any selfish claims on the other. It is giving yourself to your mate while allowing him or her the freedom to be himself or herself. It is sometimes easier to have unconditional love— love that says, "there is nothing you can do to keep me from loving you"—for one's children than for one's mate. For most marriages to have this kind of love, the work of the Holy Spirit is needed. God's plan, based on what we know of human sexuality, is for *eros* to mature into *agape,* without itself getting lost along the way. And don't forget *phileo,* that demonstrated natural affection we talked about on page 21.

Mutual submission is a third ingredient for a fulfilled marriage. Ephesians 5:22–33 sets forth the marriage relationship as it was designed by God.

> Wives, submit to your husband as to the Lord. For the husband is the head of the wife as Christ is the head of the church, his body, of which he is the Savior. Now as the church submits to Christ, so also wives should submit to their husbands in everything.
>
> Husbands, love your wives, just as Christ loved the church and gave himself up for her to make her holy, cleansing her by the washing with water through the word, and to present her to himself as a radiant church, without stain or wrinkle or any other blemish, but holy and blameless. In this same way, husbands ought to love their wives as their own bodies. He who loves his wife loves himself. After all, no one ever hated his own body, but he feeds and cares for it, just as Christ does the church—for we are members of his body. "For this reason a man will leave his father and mother and be united to his wife, and the two will become one flesh." This is a profound mystery—but I am talking about Christ and the church. However, each one of you also must love his wife as he loves himself, and the wife must respect her husband.

It would be good for both husband and wife to pray and meditate on this passage and to discuss the meaning of God's words concerning the sacred relationship of marriage, which He designed. This text is not a judgment on who is better; it is not a ranking of one gender over the other. After all, Paul teaches in Galatians 3:28 that male and female are equal ("You are all one in Christ Jesus"). It is a teaching about a relationship and the personal roles in making that relationship work. The ultimate destiny of every marriage depends on a couple's success or failure in applying these principles. Women (and men) who get stuck at the "Wives, submit to your husband" part need to read on to the "Husbands, love your wives, just as Christ loved the church *and gave himself up for her*" (emphasis ours).

For a wife to submit to her husband as to the Lord, it helps to know she is loved by her husband; for a husband to love his wife as Christ loved the church, it helps to know that his wife respects him. The man needs to know he is honored; the woman needs to know she is cherished. Our God certainly understands the psychology of the sexes! For both of them to maintain this relationship consistently, it must be founded on Christ.

The Husband's Role

God has given the husband the prime responsibility for making the marriage relationship work, which is as it should be since he has been made the head. "Husbands, love your wives, just as Christ loved the church and gave himself up for her. . . . Husbands ought to love their wives as their own bodies." These are words of deep love. This is love as Christ loves His church—a sacrificial, unselfish, and unconditional love—a love strong enough that a husband would give up his life for his wife. It may be easy to imagine the romantic idea of actually dying for your wife, to save her life by giving up yours. And if that moment should ever come, many husbands would not hesitate (at least we would like to think that). Yet "gave himself up for her [the church]" has a broader meaning here as well. For three years Jesus dedicated His life, gave up Himself, died to Himself moment by moment, day by day, for the well-being of his followers. This is how a husband is to measure his love for his wife.

A husband may say, "Of course I love my wife." But he must not only love his wife, he must also demonstrate his love to her so often and to such a degree that she knows she is loved. Love is primarily an act of the will. If a husband genuinely loves his wife and has a strong commitment to their relationship, he will show signs of that love and commitment toward her. A woman who can feel her husband's love and commitment will take great delight in submitting to him. And a husband who can feel that his wife respects him increases his love and commitment; as a result the marriage operates at an increasingly higher level.

The Wife's Role

"Now as the church submits to Christ, so also wives should submit to their husbands in everything. . . . and the wife must respect her husband." The Greek word translated "submit" is derived from the same word meaning "to yield" in the sense of yielding to another's authority. This does not imply that one person should control another; this concerns the smooth running of the relationship. This passage does not say that women should submit themselves to all men; this advice is strictly for the submission of wives to their husbands. It implies respect for the husband, not because he is a man, but because he is the husband. When he says "I do," he is also taking on the responsibility this headship brings with it.

"As to the Lord"

The final message in God's design for the marriage relationship in Ephesians 5 is found in the phrases: "as to the Lord," "as the church is subject to Christ," "as Christ also loved the church." They imply love and submission toward one another of the same quality we have for the Lord. We are commanded to see Jesus in "the least of these" (Matt. 25:40). How much more then are we to see Jesus in our spouses? And when we do this, the commands to love sacrificially, submit, and respect suddenly become easier.

When Your Marriage Is Struggling

As one of our happiest, proudest accomplishments, we marked our thirtieth wedding anniversary in 1996. This is how we know there is a God! Seriously, if left to our own human resources, we wouldn't have made it to three years, or even three months. Looking back at the history of our life together, we can only shake our heads in amazement that our marriage not only survived but is now thriving beyond what we could ever have imagined.

It was not always so. There were times when one or the other of us could have easily walked away. Sometimes it was the marriage itself, sometimes the strain of circumstances, and sometimes it was personal struggle causing our marriage to be stretched to the point of breaking. If you recognize that your marriage is at one of these points, so that our discussion of Christian commitment to God and to one another just sounds like so much fluff, pray and ask God to show you where to go for help. There will be just the right book to read, a long overdue talk with one another, or with your pastor, or there may be a professional counselor you need to find. We have done all of these things over our thirty years, and we will continue to as long as the two of us are alive. It is not a shame to need help with your marriage or your personal struggles. It is a shame to not seek it when you need it.

One book, of the many we have read, that we found to be a foundation for all we needed to learn about Christian marriage, is titled *Under the Apple Tree: Marrying, Birthing, Parenting.* We have listed it, along with our other favorites, in the bibliography at the end of this book.

COMMITMENT TO GOD'S DESIGN FOR PARENTS

As you begin your parenting career, you will be bombarded with advice on how to care for your baby. All of your well-meaning friends and relatives are going to offer you their personal how-tos of babycare. Even the advice you'll hear from doctors is based on personal opinion. Dear parents, bear in mind that because you love your baby so much, you will be vulnerable to any advice that may claim to make you a better parent or your baby a better child. Being able to evaluate advice is not easy for first-time parents when they have little or no experience with babies. In our many years of teaching parents, we have discovered a way you can know with confidence whether or not any advice is helpful.

Three goals for you as parents will form the basis for a relationship with your child: (1) knowing your child, (2) helping your child feel right, and (3) enjoying your child. For Christian parents there is one more goal: leading your child to faith in Jesus. Advice and parenting choices need to be evaluated in the light of these four goals. Much of this book is devoted to exploring God's design for parenting and child care and how His design is meant to help parents reach these goals.

Initially, we stated these goals in terms of how to discipline children. Then we realized that since everything parents do with and for their baby from the very beginning falls into the category of discipline, these are the goals for all of parenting. We will discuss them more fully in the chapters on discipline.

We know that the only way to be able to discipline and teach someone is to know that person well. Psalm 139 makes this clear: "O LORD, you have searched me and you know me. . . . you perceive my thoughts from afar. . . . you are familiar with all my ways. . . . If I rise on the wings of the dawn, if I settle on the far side of the sea, even there your hand will guide me, your right hand will hold me fast" (vv. 1,2b,3b,9–10). Helping your child feel right (see box, p. 33) is akin to verses 13 and 14: "For you created my inmost being; you knit me together in my mother's womb. I praise you because I am fearfully and wonderfully made; your works are wonderful, I know that full well." This certainly sounds like a person who feels right and who is enjoyed by God. Psalm 149:4 tells us: "For the LORD takes delight in his people." Surely, He wants us to delight in (enjoy) our children. Back to Psalm 139, we read: "Search me, O God, and know my heart; test me and know my anxious thoughts. See if there is any offensive way in me, and lead me in the way everlasting" (vv. 23–24). What a wonderful parallel we can draw from this Scripture for our goals as parents.

Parenting Choices

As you care for your baby, you will develop your own parenting style. We like to think of parenting as a relationship that develops naturally with your baby. From this relationship the how-tos automatically unfold. A flurry of books and articles on quick-and-easy parenting methods has surfaced in the past few decades. They seem to convey that new parents can choose a system of child

HELPING YOUR CHILD FEEL RIGHT

Throughout this book we refer to "feeling right." To avoid misunderstanding, let us define what we mean by that. Helping your child feel right means that as parents you do whatever you can to establish a source of well-being in your baby. That is your job description. You attend to all of your baby's physical and emotional needs, and as he grows you also attend to his mental and spiritual needs. When a baby and child feels right, he is more likely to want to act right, want to please his parents, and be a joy to those around. Helping a child feel right incorporates such things as positive relationships, conscience, and sensitivity (to name a few). As the child grows, he learns that feeling right is what adults mean by having inner peace and the inner witness of the Holy Spirit. (Luke 2:52 says this of Jesus at the age of twelve: "And Jesus grew in wisdom and stature, and in favor with God and men." When each of our children has his or her twelfth birthday, we give him or her this verse as our way of acknowledging this important process in our child's life. Eugene Peterson says it this way in *The Message*: "And Jesus matured, growing up in both body and spirit, blessed by both God and people." This is the ultimate goal we all have as parents.)

When we say "helping your child feel right," we do not mean that the emotions are a reliable measure of spiritual well-being. We don't mean that good feelings always produce right behavior. Behavior sometimes has to precede "feelings" just because something is the right thing to do, a concept children learn gradually with the patient help of their parents. We certainly do not intend this phrase "helping your child feel right" to mean making "the little darling" feel good at all costs. That would be a fatal direction for parents and child.

care that fits most conveniently into their own lifestyles. These options are designed to appeal to busy parents whose first concern is their own lifestyle and who expect their children to conform to it. We do not feel this style of "convenience parenting" is in accordance with God's design. This parenting style can actually interfere with those four goals discussed on page 32. Be mindful of the Father's advice, "Train (or start) a child in the way he should go . . ." (Prov. 22:6), meaning the way God has planned for this child. Seek to determine God's way for your baby. Then help your child grow up in that way even though it may not be the most convenient way.

The catch phrases of convenience parenting are: "Don't be so quick to pick up your baby every time he cries"; "Don't let your baby manipulate you"; "What? You're still nursing? You're making him too dependent"; "Don't let your baby sleep with you; she may get into the habit"; "You're going to spoil her"; "You have to show him who's in charge"; "You've got to get away from that kid." These common admonitions from trusted advisors tell mothers not to use their intuition, but rather to depend on arbitrary rules and schedules instead. Convenience parenting can keep you from knowing your child, keep your child from feeling right, and ultimately can keep you from fully enjoying your child. We believe that convenience, or detachment, parenting is not in accordance with God's design.

Attachment Parenting

The type of parenting we believe is God's design for the father-mother-child relationship is a style we call "attachment parenting." Our intent in recommending this style of parenting to you is so strong that we have spent more hours in prayerful thought on this topic than on any other topic in this book. Attachment parenting is not just our own theory developed in raising our own eight children. It is a parenting style we have learned from (1) studying attachment theory in the research literature and reading the works of respected authors, both Christian and secular, (2) observing and recording parenting styles throughout the past twenty-five years of pediatric practice, and (3) becoming involved in parenting organizations whose principles we respect. We have a deep personal conviction that this is the way God wants His children parented.

This attachment discussion refers mostly to the mother, not because father has a minor role in parenting, but because in those first two years of a child's life the mother is the main attachment figure. However, there is still plenty of room for father-infant attachment. Also, mother-infant attachment is difficult to achieve unless the father provides a supportive environment. Problems in the parent-child relationship are not a fault in the design or the Designer; they are a result of a breakdown in the support system that allows a mother to follow God's design.

What is attachment? Mother-infant attachment is a special bond of closeness between mother and baby. Mother's care enables the young of each species to thrive and, for human babies, to reach their fullest potential. Babies come equipped with behaviors that help mothers deliver the right kind of care. God has placed within mothers both the chemistry and the sensitivity to respond to their babies appropriately. This maternal equipping is what is meant by the phrase "mother's intuition." It helps her get attached to her baby.

ATTACHMENT PARENTING VS DETACHMENT PARENTING

Why is attachment parenting preferable to convenience, or detachment, parenting? Compare these two styles and the effects they have on the parent-child relationship.

Attachment Parenting Advice	*Detachment Parenting Advice*
"Be open to your baby's cues."	"Don't let your baby run your life."
"Take your baby with you."	"You've got to get away from that kid."
"Throw away the clock and the calendar."	"Get that baby on a schedule."
"Respond promptly to cries."	"Let your baby cry it out."
"Travel as a family unit."	"You and your husband need to get away."
"Sleep wherever you all sleep best."	"Don't let your baby sleep in your bed; she'll get used to it."
"Let your baby sleep when he is tired."	"Put him down at 7:00 and let him cry; he'll learn to sleep."
"Wean when both of you are ready."	"What, you're still nursing?"
"Let her decide when she is ready to be independent."	"You're making her dependent."
"Allow discipline to flow naturally from harmony with your baby."	"You're spoiling him; he'll never mind."
"Let authority flow from trust."	"She's controlling you."

Attachment Parenting Results	*Detachment Parenting Results*
You develop confidence in your own parenting abilities.	You do not trust your parenting; you rely on outside advice.
You know your child well.	You and your baby may have a strained or distant relationship.
You develop realistic expectations.	You compare your baby to other babies.
You adjust more easily to your new lifestyle.	You more easily resent your baby's demands.
You enjoy your baby more.	You need more alternative fulfillment.
You are more discerning of advice.	You are vulnerable to unwise advice.
You keep pace with your child.	You play catch-up parenting.
Your child learns to trust.	Your child doesn't learn trust.

Some mothers are able to attach with their babies easily; others have to work at it and need all the help they can get. The skills for attachment certainly don't come easily to many women in our culture because we have lost, to a great extent, the benefit of a close-knit society where the young ones can learn by watching the experienced ones. This is the reason why we have books and classes on parenting, and support groups to take over where families and communities no longer function.

The Benefits of Attachment

When a mother and baby are attached, mother's sensitivity and baby's behavior are allowed to be in harmony with each other. Baby gives cues; mother, because she is open to baby's cues, responds. Baby likes the response and, because mother's responses are trustworthy and predictable, is motivated to give more cues. As a result, the mother and baby work out a communication system, and they feel comfortable together. As this happens, the mother's responses become more spontaneous and the how-tos of baby care—when to feed, when to change a diaper, when to help a baby fall asleep—flow naturally. How do you know that you are building this attachment with your baby? When you have a feeling of rightness about your responses to your baby's cues, and when you are continually sensitive to your baby (you know what he is thinking) and meeting his needs, you are there.

What attachment parenting does for you can be summed up in one word, harmony. A harmonious relationship allows you and your baby to be more in sync with each other, to become sensitive to each other. Not only will your baby need you, as all babies do, you will actually need and want to be with your baby. This is God's way of making sure babies get the closeness they need.

Attachment parenting also creates a sustained chemical change in the mother's body. Breastfeeding stimulates the hormones prolactin and oxytocin (the milk-producing and milk-releasing hormones). These hormones make you feel relaxed and happy when you are with your baby, and give you the calming boost you need during trying times. These hormones, part of God's design, are the chemical basis for a mother's ability to relax and enjoy her baby and respond to his needs. They are, if you will indulge us in a little wordplay, the "hormoneous" relationship that parallels the harmonious relationship you are building with your baby.

You may be thinking that this attachment style of parenting is all giving, giving, giving. To a large extent, this is true. Parents are givers and babies are takers; that is how God designed them. But because of this "hormoneous" relationship, the baby can give something back to mother—more oxytocin and prolactin yields more relaxation. This mutual giving is a beautiful example of the divine design: mothering stimulates more mothering.

Attachment parenting has long-term benefits. When you get in harmony with your child right from the start, you set yourself up for an easier relationship in the months and years to come. Your child will trust you, will more readily follow your guidance, and will more want to please you. Even if you are past the baby stage with your child, realize that it's never too late to get connected, to get behind the eyes of your child and respond to his needs, not just his childish behavior. The response required when a child is older is much more difficult, as is anything that must be done once the natural time for it has passed, but the rewards are tremendous.

Attachment parenting also can give your child an appropriate model to follow when he or she becomes a parent. Remember, you are parenting someone else's future husband or wife, father or mother. How your child is parented influences how he or she will parent. The lack of healthy models causes confusion in many young parents today.

Answers to the Detractors of Attachment Parenting

There are people who say, "I'm not going to let this tiny baby dominate me; I'll get her on *my* schedule. I'm in charge here." Being open to your baby's cues does not mean that you are losing control. There is more to being in charge than setting your own hours for sleeping and waking. The way you convey your authority to a tiny baby is by showing her that you can help her handle her problems. You can help her feel right. Being

WHAT WOULD JESUS DO?

Isaiah 49:15 teaches us that ignoring a baby's cries, a baby's need to be held, is unnatural.

"Can a mother forget the baby at her breast and have no compassion on the child she has borne? Though she may forget, I will not forget you."

Jesus taught us much about compassion. He was often responding to the crowds and to individuals with compassion. Respond to your baby with compassion. If you need guidance, ask yourself, "What would Jesus do?"

AVOIDING THE SHEEP SYNDROME: BECOMING DISCERNING

As you develop your parenting style, and throughout your entire parenting experience, it will be important for you to be discerning while listening to parenting advice. Love for your baby makes you vulnerable to any advice that promises to turn out a better baby and opens up opportunities for false prophets of bad baby advice. If you blindly follow false prophets in the field of parenting, you run the risk of becoming a sheep and falling prey to a phenomenon we call "The Sheep Syndrome." When attending a parenting class or being on the receiving end of well-meaning advice, use discernment about whether the advice is accurate, biblical, and whether it fits your individual baby and your family situation. Try these exercises to improve your discernment:

1. **Trust your intuition.** Remember, God would not have given you a child without also giving you the wisdom to care for her. All parents, especially mothers who practice attachment parenting, have built-in sensors to what is best for their baby. Before buying into a doctrine of parenting, run it through your internal sensor. You be the judge.

2. **Beware of the authoritarian approach.** Be discerning in classes that offer quick fixes and boast that theirs is the only way or even, presumptuously, "God's way." Complex parenting problems do not have easy answers. Children have such unique temperaments and parents such diverse lifestyles that there is seldom one way to deal with parenting issues. Shun rigid classes; it's better to choose classes that give you the basic tools on which you can build a parenting style that works for you and your child.

3. **Do the class teachings help you develop sensitivity?** Our friend Susan was visiting a new mother who was fresh out of a parenting class taught at her local church. Her newborn began crying and exhibiting other hunger cues. The new mother continued her conversation, seemingly oblivious to her newborn's crying. Susan asked if the mother wouldn't rather attend to her newborn. The mother replied, "No, it's not yet time for his feeding." This well-meaning mother was following the dictates of the teacher's manual instead of her God-given maternal instincts. She had become desensitized to her baby's signals and to her own. She had become a sheep, following a blind guide.

AVOIDING THE SHEEP SYNDROME: BECOMING DISCERNING (CONT.)

4. **Check out the teachings with wise parents.** Surround yourself with wise and experienced parents. These persons will be your most credible advisers. List your concerns and run them by your advisers. Because parents are so vulnerable and babies are too valuable for you to get advice from only one person, we use this model in all of our teaching. Before our major writings go to press, we run them by wise parents and professionals whom we call our "board of directors."

5. **If it isn't working, drop it.** Do the teachings draw you closer to your child or create a distance between you and your child? Is your baby thriving physically and emotionally; for example, appropriate growth and development, emotional sparkles, adept at giving cues? Are you growing in your ability to read and respond to your baby's cues, or are you becoming more confused?

6. **Watch for the biblical twist.** Do the class teachings fit the Bible or does the teacher twist biblical teachings to fit his or her own preconceived biases? If the teachers are using Scripture, do they apply Scripture correctly and in context? Do their teachings square up with the whole of Scripture? This is especially characteristic of heavy-handed, spank-controlled dogma that bases the entire parenting philosophy on the "rod verses"—those Old Testament proverbs that are prone to individual interpretation (or misinterpretation). We recently reviewed a parenting class manual that promotes "parent-controlled" feedings and claimed a biblical basis for this. Not only is there no scriptural basis for this feeding practice, but it is also scientifically unsound.

7. **What are the credentials of the "shepherd(s)"?'** Do the teachers have a lot of practical experience (i.e., cared for or parented lots of children)? Have the teachers studied children professionally for many years? Do they seem to be knowledgeable and sensitive? It's okay to be a sheep if you have a wise shepherd. Christ provided such a model—and He had credentials.

open to her cues provides the conditions for developing trust in three relationships: (1) you trust your baby to give you the cues to tell you what she needs; (2) you trust yourself and your ability to respond to your baby's cues appropriately; and (3) you trust that God's design for a mother-baby communication network will work if allowed to operate as designed. When your baby cries in the middle of the night (for the third time) and you respond, don't feel you are "giving in"; you are simply giving.

God would not have designed a system of child care that does not work. We know that mothers are designed to be responsive to their babies. For example, researchers have found that the bloodflow to a mother's breasts doubles when she hears her baby cry. (This is just one example. We will discuss this much more in chapter 9, "Responding to Your Baby's Cries.") If you are a mother who struggles with knowing what your baby needs, respond sensitively and consistently to your baby without hesitation and you will find your shaky confidence maturing. Try to see this process as a learning experience. For example, your baby cries, you pick him up; your baby is restless at night, you sleep with him; your baby needs to be held a lot, you hold him or use a baby carrier to "wear" him. By freely responding, you become more confident in the appropriateness of your response.

What if you are confident in your parenting ability but are blessed with a very demanding baby (see chapter 10, "The Fussy Baby")? Consider the law of supply and demand. When your responsiveness and your perseverance increase in proportion to your baby's needs, you stay in harmony, in sync, with each other. However, if you succumb to outside pressure not to be open to your baby and you restrict your responses, you will quickly lose harmony with your baby. This seriously interferes with the goal of knowing your child. In subsequent chapters, important attachment principles will be addressed that help the mother-baby relationship develop according to God's design.

Parenting Practices that Enhance Attachment

In our years of growing as parents ourselves and watching the parents of the children in our pediatric practice, we have identified some parenting practices that are key to the attachment style. Because of the great variability in family situations, you may not be able to incorporate all of these practices in your parenting all of the time. But to the extent that you can, you will find your attachment to your baby greatly facilitated and enhanced. In fact, attachment is the natural outcome of these practices, which have as their central purpose an understanding of what babies need. These practices include: having a safe and satisfying birth experience that can enhance bonding, breastfeeding, babywearing (explained in chapter 11); responding appropriately to baby's cries; supportive father involvement; gradual weaning; and wise boundary setting. Each of these practices will be explored chapter by chapter. At the end of chapter 8, "Nighttime Parenting," there is a testimony that sums this up beautifully (see page 200. Also see our bibliography for information on *The Nurturing Parent,* a journal dedicated to the concepts of attachment parenting).

Any Guarantees?

Practicing attachment parenting does not guarantee that your child will always obey you, never make unwise choices, or never turn from God's will. It does mean that your child will have experienced God "with skin on," making it easier for her to recognize the God of the universe in His timing. There are three reasons why you cannot claim full credit or blame for your child's future: (1) every child comes wired with a unique temperament; (2) throughout life, your child will be bombarded with trials and temptations and alternatives in lifestyles; and (3) God has given your child a free will. Comparing childrearing with planting a garden may help you understand this concept. Certain styles of care give seeds a better chance of becoming healthy plants. However, each plant is unique, and the fruit each bears will also be vulnerable to the forces of nature. Your child is subject to forces beyond your control, including his or her free will. You can understand why even the most well-attached child will bend a little (or a lot!).

Because God knows children will have erring, human parents, He builds into each child an ability to adjust to a wide range of parenting styles. Most children have a wider acceptance of parenting styles than parents have of childish behavior. However, the closer your style of parenting is to God's design, the less your children will need to tap into their reserves of resilience. As a result, certain undesirable behaviors of childhood, "diseases of detachment," are less common (fearfulness, tantrums, depression, withdrawal, distancing).

So, yes, attachment parenting involves a lot of giving. Giving is a concept that stretches humans. It is a scary thing for us. Yet, it is a concept God wants us to master. There are nearly two thousand references to "giving" in the Bible. This is what Christianity is all about. Once we have received God's love and forgiveness, we are called to love others as we love ourselves. The great maturity that comes from parenting is that we learn about giving. Parenting according to God's design helps both parents and children grow to be giving persons.

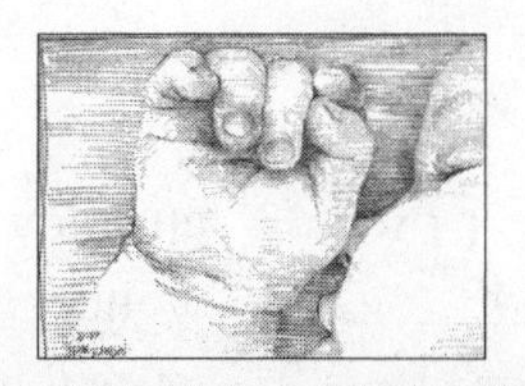

CHAPTER TWO

Fathering: Commitment to Being **A Spiritual Leader**

Fathering is tough, and Christian fathering is even tougher. So many other demands compete for your attention and threaten to pull you and your family further and further away from God. Fathers, I (Bill) am writing to you not as one who has his spiritual act together but as one who has made many mistakes in his own fathering, as one who has confused his priorities, and as one who is still struggling daily to be a spiritual leader in his own home. For those of you who are also struggling, the following suggestions may help you become spiritual leaders in your homes and help you lead your children to faith in Jesus.

Because the stakes are high, a plan for spiritual leadership is necessary. The vital importance of planning hit me in 1968 when I visited the NASA space center in Houston, Texas. In a large room was a huge chart showing the master plan for going to the moon. At one end of this chart was the nation's commitment to put a man on the moon. At the other end was the final goal, the landing of a man on the moon. In between the commitment and reaching the goal were thousands of obstacles to be overcome and problems to be solved. One by one these obstacles were checked off as NASA neared the final goal. All during this process the U.S. government reaffirmed its commitment to get to the moon by continuing to provide financial backing.

HOW TO BE AN EFFECTIVE SPIRITUAL LEADER

For some fathers, becoming effective spiritual leaders may seem as difficult as putting a man on the moon, but the components of the plan are similar: (1) make the commitment; (2) define your priorities; (3) define your goals; and (4) define the obstacles that keep you from reaching your goal.

Make the Commitment

At the core of fatherhood lies commitment. My main goal in this life is to return to my Father in heaven. The second goal in my life is to lead my children there also. You can make this commitment too, and once you have, do as God commanded in Deuteronomy: fix this commitment in your heart; reaffirm this commitment when you get up and when you lie down. Attach this commitment to the dashboard of your car, to the door of your office; place it on your desk; seal it to the doorframe of your house. In today's busy life the father is often overcommitted and overinvested in the things of the world and undercommitted and underinvested in his ultimate goal and the care of his children. Making the commitment is the first step toward becoming the spiritual leader in your home.

Define Your Priorities

A father gets a tremendous amount of advice from the Christian media on how to father and how to be a spiritual leader. He may wonder, *Do these preachers really know how tough it is out there in the real world? Do they understand my job pressures, paying the bills?* It isn't easy to spend time with Scripture every day when you have barely enough time to get your job done; it isn't easy to "give thanks" in everything (1 Thess. 5:17) when you are struggling to hold onto your job; it isn't easy to say, "Don't worry, the Lord will provide" (see Phil. 4:19) when your mortgage payment is overdue. It's tough to lead your children to Christ when you're not sure where you stand yourself. Being a Christian father is the longest and most challenging race you will ever run; the reward for finishing the race is, as Paul says in 2 Timothy 4:7–8, the crown of righteousness. *The Message* puts it like this: "This is the only race worth running. I've run hard right to the finish, believed all the way. All that's left now is the shouting—God's applause!"

To make this commitment stick, it is necessary to continually define your priorities and reaffirm your position. The order of importance that I believe God sets for us is (1) God, (2) family, (3) job, and (4) church activities. This is not a rigid measuring of relative amounts of time that should be invested in each area, but recognize that all these priorities are interrelated. Being a God-centered person is necessary to being a God-centered father of your family. Meeting your job priority is easier if you are first right with God and with your family. However, it is unrealistic to play down the importance of your employment outside the home. Job satisfaction is important. If you aren't satisfied with your job and your ability to provide for your family, your sense of self-worth is affected. As your child's self-image affects his behavior, so does your self-image in your job affect your relationship with your family and ultimately your openness to God. (Your mate needs to be mindful of this.) Still, a job should be primarily a means to an end, not an end in itself; it should be a means for providing for a family, a means for serving God, a means for ministering to the community.

What gets many fathers into trouble is devoting so much time and energy to their jobs that their jobs begin to dominate their lives and compete with God and their families for their attention. This goes against God's will for us. God promises to bless those who put Him first: "Blessed is the man who does not walk in the counsel of the wicked. . . . But his delight is in the law of the LORD. . . . Whatever he does prospers" (Ps. 1:1–3). "Seek first his kingdom and his righteousness, and all these things will be given to you as well" (Matt. 6:33). In plain everyday English, that translates to "Steep your life in God-reality, God-initiative, God-provisions. Don't worry about missing out. You'll find all your everyday human concerns will be met" (*The Message*).

Define Your Goals

To be a spiritual leader in your home, you must have a well-nourished spiritual life. Fathers, take the time to get your own spiritual house in order. Take periodic spiritual inventories (at least once a year) of where you are relative to where you were and where you would like to be. Your spiritual growth chart should be as up-to-date as your career growth chart. To work toward these goals, define and eliminate the obstacles to your growth in faith and emphasize those things that encourage it. No one can give what he does not have himself.

Here are goals to strive for in your spiritual life—goals that Christ Himself has given to committed believers:

- Love the Lord and love your neighbor as yourself.
- Fear God and keep His commandments.
- Pray for wisdom to make the spiritual decisions that lead you and your family toward your ultimate goal.
- Study Scripture and apply it in your life.
- Live a Christ-centered life in relationship with God as your Father.

Define Obstacles to Your Growth

In an increasingly materialistic world, there are many obstacles to spiritual growth. These obstacles will be different for every man, but I will mention some of the major ones confronting most fathers today.

For many, debt is an obstacle to spiritual growth. Many people are financially overextended, especially in a system that offers easy credit, and even rewards some kinds of debt with lowered taxes and easy write-offs of losses. I wonder if some day, as we stand before the pearly gates in front of the Ultimate Accountant, He might check His ledger and announce, "Mr. X, your life has been a series of write-offs. You wrote off your wife, you wrote off your children, you wrote off your friends at lunch and during recreation. If it weren't for My Son's magnificent work on the cross, in which you have come to believe and hope, I would have to write you off."

Debt weighs especially heavy on those in the world of business. In my pediatric practice, I see how their children are affected by their parents' money worries. Children often inherit a sense of financial pressure from the atmosphere at home. Jesus really meant it when He said, "Do not worry about your life, what you will eat or drink; . . . your body . . . clothes . . . tomorrow" (Matt. 6:25–34).

Before making a purchase, consider these questions:

- Do I need it more than I want it?
- Will it directly or indirectly contribute to my spiritual growth and/or that of my children?
- Can I afford it? Could the money be spent better elsewhere?
- Will I worry about it?

You'll find that many purchases don't stand up to this kind of scrutiny, and you and your family will be better off without these things.

Perhaps the greatest obstacle to spiritual growth for all Christians is materialism, a preoccupation with satisfying ourselves with the world's attractions. "For where your treasure is, there your heart will be also" (Matt. 6:21). These words spoken by Jesus expose a stumbling block for many Christians in our affluent society. Families will continue to struggle with having their hearts in the wrong places as long as fathers pursue treasures in all the wrong places. One of the main goals for my spiritual leadership is to teach my children to be filled by spiritual treasures rather than by material turn-ons. Of course, the only way to teach my children this is for me to live this way.

PRACTICAL TIPS FOR CHRISTIAN FATHERING

Consider the spiritual leadership of your children as a business venture. The competition for the values and minds of your children is tough. Your competitors have money and experience, and they are intensely motivated. The following practical "business tips" can help you beat the competition and secure the hearts of your children.

Be a Role Model

Role models have a powerful effect on your children's behaviors and values. Make it your business to be a positive role model. Children see your values in your daily living. What is important to you becomes important to them. If God has blessed you with riches, please realize there is nothing intrinsically un-Christian about wealth. The Bible tells of many men to whom God gave prosperity because they walked in His ways. It is the attitude toward wealth that can go wrong. It is no sin to be rich; it is a sin to let your wealth dictate your actions.

Children are naturally attracted to big cars, fancy houses, and any expensive "toys" their fathers may have. The adage "the only difference between men and boys is the price of their toys" has a lot of truth in it. Children astutely watch how their fathers value their own possessions. Are you constantly talking about your grown-up toys, playing with them, talking about how you are going to pay for them, expressing your delight in them, and getting angry when they are broken or don't give you the gratification you expect from them? Do you spend most of the weekend getting turned on by the electronic stimulation the competition is constantly turning out? Do you fail to fit God into your busy schedule, skipping Sunday school and church for other, more glamorous pursuits? Do you doze off in front of the television instead of making time for a ten-minute bedtime prayer? If your children see this role model, they learn one important lesson: toys are more important than God.

God had the foresight to know that the competition against Him would be great. To meet this competition head-on He gave parents His Word, which includes a set of rules for a successful Christian childrearing business. If we follow His business plan, He promises help in winning out over those who try to seduce our children. God understands the importance of modeling. In addition to *telling* us how to live, He sent Jesus to *show* us how to live. The concept of imitation is mentioned four times by Paul (see Eph. 5:1–2; 1 Cor. 4:15–16; 1 Thess. 1:6; 2:14). Imitation is what children do with what we model to them. "For in Christ Jesus, I became your father through the gospel. Therefore, I urge you to imitate me" (Eph. 5:1–2, *The Message*). Paul was not asking them to do anything he was not already doing himself.

Begin Early with Small Things

The critical period for your children to be influenced by role modeling is when they are three to six years of age. At that time, they view the world through the eyes of their parents. What is important to you is important to them. If they constantly hear that "Toys are the real thing," they will believe it; if they constantly hear that "God is the real thing," they will believe that.

By four to six years of age children should be able occasionally to delay their gratifications. Young children are very food-for-pleasure oriented; therefore, food is one of the easiest and most available tools for teaching delayed gratification to them. Perhaps, as the old saying goes for a man's heart, the best way to a child's soul is through her stomach. The young child might hear you occasionally say, "I would like to have a piece of pie, but I really don't need it." That child will learn, "It makes me strong to say no now and then to myself." Your modeling of the concept of prayer and fasting is more important than your words. Also, be prepared to step in with personal attention as a substitute for what your child has given up.

One day years ago, I was talking to our seven-year-old son, Peter, about being strong, saying no, and giving up certain food pleasures; he had been complaining about being refused a second helping of ice cream. He promptly reminded me that the night before I had become angry because Martha had neglected to purchase my favorite ice cream to go along with the pie she had made. And just recently our four-year-old, Lauren, came up with the observation that it isn't good for us to have everything we want. Believe me, they are always watching, always soaking it in.

Teaching young children how to give up small things occasionally, such as a toy at the checkout counter, sets the pattern for saying no to more elaborate material things when they are older. If a child is going to make it as a Christian in today's world, she must learn to say no to self. This is a big step in becoming a responsible Christian. Let your children see you say no to yourself occasionally in ways with which they can identify. Jesus' words to this effect are recorded in three of the Gospels, practically verbatim: "If anyone would come after me, he must deny himself and take up his cross and follow me" (Matt. 16:24; Mark 8:34; Luke 9:23). He must have wanted to be sure we didn't miss this instruction. (Luke added the word *daily* just in case anyone would wonder.)

Provide an Alternative to Materialism

Too much materialism is not healthy for your child, but if he is told constantly what he can't have, he will rebel against your whole system, feeling that "it's no fun to be a Christian." In Deuteronomy, chapters 6 and 11, God foresaw difficulty in this area. His advice was to saturate the child's environment with things of the Lord instead of things of the world. Fill your children with

FATHER VERSES

The following Scripture verses are particularly helpful to fathers who are struggling to be spiritual leaders in their families. In these references, God could be talking directly to fathers. Memorize these verses, meditate on them, fix them in your hearts:

Matthew 18:1–6	Exodus 20:4–6
Luke 12:16–21	Deuteronomy 6:4–9
2 Corinthians 12:14–15*	Proverbs 22:6*
Ephesians 6:4	Jeremiah 17:7–8
Colossians 3:21	

* This is how it reads in *The Message:*

"Children shouldn't have to look out for their parents; parents look out for their children. I'd be most happy to empty my pockets, even mortgage my life, for your good" (2 Cor. 12:14–15).

"Point your kids in the right direction—when they're old they won't be lost" (Prov. 22:6).

spiritual goodies, things of eternal value, when you are in control of what goes into them, lest they fill themselves with worldly things at a later age when they are beyond your control. The most important alternative to materialism that you can give your children is yourself. A child will prize focused attention from a parent more highly than the latest gimmick from the toy store.

Teach Your Children to Share Their Wealth

If God has blessed you with an abundance of material wealth, please don't hoard it for yourself. Use it to enrich the lives of the less fortunate. If you have a summer home or winter place, share it with those who can barely afford one home. Invite your church's youth group to use your large van for a weekend trip. Let your Father in heaven and your child on earth see where your heart is. (They are the only persons who need to know about your philanthropy.) Encourage your children to be a friend to disabled children, or to the child who seems to have no friends. Invite them along on family outings. You can teach sharing to your children in a multitude of ways, beginning with your own attitude of generosity to visitors.

Pray and Read God's Word

You cannot be a good father without outside help. Prayer and study of Scripture are necessary. Throughout the Bible God tells you how to be a model father to your children.

The most important factor in teaching Scripture to your child is your own attitude toward the Word of God. Your child is focusing on one big point: how important is the Bible to my dad? If you behave as if it is important to you, then by the principle of modeling, the Bible becomes important to him.

Does your child see you reading Scripture frequently? Do you rely on the Bible to solve both major and minor problems when they arise? Can you quickly refer to the appropriate verse when your child gives you an "opener" and would appreciate an answer not only from his dad but from God? When your children ask for your opinion or advice on a subject, think how much more meaningful it is if you give them your own opinion and then mention an appropriate scripture to back it up. This drives home to your children the important point that their father's life is directed by God's Word.

Ideally your child would see you spending as much, if not more, time in God's Word as you do in the books relating to your interest or hobby. But five or ten minutes a day would be a great start. It is inexcusable for a Christian father to be illiterate in Scripture. Recently, Martha gave me a copy of *The Message* by Eugene M. Peterson. This paraphrase of the New Testament and Psalms and Proverbs is the perfect antidote for anyone who can't quite get excited about reading the Bible. To quote a sentence from Peterson's introduction: "The goal is not to render a word-for-word conversion of Greek into English, but rather to convert the tone, the rhythm, the events, the ideas, into the way we actually think and speak." I can't put it down easily. I'm drawn to keep reading, to soak up more about who Jesus is and what He wants to give me.

Pray daily together with your child for two things: (1) for guidance and wisdom as a father, and (2) for God to fill your child with the Spirit by whom his or her behavior will be directed. Praying does not come easily, especially for new Christians. Don't fear that your words won't sound quite right. Just as your Father listens to your heart and not your words, your child is more sensitive to your attitude and sincerity of prayer than your verbiage. Again, you are role modeling; your child sees that "prayer is important to Daddy, so I want to pray too."

Children need to learn the power of prayer. To illustrate this, let me share two situations that occurred in our family from which our children learned the power of prayer.

Sailing is our family hobby. Years ago my two oldest sons and I were sailing with some friends down New York River past the Statue of Liberty, which was a very moving and patriotic experience for us. We then sailed out toward the ocean through the busiest shipping channel in the world. A pea-soup fog set in, but I was not worried because I knew we were protected by our radar system. We were surrounded by so many ships entering the harbor that our radar screen looked like a video game. It was night and we were leaving the harbor and entering the ocean when our radar system stopped. I was scared. (A father is allowed to be scared but never out of control in front of his children.) My sons and I knelt down and prayed, and soon thereafter the radar system came on again and we continued safely through the fog. My sons certainly learned the power of prayer in this situation, but also learned, by role modeling, that their father relies on prayer and believes in prayer power.

The next story illustrates the power of prayer in healing. Medicine is a humbling profession, especially in pediatrics. Often the pediatrician must say to the parents of an extremely ill child, "There is nothing more I can do; we must pray."

Some years ago, I cared for a three-year-old boy who nearly drowned in a swimming pool. He was resuscitated, brought to the hospital, and placed on life-support. I had to say to the parents, "We are doing everything humanly possible to save your child's life." When they asked what they could do, I said, "Pray." By all medical standards this child had a very slim chance of surviving and an even slimmer chance of surviving without brain damage. Five days later the child awoke, and all life-support systems were gradually discontinued. When he left the hospital a week later, he seemed to be a normal child. One year later he showed absolutely no evidence of brain damage from the accident.

My children were involved with praying for the complete healing of this child. Since I involved them in daily prayer for the child's health, they learned the power of prayer and healing. As a father, I hoped that this vivid illustration of God's answer to prayer would make a lifelong impression on my children, prompting them to go to their heavenly Father in times of need. But you don't need to wait for a big crisis to pray. When a toy is missing, or my pager, I say, "Let's ask Jesus to help us find it. And, remember, He doesn't want us to worry about it." We pray when tests are looming, when one of us is traveling, when someone has a fever or sore throat, or when little ones can't get ahold of runaway emotions.

There are three times during the day when prayer is most meaningful to children: (1) in the morning as they begin the day, (2) at mealtimes when it becomes part of family communication, and (3) before bedtime, to thank God for the blessings of the day. The first words that come out of your mouth in the morning and the last words at night could contain a message from the Lord. "God bless your day, Matt." As spiritual leader, you can help your child begin and end the day with the Lord. This modeling carries over into your child's view of God: "If God is top priority in Dad's thoughts, He must be a very important person, and therefore He will be top priority in my thoughts."

When you pray together, the content and the attitude of your prayers have a great influence upon your children. Use prayer as a means of conveying to them how you want them to relate to you. You've often heard that your concepts of God are determined in some ways by the kind of relationship you have or had with your father. As your children hear how you pray to your heavenly Father, they will be learning how they can look toward you, and therefore toward God. If your children hear you submit to and obey God's authority, they will pick up on how they can submit to their father, and their respect for authority in general will be raised to a higher level.

Give Your Children Memories

Remember Bob Hope's theme song, "Thanks for the Memories"? One of the most beautiful gifts you can give your children is to fill their receptive minds with vivid memories of their father in various roles—as a Christian, as spiritual leader in the home, as husband to their mother, as a fun friend, as provider, and as someone who made his children a top priority. Memories keep the model you set for your children ever available in their minds.

Fathers often underestimate how an apparently insignificant event such as a ball game or a walk to the store can make a vivid and lasting impression on a child. To illustrate this, ask a group of teenagers to recount some of the memorable moments they have had with their fathers. One time in our Sunday school class I asked a group of young fathers to recount some pleasant and some unpleasant childhood memories they had of their fathers. The responses indicated that unpleasant experiences were remembered more quickly than pleasant experiences, but how their fathers walked with God was one of the most vivid good impressions. The other lasting memories formed around the priority sons had in relation to fathers' jobs. As one man shared with me, "In our house there was no doubt where I stood. My father's job came first, and I was a distant second."

Be a Hero in Your Family

This is a hero-worshiping society. Advertising agencies capitalize on this hero worship by employing movie stars and sports figures to advertise products. If these heroes eat a certain candy bar or wear a certain piece of clothing the child believes that he must do so also. I once asked a group of six-year-old boys to think about their favorite heroes and whom they would want to be like when they grew up. I received many answers, but not one child gave me the answer I was hoping for—"my father."

Spend Time with Your Children

One of the greatest challenges in fathering is having enough time for your child. Many demands on today's father rob him of parenting time. In answer to this dilemma, many writers have promoted the concept of quality time: the amount of time you spend with your child is not as important as how you spend it. There is certainly an element of truth in the quality-time concept, but quality time is certainly not a substitute for quantity time.

Children are spontaneous in their actions, and their moods determine their receptivity to guidance. If a father is not around when something exciting or important happens, or if he tries to guide when a child is not in the mood to be guided, both the father and the child miss the opportunity for a teachable moment that may not come around a second time. Study your children to know them better. Spend quantities of high-quality time with them. There is no substitute for simply being with your children. Be available, be approachable, be "on call" for them.

One of the best compliments my children have ever given me came from Peter, who was four years old at the time: "Dad, you're fun to be with." If you are a fun father who spends both quality and quantity time with your child, your job as a spiritual leader is given a real boost.

Establish Special Times

It is often difficult for a busy father, especially if there is more than one child, to know where he stands with his child and what his child is thinking about life. To solve this problem in our own family, I have instituted the practice of "special time" with each of my children at least twice every month. I rearrange my schedule to take him or her to a lesson (instead of Mom), or we pick something fun to do, or we just decide to have a meal together, just the two of us.

This special one-on-one time seems to increase father-child rapport. It conveys that you care enough to take time out of your busy life to "hang out" together, just because you want to. Second, you give that child focused attention. He does not have to compete with other children or adults for your attention, nor must you compete for his. Third, it gives you a time to take inventory in the following important areas:

- How your child feels about himself.
- How your child feels about you.
- How your child relates to the world and how she sees her place in the scheme of things.
- How special needs or problems are affecting him.
- What does your child think about God? Does she see herself as someone special in His eyes?

As your child gets older, keep things light. Resist the temptation to preach, or your child will shut you out. You want him to look forward to these outings because he enjoys your company. He should not feel as if an oral report is necessary or that this is a time to be quizzed and drilled.

Avoid vague openers: "How are you feeling?" or "How's your spiritual life?" You want your older child to enjoy communicating with you on topics that are important to him. Listening carefully will tell you a lot about your child's self-image and his emerging value system. You can gradually ease into topics that are important to you. Whenever I am spending this time with one of my teenagers, the most pressing items on my agenda are (1) how she feels about herself and (2) how she feels about God. However, teenagers are very private and usually will not disclose their full feelings. As frustrating as this may be for a father, pressing a child to go deeper than he or she is comfortable with is doomed to failure.

During your special time together try to leave your child with the following messages:

- I love you more deeply than you ever can imagine.
- I am interested in how you feel and what you do.
- I want to be involved in your life—to help, not to interfere. I am available for advice, not because I am smarter or because I don't trust you, but because I have lived longer and have profited by the experience of time.
- My most important wish for you is that you learn to love God.

You are not hitting your child with each of these heavy messages as though you were reciting the Ten Commandments to him. You are subtly discussing them in between bites of pancakes, an account of the last football game, or comments about various friends. The way you listen and respond will send as great a message as any profound advice you offer. In answer to your concern about how your child understands God, you may get a simple but meaningful response, such as, "Dad, He's awesome."

SPIRITUAL LEADERSHIP BENEFITS YOUR MARRIAGE

What's in it for you? How do fathers who are effective spiritual leaders in their families ultimately profit from this leadership? Once you step into the role of spiritual leader in your home you will find that your family relationships operate on a much more meaningful level. Your wife has more respect for you as the chairman of your own home than she would have if you were chairman of your own corporation. One of the greatest gifts you can give your wife is your involvement in your children's lives. Men often fail to appreciate the incredibly deep desire mothers have for the well-being of their children. You as a father have this desire also, but in some ways it seems to run more deeply in mothers.

When you are the spiritual leader in your home, the respect you will receive from your wife will be beyond your greatest expectations. Why does it seem to work this way? Because this is God's order in the family. When the husband shows his commitment to his family by being caring and involved, both the wife and the children profit, and the entire family relationship operates on a more rewarding level.

Fathers who have their spiritual houses in order earn respect from their children. Obedience is certainly their God-given right as parents; however, respect results in obedience from the heart. Esteem for the person of the father, an admiration of his personal qualities, makes children want to obey him. This is the beautiful level of discipline that you as an effective Christian father can achieve. If you have provided your children with a Christian model like Christ gave His disciples ("His children"), your children will follow you because they want to, not because they have to. Achieving this respect will give you a tremendous lift in your self-image. As your self-worth increases, you will become more comfortable interacting with your children, and your father-child communication will operate on a higher level.

What's in it for your children? Do children reared in a home where their father is the spiritual leader feel or act any differently? The answer is a resounding yes! The children have direction. They show direction in the "three Ms" of Christian goals: a Master, a mate, and a mission. How fathers love and serve their Master, how they love and serve their mates, and how they work toward their mission in life will leave lasting impressions on their children. Children who have strong Christian fathers see them working on these goals and therefore learn to value the Christian life.

Second, because these children have direction, they also have self-worth. They feel positive about themselves because they have purpose in life. I feel that the source of the problems facing today's troubled teenagers is a poor self-image and lack of purpose and direction in life. They have no sense of belonging, so they lack identity. The reason for this is that they have not experienced strong spiritual leadership. I learned this in a personal way when my son Jim wrote a paper about how being a Christian changed his life. His comment that spoke volumes was "Now I have a purpose to my life, and I know why I'm here."

Third, these children have proper priorities. They are able to say no to those things of the world that compete with their relationship with God, and this is very difficult for most teenagers to do.

Remember, your children may not give you immediate feedback during your many years of raising them. Parenting is not a pastime that provides instant gratification. The effects of spiritual training may appear very slowly; you may not see the full fruits of your labor until your children are much older.

Fathers, when you stand before your Father in heaven and are held accountable for rearing your children according to God's plan, what will your judgment be? Christian fathering is indeed a long-term investment.

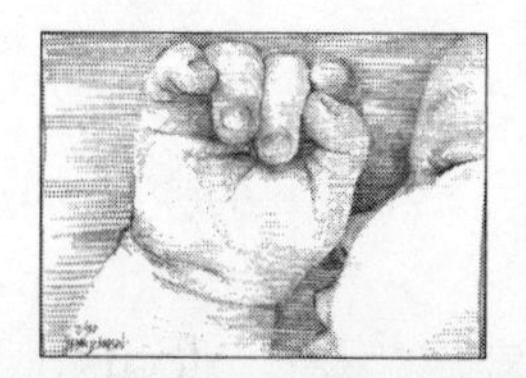

CHAPTER THREE

Pregnancy to Delivery

THE PREGNANT COUPLE

"God blessed them and said to them, 'Be fruitful and increase in number'" (Gen. 1:28). People have been following God's directive, while not always realizing that there is blessing attached to it. What a difference that blessing makes. When a man and woman become fruitful, it is because of God's blessing. Pregnancy announces to the world that you as a couple have taken part in a unique act of creation, with the Creator of the universe.

Pregnancy is an awesome time of waiting and preparing physically, emotionally, and spiritually. The most profound change ever to happen in the life of a couple is about to occur. Having a baby will change your lives in ways you would never dream possible. If this is not your first baby, you already know this. Cooperating with God in forming and shaping your child will surely drive you to your knees both in praise and supplication. But for now, thank God you are pregnant!

We use the term *pregnant couple* because although the mother alone physically carries the baby, both mother and father are preparing for parenthood, spiritually carrying the baby and nurturing each other through pregnancy. As the baby is growing to maturity, the Christian couple also will ripen spiritually if they stay open to what

PSALM 139:13–16

For you created my inmost being;
You knit me together in my mother's
womb.
I praise you because I am fearfully and
wonderfully made;
Your works are wonderful,
I know that well.
My frame was not hidden from you
when I was made in the secret place.
When I was woven together in the
depths of the earth,
your eyes saw my unformed body.
All the days ordained for me
were written in your book
before one of them came to be.

Meditation on Psalm 139:13–16

Sculpture within sculpture
And form within form resides.
Shape and splendid texture,
Like tapestry woven, now hides.
Precious miracle resting,
Then sensing the time is right,
It springs from protected nesting,
Bringing God's genius to light.

Martha Sears

God wants to do in their lives individually and as a couple. Our pregnancies helped us focus on our couplehood.

Prayer and Pregnancy

One custom we enjoyed as a pregnant couple was a nightly prayer ritual of laying our hands upon "our" womb. Our prayer would go something like this: "Father, we thank You for giving us this tiny life within. We acknowledge You as the architect of our developing child. Watch over every dividing cell, every organ, every system as the child You are building nears completion. Into Your hands we commit our child." (Psalm 139:13–16 is a beautiful prayer to use during pregnancy.)

In addition to praying for the health of your preborn child, you might also pray daily together for your own health and the health of your marriage. Daily prayer, beginning early in pregnancy, gets Christian parenthood off to the right start. Talking to your child in the womb and praying daily for him or her acknowledges that your fetus is already a member of your family. Prayer during pregnancy sets the stage for the moment of birth when you truly can thank God for answering your prayers. Francis and Judith McNutt have written a unique book entitled *Praying for Your Unborn Child: How Parents' Prayer Can Make a Difference in the Health and Happiness of Their Children* (see bibliography for a more complete description).

The daily pregnancy prayer and the ritual of laying on hands may be the father's first act as the spiritual leader of the family and his first step toward commitment and involvement with his children. In our family, this nightly ritual for our preborn babies became such a habit that after their births Bill couldn't get to sleep without first laying his hands on our newborn's head and praying. We felt God using this prenatal bonding experience to deepen our attachment to our babies.

Feelings about an Unwanted Pregnancy

For a variety of personal reasons you may not want to be pregnant, and when a menstrual period is missed, the question of pregnancy arises. This situation gives you a real opportunity as a Christian couple to put God's will before your own. Before you have a pregnancy test to confirm your suspicion, pray that you can joyfully accept God's will in the result of the test. Prepare your minds and hearts to embrace what God has designed for you. It is important to begin this prayer before the test, because your reaction to the results of the test can affect your attitude toward your pregnancy and can ultimately affect your child's sense of being welcome. Accepting the will of your Creator and putting aside your own desires is a difficult task, but one that will lead you to Christian maturity. Also, remember who is forming and knitting together this new life in the womb!

How Pregnancy Changes Your Marriage

The responsibility of a child can bring a higher level of maturity to your marriage relationship; pregnancy can increase your commitment to one another. However, if your marriage is shaky, you are particularly vulnerable to the emotional upheaval of pregnancy. A baby does not usually stabilize a marriage that lacks a strong foundation. This is why it is important to establish a strong Christian marriage before, or at least during, pregnancy.

In chapter 1 we talked about mutual giving as the hallmark of a fulfilled Christian marriage. When you are aware of and sensitive to each other's needs and how to respond to them during pregnancy, you are making a good preparation for parenting. In parenting, this giving is taken one step further—you will both be giving to a third person. In pregnancy, you continue the process of coming out of yourselves and prepare to give unselfishly to your child. In some respects, giving to your child is easier than giving to your spouse since a child is a biological extension of yourself, babies are more dependent, and their needs more obvious. On the other hand, babies are all unique individuals, and you must prepare yourselves to accept the child you are blessed with, whether easygoing or more demanding.

The many physical, emotional, and spiritual changes that occur during pregnancy will help you mature into Christian parents. Learning about these changes will help you be sensitive to each other's needs.

The first trimester. Pregnancy is not just growing a baby; it is the start of new relationships in the family. Pregnancy brings a sudden shift to the couple's relationship. The physical changes are obvious, but there are also accompanying emotional changes due to the effects of the hormones of pregnancy. For example, the hormone prolactin, which causes the mother's breasts to develop in order to nourish the baby, also cause her to feel more maternal.

Husbands need to be aware that the hormones necessary for the development of the baby can also be responsible for the uneven emotions experienced by their pregnant wives. Pregnancy is a stage of development, much like adolescence, and ambivalent feelings are normal. One minute a pregnant woman may feel like praising the Lord for her pregnancy, and the next minute she may have doubts or realize a frightening identity crisis: "I am going to be somebody's mother, but what will happen to the 'me' I know now?" She may experience the positive feelings called the "pride of pregnancy," which is the proof of her fertility and a delight in nourishing another life within her own body. And she may have negative feelings: fear of miscarriage, fear of becoming less attractive to her husband, ambivalence about leaving her job, or worry about her capabilities as a mother. The more unpleasant the woman's symptoms of pregnancy (for example, morning sickness), the more these negative feelings may increase. It's hard to handle complicated emotions when you feel horrible. The first trimester is a period of acceptance and adjustment for both of you, so most of your prayers can be directed toward this.

The second trimester. The second trimester is usually a quieter period. The concerns of the first trimester and the discomfort of morning sickness and fatigue probably will

SEXUAL FULFILLMENT DURING PREGNANCY

Many couples are pleasantly surprised at the woman's greatly increased sexual desire, especially during the middle months. Toward the end of pregnancy, a woman's sexual interest may diminish as she is physically more limited or if she has fears of inducing premature labor. (This fear is unfounded in normal pregnancies.) Often it is the man who becomes reluctant to have sex for these same reasons, concern for the baby and his wife's comfort. They both may struggle with psychological obstacles to sexual expression—the man feeling there is something unnatural about lovemaking now that his wife is so changed, the woman feeling she is less desirable. Inventiveness in sexual techniques will be useful at this time, along with a mutual sensitivity to the fact that growth brings change. *Making Love During Pregnancy,* by Elisabeth Bing and Libby Colman, is sensitively written and illustrated, and is especially helpful for first-time expectant couples. Cliff and Joyce Penner's book, *The Gift of Sex: A Christian Guide to Sexual Fulfillment,* is a wonderful book to encourage couples at any time during their marriages, especially when one or both of them may be struggling to understand and appreciate the gift of sex, including the spiritual aspects of this union God designed.

have lessened. The highlight of this period is feeling your baby move (around sixteen weeks for the mother and twenty weeks for the father). When you can both finally feel your baby kicking together, you will be moved to a higher level of bonding. This is especially true for the father because he now knows firsthand there is really a baby in there! Feeling your baby move is a high point of prayer and praise during your pregnancy.

Dependency feelings run high in the second trimester. The wife may feel an increased dependence on her husband as the protector and provider and often may express her own need to be "mothered" and loved, as he is instructed to do so beautifully in Ephesians 5:25–29. The husband also will depend upon his wife to nourish the child within her.

Pregnancy is a good time for you to share positive and negative thoughts about your present and future role changes. Good communication and a sincere appreciation of the emotional and physical changes during pregnancy can mean the difference between regarding pregnancy as a richly rewarding experience and seeing it as a low point of your marriage.

If, by the beginning of the second trimester, you and your spouse are finding it difficult to praise God for the life all three of you have created, and if you are struggling with being mutually sensitive to each other's needs, then you should seek professional counsel. Communication problems during pregnancy usually stem from one partner not being aware of the ambivalent feelings within the other person or of how these feelings are responsible for his or her behavior. Anticipatory guidance, an effective counseling tool during pregnancy, can help you talk with one another more effectively and prepare for many of the reality changes ahead. With prayer and consultation, pregnancy can be a high point of your experience with communication in marriage since there certainly is a lot to talk about.

Marital disharmony contributes to a woman's vulnerability to anxiety and depression during pregnancy. Although these are normal to a point, depression and anxiety in Christian parents may signify a breakdown in the living out of God's order for marriage and parenting. God ordained that a marriage have a firm foundation before a child is brought into the relationship. Perhaps much depression and anxiety during pregnancy arises from concern for what will happen when a child enters a home that is wobbly because the spiritual foundation is weak. And the skills necessary for successful, natural childbirth also require that a couple be spiritually in tune.

The third trimester. Even before the third trimester the wife's pregnancy will be showing in all its glory, and, like most women, she will be experiencing tremendous pride in her fullness and in the special status that is given to pregnant women. Offers of help will come from all around. Some of the anxiety levels that appeared during the first trimester and settled down during the second trimester will peak again in the third trimester in anticipation of the birth.

In spite of the radiant glow around pregnant women, at times they may not feel so radiant. In the third trimester, the wife needs constant reassurance from her husband that he loves her in this "state." Special attention to good grooming, and taking care of herself (as in being nice to herself, not just looking good for others), will do wonders for her self-image at this stage.

The final month. In the final month of pregnancy your anticipation level will be high. Although many women leave their jobs in the final month, others continue to work until the last minute to avoid the anxiety of waiting. Whichever you choose, make rest a priority. You may have trouble sleeping, partly because of a restless mind and partly because you just cannot find a comfortable sleeping position. Sleep, however, will come when you can let God bring His peace to your mind. He knows you need your rest. The best spiritual aid for sleeping we know is to relax by reading your favorite psalms. Getting comfortable in a side-lying position using several regular pillows or a body pillow to support your limbs and ease the strain on your back muscles will help you relax better.

God's design includes a nesting instinct that leads women to do the things necessary to prepare for the baby's coming. They may seek quiet times in the final month of pregnancy when they can tune in to the child inside and feel that this child is a person within the family. This time of peace and quiet is a time to relax, slow down, and devote more time and energy to bonding with and welcoming your child. This is all part of the attachment process that began early in pregnancy and continues after birth.

Tuning in to the nesting instinct may also result in a sudden burst of energy that inspires a mother to clean the house and have everything just right for the baby. Be careful not to overdo it and wear yourself out. Starting labor in an exhausted state is not good.

A word about preparing a nursery. It is more important for a Christian couple to prepare their minds and souls for the coming of their baby than to prepare a room. We have noticed throughout the past decade that many expectant couples are shifting their priorities and seem less preoccupied with the properly appointed nursery. This has long been the case in our family. A few months after the birth of our fourth child, we opened

COVERING THE BASES

The following Scripture verses are like bookends, holding up both ends of the spectrum of concerns a new father-to-be may have. With these two Scriptures you can overcome your uneasy father feelings and prepare yourself for being a Christian father. Managing those father feelings and growing toward being a God-centered Christian father during pregnancy will lay the foundation for you to become an enthusiastic Christian father when your child arrives. You'll have all your bases covered.

Ephesians 5:25: "Husbands, love your wives, just as Christ loved the church and gave himself up for it."

Philippians 4:19: "My God will meet all your needs according to his glorious riches in Christ Jesus."

our house as part of a tour of homes benefiting a local church charity. We were amused to see the confusion in the eyes of visitors when they exclaimed, "But where is the baby's nursery?" Our baby's "nursery" was right where God led us to have it—her little cradle was next to our bed, and within a few months she graduated into our bed.

Father Feelings during Pregnancy

Though God has blessed the mother with the privilege of carrying, birthing, and nourishing a baby, the father does plays a vital role in pregnancy, birth, and child care. The father also has adjustments to make during pregnancy and will need to pray, to plan, and to prepare his heart for the new arrival. He will also need emotional support from family and friends, and especially his wife.

When the pregnancy is confirmed, most men feel pride in their masculinity and fecundity. Then the reality of another mouth to feed sinks in; the responsibility of caring for his family can begin to weigh heavily upon him. In addition to the new dependent now growing in the womb, your wife may become more dependent on you throughout the pregnancy. These increased demands may make you question your ability both to father the baby and "mother" the mother. Economic worries are among the earliest concerns of the new father. Like many fathers, you may exaggerate this worry way out of proportion. You don't have to think about college tuition prenatally.

Some men actually experience pregnancy-like symptoms, such as nausea or weight gain, during their wives' pregnancy,

GETTING ENOUGH PROTEIN

Counting protein is the most important part of planning your day's nutrition. Seventy-five to 100 grams is what you should aim for. Some days you'll be high, even over 100; other days you'll barely make 75. If you consistently fall in the low range, try having two eggs every day since they are easy to prepare. Or, combine grains and legumes to make a complete protein, for example, beans and rice. An easy way to count protein is to follow this rule of thumb—there are about *seven* grams of protein in each of these *seven* items:

- 1 large egg
- 1 cup of milk
- 1 ounce of meat, poultry, fish
- 1 ounce of cheese
- 1½ tablespoons of peanut butter
- 1 cup of yogurt
- 1/2 cup cooked, dry beans

If you have all seven, you will get about 50 grams of protein. By increasing any category you choose (for example, you have a four-ounce serving of chicken and an extra egg), you have added four "7s" to the total, making your protein count 77 grams. To raise that to about 100 grams, you could have an extra two cups of milk (14 grams) and another ounce of cheese, or you could have three ounces of tuna fish. Between *eleven and fourteen* "7s" is your daily goal.

showing a subconscious desire to share in their wives' physical condition. Other fathers do not envy pregnancy at all, and they regard this period as a necessary nuisance before having a baby. Husbands, if this is your attitude, you may tend to focus on your baby's arrival and subconsciously ignore the pregnancy and with it your wife. However, your wife's physical and emotional changes will be hard to block out, and they will serve as a reminder of the reality of the family pregnancy.

Toward the end of the pregnancy you may have worries about how the baby will affect your marital relationship. These feelings, and all of those listed above, are normal during pregnancy. The following tips may help you handle these uneasy feelings.

Take stock of your situation. As the fetus matures, so will you. The challenges of pregnancy are an opportunity for you to ripen spiritually and become a more mature man. Pregnancy can be inventory time in your personal life: a time to take stock and define your priorities. It is a time to account for where you have been and where you are going. Specifically, take a hard look at how you are walking with God and how you are relating with your wife. If your life and your marriage are God-centered, your fathering will be too. Are you sensitive to your wife's needs? How is your career affecting your marriage? It is important to put your marriage before your job at this stage so that later you can put your fathering before your job.

Get involved in the pregnancy. The earlier you are involved, the more involved you will be throughout pregnancy and in the years of childrearing to come. Participate in the choices you and your wife will make early in your pregnancy: which doctor or midwife, childbirth class, pediatrician, birthing environment, and so on. Accompany your wife on her visits to the doctor or midwife. The more involved you are, the more you will know about what is going on, and the more comfortable you will feel. Your fathering career will be off to a confident start.

Help prepare the nest. Assist your wife in the tasks of getting ready for the baby. Become interested in the shopping trips, admire the shower presents, and start a checklist of things that need to be done around the house. A word of advice: respect your wife's nesting urges. If major lifestyle upheavals are necessary, such as moving to a new house or changing jobs, avoid making these changes in the last couple of months of pregnancy, or too soon after birth.

Pray daily that God will give you the wisdom to be a husband and father according to His design. Ask God to prepare your heart and soul for the arrival of this new life He has entrusted to your care. Both husband and wife are blessed when they are involved together and with God in the formation of a new family unit. This blessing will carry over into your commitment to your wife and to your child, and this commitment will be the foundation of your family life.

MOTHERING YOUR PREBORN CHILD

Taking care of your baby begins long before you are able to hold your baby in your arms. More is discovered every year about what babies need in the womb to have the best chance of being healthy throughout their lives. Some of what you can do even begins before conception, for example, good nutrition.

Nutrition during Pregnancy

Good prenatal nutrition, or the lack of it, can affect the health and development of your baby profoundly. When you eat right, your baby can grow right, meaning fewer congenital defects and better brain growth. For yourself, the benefits are lower risk for gestational diabetes, toxemia, anemia, leg cramps, heartburn, obesity, and complicated or premature labor. The main nutritional requirements for all growing persons (in this case, mother and baby) are proteins (at least seventy-five grams per day), calories (approximately five hundred extra), vitamins and other phytochemicals from fresh fruits and vegetables and whole grains, and iron. Each day you should eat the following number of servings from the five basic food groups:

- 5 grains (whole grain breads, cereal, rice, pasta)
- 3–5 vegetables (fresh or frozen; raw whenever possible)
- 2–4 fruits (fresh or frozen; raw is best)
- 2–3 dairy (milk, yogurt, cheese)
- 3–4 protein (meat, poultry, fish, eggs, dry beans, nuts) (See box on p. 65.)

Note: If you are intolerant of dairy products, increase the protein in the meat group and supplement your diet with other sources of calcium.

What is a healthy weight gain during pregnancy? This varies from woman to woman, but there are some general guidelines. At one time, strict limits were placed on weight gain. Providing you are eating nutritious foods, such limits are not necessary. Weight gain is an individual situation that should not be controlled by anything except good nutrition. The usual weight gain during pregnancy is around thirty pounds, give or take a few, distributed as follows:

- Weight of baby: 7½ pounds
- Weight of placenta: 1½ pounds
- Weight of uterus: 3½ pounds
- Weight of amniotic fluid: 2½ pounds
- Weight of extra blood volume and fluids: 8½ pounds
- Weight of breasts: 1 pound

Any weight over this total 24½ pounds will be fat, a certain amount of which is healthy.

A general guide for weight gain during pregnancy is three pounds during the first trimester and about three to four pounds per month thereafter. A woman who is underweight to begin with should show a larger weight gain, adding catch-up pounds early in her pregnancy. If you are overweight, pregnancy is not the time to try to diet in order to be closer to your ideal weight after you give birth. Eat plenty of nutritious food to nourish your preborn child properly, and avoid indulging in high-fat, empty-calorie treats.

It is unlikely that expectant mothers will put on too much weight by indulging in the foods suggested here. Most women gain excessive weight because they eat the wrong kinds of foods. Avoid junk food and high-fat meals. Nibble on nutritious snacks between meals. Use fats, oils, and sweets sparingly. Do not skip meals, and above all, *avoid crash diets* during pregnancy.

Your appetite and food consumption should parallel your pregnancy. It may be hard to eat well in the early months when your stomach is queasy; frequent snacking on food you can tolerate, especially protein, will help to decrease nausea. During the last three months of pregnancy you may be consuming an extra five hundred nutritious calories a day without excessive weight gain. You may be subject to certain cravings, many of which are high in fat as well as the complex carbohydrates and protein you need. You do deserve to pamper yourself occasionally, but it is not wise to overindulge. If you feel well, eat mostly nutritious foods, and show no evidence of unhealthy water retention, there's no need to worry about your weight gain.

What to Avoid during Pregnancy

Certain chemicals are known to cause defects in the preborn baby; these are called teratogens. Only a few drugs have absolutely proven to be teratogenic; however, knowledge of subtle teratogenic effects is incomplete. No one knows if a teratogen that harms the baby in large doses will harm it more subtly in smaller doses. It is possible that very low levels of some chemicals may cause very subtle malformations that are difficult to identify.

Drugs and medications. You should seek professional medical advice before taking any drug during pregnancy, even an over-the-counter medication. When you take a drug, your baby also takes the drug; but unlike you, he is a rapidly developing organism with limited capabilities to get rid of the drug. The time of highest risk to the baby is during the first trimester of pregnancy. It is best not to take any remedies, even over-the-counter ones, such as aspirin or nasal sprays, if you suspect you could be pregnant. (Home pregnancy tests can give you that information.) During pregnancy refrain from taking any medications unless directed by your physician.

And, of course, Christians know drugs like marijuana and cocaine abuse their bodies,—the temples of the Holy Spirit. At this writing, marijuana has *no proven* detrimental effects to the resident of the womb. It is known, however, that marijuana can damage brain cells and reproductive cells in experimental animals and probably also in humans. Common sense should dictate that it would be risky to smoke marijuana during pregnancy. Cocaine has been proven to be definitely harmful to the baby.

Nicotine. This is another drug that is abusive to our bodies, and it is even more so to the baby in the womb. Do not smoke during pregnancy; do *not* compromise your baby's health. Nicotine decreases the blood supply to the placenta and therefore to the baby. Your smoking can cause your baby to be premature, to have diminished brain growth, and to be smaller than normal; this risk increases in proportion to the number of cigarettes you smoke each day. (This also means a greatly increased risk for Sudden Infant Death Syndrome.) It is hard to quit smoking, but the health benefits for you and your baby, now and after birth, will be well worth the effort. Secondhand smoke can also be harmful; insist that others not smoke around you.

Alcohol. "You are going to conceive and have a son. Now see to it that you drink no wine or other fermented drink" (Judg. 13:3–4). These were God's words to the mother of Samson. It would be good if every pregnant woman could be so directly instructed. Experts now recognize that alcohol is potentially very harmful during pregnancy. Excessive alcohol consumption during pregnancy can cause a large spectrum of abnormalities, referred to as "fetal alcohol syndrome"—small baby, unusual facial features, and mental retardation. Nearly every organ can be affected by alcohol in the fetal blood, and the greater the alcohol consumption, the greater the severity of the fetal malformations. How much alcohol can you drink without causing damage to your baby? The threshold for safe alcohol consumption is unknown. It is known that a lot of alcohol harms the baby a lot, but it is not known whether a little alcohol harms the baby a little. It is known that five or more drinks at one time early in pregnancy, or an average of two drinks per day throughout pregnancy can harm your baby. Because no one knows the exact threshold effect of alcohol, it seems wise not to drink any alcohol during pregnancy. Unfortunately, many heavy drinkers are also heavy smokers. This can be a disastrous combination.

It is interesting how God designed the human body to care for itself by sending out warning signals. During pregnancy, many mothers have a natural distaste for cigarettes, alcohol, and caffeine.

Caffeine. At this writing, it is uncertain whether caffeine is harmful to the human fetus. However, caffeine that has been given in very large doses to experimental animals does result in malformations in their offspring. And we do know that caffeine does interfere with the absorption of certain nutrients. Until this caffeine question is settled, the Federal Food and Drug Administration advises pregnant women to limit their consumption of products containing caffeine as a precautionary measure. These include coffee, certain soft drinks, tea, and chocolate. Some over-the-counter pain and cold remedies also contain caffeine; their labels usually identify their content.

Prenatal Bonding

Being in harmony with your baby is one of the most important aspects of God's design for parenting. This harmony begins during pregnancy. Research on fetal awareness has shown that the emotional state of the mother during the last three months of pregnancy can affect the emotional development of the baby. How a baby in the womb also senses joyful emotions is beautifully illustrated in Luke 1:44. When Mary greeted Elizabeth, the baby leaped for joy in Elizabeth's womb. Likewise, when a pregnant mother becomes anxious or stressed, levels of stress hormones cross the placenta into the baby's circulatory system and can cause the baby to be agitated as well. In other words, when mother is upset, baby is upset. Constant exposure of the baby's developing brain to stress hormones can result in an overcharged nervous system, accounting for the common statement made by parents of a hypersensitive baby, "He came wired that way." (Chapter 10 includes a thorough discussion of temperament, which is determined both by genetics and by environment, including womb environment.)

The idea that your emotional state during pregnancy can influence the baby's personality creates awesome responsibility. You can create a peaceful womb experience by following these suggestions.

Resolve stress promptly. Every mother experiences some stress during pregnancy because there are so many changes in so many areas of life. How quickly and effectively you deal with this stress is the important issue. Researchers in fetal awareness believe that temporary stresses do not appear to have any lasting effects on the fetus. Chronic, unresolved conflicts and anxiety throughout most of the pregnancy are more likely to disturb the baby. Keep in mind that your baby shares your emotions, and find positive ways to handle the stress in your life.

Talk and sing to your baby. Give your baby pleasant womb memories. Studies have shown that infants respond to the familiar voices that talked and sang to them *in utero.* Newborns were better able to attend to their fathers' voices if they had talked to them a lot before birth, and children were able to learn songs more easily that their mothers had sung to them while they were in the womb.

Play harmonious, calming music. Preborn babies are calmed by soothing music, such as Vivaldi, Mozart, and classical guitar, but they are agitated by rock music.

Do your best to stabilize and strengthen your personal life and your marriage relation-

ship, seeking counseling if necessary. We can't help feeling that the baby inside you senses the commitment that awaits him or her after birth. The following Scripture passages will help you encourage a peaceful womb environment and manage your emotions during particularly stressful times.

Psalm 4	Psalm 22:9–11
Psalm 37:1–11	Psalm 71:1–6
Psalm 127	Psalm 139
Proverbs 3:5–6	Proverbs 17:22
Isaiah 41:10	Matthew 11:28–30
John 14:27	Philippians 4:4–9
1 Peter 5:7	1 John 4:13–18

MAKING IMPORTANT CHOICES ABOUT BIRTH

Parenting begins long before your baby is born. There are many important decisions to make during pregnancy (or ideally even before pregnancy!) that will affect how you begin your life with your new baby. The more time you can have to do your homework, the better. If you only have a few months before your baby is born, pray for God's guidance as you explore all the options open to you in today's birthing world.

Very early in the pregnancy, a Christian couple should seek answers to the following questions:

- Are there support groups and/or parenting classes available in our church or other churches that support the type of philosophy, laid out in this book?
- What childbirth classes are available in our community? Are any of them taught by a Christian, or even with a Christian emphasis?
- Who will be the best doctor or midwife for our pregnancy and delivery?*
- Should we hire a professional labor assistant to be with us during the birth?
- Who will be the best pediatrician or family doctor for our baby?*
- Where should we have our baby, and what birthing alternatives are available in our area?

Choosing a Christian Support Group

Just as a good Bible study group is helpful for the beginning Christian, some type of support group or parenting class is helpful for first-time parents. Support groups consist of parents who share their problems and encourage one another. More experienced

*It is unwise to compromise competence just to get a Christian doctor or midwife. Seek out a health care provider who is professionally competent, whom you feel comfortable with, and who is also a Christian; if this combination is not available, select the best provider, and hopefully one who is pro-life.

parents help new parents, and the support group functions as an extended family.

Your support group can assist you in making basic decisions during your pregnancy. It can also help you develop your own parenting philosophy and at the same time make you more aware of the available resources in your community. Look into some of the following support groups early in your pregnancy.

Parenting classes, possibly within a local church. Some churches, especially very large congregations, offer parenting classes, such as those created or recommended by Apple Tree Family Ministries (P. O. Box 2083, Artesia, CA 90702-2083; (562) 925-0149 or toll free (888) 925-0149). These classes may be directed to pregnant and first-time parents. If your church does not offer such classes, ask your midwife or doctor to recommend other classes in your community.

La Leche League International (LLLI). LLLI is perhaps the largest mother-to-mother support organization in the world. It was started by a small group of mothers in 1957 for the purpose of providing breastfeeding information and support at a time when a large majority of mothers did not breastfeed. Although this group is a secular one, the principles held by LLLI are applicable to Christian parents. Monthly meetings are held in the home of a local La Leche League member. Each leader, besides having long-term breastfeeding experience, has special training in counseling new mothers about common concerns of breastfeeding and parenting. She also enjoys access to a lending library, a board of medical consultants, and her own continuing education that she passes on to you. We strongly recommend that you attend a series of La Leche League meetings during pregnancy. Although most mothers at first come to La Leche League for breastfeeding help, they tend to stay involved because of the support they find for their parenting style. (LLLI: P. O. Box 4079, Schaumburg, IL 60168-4079; 1-800-LA-LECHE or 847-519-7730). It is helpful to keep in mind that as with any secular organization, there will be a variety of spiritual views represented.

Choosing Childbirth Classes

We highly recommend that first-time pregnant couples attend a childbirth class starting around the sixth month of pregnancy. If possible, find a Christian childbirth class that uses biblical principles to explain God's design for childbirth. Most hospital-based childbirth classes teach couples what the hospital and the doctors consider important. They will prepare you to be a good patient, but this may not be the best choice for you. A better choice would be a reliable private teacher or classes offered by a consumer-based organization that will help you prepare for the birth you want. The following list names the more popular organizations that teach childbirth classes. They differ mainly in the techniques used for relaxation and coping with the stress of childbirth. Christian childbirth classes often incorporate the best techniques from several organizations.

- Apple Tree Family Ministries—a Christian organization (see information on page 72.)
- The American Academy of Husband-Coached Childbirth—also known as the Bradley method®—P. O. Box 5224, Sherman Oaks, CA 91413-5224, (800) 423-2397; (800) 42-BIRTH in California
- International Childbirth Education Association (ICEA)—P. O. Box 20048, Minneapolis, MN 55420, (612) 854-8660
- The American Society for Psychoprophylaxis in Obstetrics (ASPO)—also known as the Lamaze method—1840 Wilson Boulevard, Suite 204, Arlington, VA 22201, (800) 368-4404
- NAPSAC (National Association of Parents and Professionals for Safe Alternatives in Childbirth)—P. O. Box 646, Marble Hill, MO 63764, (314) 238-2010; request their consumer guide to childbirth education organizations

PLAN AHEAD FOR POSTPARTUM CARE

The controversy in the health insurance industry over how soon a new mother and baby should leave the hospital brings up an important issue. Mothers and babies have tended to do better once they get home to the familiar nest. That's not because they don't need the care, but because home is a friendlier place, the appropriate place for both newborn and mother. What needs to happen is for health care to provide continuing care at home so that breastfeeding can be monitored and the new mother taught basic newborn care. It is not right that new mothers are sent home to care for newborns before they are ready, just to save on the cost of additional days in the hospital. Home care, in the form of a postpartum *doula* (from the Greek word meaning "servant"), can provide all the lactation help and infant monitoring that mother and baby need at a fraction of the cost of extending the hospital stay. Ask your insurance company about how they will work with you to be sure you can get the care you need. Ask them to consider covering the cost of a *doula* in order for you to be able to have a shorter hospital stay. (See p. 78 for how to find postpartum services through DONA.)

Choosing Where to Deliver Your Baby

Many childbirth choices are available for today's couples. Where and how you deliver your baby are probably two of the most important decisions you will make during your pregnancy. These decisions should be made with much prayer and consultation.

Many variables go into making the right decision: Is this your first baby? Are you anticipating any obstetrical complications? What will your insurance pay for? How far do you live from your hospital or birth attendant? How important to you are the setting and the environment of your childbirth experience? The following options are available for you to consider.

A traditional method of delivery. We only mention this option to discourage it. Fortunately, gone are the days (or at least they should be) when pregnancy was viewed as a disease and a woman went to the hospital to be delivered by means of a medical and/or surgical procedure. Childbirth classes were not encouraged. A father was made to feel unclean and inept and was banished to the waiting room while the mother labored and delivered alone. The lonely, laboring, medicated mother was required to remain on her back, a position that increases back pain and lessens the blood flow to the uterus. The mother was then moved to an operating table, still on her back, and strapped into stirrups. After the birth, mother and baby were taken to separate rooms to "recover" from this operation of birth, and the father viewed his baby through the glass windows of the nursery. The baby was fed a scientifically tested formula that was supposed to be as good as and certainly more convenient than what the Creator had designed. Fortunately, nearly all couples today have the wisdom to demand more from the birth event than what these antiquated practices provide.

Birthing or LDR rooms. Most hospitals now offer a childbirth option called the labor-delivery-recovery room or the birthing room. It is located within the obstetrical unit of the hospital and is sometimes referred to as an ABC (alternative birth center). At first glance this room (or suite of rooms) looks like a normal bedroom; it is designed to convey a homelike atmosphere. Furnishings may include colorful curtains and bedspread, plants, rocking chair, stereo, kitchenette, labor tub, and similar conveniences. The bed does not look like a delivery table but resembles most hospital beds (or even a homey queen-size brass bed) and is adjustable for the laboring mother. Some rooms have birthing chairs. All the medical and surgical equipment that may be needed is unobtrusively but efficiently near at hand.

The laboring couple is admitted to the birthing room. They labor together in this room, deliver in this room, recover and even spend their postpartum course in this room. They are not transported from room to room as they would be in traditional births. A very important feature of the birthing room is that the baby can stay with the mother from birth to discharge from the hospital and is taken into the nursery only if the mother wishes or medical complications occur. The birthing room represents more than just a physical facility. It represents an attitude that birth is a normal process in life until proven otherwise. (Be sure the birthing room you choose has this attitude, as well as the proper physical appointments.)

One more important factor for an expectant couple to consider in choosing a hospital is the level of newborn intensive care available should medical complications arise during or after birth. If a complication occurs around the time of birth, it is usually with the baby. Therefore, parents should base their choice of a hospital on the newborn care facilities as well as the facilities available for mother care.

Birthing centers. Free-standing birthing centers are located and run separately from any hospital but are usually within minutes of a medical facility to which the laboring mother can be transported if complications arise. Birth centers are staffed by certified nurse midwives (or by lay midwives in some states) who are supervised by physicians. Some are even owned and operated by physicians who rely on midwives to provide some or most of the prenatal and birth services. In this type of birth environment couples can find a homelike setting without the medical mindset still encountered in hospital birthing rooms.

A well-trained and experienced midwife is the ideal birthing attendant because her mindset is dedicated to the concept that birth is a normal, healthy process for at least 90 percent of all women. She is also able to discern which women will need the services of an obstetrician and she is wise enough to screen her clientele carefully. Midwives also practice in many hospitals. Many midwives are dedicated Christian women who see their profession as a ministry God revealed in Scripture (Exod. 1:15–21).

Home births. The home-birth movement arose because the traditional system of maternal care failed to recognize an honest consumer need. Increasing numbers of Christian couples have reacted to the childbirth-is-a-disease-needing-treatment attitude by taking the birth event back to the home.

Because of the possibility of obstetrical complications, both the American Academy of Obstetrics and Gynecology and the American Academy of Pediatrics do not endorse giving birth at home. Yet good studies have shown that when a baby is born at home, the safety and outcome is as good or even better as long as the birth is attended by a qualified midwife or physician and the mother is carefully screened for risk factors. We understand the feelings of couples who wish to give birth at home.

We can speak with some insight into this dilemma, since four of our own seven births were at home. It is a beautiful experience for parents and baby. As with all the options of childbirthing environments, prayer and consultation are needed before choosing to have a home birth. We know that there are couples whom God will lead toward safely attended home births. (For an in-depth discussion of how to prayerfully and wisely make the decision to have a home birth, we refer you to a chapter in Helen Wessel's book *Under the Apple Tree,* entitled "No Place Like Home" [see bibliography]). One answer to help more hesitant parents is to have more sensitive birthing environments in hospitals or birthing centers.

Use prayerful discernment in deciding where to birth your baby. We encourage couples choosing a hospital birth to choose a hospital that has a genuine alternative birthing center. The choice between "natural" or "technological" childbirth should not be an either-or decision. Thank God for the technological advances that have saved the lives of many mothers and babies. We want to see modern maternal care rely not only on a blend of parental intuition and medical science, but also on a true understanding of God's natural design and efficiency for the birth process that will work well in most cases, if not hindered.

Choosing Your Doctor or Midwife

In perhaps no other area of healthcare is the art of provider-client communication as important as in pregnancy. The following suggestions will guide you in selecting a healthcare provider whom you can trust to work with you to achieve the birth you want.

It is quite advisable and customary to interview healthcare providers before choosing the right one for your family. When making your first appointment, let the receptionist know you are making the appointment solely to discuss your philosophy of childbirth and whether this particular provider can meet your needs. Take a written list of questions specific to your needs. Early on in your pregnancy you may have no idea of what questions to ask. There is so much to learn before you can even know what your questions are, let alone be able to evaluate the responses you will get to your questions. Reading chapter 4, "The Birth of Your Baby," will be a way to start gathering information. Check the bibliography for other books to read. There are many things you will need to decide, and as a consumer of health care it is your responsibility to be informed so you can make the choices that will be best for you and your baby. The motto of the International Childbirth Education Association (ICEA) is "Freedom of choice through knowledge of alternatives." Ideally, as you read, learning what your options are, you can prepare a list of questions to ask your prospective birth attendants. Realistically, however, most women don't do this reading until they have already chosen who will attend their baby's birth. If you find you are having increasingly difficult differences in your birth planning, you may have to make the decision to change healthcare providers.

Because of the increasing numbers of informed and discerning parents, most doctors are becoming more flexible about offering alternatives during labor and delivery to meet the parents' requests. As you ask a doctor to be sensitive to your needs, please be sensitive in return. The physician you are speaking with is a highly trained professional who has a sincere interest in the medical safety of your childbirth. For this reason you will probably receive an answer like this: "I respect your desires completely, but I must, for the best medical interest of yourself and your baby reserve the right to intervene medically should the need arise. You will have to trust my judgment." A Christian doctor may add, "We must pray that God will give us both the wisdom to trust each other's judgment." Your doctor is asking of you the same respect and flexibility that you are asking of him or her. This is easy once you have found a professional with whose philosophy you are comfortable.

Using a Professional Labor Assistant

The newest members of the obstetrical team are professional labor assistants (PLA's). Also known as *doulas, monitrices,* or *labor support persons,* these women, who are often nurses, childbirth educators, or midwives, provide psychological support and practical help during labor and delivery. The PLA you choose will get to know you as a couple, work with you to develop a birth plan, and help you both understand how she sees her role in helping you grow as a couple through this experience. You will want a PLA whose marriage philosophy, as well as her birth philosophy, is in line with yours. During labor she will do everything she can to help your labor progress well, from simply suggesting changes of position to helping you interpret medical information so that you can participate in decisions about your care. The calm and helpful presence of a PLA can shorten your labor and increase the chances that your birth will turn out much as you hoped. Fathers greatly appreciate the presence of the PLA, as her expertise takes the pressure off husbands cast in the role of "coach," enabling them to do what they do best—support and love their wives.

We believe that PLA's are the future standard of excellence in care for expectant families. To find one near you, ask your doctor, your midwife, or your childbirth instructor. Or you can contact Doulas of North America (DONA), 1100 23rd Avenue, Seattle, WA 98112, (206) 324-5440 (ATFM, p. 72, is a source for finding Christian *doulas*.) In some situations, health insurance companies can even be persuaded to cover the PLA's fee. Before choosing a PLA for your birth, interview her as you would a doctor or midwife: What services does she provide? When will she come to you during labor? What are her qualifications and training? How many births has she attended? What in general is her philosophy of childbirth and, in particular, how a couple matures through childbirth? Choose someone with whom both of you feel comfortable.

Choosing Your Pediatrician

If you've chosen a family practice physician for prenatal and birth care, she or he will probably continue to care for your baby. Otherwise, when selecting a pediatrician, follow basically the same guidelines for choosing your own health care provider; consider the doctor's competence, communication abilities, and his or her walk with God. It is important to have a face-to-face interview with the pediatrician during pregnancy. Otherwise, your first meeting with this doctor will take place in the hospital shortly after delivery when he or she makes the initial examination of your newborn. This initial patient-doctor communication is often compromised by the confusion or hubbub of a busy hospital unit, an extremely tired mother, or a hurried doctor. Interview your prospective pediatrician during the latter months of your pregnancy. This prenatal visit will give the pediatrician an idea of what you really want and also will increase his or her respect for you as prospective parents.

Bring a written list of your most pressing questions and concerns. Attempt to keep the interview brief since most pediatricians do not charge for this prenatal visit. Respect the doctor's time.

Ask your prospective pediatrician his or her philosophy about the aspects of childrearing that are most important to you. What is the doctor's overall philosophy of early parenting? You will want it to be compatible and supportive of your own views. Ask how he or she will be involved in the care of your baby after birth. How do you reach the doctor in case of emergency?

Avoid negative openers. Nothing is more nonproductive than opening the interview with a list of "I don't wants"; for example, "I don't want my baby to have any bottles in the hospital." It is more helpful to ask, "How can I avoid having any bottles given to my baby in the hospital?" Remember, your reason for doing the interview is to determine if you and your prospective pediatrician are on the same wavelength. Negative openers close your mind to the possibility that you may, in fact, learn something by your doctor's response, something you may not have considered before your interview, although you were certain you knew all the angles. Negative openers may also close the doctor's mind toward you and set up a barrier to future communication.

To help you get the most out of your prenatal visit with your pediatrician, look at this visit through the doctor's eyes. All during the interview he or she is filing away bits of information from which to draw conclusions about his future level of service to you. Here's what might be going on in the pediatrician's mind: *These parents are certainly off to the right start. Parenting seems to be a top priority in their lives at this moment. They have taken time to interview me, and I can tell from their questions that choosing the right pediatrician for their baby is also a high priority. These parents care, which makes me want to care. Therefore, I will make a special effort to be a good pediatrician for them.*

A caring doctor and intuitive parents are a winning combination that brings to your child the high level of medical care that most parents and children want and deserve. Some parents feel confident enough in their parenting that they want a lesser level of involvement of the doctor in their family; he is on standby should a medical problem arise. Other parents, especially first-time parents, often want a highly involved doctor who becomes a trusted extra member of the family.

One of my most memorable new-patient visits was from a couple who said to me, "We'll pray for you; we always pray for our doctors." That simple statement said it all. From then on I knew what kind of a relationship I would have with that family.

CHRISTIAN CHILDBIRTH

Marriage, birth, and death are important events in a person's life. No Christian would dream of approaching them without the support of prayer, Scripture, ministry, and fellowship. If you are properly and prayerfully prepared, your baby's birth will most likely be a good experience. Christian couples should equip themselves with knowledge about the birth process, techniques for coping and preventing pain, and the reassurance of God's promises for them in pregnancy and in childbirth. These promises are a tremendous source of strength and blessing, but a source that is often untapped. These scriptural promises will be explored later in this chapter, in the section on Christian childbirth classes, which combines

SURGICAL BIRTH CAN BE PREVENTED—MOST OF THE TIME

In American hospitals 25 percent of mothers give birth by cesarean section. Why does the divine design for childbirth go wrong 25 percent of the time? Does this mean that the Creator made a mistake in how birth was meant to happen, or could it be that our interference with the divine design creates these alarming statistics? When mothers are given proper prenatal education and preparation, when they have appropriate support during labor and freedom to move with their bodies, cesarean births should be necessary for only about 5 percent of women. "Failure to progress" is the biggest reason for doing a cesarean. This diagnosis usually means that fear and tension are inhibiting the body's ability to do its work. It is also sometimes due to doctors' expectations of how fast the labor should progress, not allowing for variations that can still be considered normal. We need the option of cesareans for true cases of failure to progress, where the mothers become overwearied and nothing else is working, or for those unusual situations where the baby simply cannot make it through the birth canal. We also need a much broader definition of what's normal.

Vaginal Birth after Cesarean (VBAC)

The old adage "Once a cesarean, always a cesarean" is no longer accepted by even the most conservative obstetricians. *At least* 70 percent of all women who have had previous cesarean births can have a vaginal birth with subsequent pregnancies. In his book *Birth after Cesarean: The Medical Facts* (see bibliography), obstetrician Dr. Bruce Flamm presents the results of his research and describes how women can work with their doctors in avoiding unnecessary surgery.

Much attention has been given to reducing the cesarean rate both by professional committees and by lay organizations such as International Cesarean Awareness Network (ICAN). Contact ICAN for more information on VBAC and for the location of a chapter in your area. They hold meetings to educate couples about what they can do to lower their risk of having a cesarean and to increase their chances that a VBAC will be successful, even if a woman has had several cesareans. They also provide support for women who have had cesareans or other disappointing birth experiences. International Cesarean Awareness Network, 1304 Kingsdale Avenue, Redondo Beach, CA 90278, (310) 542-6400.

physical and emotional training with thorough spiritual preparation.

Overcoming Fear and Pain

Fear and the tension that results are the source of much of the agony that we have come to associate with childbirth. Dr. Grantly Dick-Read was the first to write about the effects of fear on women in childbirth. His research was not easily accepted by his professional colleagues because, at that time, the answer to pain in childbirth was anesthesia. In the 1940s Dr. Dick-Read published *Childbirth without Fear* (now in its fifth edition) in which he described how women could break the fear-tension-pain cycle and have positive birth experiences. As a result, *natural childbirth* became a household term. Dr. Dick-Read recognized that childbirth is not intended by God to be a time of suffering. This truth is borne out beautifully in God's Word. Scriptures refer to childbirth as a joyful time. In Genesis 21:6 Sarah says: "God has brought me laughter" when Isaac was born. In Luke 1:57–58 we read, "When it was time for Elizabeth to have her baby, she gave birth to a son. Her neighbors and relatives heard that the Lord had shown her great mercy, and they shared her joy." Jesus used the birth of a baby to describe the joy His disciples would have when they saw Him resurrected (John 16:21).

For Helen Wessel's book *The Joy of Natural Childbirth* (fifth edition of *Natural Childbirth and the Christian Family*), she researched the Hebrew meaning of certain terms relating to childbirth. She shows how modern translators of the Bible have done childbearing women a disservice. For example, Genesis 3:16 reads, "To the woman he said, 'I will greatly increase your pains in childbearing; with pain you will give birth to children.'" The word *pains* in the first half of the verse is translated from the Hebrew root word *itstsabon*, meaning "sorrow" or "toil"; it is actually referring to a mental state rather than to a strictly physical state. In Genesis 3:17 God said to Adam, "Cursed is the ground because of you; through painful toil you will eat of it all the days of your life." The *toil* applied to Adam is translated from the same Hebrew word *itstsabon*. Cultural programming about birth has caused the word to be translated *pain* for Eve but *toil* for Adam.

Basically, God was telling Adam and Eve that having sinned, they both would have to work hard to bring forth the fruit they desired. God was actually telling Eve that as a consequence of her disobedience she would have to struggle mentally and physically to give birth to children that He could have freely and easily given her had she not broken communion with Him by sinning. Today's women must also live with the toil of labor and with a mental state of concern that all will go well with their little ones. The so-called "curse of Eve" in which women are supposed to be punished by pain and suffering during childbirth actually has no scriptural basis. God cursed the serpent (Genesis 3:14) and the ground (Genesis 3:17), but not Adam or Eve.

Many Christian childbirth educators do not accept that a woman must suffer pain in childbirth; they teach expectant women not to expect severe pain and suffering during their birthing experiences. Hard work in labor is not "suffering" any more than hard work in farming the land is suffering. Most childbirth educators feel that a mother benefits from being able to experience the full sensation of her body in labor. They feel that using anesthesia to abolish all feeling denies the sensuality of birth. No one wants a mother to suffer during childbirth, but mothers often regret giving birth with no physical sensation. Some studies have suggested that the reality of participating in the entire birth experience, as long as the pain is manageable, has significant benefits for successful bonding in the newborn period and for the mother's postpartum adjustments. And certainly, a negative birth experience in which fear, pain, and the inability to manage predominate can negatively affect a mother's postpartum adjustment and interfere with bonding.

How Fear Can Do Harm

The natural birth process that God designed is an awe-inspiring miracle to witness or participate in. Only God could have figured out the way in which hormones, muscles, bony structures, and emotions interrelate so intricately in labor and birth. Even though God's design is so perfect, Satan can still rob women of the wonder and the beauty of birth through deceitful fear. Fear works against the woman in the birth process.

The birth muscles—the uterus and the birth passage—are meant to work together gradually and smoothly so that there need be no suffering, only some very intense physical and emotional sensations. The opening of the birth passage is meant to be coordinated with the muscular contractions of the uterus so that the intense force does not become unbearably painful. When fear enters the process, tension results, and the muscles of the birth passage become rigid and resistant, causing terrible pain because the baby is being pushed down against those hard, unyielding muscles. This can lead to serious problems for mother and baby because labor stops progressing, which can result in fetal distress. The use of drugs as the only answer to the fear-tension-pain cycle is to ignore what God would have us know. There are better ways to deal with this problem. By learning why the physical sensations occur, by using relaxation techniques, and by learning how to work *with* rather than against their bodies in labor, most women do not have to suffer or be drugged to give birth.

This is not to say that the birth process is painless, but natural childbirth classes teach you to interpret birth sensations for what they really are—part of the normal physiological process for which the female body was designed. Birth is hard work. The exertion is intense, as is running a hard race. At times during a race the runner feels pain. This is a productive, positive type of pain that drives the runner toward the finish line. It is far different from the pain of a traumatic injury that is the body's signal to stop and pay attention. Severe pain in childbirth is not normal, but is a sign of an underlying problem. If that problem can be corrected (or avoided), intolerable pain can be reduced to the level of an acceptable sensation that you can tell feels right and is nothing to fear. If that problem cannot be corrected, then medical and surgical intervention is to be used appropriately and without condemnation.

The Sources of Fear

What are some of the sources of fear? Where does this destructive emotion come from that takes over our minds and causes such counterproductive tension in our bodies? There are as many answers to these questions as there are women giving birth.

Some mothers' fears originate in horror stories passed down from one generation of women to another. Many of these women from the past experienced birth as a dreadful and sometimes fatal event. These fears may be further validated by a woman's own past labor experiences, for which she may have been unprepared. Fear can also come from a deeply disturbed attitude about the pregnancy—unwanted pregnancy, economic insecurity, husband-wife problems, unsupportive or interfering relatives. A woman also may have fears that her baby will not be normal or that she will not be a good mother.

Many women fear being in a hospital. Somewhere inside herself she feels that something will go wrong with her delivery. The hospital environment can reinforce this kind of fear. The mother is hooked up to an intravenous line for fear of dehydration, in case of "failure to progress," or in anticipation of the need for emergency medication. Electronic fetal monitoring is used in case baby experiences distress during labor; and the delivery room is set up like an operating room lest something go wrong and an operation is necessary. Those "in case of" practices by the doctor may be interpreted "for fear that" by the mother. A good childbirth class can help overcome many of the fears that our culture has perpetuated, and prepare the mother for understanding the basis of such fears.

How a Christian Childbirth Class Functions

In a Christian childbirth class, just as in a secular class, couples learn about pregnancy, labor, and birth so that fear of the unknown is no longer an obstacle. The sensations of giving birth are less difficult to cope with when the couple understands what is happening and how they can cooperate with the process.

A Christian childbirth class is led by a qualified childbirth educator. Couples are part of a small, intimate support group that learns and prays together. The series of around eight to ten classes starts in the sixth month of pregnancy and meets once a week for about two hours, usually in the comfort of the instructor's home. Often one of the fathers opens class with prayer, committing their special time together to learning God's path for each couple in their childbirth experience.

The classes provide the same basic ingredients of any good childbirth class—exercises, relaxation, breathing, information on the physiology of pregnancy and birth, comfort measures, information on various medications and procedures, and specific instructions on how the couple can work together to cope with the challenges of labor. Options in childbirth are covered, such as birthing rooms, siblings at birth, bonding, and rooming-in. Nutrition is emphasized, and things to be avoided during pregnancy are discussed. During the class, couples share experiences from previous births. These can be a great encouragement and lesson for first-timers.

A good class usually provides a lending library and presents slides or films showing labor, birth, and the surrounding events. Breastfeeding information and discussion of life with a new baby are important. Postpartum adjustment can be a big shock physically and emotionally to first-time parents, so discussion and sharing in this area are important. (Read chapter 5 before your baby is born. See also page 226, "Have Realistic Expectations.")

In addition to teaching the art of relaxation in combating the physical effects of fear, a Christian childbirth class studies scripture verses about fear. Meditation on these verses will show that faith is the antidote to the fear. Isaiah 41:10 is a great source of strength: "So do not fear, for I am with you; do not be dismayed, for I am your God. I will strengthen you and help you; I will uphold you with my righteous right hand." Imagine being cradled in the arms of your Father-Creator during labor! As stated in 1 Peter 5:7, you can "Cast all your anxiety on him because he cares for you." As you are held by Him in labor, hear Him saying your name, soothing away your fears with the promise of Isaiah 43:1: "Fear not, for I have redeemed you; I have summoned you by name; you are mine."

The message of 1 John 4:18 is definite: "There is no fear in love. But perfect love drives out fear." What greater expression of love is there than giving birth—giving love by bearing what was conceived in love, a new person with whom to share God's love? God wants us to overcome our fears and look to Him, as Jesus said in John 14:27, "Peace I leave with you; my peace I give you. I do not give to you as the world gives. Do not let your hearts be troubled and do not be afraid." The world makes childbirth a thing to be feared, but Jesus, the author of life, said, "Do not be afraid." Second Timothy 1:7 says that God did not give us a spirit of timidity (or fear); that spirit comes from Satan. He gives us a spirit of power, of love, and of self-discipline. Second Corinthians 10:5 encourages us to "take captive every thought to make it obedient to Christ."

Fear in childbirth, as we already discussed, can result in a long line of undesirable effects—even to the point of affecting your total commitment as parents. Mothers who have negative birth experiences have high risks of postpartum adjustment problems. This is one of the many ways Satan defeats the strength and unity of the family.

Your family's birth event needs to be bathed in prayer and faith so that the evil one cannot get you off to a bad start. Faith predominates over fear, so even if you do find yourself in need of a surgical or medical intervention, you will be able to turn it over to God and proceed in a spirit of faith, not fear. During childbirth preparation, you will learn how to overcome fear and tension together and how to work with the labor process. You will have the best labor support system available—the promises of God. You can look to Him as the Great Physician and rest secure in His care so that childbirth without fear can be a reality.

Martha taught natural childbirth classes for eight years, and four of those years were specifically for Christian couples. Bill looked forward to opening up our living room once a week to the joyous instruction of expectant couples. We especially enjoyed the "show and tell" night. A few weeks after everyone in the class delivered, couples and their babies met for a postnatal discussion class in which they shared how beautifully God worked in their miracle of birth. It was also a night of prayer and praise—prayer for the new parents as they worked on postpartum adjustment problems, and praise for the new lives God had given them. Couples in a Christian childbirth class often decide to continue meeting as a support group for Bible study as they progress through the challenges of parenting.

A Christian childbirth class is the ideal. If there are none nearby, find the best natural childbirth class you can (not always the one taught at the hospital, where often what you learn is how to do what the hospital wants). Supplement this class with the books recommended in the bibliography. Start reading early to help you judge which is the right class for you. (*Childbirth without Fear*, *The Joy of Natural Childbirth*, and *Under the*

Apple Tree are excellent resource books.) Couples must take their childbirth class seriously, giving it top priority in their schedules. Being thoroughly and competently prepared for the birth of a child reaps benefits well beyond the amount of time invested.

SCRIPTURE HELPS

Scripture references guide the study of various other childbirth topics. For example, for the discussion of physical conditioning:

Proverbs 31:17—"She sets about her work vigorously; her arms are strong for her tasks."

Exodus 1:19—"The midwives answered Pharaoh, 'Hebrew women are not like Egyptian women; they are vigorous and give birth before the midwives arrive.'"

2 Chronicles 15:7—"'But as for you, be strong and do not give up, for your work will be rewarded.'"

For nutrition, use:

3 John 2—"Dear friend, I pray that you may enjoy good health and that all may go well with you, even as your soul is getting along well."

1 Corinthians 6:19–20—"Do you not know that your body is a temple of the Holy Spirit, who is in you, whom you have received from God? You are not your own; you were bought at a price. Therefore honor God with your body."

For labor and birth, read:

Psalm 22:9–10—"Yet you brought me out of the womb; you made me trust in you even at my mother's breast. From birth I was cast upon you; from my mother's womb you have been my God."

Isaiah 66:9—"'Do I not bring to the moment of birth and not give delivery?' says the Lord. 'Do I not close up the womb when I bring to delivery?" says your God."

Psalm 71:6—"From birth I have relied on you; you brought me forth from my mother's womb. I will ever praise you."

SCRIPTURE HELPS (CONT.)

For relaxation, refer to:

Matthew 11:28–30—"'Come to me, all you who are weary and burdened, and I will give you rest. Take my yoke upon you and learn from me, for I am gentle and humble in heart, and you will find rest for your souls. For my yoke is easy and my burden is light.'"

Psalm 37:7b—"Be still before the LORD and wait patiently for him."

The possibilities of relating Scripture to childbirth are endless and creative. Verses can be copied on index cards to be used during difficult moments of the labor.

CHAPTER FOUR

The Birth of **Your Baby**

The long-anticipated event is near—you are beginning labor. You are excited and well prepared. With help from God you have developed the confidence that you will be able to cope with labor and delivery. Childbirth classes have prepared your mind and body for the work of childbirth, and with prayer you have prepared your heart to accept the child that God will give you.

Many couples prepare themselves for the ideal delivery, and when medical complications necessitate a departure from the "natural" way, they are disappointed. "I feel like a failure," one mother who needed a cesarean section confided in us. As your labor begins, pray a prayer of acceptance asking God to give you the strength to cope with whatever type of labor and delivery you are blessed with. Everything about labor varies greatly from woman to woman and even from one pregnancy to the next for the same woman. Still, all labors follow a basic pattern, and it's good to know what to look for along the way.

THE STAGES OF CHILDBIRTH

Stage 1: Labor

The process of labor has three distinct phases, and you will feel different in each one.

Early labor. Labor usually begins with mild contractions ten minutes or more apart. At first you may wonder if this is the real thing, especially since contractions may come and go. You've gotten used to having some contractions before labor—the warm-up contractions called Braxton-Hicks. Now, early labor is another kind of warming-up period. These early labor contractions are thinning the cervix (the muscle that holds the uterus closed), but this can be a very slow process, especially for first-time mothers.

The most important thing you can do during early labor is rest. Relax and try to sleep if you can. This is easier said than done because you will be very excited. Now is when to start using the relaxation skills you learned in class, remembering to pray for help in staying peaceful. Eat lightly and remember to drink fluids. Save your energy for the hard work ahead.

You may want to call your midwife or doctor during early labor (though not if it's 3:00 A.M.), but in most situations it's wise to stay at home until contractions are well established, regular, and around five minutes apart.

Active labor. When contractions require your full attention and are coming every three to five minutes, you are probably in active labor. These contractions dilate your cervix, opening the "baby door." It is important to continue to use your relaxation techniques so that tension does not interfere with the process of opening up.

Transition. Toward the end of the first stage, you enter transition, the most intense part of labor. Contractions come quickly, with little time in between to rest and recover. Women often become irritable and panicky at this stage and need lots of reassurance from their husbands and birth attendants. This may be the point when you feel it's time for pain medication, but actually the worst will soon be over. It takes twenty to thirty minutes for epidural anesthesia to take effect, and by then you may be ready to push your baby out, which is a much easier sensation to handle.

Stage 2: Pushing and Delivery

Pushing is hard work, but very satisfying. This is the second stage of labor, the one that will bring your baby out into the world for you to see. Being upright helps, as does the squatting position. Your birth attendant will help you know when to push and when to ease up to avoid tearing of the skin and muscle surrounding the birth canal (the perineum).

Stage 3: Delivery of the Placenta

Once your baby is born, you may be so preoccupied with holding her and admiring her that you pay little attention to the third stage of labor, the delivery of the placenta. It takes a few more contractions for the placenta to separate from the uterine wall and be expelled, but these contractions are mild compared to what you've just experienced. Putting your baby to your breast will help your uterus contract, and prevent hemorrhaging.

PREPARING YOURSELF FOR BIRTH

Childbirth classes will offer you more detailed information about labor and birth, along with suggestions for handling the challenges of each stage. To reinforce what you learn in childbirth classes, here are some tips on coping with labor and preparing to birth your baby with joy and confidence.

Learn to Trust Your Body

Be confident in your body's ability to give birth to a baby. Reflect on the concept of Creator. God designed all the organs in the human body to work well—and most of the time they do. For the majority of mothers, birth is a normal physiological process. A woman's entire reproductive system works well as long as she takes care of it and no one interferes with it. Trust that your body is built to give birth. Be confident that birth will go well for you. Remember Isaiah 66:9—"'Do I bring to the moment of birth and not give delivery?' says the LORD."

Too many voices in our culture are saying that women are incompetent in this area. You are told you need routine assistance from technology, often very complicated technology. We believed that lie with the birth of our first child—spinal anesthesia and forceps were pushed on us, and we did not question that approach. The stories of all our births, and what we learned, are told in the first chapter of *The Birth Book* (see bibliography). Our biggest lesson was to take responsibility for our own births.

Women who lack confidence in their bodies are at risk for having a less than satisfying birth experience. They are more likely to hand over responsibility for the birthing decisions to someone else. They are then set up for a medical and technological childbirth, even a cesarean section. This type of birth can further weaken an already shaky self-image. A woman with this experience is often left with the feeling "My body couldn't do it," which translates into "I couldn't do it." This can cause a woman to be full of doubt about her mothering abilities, which can interfere with the unfolding of the mother-baby relationship.

In contrast, a woman with confidence can take primary responsibility for her birthing decisions, and the couple can direct the birth she wants. For many women, birth becomes the high point of their sexuality and femininity. When a woman masters the task of giving birth, whether it be a completely positive experience or one that is incredibly challenging, she has bragging rights. Taking responsibility for your baby's birth, knowing that God is carrying you through it, means that even if you do wind up needing a cesarean, you have bragging rights. "I can do everything through him who gives me strength" (Phil. 4:13).

Explore the Best Positions for Your Labor and Birth

Most people's preconceptions about labor start with the picture of a mother lying on her back in bed. Your hospital room will have a bed in it, so this may seem the obvious thing to do. But back birthing is neither comfortable for the mother nor healthy for the baby. The more you can stay off your back during labor, the faster your labor will progress and the less it will hurt. Lying on your back tenses your pelvic muscles, which need to relax as the baby descends; and tense muscles hurt more. Lying on your back allows your heavy uterus to press on the major blood vessels running alongside your spine, lessening the blood supply to the uterus and to your baby. And in this position you would be pushing your baby *uphill*. The more time you can spend out of bed and moving around during labor, the better birth you are likely to experience.

There is no one right position for laboring or giving birth, only the ones that work for you. Stand, walk, kneel, squat as you explore what positions ease your discomfort and speed the progress of labor. Women are so accustomed to being confined to bed during labor and birth that they may not realize what a valuable labor asset moving can be. Moving in response to signals from your body helps the baby to twist and turn to find the path of least resistance through your birth passage. Being upright allows gravity to help bring the baby down. Squatting widens the bones of your pelvis. Most important is your freedom to move and experiment with whatever labor and birthing positions work for you. Feel free to improvise and be sure your birth attendants and birthplace encourage you to go with the urges of your body during labor. You are birthing your baby, and you have the right to choose your position. You can stand during labor, embracing your husband, supported by his caring arms. You can give birth in a vertical, side-lying, or squatting position (or even on all-fours) if your birth attendant is willing and able to accommodate you. Women who have the most satisfying birth experiences assume various positions at different stages in their labor. The important thing is for you, not someone else, to choose your best birthing position. You are more likely to try different positions if you have practiced them and conditioned yourself for them during pregnancy.

Use Technology Wisely

It is a wise couple who remembers that there are appropriate and inappropriate uses for technology. The laboring woman must be wary of medical interference in God's design for the birthing process. While tests and technology can be lifesaving in some circumstances, and can also contribute to a safe and satisfying birth, some hospital routines and interventions can lead to a spiral of interventions, each leading to another until finally the obstetrician determines that a cesarean is necessary.

Just entering the hospital and putting on a hospital gown is enough to slow down labor in many women. Being confined to bed or having one's freedom to move around encumbered by an I.V. or a fetal monitor can also slow down contractions. A drug may then be used to get the labor moving again, but the contractions that follow the use of artificial stimulation are usually much more intense, raising fear in the mother and making it more difficult for her to cope. So then she gets pain-killing drugs or epidural anesthesia, which can depress labor or give the mother less control over her muscles when it's time to push the baby out. This can lead to needing a forceps or vacuum extraction or a cesarean, with greater risks for both mother and baby. This spiral can leave a mother feeling passive or even victimized rather than confident. Taking responsibility for your birth experience is the best way to minimize the inappropriate use of technology. Do not enter labor expecting to "be delivered"; instead, plan on giving birth. If you need a high-tech birth, educate yourself about the benefits and risks of technology so that you can be part of the decision process.

Learn Self-Help Techniques to Relax and Ease the Discomforts of Labor

Women do not have to suffer or be drugged to give birth. It is not wise for a woman or her baby to be so heavily anesthetized that she is disconnected from her sensations during labor. Pain has a purpose, compelling a woman to make changes, to do something to relieve it; and in making these adjustments in her body, she often increases the progress of labor and helps her baby's well-being. Unmanageable pain is not normal during labor; rather, it is your body's signal that you need to make a change.

The most important thing you can learn in preparing for childbirth is how to relax. If the class you choose does not spend much time on this, ask your instructor to refer you to other sources of instruction. Several of the books on childbirth in our bibliography teach relaxation, and Helen Wessel's books add the spiritual dimension that is so important for true relaxation. Total release in body, mind, and spirit will be your best tool in labor. The concept of giving birth is difficult to appreciate apart from relaxation and release. If you struggle in this area, consider getting some prayer and counseling.

HELPING LABOR PROGRESS

Use the following natural techniques to ease the discomfort and speed the progress of labor—think PROGRESS to help you remember.

P *Prayer and Proper Position*—pray for peace and strength during labor. Change positions frequently if, for medical reasons, you must stay in bed. Walk a lot during early labor.

R *Relax and Release* your mind and muscles through massage; mental relaxation; imagination (as seen in Psalm 23: "He makes me lie down in green pastures, he leads me beside still waters"); slow, deep breathing; and relaxing music.

O *Output*—urinate every hour; a full bladder creates painful spasms.

G *Gravity* helps; be upright: sit, kneel, squat, stand, walk.

R *Rest* between contractions and let go of any tension from the previous contraction; don't fearfully anticipate the next one.

E *Energy* check—snack when hungry; drink to avoid dehydration.

S *Submerge* in water if the going gets rough; best is a labor pool, otherwise a tub or shower.

S *Support* throughout labor, from husband and labor assistant.

The Truth about Pain in Childbirth

Childbirth is an intense experience, and substituting the word *contraction* for the word *pain* does not hide the fact that it can hurt. But it should be a good pain, one closely connected to pleasure. Allow yourself to experience it rather than resist it—be willing to turn entirely inward and concentrate on your body. Acknowledge the sensations of labor for what they are—the way being paved for your baby to emerge. The sensations are only frightening if you don't understand them. Ride along with the emotions of labor as well: happy and excited when it begins, serious and intent on the work as it continues.

Find out what childbirth was like for other women. Talk with the ones who have positive, constructive things to say. Ask them what helped the most. One woman said that having her feet rubbed the whole time got her through it. Another woman said she needed to know it was okay to make low, throaty sounds and moans during transition.

There is a point in many labors where the birthing woman experiences self-doubt or becomes very cranky. Feelings like this often come when contractions are most intense, with little time to rest in between. This happens near the end of the first stage of labor, shortly before it is time to actively push the baby out. This is not the time to call for pain relief but to know that moments of trial and of doubt are all part of the experience. Remember that the authors of the Psalms, who could shout aloud to God with praise, also had dark moments of doubt in difficult times. You may be considering asking for pain relief. Instead, hang on to the Lord and realize that your baby will soon be in your arms.

Natural childbirth does not mean that you passively suffer through pain, but that you find ways to cope and to correct problems. Childbirth classes will teach you ways of coping with and preventing pain during labor. Changing positions, getting into a tub of water, standing in a shower, having your back rubbed, being lovingly supported and comforted by your spouse—these comforting measures can all help your body do its work more efficiently. The more you can work with your body, instead of fighting it, the easier it is for your baby to be born. Remember, if the pain becomes unmanageable, that is your signal to check your PROGRESS (see box, page 94). After twenty minutes or so, if the pain continues, *then* there is always the option of medical relief. Ask yourself, "Am I coping, or am I suffering?" Pain can be letting you know there is a problem; sometimes the solution is as simple as a change in position. If the problem cannot be corrected, medical or surgical intervention may be necessary, and we can be thankful that God has blessed our modern age with technology that has helped to make childbirth safer for both mother and baby.

Water—An Excellent Relaxation Tool

Relaxation skills during labor do work to decrease or eliminate pain, but not all women are able to master the art of total body relaxation even during pregnancy. Once labor begins and escalates, the inability to relax takes its toll. Immersion in a warm tub (98 to 100 degrees, body temperature), deep enough to cover the mother's abdomen, is a very simple, drug-free method of enabling a tense, laboring woman to fully relax so that her uterus can get on with the work of birth without the obstacle of tension and pain. The buoyancy of the water enables the mother to more easily support her body and relax during the contractions. As she relaxes, her stress hormones decrease and the natural birth-progressing hormones (oxytocin and endorphins) flow uninhibited.

During the labor with our seventh baby, Martha experienced excruciating suprapubic (low front) pain. After trying the all-fours position and other comfort measures without relief, she got into our large tub. She was finally able to relax enough and the pain melted away. When birth was imminent she got out of the water to deliver, and then we saw the reason for the unusual pain—the baby's hand came out wedged alongside his head, a compound presentation.

Labor tubs are intended to be used to ease the pain and improve the progress of labor. Some women actually give birth in the water, and studies show lower rates of infection than in traditional births and no detrimental effects on the baby.

Use Medical Pain Relief Wisely

If you leave pain relief up to your doctor and don't use all the self-help labor aids at your disposal, you are likely to be disappointed. A pain-free birth without risks is a promise your doctor can't deliver. Be sure you understand the risks and the benefits of using medication during childbirth. By participating in the decision to use medical pain relief and by doing your part to lessen the need for drugs, you increase your chances of having a satisfying birth and a drug-free baby. While medication, such as epidural anesthesia, decreases pain in childbirth, it also decreases your participation in one of the high points of your life. Having a completely anesthetized birth leaves many women with long-term memories of a less than satisfying birth experience. There are situations, however, when the wise use of anesthesia and pain relievers helps labor progress (for example, if the pain is overwhelming and you are becoming exhausted) and contributes to safer and more satisfying birth. Your childbirth class should address the risks and benefits of using drugs during childbirth.

Avoid Episiotomy

Episiotomy is the incision made in the perineum (the skin and muscle between the birth canal and the rectum) just before the baby's head emerges. Once done routinely for nearly all physician-attended births, episiotomy is being reevaluated and avoided by more and more birth attendants. Research is showing that babies do fine and mothers do better without episiotomy. By having perineal massage and support, avoiding the rush to push the baby out, and assuming a more vertical birthing position, you can spare yourself having episiotomy. Many women speaking from personal experience state that recovering from tear stitches is much easier than recovering from episiotomy stitches.

The reason we want you to come to your birth armed with prayer and trained in many self-help measures is that a satisfying birthing experience gives a woman a head start toward a satisfying mothering experience. Spending the early weeks of motherhood healing physical and emotional wounds is not a good way to begin life with a new baby.

THE FIRST HOUR AFTER BIRTH

During your pregnancy you began to form a bond with your baby as soon as you became aware of the precious life growing inside. Now, you can see and hold this little person, whom before you knew only by the bulge, the movements, and the heartbeat you heard. Inside, you gave your whole body to nurture your baby; outside, you continue to give—your face, your voice, your arms, your touch, your scent, your breast. This continuum of mother-infant (and father-infant) attachment work is important; it should never be interrupted unnecessarily by hospital routines and procedures.

The first hour after birth is a sensitive period, a time when your baby's whole physiology is attuned to drinking in who you are with all of his senses alert. After an hour or so, baby will fall into a deep sleep, so unless a medical complication prevents it, your baby should be placed immediately onto your warm, soft abdomen and breasts. This initial family time should be spent touching, stroking, gazing at, talking to, and suckling your baby. This is a special time in which mothers and fathers are very high from the excitement of birth, and babies are in that state of quiet alertness that comes right after birth. Neither you nor your newborn should be deprived of this special time to look at one another, speak and listen to each other, enjoy skin-to-skin contact, and bask in each other's presence.

Does this early bonding benefit you and your baby beyond the good feelings of the moment? Medical science is continually examining what mothers have known and God has designed from the beginning. Klaus and Kennell, prominent researchers in the field of bonding, found that mothers who have contact with their babies immediately after birth are more successful at breastfeeding, talk with their infants more and use more descriptive speech, spend more time in the face-to-face position of eye-to-eye contact, and touch and groom their infants more.

What happens when a medical complication, such as a cesarean delivery or fetal distress, temporarily separates mother and baby after birth? Is this parent-baby relationship permanently affected by a temporary separation, or can you make up for the time you were separated (delayed bonding)? This is an important question.

Parents who are unable to be with their baby immediately after birth should not feel guilty that their relationship has been permanently affected. Immediate bonding after birth is not like a one-time only glue that cements the parent-infant relationship forever. Many steps must be taken throughout the first days, weeks, and months of infancy to create a strong parent-infant attachment. There is no scientific rationale for concluding that being deprived of this initial bonding can permanently affect the parent or child. However, bonding during this biologically sensitive period does give the mother-infant relationship a head start. Spending lots of time with your baby in the weeks to come will help you overcome any disappointment you may feel if early bonding opportunities were disrupted.

Bonding Tips

The following suggestions can help get you off to the right start with your baby.

Prepare for birth. A positive birthing experience encourages maternal bonding; a negative birthing experience often negatively affects a mother's first meeting with her infant. Two factors that greatly increase the likelihood of having a positive birth are taking a quality childbirth class and having the presence of a supportive husband or friend during labor and delivery. The presence of a professional labor assistant also helps.

Pain-lessening drugs given to the mother during labor can decrease the mother's and the baby's receptiveness to one another after birth. Mothers who have been well prepared for birth require few, if any, drugs during labor. If you do have a negative birthing experience in which fear and suffering predominate or medical complications occur, realize that your feelings of attachment to your baby can be temporarily affected. Ask God for help with your feelings of disappointment in the birthing experience. Pray for healing and spend as much time with your baby as possible from here on. Taking pleasure in your baby can help make up for a bumpy beginning.

Touch your baby. Ideally, immediately after birth your baby should be "skin-to-skin" on your abdomen, with your arms around baby and a blanket over your arms. Recent research by Klaus and Kennel shows how infants whose mothers were not medicated and who were not separated at all from mother were able to make crawling movements along mother's abdomen and reach her breast by themselves and then attach themselves to the breast. Touch is a powerful motivator! Your newborn benefits greatly from the stimulation she receives from skin-to-skin contact. Gently stroke your baby,

touching her whole body. Mothers and fathers naturally touch their babies differently. It is moving to see a new mother stroke her baby's entire body with a gentle caress of her fingertips and to see the new father place his entire hand on his baby, as if symbolizing his commitment to protect the life he has fathered.

Look at your baby. Your newborn can see you best within the distance of twelve inches. Because they are in the state of quiet alertness after birth, newborns will open their eyes much more during the first hour after birth than they will an hour or two later when they are sleeping soundly. The feedback you will receive from staring into your newborn's eyes may trigger a rush of beautiful mothering feelings. Ask the nurses to delay putting eye ointment in baby's eyes (given to prevent eye infection) until after the bonding period, since this ointment may lessen your baby's ability to open his eyes.

Talk to your newborn. Mothers naturally speak to their newborn babies in a high-pitched, rhythmic voice. Your newborn's ears are already attuned to your speech, and you may notice that your baby moves rhythmically in response to your voice. Babies usually also recognize dad's voice and look to see where it's coming from. This reminds us of Jesus' words in John 10:4: "His sheep follow him because they know his voice," speaking of Himself as the Good Shepherd.

Breastfeed your baby right after delivery. Some babies have a strong desire to suck immediately after birth, and others are content simply to lick the nipple. How eager they are depends on several things: use of pain medication, temperament, and the need for calming that sucking provides. Medical research clearly demonstrates that babies should be close to the breast immediately after birth so they can explore. Sucking and licking the nipple release the hormone oxytocin into your bloodstream. The oxytocin increases the contraction of your uterus and lessens postpartum bleeding. This early sucking also stimulates the release of the hormone prolactin, the milk-producing hormone, which also enhances your mothering abilities after birth.

Have some private time. If no medical problems occur, a perceptive hospital staff will leave mother, father, and baby alone for a while after birth. This should be a time of peace and privacy as you celebrate the birth of your child. It is time when all three of you can embrace each other. It is a time to acknowledge God's presence in the room (if you haven't already) and to pray a prayer of thanksgiving for the precious life that He has given you. After the baby's initial hour of alertness, he probably will reward you with several hours of deep sleep. The ecstasy of the birth event may not fade for many more hours, but the tiredness of your body will help you appreciate some much-needed rest.

Rooming-In

Who will be your baby's primary caregiver in the hospital, you or the nursery staff? In most hospitals there are several options available. One possibility, which we strongly discourage, is giving the job of caring for your baby to the nursery staff, who will bring your baby out to you on a predetermined schedule or at their convenience. In our opinion, this option should be reserved only for sick mothers and sick babies. Not only does it deprive you of the joy of caring for the life you nourished for so long, but it delays mother-infant attachment and causes the mother to worry. This scheduled newborn care puts the mother in the role of secondary caregiver, a role not at all in accordance with God's design. Hospitals should not consider mother's presence as something to be dispensed to the baby in concentrated doses at prescribed times.

A second option is modified rooming-in. In this option the newborn spends most of the day with mother but spends the night in the nursery and is brought out as needed for night feedings. In theory, this type of rooming-in seems attractive, and the mother apparently gets the best of both worlds. Actually, all the back-and-forth to the nursery often becomes confusing to both mother and baby, and baby may wind up spending a lot of time in the nursery.

The third option, and the one we strongly encourage, is full rooming-in. In our opinion, healthy mothers and healthy babies should stay together from birth to the time of discharge from the hospital. This is becoming much more common now that many hospitals have LDR rooms—one private room where mother spends her entire hospital stay, labor, delivery, and recovery. (Fathers are often invited to stay too.) Rooming-in is even an option for mothers recovering from cesareans, especially if dad or a friend is available to help the mother manage baby. Full rooming-in will allow you to become familiar with and to practice your intuitive mothering skills at a time when the hormones in your body are programming your maternal instincts. Studies have shown that infants who room-in with their mothers cry less and more readily organize their sleep-wake cycles. As a former director of a university hospital newborn nursery, Bill noticed that mothers and babies who fully room-in together enjoy the following benefits:

1. The mother has fewer breastfeeding problems. Her milk supply is established sooner, and her infant gets more practice with breastfeeding.

2. The newborn has less jaundice, probably because she nurses more often.

3. The mother actually seems to get more rest since she experiences less separation anxiety, and the newborn will sleep most of the time anyway.

4. Babies in a large nursery are soothed by tape recordings of a human heartbeat. Rather than being soothed electronically, the baby who is fully rooming-in with his mother can be soothed by the real thing.

5. The newborn seems more content because she interacts with only one predictable caregiver, her own mother. The rooming-in mother feels much more competent and intuitive in the care of her newborn once they get home.

6. Research has shown that the rooming-in mother has a lower incidence of postpartum depression.

Rooming-in allows mothers the best of both worlds. The attending medical personnel are nearby to function as advisors while mothers are able to get acquainted with their baby's needs and become comfortable handling their babies. Mothers and babies leave the hospital well acquainted with each other, even if their hospital stay is short because of insurance requirements. Best of all, rooming-in respects God's plan for the family. It fits the natural progression of attachment—mother's womb to mother's room.

ROUTINE HOSPITAL PROCEDURES

Apgar Scoring

Within the first five minutes after birth, your newborn will be evaluated using a scale called the Apgar score, which is a measure of the general health of newborn babies. The Apgar scoring is performed at one and five minutes after birth, and your newborn is given from zero to two points for each of the following parameters: color, breathing efforts, heart rate, muscle tone, and crying. An infant who receives a score of ten has received two points for each of these parameters, indicating that each system was functioning at its maximum; a score toward the lower end of the scale (four or five) indicates that some of these systems are not functioning at their maximum within the first five minutes after birth.

Since it is often customary to tell the parents the Apgar score, you should know its real meaning in order to alleviate any anxiety you may have. Infants who are pink all over, cry lustily, breathe normally, have good heart rates, and show strong muscle movements are given scores of ten. Most of the time, however, healthy newborns do not achieve scores of ten. It is quite normal for the hands and feet of a newly born baby to be somewhat blue because it takes a few minutes for the newborn's circulatory system to become adjusted to his postnatal environment.

Another problem with the scoring is that some newborns are born in the state of quiet alertness and therefore are not crying; but the newborn loses two points for this on the Apgar score. A baby who scores ten is not necessarily more healthy than a baby who scores seven or eight. The Apgar score is only valid if done by a trained medical person whose only responsibility in the delivery suite is to calculate that score. The Apgar number given to the parents after birth has little or no predictive value as to the health of the baby. A lower score should not be a source of anxiety to parents. It only serves to alert the attending medical personnel to observe the baby more closely over the next few hours for circulatory or respiratory problems.

Medications and Weighing

After birth your newborn will be given an injection or oral dose of vitamin K to prevent a rare condition that causes infants to bleed internally. It is also a law in most states that your baby be given some medication in both eyes in order to prevent any infection of the cornea that may have been picked up during passage through the vaginal canal. Silver nitrate, which temporarily irritates the eyes, has now been replaced by a milder but equally effective ointment such as erythromycin. It is not necessary that these be done immediately after birth. Parents who wish to have the special time of bonding and prayer after birth can request the nurses to delay routine procedures, including weighing, measuring, cleaning, and diapering. All of these things can be done in your room so baby does not have to be taken away.

PKU Testing and Thyroid Testing

Phenylketonuria (PKU) is an extremely rare metabolic disorder occurring in approximately one out of fifteen thousand infants. If diagnosed within a few days after birth, it can be treated with a special diet. If left untreated, it can result in brain damage. The PKU test, required by law in most states, is usually done just prior to discharge from the hospital, and it is conducted with a few drops of your baby's blood. This disease is rare, so there's no need to feel anxious about the results of the test. Your baby's blood is also analyzed for sufficient thyroid hormones. Congenital hypothyroidism (low thyroid at birth) occurs in about one out of five thousand infants and can cause retardation if untreated. The earlier this disease can be detected, the more effective is the treatment.

Jaundice

Almost all newborns develop some degree of jaundice, and parents often are made to worry about what is really just a normal physiologic process. Jaundice is the yellow color in a baby's skin caused by a buildup in the blood of a yellow pigment called bilirubin. Bilirubin is produced by the breakdown of worn-out red blood cells. Bilirubin is usually disposed of through the liver and intestines and does not reach high enough levels in the blood to cause yellow deposits in the skin. But when many blood cells are broken up very quickly or if the liver is unable to get rid of the excess bilirubin fast enough, this excess bilirubin is deposited in the skin, giving the yellow color.

Newborns are susceptible to two types of jaundice: normal and abnormal. The term *normal jaundice* (also called "physiologic jaundice") is used because almost all babies have some degree of jaundice. While still in the womb, they need a higher number of red blood cells to carry oxygen. After birth, they need fewer of these cells, but because of the immaturity of the liver and the intestines they can't dispose of the excess quickly. The result is jaundice.

Rarely, jaundice can be a symptom of other problems, so your pediatrician will watch to see whether your baby's jaundice is normal or whether it is due to some abnormality. In abnormal jaundice, bilirubin levels could go high enough to cause brain damage in a sick newborn or premature baby. The cause of this type of jaundice is usually blood group incompatibility (such as the Rh factor difference in mother and baby) or an infection.

Normal newborn jaundice can create a lot of unnecessary worries for new parents, especially when it is overtreated. In many cases jaundice is a reflection of the fact that God's design for mother-infant togetherness has been tampered with. Bilirubin levels can be higher in breastfed babies; these higher bilirubin levels may be the result of not enough breastfeeding. Babies who are allowed to room-in with their mothers and who are breastfed on demand have much less jaundice than those who do not room-in and do not feed frequently. Studies show that the more frequently mothers breastfeed in the hospital, the lower the bilirubin in their babies. Frequent nursing promotes frequent stooling, and bilirubin leaves the body in the stools.

Unfortunately, in the past mothers often were advised to stop breastfeeding because the breast milk was assumed to cause the jaundice; but rarely is breast milk itself actually the cause, and even then it need be stopped for no more than 48 hours. There is no evidence that normal newborn jaundice is harmful to full-term, healthy babies. (Jaundice is still a concern in premature infants or those who are ill, and it is treated more aggressively in these babies.) In most situations, the best solution to jaundice is to continue breastfeeding frequently (or pump your milk to supplement feedings if baby is not getting enough) and wait for it to go away on its own.

If your doctor does feel that your baby's jaundice should be treated, he or she will probably order phototherapy. Your baby will be placed under a special light that dissolves the bilirubin in the skin, allowing it to be disposed of more quickly through the kidneys. You can take baby out from under the lights to nurse.

Regardless of the cause of your baby's jaundice, there is seldom a reason to separate you and your baby. One of the best ways that you can prevent or lessen your baby's jaundice is by keeping your baby with you in the hospital and breastfeeding frequently. Since the jaundice can increase once your baby gets home, your doctor may ask that baby be brought back to the hospital for a follow-up blood test to check the bilirubin level. Phototherapy can be administered at home, if your doctor feels it is necessary. Whatever the cause of your baby's jaundice, it is necessary that both the bilirubin level of the baby and the anxiety level of the parent be appropriately diagnosed and treated. Jaundice should not be allowed to interfere with breastfeeding or with your developing a positive relationship with your baby.

HEALING THE LESS-THAN-PERFECT BIRTH

Sometimes, despite all the planning and preparation, births do not go as parents hope. Problems occur that necessitate medical or surgical intervention to safeguard the health of the mother and the baby. If you have done your homework and have talked through all the decision making with your doctor or midwife as it occurs and prayed for God's direction throughout labor, you can have confidence that the choices made were the best ones possible in your situation. This will make your job of coming to terms with disappointment much easier.

If your childbirth experience turned into one in which pain became suffering and you experienced a great deal of fear and anxiety, it will take some time after the birth to put everything back together in your mind. Even if the baby is beautiful and you both are healthy, you may feel a sense of loss at not achieving the birth you hoped for. It is important to acknowledge these very real feelings and talk about them with someone who can be supportive and understanding. This might be a friend, your nurse, your childbirth educator, or someone in a cesarean support group (see ICAN, p. 80). Ask the Lord to comfort you Himself and bring healing. Try not to be hard on yourself, as though somehow it could have been your fault. Pray that you can learn from any mistakes, and thank God that "we know that in all things God works for the good of those who love him" (Rom. 8:28).

Unhappy feelings about the birth can sometimes get in the way of your developing attachment to your baby. The best medicine for this is large, frequent doses of your baby. As you hold her and enjoy the physical sensation of her, nurse her, and look into her face, you will find that your love for her will bubble up and drown out the grieving.

CIRCUMCISION

Circumcision is the cutting away of the covering of skin (foreskin) that encloses the glans (head) of the penis. Up until recent years circumcision was considered routine for newborns, but parents have begun to ask if circumcision is really necessary for their babies. In the following discussion, we will present some information and considerations to help Christian parents make an informed choice regarding circumcision.

Biblical Basis for Circumcision

In Genesis 17:10–12, 14, God commanded Abraham to circumcise the males in his household:

> This is my covenant with you and your descendants after you, the covenant you are to keep: Every male among you shall be circumcised. You are to undergo circumcision, and it will be the sign of the covenant between me and you. . . . Every male among you who is eight days old must be circumcised. . . . Any uncircumcised male who has not been circumcised in the flesh, will be cut off from his people; he has broken my covenant.

It is clear from this verse that, according to Mosaic law, all Jewish males were to be circumcised, and Mosaic law was followed concerning Jesus' circumcision: "On the eighth day, when it was time to circumcise him, he was named Jesus" (Luke 2:21).

However, in the New Testament there was much controversy about circumcision among early Christians as the church grew to include Gentiles as well as Jews. Some of the Jewish Christians, from the party of the Pharisees, believed that the Mosaic law should be followed and that a Christian could not be saved unless he was circumcised (Acts 15:1, 5). Paul, however, taught that circumcision was not necessary for salvation, and Peter made that teaching official when Paul conferred with him in Jerusalem (see Acts 5:2–11). Many verses state that circumcision is not necessary: "Circumcision is nothing and uncircumcision is nothing. Keeping God's commands is what counts. Each one should remain in the situation which he was in when God called him" (1 Cor. 7:19–20). "Circumcision is circumcision of the heart" (Rom. 2:29). "For in Christ Jesus, neither circumcision nor uncircumcision has any value" (Gal. 5:6). "Neither circumcision nor uncircumcision means anything; what counts is a new creation" (Gal. 6:15).

Should Your Baby Be Circumcised?

Whether or not your newborn son should be circumcised is your decision to make. It is an issue you need to consider carefully, with thought, prayer, and discussion between both parents. Here are some questions you may have as you gather information about circumcision.

How is circumcision performed? The baby is placed on a restraining board and his hands and feet are secured by straps. The tight adhesions between the foreskin and the penis are broken free with a metal instrument. The foreskin is held with metal clamps while a cut is made lengthwise into the foreskin. A metal bell is placed over the head of the penis, and the foreskin is pulled up over the bell and cut all around, leaving the head of the penis uncovered.

Is circumcision safe? Does it hurt? Circumcision is usually a safe surgical procedure—there are rarely any serious complications. However, as with any surgical procedure, there are occasional problems such as bleeding, infection, or injury to the penis. Yes, it does hurt. The skin is clamped and cut, so of course it hurts. A newborn baby has painful sensations in the skin of his penis; it is wishful thinking to believe that this procedure does not hurt. God has endowed babies with a mechanism by which they can withdraw from pain. Many babies will initially scream and then withdraw into a deep sleep toward the end of the operation. The sleep is a mechanism for withdrawing from pain—not a sign that everything is all better. Circumcision, in fact, upsets a baby's entire physiology.

Can the baby have anesthesia to lessen the pain? Yes. A local anesthetic can be used. Ask your doctor about this. There is plenty of reason to state that an infant has the right to an intact foreskin. At the very least, we believe he has the right to painless surgery. If your doctor is not aware of this technique, he or she can find a description of the procedure in the *Journal of Pediatrics*, vol. 92 (1978), page 998.

Does circumcision make hygiene easier? The glands in the foreskin secrete a substance called "smegma." In the adolescent and adult male this secretion can accumulate beneath the foreskin, but it is easily cleansed during bathing.

What happens if the foreskin is left intact? Leaving the foreskin intact protects the penis from irritation and infection from wet diapers. At birth it is impossible to make a judgment about how tight the foreskin will remain since almost all boys have tight foreskins for the first few months. Around one year of age many foreskins begin to retract from the head of the penis. This happens by itself gradually, over time, as a result of the natural occurrence of erections that boys will experience.

By three years of age, 90 percent of uncircumcised boys have fully retractable foreskins, and by puberty all normal foreskins retract. Once the foreskin retracts easily, it becomes a normal part of male hygiene to pull back the foreskin and cleanse beneath it during a bath. While it is true that infection from the secretions beneath the foreskin is more often a problem in uncircumcised males, simple hygiene will prevent this problem.

No one should ever forcibly retract the foreskin. Doctors unfamiliar or uncomfortable with the care of an intact foreskin may not realize that the foreskin will retract on its own. Be sure any doctor who examines your son knows not to force the foreskin back. By forcibly retracting the foreskin the child is hurt and the tissue is damaged. This tissue damage can result in infection of the foreskin or even of the urinary tract.

If the foreskin does not retract naturally, will circumcision be needed later on? Circumcision is *very rarely* necessary for medical reasons. If the foreskin does not retract, it can become tight enough to obstruct the flow of urine. This condition, called "phimosis," requires circumcision. If circumcision for phimosis is necessary later in childhood or adulthood, anesthesia is used.

If our son isn't circumcised, won't he feel different from his friends? Parents cannot predict how their son will feel if he is circumcised or intact. Children generally have a wider acceptance of individual differences than adults do. The number of circumcised boys has been steadily declining in recent years as more parents begin to question routine circumcision. So, your uncircumcised child will likely not be unusual, as he might have been in the past. You simply tell your son that he was allowed to keep his foreskin.

My husband is circumcised. Shouldn't my son be the same as his father? Some fathers have strong feelings that if they are circumcised, their sons should be, and these feelings should be explored. Many fathers change their minds once they are fully informed.

We have a son who is already circumcised. Should brothers in the same family be the same? Many parents feel that sameness is very important among the males of the family since little boys do in fact compare the styles of their penises. Realize that no two children are alike anyway. Often hair color, eye color, height, weight, and body type are all different in the same family. This would be just one more difference. Your problem will most likely not be in explaining to your intact child why he is intact, but rather in explaining to your circumcised son why he was circumcised.

Do circumcised boys experience any particular problems? Some mothers report that their babies do not breastfeed as well for a few days after circumcision, and seem harder to settle, probably due to the disturbance in baby's physiology. Also, the foreskin acts as a protective covering of the sensitive head of the penis. Removal of the protective foreskin allows the head of the penis to come in contact with ammonia in the diapers. Sometimes this irritation causes circumcised babies to develop painful sores on the tip of the penis.

Does circumcision prevent any disease? Circumcision does not prevent cancer of the penis, as some have thought. Cancer of the penis is a very rare disease anyway, and it occurs more frequently in males who do not practice proper hygiene. Nor does circumcision prevent cervical cancer. Cancer of the cervix is not more common in the sexual partners of intact males who practice proper hygiene. Circumcision also does not prevent sexually transmitted diseases.

Does circumcision make sex more pleasurable for a man? The head of the penis is very sensitive, and this sensitivity will lessen if the protective foreskin is cut off. Some men who have been circumcised as adults and who compare their sexual experiences before and after have claimed that their penises were more sexually sensitive before the foreskins were removed. Because of this consideration, a custom developed many years ago to do a partial circumcision in which only a small part of the foreskin was removed, thus allowing the foreskin to cover about half of the head of the penis. In our opinion, partial circumcision should not be done because the part of the foreskin still covering the penis can become tighter and the circumcision may have to be repeated later on if adhesions form between the partial foreskin and the head of the penis. This also defeats the whole purpose of the circumcision because foreskin care is still necessary. In many ritual circumcisions a very generous amount of foreskin is removed. More problems arise from circumcisions in which not enough foreskin has been removed than in circumcisions that have removed too much.

When should the circumcision be performed? Genesis 17:12 states, "Every male among you who is eight days old must be circumcised." The probable reason for this was that the newborn baby's blood clots faster by the eighth day. Today, it is medically unnecessary to wait until the eighth day, but for those babies who do not receive vitamin K shortly after birth, it would be wise to wait until the eighth day for circumcision. Usually circumcision is done in the hospital within the first couple of days after birth for convenience. Up until recent years it was often the custom to do the circumcision immediately after delivery. Because of the increasing regard for the feelings of the newly born baby and the emphasis on the bonding period after birth, this practice fortunately is being gradually disregarded. Circumcision shortly after birth is incompatible with the trend toward gentling the newborn baby and making his new environment comfortable.

How do we care for the circumcised penis? The nurses or your baby's doctor will tell you how to care for the circumcision site. For a few days apply a protective lubricant every time you change a diaper. It will take about a week to heal, being swollen first, then getting a yellow scab. Watch for signs of infection—the entire penis would be red, warm, swollen, and the scab draining pus. Also, report bleeding of more than a few drops.

How do we care for an intact foreskin? If you choose to leave your baby's foreskin intact, all you have to do is *leave it alone.* We call this the "uncare" of the foreskin. In most babies the foreskin is tightly adhered to the underlying head of the penis during the early months. The foreskin gradually loosens itself, but it may not fully retract until the second or third year, although this varies considerably from baby to baby. Leave the foreskin alone until it begins to retract easily. *Do not forcibly retract* the foreskin since this may prematurely break the seal between the foreskin and the head of the penis, allowing secretions to accumulate beneath the foreskin. When the foreskin retracts naturally, gently clean out the secretions that may have accumulated between the foreskin and the glans of the penis. This should be done as part of the child's normal bath routine. Usually by three years of age, when most foreskins are fully retractable, a child can easily be taught to clean beneath his foreskin as part of his bath.

HOME WITH BABY

There are a lot of questions you'll have when you think about having your baby all to yourself to care for. In chapter 11 you'll read about what you need to know once you're at home on your own.

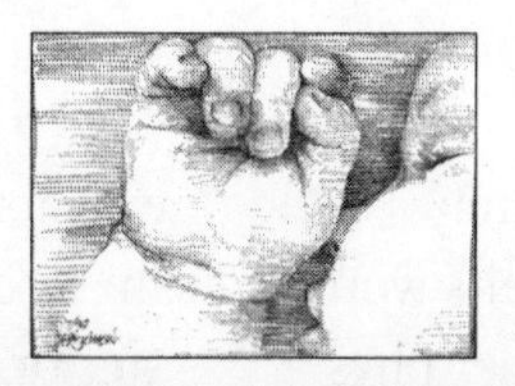

CHAPTER FIVE

Postpartum **Parenting**

Bringing home your newborn brings home reality that your family has grown. The euphoria of giving birth begins to wear off, and you as a couple will experience some degree of difficulty adjusting to life with a new baby, especially a first baby. Most certainly for mothers this is a stressful time. With the help of the Lord and her husband, the new mother can cope with these stresses and make a positive transition into motherhood.

THE MOTHER'S ADJUSTMENT PERIOD

Women having their first baby, even if it is by adoption, experience the most transforming event of their lives (other than spiritual rebirth). For the first time ever a woman is completely responsible for another life. Throughout pregnancy the responsibility was just as real, yet it was carried out passively. Now her baby depends on her active caregiving for its very life—physical and emotional. The mother finds herself putting her newborn's needs first moment by moment, day after day.

This is not only a new concept she must learn, and quickly, but it is a difficult one, at best, if she has no solid footing for what she needs to do. Our culture does not traditionally supply that solid footing. Other present-day cultures, as well as past cultures (including the Hebrew culture of two thousand years ago), provide for a new mother to have the full support of the community. They do much more than bring in a week's worth of dinners. They care for the mother physically; they take over the running of her household so that she can rest and take care of her baby and bond deeply with her baby. She may even be cared for in a special place, away from her domestic duties, so special and set apart is this time (a month or two, or even six!).

(In the Bible, a new mother was excused from attending the sanctuary until a specified period of time after the baby's birth [Lev. 12:1–7], and from involvement with religious items even in the home. Though the particulars may differ today, the principle remains the same: a "baby moon" is a good idea while the mother recuperates from childbirth and family members adjust to new roles. This is especially important with a first baby, but time for rest and adjustment is valuable with subsequent babies as well.)

"If birth is so wonderful and my baby is a precious gift from God, why do I feel so overwhelmed?" As we've mentioned, many cultures around the world recognize this sensitive period following birth and grant women an extended period of rest following childbirth. They provide a *doula*—someone to help with routine tasks so mother and baby can be together. Since our culture has no such tradition or provision, each individual family must see to it that somehow a new mother is not abandoned to her own slim resources. A mother or mother-in-law, sister or aunt, cousin or best friend can be brought in to help, in succession if need be. Since these people may not be readily available (they all work or have families in other states), a new profession has sprung up to fill this gap. (See details and resources in the section entitled "The Father's Postpartum Role" page 119.)

Many if not most young couples cannot afford to hire this help, but they cannot afford to be without it either. (No one thinks to budget for a *doula.*) Since our social community no longer performs this function, and hasn't for the greater part of this century, how wonderful it would be if churches would provide this service. Think of the testimony to the world we would be giving: "Those Christians really know how to care for one another."

The price we pay as a society for not taking care of our new mothers is reflected in our statistics on postpartum depression and related difficulties, including poor mother-infant attachment. About 50 percent of all women giving birth in North American hospitals experience some degree of after-baby depression. One hundred thousand women are treated in outpatient clinics for varying degrees of postpartum difficulties, and about four thousand women per year are hospitalized with se-

SIGNS OF POSTPARTUM DEPRESSION

Signs of postpartum depression include:

- Extreme fatigue
- Episodes of crying, anxiety, and fear
- Confused thoughts and difficulty in concentrating
- Insomnia (even if baby is asleep)
- Periods of nervousness and tension
- Loss of appetite
- Feelings of failure and panic
- Fear of going crazy
- Worry about physical appearance and unattractiveness, with diminishing desire to groom yourself
- Negative feelings toward husband
- Irritation by trivial things—tendency to "make mountains out of mole hills"
- Heart palpitations
- Shaky feelings

Serious depression needs professional attention. If you have more than two or three of these symptoms, and if these symptoms do not go away after trying the suggestions in this chapter, consult your doctor for advice. For more information on postpartum depression, call DAD (Depression After Delivery) at (215) 295-3994 or (800) 944-4773.

vere psychiatric disturbances within six months after giving birth.

The difference between the "baby blues" and postpartum depression is a matter of timing and degree. Most women experience some degree of temporary, mild depression within a few days or a week or two after giving birth. These emotional changes are due in part to the fact that often in human adjustment, a low follows a high. Shifting hormones and lifestyle changes are other contributing factors.

Even without postpartum depression a woman can experience doubt and frustration—doubt about her mothering abilities and often frustration at her apparent lack of success. These feelings may lead to some negative feelings toward her baby, then to feelings of guilt for having had these seemingly terrible feelings. Mothers, remember that it is not unusual (or unchristian) to experience this difficulty, but it is unhealthy if it gets out of hand. Talk about these feelings with a friend who is an experienced mother, and also with your health care provider. Let your husband know you are struggling so he can pray with you and do what he can to support you. Be sure he knows you do not blame him for how you feel, and don't expect him to have all the answers. He's as new to this as you are!

WHAT CAUSES POSTPARTUM TROUBLES?

Most postpartum difficulties are caused by too many changes too fast, and depression is a signal that a woman has exceeded her physical and psychological capabilities to adapt to these changes. She should not consider this a weakness in herself but realize instead that her stress level exceeds her individual ability to cope. The usual stresses contributing to postpartum depression are both physical and emotional.

RISK FACTORS FOR POSTPARTUM DEPRESSION

During pregnancy and delivery a woman can identify certain factors that may increase her risk of postpartum depression. If you have any of these risk factors, pray and seek counsel during pregnancy and in the early postpartum period.

1. A previous history of depression or difficulty coping with combined stresses.
2. Exchanging a high-status career for motherhood, with ambivalent feelings about the status change.
3. Feelings of this pregnancy being unwanted, or ambivalent feelings of how a child will fit into the current lifestyle.
4. Marital discord and unrealistic expectations that a child may solve marital problems.
5. A negative birth experience in which fear and pain predominate.
6. An ill or premature baby.
7. Any situation that separates mother and baby and interferes with a close mother-infant attachment shortly after birth.

Physical and Chemical Changes

In the postpartum period a woman's body chemistry is going through tremendous change, adjusting from the pregnant to nonpregnant lactating states. Hormone levels are fluctuating and this brings changing moods and feelings. Sleep cycles also undergo a tremendous change. The mother has had to adjust her sleep needs to fit the baby's sleep cycles, which may be unpredictable at first. "Sleep when your baby sleeps" is good advice, but adjusting to this new way of catching enough rest is not easy for many mothers.

Exhaustion also makes it difficult to recover from the birth itself. This is particularly true when the mother has experienced a traumatic birth (cesarean section or a prolonged and difficult labor). A difficult physical recovery from birth can be compounded by disappointment that the mother's expectations for an ideal birth were shattered by a reality in which she felt her wishes were not respected.

Emotional Changes

Especially with the birth of their first children, many women experience status changes that leave them searching for a new identity. This is particularly true of a very young mother who has no strong sense of self yet or of a woman who has had an exciting career outside the home from which she received much status and affirmation. A new mother may feel her identity is blurred: "I'm Johnny's mother, and I'm Bob's wife, but what happened to me as a person?" These are normal feelings that any person would have when his or her self-image is shifting. Another factor is a woman's expectations of motherhood and how different things are in reality. When her ideals don't materialize, a woman can feel let down. Perhaps at no other time in a married couple's life are there as many changes happening as fast as in the immediate postpartum period: change in lifestyle, role changes for husband and wife, disrupted routines, disrupted sleep patterns, changing economic status, and on and on. Whether these changes are for the better or for the worse, the reality is that they are stressful. There are new feelings to cope with.

EASING POSTPARTUM ADJUSTMENTS

Adjusting to motherhood is probably the biggest job you will ever have. There is a lot to get used to, but it can't be rushed. It takes time and a lot of patience, not just with your baby but with yourself. You need to learn how to respond to your baby and how to read his cues. Your mind needs time to adjust to your new role and sort out the reality of motherhood now that baby is here. Your body has some adjustments of its own to make and you want it to stay healthy. Here are some guidelines and suggestions to make your job easier.

Make Adequate Preparation

A woman can prepare her heart and body for the coming of her baby by following the suggestions discussed in chapter 3. During this preparation period she can get involved with various parenting groups, such as La Leche League, that can serve as positive support groups after delivery. Since postpartum depression is so common, new mothers can find comfort from other mothers in these support groups.

Be Flexible

When a woman enters labor, she can ask God to give her the strength to accept the labor and birth she has even as she plans for the "ideal" delivery. When decisions must be made about the management of her labor, she and her husband should ask questions about procedures and alternatives, state their own preferences, and work together with the medical team to ensure the health of baby and mother.

"Room-In" at Home

Continue the rooming-in you started in the hospital at home (see chapter 4). Mother-infant detachment is one of the contributing factors to postpartum depression. Positive interaction with baby is often a powerful antidote to baby blues. Keep baby near you as you rest. Keep him in your arms or in a sling as you move about the house. Consider the following new mother's experience:

> After the birth of my first baby, I went through an experience that I was in no way prepared for: postpartum depression. The tension and stress I felt from suddenly becoming a new mother caused me to actually be scared of my baby at times. Compounding my tensions was the thought that since I'd be returning to work soon, I felt like I would be "abandoning" my baby. All of these doubts and uncertainties were manifested in a bout of insomnia that stretched for four days.
>
> I'd lay my baby in her crib at night, then go to my room and just pray that I would get some sleep before she woke up for her next feeding. This was a bad mistake. While I tried to force myself to relax, I was aware of every turn, gurgle, and sigh that she was making in the next room.
>
> By the time I called my pediatrician, I was desperate for help. He suggested that I bring her into bed with me at night. I tried it, and although I was slightly nervous at first, afraid I would

> roll onto her, I quickly found that I was able to sleep and relax when she was next to me. I also think that having a family bed has brought us closer together as mother and daughter. Spending the night together, holding her and then breastfeeding her when she wakes up has made me feel less uncomfortable about leaving her with a sitter during the day. Besides, like my husband says, what better way to start a day than to wake up with your lover and your child next to you!

Avoid Extreme Fatigue

Although being tired is a realistic expectation of the parenting profession, new parents can do some things to keep fatigue under control, such as obtaining help at home from friends, relatives, or hired help if that is economically feasible. This is a time for friends to rally around new parents, help with the housework, prepare the meals, and simply "mother" the new mother. In our experience, much postpartum fatigue is due less to the many needs of the baby and more to the efforts of the new mother to be all things to all people (see the section "The Father's Postpartum Role" in this chapter).

A new mother must learn how to delegate responsibilities. The housework, cooking, dishes, and laundry can be done by someone else, but no one can mother your baby as you can. One new mother with a large family shared with me, "I simply sit in my rocking chair, dressed in my nightgown, nursing my baby and directing traffic." If the baby has older siblings of "working age" (more than three years old), some of the simpler household chores can be delegated to them. Make them feel that they can help Mommy and their new little brother or sister.

Consider Yourself

New mothers need to take a few hours out each week to do something for themselves. They may protest, "But my baby needs me all day long." Yes, a new baby does need his or her mother, but what the baby needs most is a happy mother. Meeting your own needs is not being selfish. Doing nothing but giving is going to wear thin after a while. A mother's resources must be replenished from time to time. If she feels good about herself as a person, she will be happier as a mother, and her child ultimately will profit.

The special time a mother carves out for herself can be spent on a relaxing activity, some physical exercise, a hobby, or just a peaceful walk in the park. This special time will prevent burnout and make it easier to deal with the stress in your life. There are many things you can do that do not require leaving baby. Now and then a trusted mother-substitute can show up just as baby goes off to sleep and you may choose to get out alone for a bit to relax. Fathers make the best mother-substitutes, and they are handy—they come home from work every day. That's the time to take a soak in a bubble bath (together if baby is asleep!). At the very least, mothers, don't "waste" the baby's nap-times on housework (unless, of course, your sanity is threatened by the chaos around you). A good book can be read in snatches, even while breastfeeding. Or put your baby in the sling and go out for a walk together. The movement will put him to sleep, so you can think other thoughts. This is also a good time to pray. Even Jesus needed time to slip away, to sleep, to have time with the Father. (See more on this subject on p. 235, "How to Avoid Mother Burnout.")

Keep Yourself Attractive

When a woman looks good, she most likely will feel good. Give yourself permission to pay attention to good grooming. Join forces with a close friend who can be trusted to see ways you can stay beautiful. Buy something new to wear that flatters or strategically conceals parts of your postpartum figure. Get a manicure or a new haircut, or buy a new lipstick.

Eat a Balanced Diet

Avoid junk food because it can cause blood-sugar swings and contribute to postpartum blues. When you are nursing, you will need the same nutritious calories and balanced diet that you needed during pregnancy. Postpartum weight loss should occur gradually and not through crash diets. Dietary deficiencies can contribute to postpartum depression, especially combined with the stresses of pregnancy, giving birth, and new-parent fatigue. A consultation with a nutritionist who is experienced in postpartum problems may be necessary. Ask your doctor or midwife for a referral. Keep lots of healthy snacks on hand: veggies cut and peeled, ready-to-eat fresh fruit, yogurt, juices, whole grain bread, and crackers. Drink lots of water.

Avoid Too Many Visitors

In the first few weeks after coming home, limit visitors. "Thou shalt not entertain" is one of the commandments for a new mother. Remember the "help" (even if it's your mother) is there to *help you* and is not there to be entertained. The helping person should know you are going to care for the baby; she is there to take care of the household duties and other children. Clarify this ahead of time to avoid hurt feelings. Make a written list if it is hard for you to tell this person what things need to be done. Then sit still and relax while she does them.

Avoid Isolation

Do seek out friends and visitors when you want them. Surround yourself with positive people. Avoid negative advisors who may try to pressure you into a mothering style that does not feel right to you. Mothering in a way that basically goes against your God-given inner wisdom is a setup for postpartum depression. The human, emotional organism is not equipped to operate for long outside God's basic design. Any advice that does not feel right to you and is not working should be dropped.

Exercise

Force yourself to get at least a half hour of sustained exercise each day even if it is simply walking in the park with your baby in a front carrier. Physical exercise is absolutely mandatory for a new mother. Tiny babies are very portable. Nothing in the mother-infant contract says you must stay home all the time. Home to a tiny baby is where mother is.

Involve Your Husband

Be specific in telling your husband what you want (laundry or dishes done, a cleaning service, help with the other children, and so on). Remember, your husband is undergoing some postpartum adjustment difficulties of his own. Quite honestly, many men are slow to sense exactly what new mothers need, so you simply may have to make your needs known. Your husband may perceive a situation as insignificant and therefore ignore it, but to you it is a major deal. Tell him.

THE FATHER'S POSTPARTUM ROLE

Fathers, your wife needs mothering too. Be tuned in and sensitive to her physical and emotional needs. If your wife is having a problem with a status change, help her feel she has moved up the ladder of personal worth and not down. Be sure to express genuine love and support, "You are doing the most important job in the world, mothering our child."

Be aware of the many physical and emotional changes going on within your wife. This is a time that calls for sincere, high-level communication in which you empathize with her feelings: "You must feel very tired. How can I help?" Also, realize that your wife may be somewhat reluctant to ask for your help since she may feel this is a sign of weakness. She may feel that she should be superwoman: the perfect wife, the perfect mother, the perfect hostess, the perfect housekeeper, the perfect everything.

With so many demands on the new mother, the responsibility falls to the father to be sure she is not drained of energy. In many primitive cultures in the world a new mother often has a *doula* (from the Greek word meaning "servant"). A *doula* is a person who can take over the household chores and free the new mother to recover from the birth and care for her baby. Anyone can be a *doula* to the new mother, even the father. And if there are tasks he can't take over himself, he must enlist the support of others. It is part of the father's role to see that this kind of in-depth help is provided for his wife and his new baby. Money spent on hiring this help would be more appropriate than receiving dozens of cute little outfits and toys baby doesn't need. When your friends ask, "Is there anything you need?" be ready with an answer: "Yes, could you bring over supper tomorrow night?" Contact DONA (Doulas of North America) for how to find a professional postpartum *doula*—1100 23rd Avenue, Seattle, WA 98112, (206) 324-5440. ATFM (Apple Tree Family Ministries) is a source for finding Christian *doulas*—P. O. Box 2083, Artesia, CA 90702-2083, (888) 925-0149 or (562) 925-0149.

Watch for problems. Be sensitive to the early signs of depression: insomnia, loss of appetite, unfounded nagging, lessening attention to grooming, not wanting to get out of the house. If these red flags appear, take steps immediately. Seek professional counsel before these early warning signs progress into a full-blown depression and you wind up being both mother and father while your wife is recovering.

Respect the nesting instinct. During the final month of pregnancy and for the first few months after birth, the mother needs a stable nest. Avoid making major changes near the time of childbirth. This is not the time to change jobs, move into a new house, or move across the country. Remember, the nesting instinct is very strong in a new mother.

Control visitors. Be sure that well-meaning friends and relatives help instead of hinder the new mother. A long visit from family members, or even too many casual drop-ins in the first few weeks can be very draining, especially when baby is up a lot at night. The new mother needs time to rest or sleep rather than entertain yet another visitor. If someone comes at a bad time, say so.

Care for older children. Take charge of most of the physical maintenance of the older children. This frees your wife to concentrate on their emotional needs, which often go up when a new baby arrives; they also want mother's prime time.

Show love. You may say, "Of course I love my wife." But do you show it? Because of the previously mentioned reasons, your wife will have problems with her sense of well-being during the postpartum adjustment period. Show your love in concrete ways. This might mean bringing your wife flowers; it might mean washing the dishes. (See more on this subject on page 214, "Father Feelings and Mother-Infant Attachment.")

READINGS FOR POSTPARTUM MOTHERS

Just as you relied on the Lord for strength during pregnancy and childbirth, you can call on God for help during the postpartum period. Prayer and Scripture reading can help you cope with feelings of aloneness and depression.

Psalm 9:9–10—The Lord is a refuge for the oppressed, a stronghold in times of trouble. Those who know your name will trust in you, for you, LORD, have never forsaken those who seek you.

Psalm 27:4–5—One thing I ask of the LORD, this is what I seek: that I may dwell in the house of the Lord all the days of my life, to gaze upon the beauty of the LORD and to seek him in his temple. For in the day of trouble he will keep me safe in his dwelling; he will hide me in the shelter of his tabernacle and set me high upon a rock.

Psalm 46:1—God is our refuge and strength, an ever-present help in trouble.

Isaiah 40:11—He tends his flock like a shepherd: He gathers the lambs in his arms and carries them close to his heart; he gently leads those that have young.

John 14:27—Peace I leave with you; my peace I give you. I do not give to you as the world gives. Do not let your hearts be troubled and do not be afraid.

Matthew 28:20b—And surely I am with you always, to the very end of the age.

TEN COMMANDMENTS FOR THE POSTPARTUM MOTHER

1. Thou shalt not give up thy baby to strange caregivers.
2. Thou shalt not cook, clean house, do laundry, or entertain.
3. Thou shalt be given a *doula.*
4. Thou shalt remain clothed in thy nightgown and sit in thy rocking chair.
5. Thou shalt honor thy husband with his share of household chores.
6. Thou shalt take long walks in green pastures, eat good food, and drink much water.
7. Thou shalt not have before you strange and unhelpful visitors.
8. Thou shalt groom thy hair and adorn thy body with attractive, comfortable clothing.
9. Thou shalt be allowed to sleep when baby sleeps.
10. Look to the Lord, and He will give you strength: thou shalt not have prophets of bad baby advice before you.

RESUMING YOUR SEXUAL RELATIONSHIP

Your health care provider will schedule a six-week check-up, but some couples decide to come together sexually before that time. Once the lochia (vaginal bleeding after childbirth) has stopped, and all tenderness is gone, you don't have to wait for the six-week check-up. You will need a water soluble lubricant because the natural lubrication of the vagina will take a while to return to normal. The hormones of breastfeeding cause a woman's sexual hormones to take a back seat for a while, and this varies for each woman. If intercourse is painful, tell your health care provider what's wrong so this problem can be addressed. Don't be embarrassed to bring it to someone's attention.

CHILD SPACING AND NATURAL FAMILY PLANNING

For a variety of reasons, couples may choose to limit the size of their families or to control the spacing of their children. Christian couples will want to seek the Lord's guidance in choosing a method of family planning. For the Christian couple, the term *conception control* is more accurate than birth control, since any method that prevents the birth of a baby after conception has occurred, violating the sacredness of human life, is not an option. Before you make a decision, please educate yourself. The following information should help you make an informed choice, and we have recommended readings in the bibliography for further help.

Hormonal contraceptives—pill, implant, injection. Although perhaps the most effective method of artificial conception control, hormones have the most potential for side effects. The intricate design of a woman's hormonal system is one of God's most remarkable creations. Couples may wish to consider whether artificially manipulating these hormones to suppress ovulation may be not only medically unsafe but also not in accordance with God's admonition to regard our bodies as temples of the Holy Spirit (1 Cor. 3:16; 6:19). As Christians, we have other concerns. Hormonal contraceptives can actually do more than contracept. A certain percentage of the time ovulation is not suppressed; an egg can be fertilized but not allowed to implant. This is particularly true of the "morning after" hormones. Because we believe that human life begins at conception, we are not comfortable with this. It is important that couples not use a method that violates their conscience. Christian couples must go before the Lord and ask for guidance.

The intrauterine device (IUD). The IUD is a coil-like device that is inserted into the uterus by a healthcare professional. There can be medical complications such as infection, perforation of the uterus, or hemorrhage. The real issue for the Christian is how the IUD works. The current IUDs are abortifacient, that is, they cause abortion by preventing the implantation of the fertilized egg into the uterine wall.

Diaphragm and spermicidal foam and jelly. These methods are less effective than the pill or the IUD, but the important thing for Christians is that they are strictly contraceptive. They prevent the sperm from reaching the egg for fertilization. Many find them unattractive because they put a damper on the spontaneity of sex, and sometimes they cause allergy or infection. However, when used carefully, they can be rather efficient methods of conception control.

Condoms. Condoms are way down on this list of options. A condom alone is not very effective and should always be used in conjunction with a diaphragm and spermicide in the woman. Men often choose not to use condoms because they feel they lessen the pleasure of intercourse.

Sterilization. As both Christians and medical professionals, we are concerned to see Christian couples decide upon sterilization without prayer and consultation. We personally believe that sterilization, unless for serious medical reasons, is unwise. Before considering tubal ligation or vasectomy, consider the following: you are making a permanent decision based on your circumstances at the present time. You cannot predict what your family situation will be in the future. We have talked with many couples who wish to have sterilization reversed, even though at the time they made the decision they were certain they didn't want any more children.

As with all these matters of family planning, go before the Lord and ask for His guidance. It is a very grave matter to so completely lose your openness to life that you take this surgical step, which may not be reversible in your case. Another concern is that the safety of sterilization, especially vasectomy, is open to question. Increasing scientific evidence suggests that some males following vasectomies develop sperm antibodies that can lead eventually to diseases of the immune system.

Natural child spacing method. Frequent and unrestricted breastfeeding provides a period of natural infertility. The body chemistry behind this is uncertain, but it is generally agreed that the hormones produced by frequent sucking suppress ovulation, menstruation does not occur, and most women cannot get pregnant until their cycles resume. This is called "lactation amenorrhea." However, here a word of caution needs to be added. Breastfeeding is an effective method of conception control only when the following guidelines are followed:

1. *Under six months:* Exclusive breastfeeding with a complete openness to night nursings by sleeping with the baby and without the use of pacifiers, bottles, or cups, and without schedules.

2. *Over six months:* Baby starts taking solid food from the table, liquids begin only when baby shows interest in the cup, still no bottles or pacifiers, continued frequent breastfeeding, pacifying at the breast, sleep-sharing, and night nursing.

(Taken from *Breastfeeding and Natural Childspacing* by Sheila Kippley—see bibliography.)

In nearly every case where the mother reported that "it didn't work," there was a breakdown in one or more of these requirements, the most common being not sleeping with the baby, which discourages night nursings and promotes the use of pacifiers. The amount of suck stimulation necessary to suppress ovulation varies greatly from mother to mother, which is why a few women conceive although they apparently follow all the rules.

Studies have shown the following results in women who practice unrestricted breastfeeding as outlined above: (1) the average length of lactation amenorrhea (no menstruation and probably no fertility) is 14.5 months (the range is from two to thirty months); (2) in 5 percent of mothers, ovulation occurs before menstruation but rarely before the sixth month. *Before* six months, the chance of pregnancy is at the 1 percent level. For some women, fertility is delayed even though menstruation has resumed. This is especially true the earlier the menstrual cycles start again. *After* six months, the chances of pregnancy before your first period are about 6 percent, if you continue with unrestricted breastfeeding. Proper instruction in natural family planning can lower that to around 1 percent, about the same effectiveness as hormones.

Natural Family Planning method (NFP). God has had a way in place from the very beginning that allows couples to enjoy unencumbered lovemaking without conceiving a child until they are ready. They can do this by learning to recognize the woman's physical signs of fertility and nonfertility. The couple will need to talk about their sexuality much more openly, and take responsibility together in deciding to postpone pregnancy by avoiding sex during the fertile time.

A woman is fertile at the midpoint of her cycle, and this fertility is heralded by the appearance of a stringy, egg-white type of mucous coming from the cervix. This mucous is readily detectable at the entrance to the vagina. The onset of fertility is also characterized by a slight rise in body temperature in the morning, and by changes in the cervix that a woman can learn to detect.

When this method is used correctly, studies have shown it to be nearly 99 percent effective in preventing pregnancy. One drawback to this method is that abstinence is necessary when the woman is fertile, which is also usually at the height of her sexual interest. NFP is a way of living and loving that requires self-discipline for husband and wife. It is often this element of caring and sacrifice (see Rom. 12:1–2) that can have special benefits in building up a marriage. We encourage you to learn more by reading *The Art of Natural Family Planning,* by Dr. John Kippley and Sheila Kippley, and other related books in the bibliography.

For more information on informed choices in conception control and Natural Family Planning, contact The Couple to Couple League, P. O. Box 111184, Cincinnati, Ohio 45211, (513) 471-2000. You can request their information packet on these subjects by writing or by calling (800) 745-8252.

Allow God to plan families. Some Christians are choosing to leave decisions about when to have children, and how many children to have, entirely in God's hands by using no family planning measures. Of course most of them realize that God's plan for spacing babies involves unrestricted breastfeeding according to the natural mothering program mentioned above.

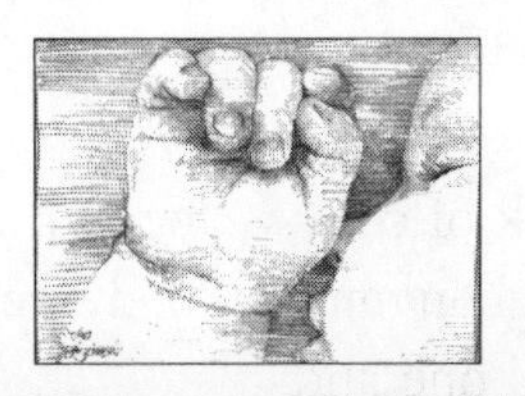

CHAPTER SIX

Feeding Your **Infant**

In her baby's first year, a mother spends more time feeding her infant than on any other parenting task. Feeding your baby according to God's design helps you enjoy this relationship more. This chapter deals with breastfeeding and formula feeding. Weaning and starting solids appear in chapter 12.

MOTHER'S MILK

We have a very important point to make at the outset of this chapter. In our opinion, unless a medical or psychological problem prevents it, every baby should be fed his own mother's milk for at least one year, and two years is even better. Parents hear confusing advice about breastfeeding and artificial feeding. Experts often say that mother's milk is best, but quickly add that modern formula is every bit as good. This just isn't true. One of the most important gifts you can give your baby is your own milk.

Human Milk for Human Babies

God designed the way in which the young of each species should be fed. He created a living nutrient, specially formulated for survival. This nutrient is called "milk." The milk for each species is unique and well suited to the young's developmental needs and its particular environment. Seal milk is high in fat because seals need high body fat to adapt to their cold environment. The milk of cows and of other range mammals is high in minerals and protein because rapid bone and muscle growth is necessary for their mobility and survival—the calf is up and running within hours after birth. And human milk is high in certain proteins and lactose, which promote growth in the brain, the survival organ of our species. Only recently have scientists begun to recognize the many functions of human milk, and what they have learned in the past few decades may be only the tip of the iceberg.

A Dynamic, Changing, Living Tissue

Your milk changes as your infant changes. An example of this dynamic process is the change in your milk's fat content. Fat accounts for a large percentage of your milk's calories. The hungrier your baby is, the higher the fat content of the milk he receives. If your baby is only thirsty, he will suck in such a way that he receives the thinner foremilk, the milk that is stored near the nipple and is delivered to the baby early in a feeding. If he sucks longer, the fat content of the milk rises, and toward the end of a long feeding he gets small amounts of very rich milk, a signal to him that the meal is over. Also, your milk has a higher fat content in the morning, when baby wakes after a longer stretch of sleep. Your milk gradually becomes lower in fat as your baby gets older because he will need fewer calories per pound of body weight as he grows.

Your milk also changes to protect your baby against germs. He needs a supply of germ-fighting elements in his blood called "immunoglobulins." The immunoglobulins, which are unique to each species, protect your baby from the germs in his environment to which he is most susceptible. Shortly after birth your infant begins making his own immunoglobulins, but they do not reach sufficient levels to protect him until he is about six months old. To make up for this deficiency, God has designed the mother to give her baby her immunoglobulins until he is able to make his own—through her blood while he is in the womb and through her milk after he is born.

The very first milk your baby receives shortly after birth is called "colostrum," which is very high in immunoglobulins. Since your newborn baby is particularly vulnerable to germs, God has designed your milk to be most protective when your baby needs it most. Your colostrum can be considered your baby's first immunization.

Long ago, mother's milk was also known as "white blood," because it contains the same living white cells that blood contains. The white blood cells in your milk fight the germs that commonly show up in your baby's intestines. Your milk also contains a special protein called "immunoglobulin A," which coats your baby's intestines, preventing the passage of harmful germs from his intestines into his blood.

The Chemistry of Breast Milk

Certain chemical nutrients are found in all milk: fat, protein, carbohydrates, minerals, iron, and vitamins. The relative percentages of these nutrients vary in each species' milk according to that species' individual needs.

Fats. You have read previously how the fat content of your milk changes to meet your baby's changing requirements. Your milk also contains live enzymes that help digest the fat. Because formula does not contain these enzymes, the fat in formula is not totally digested and some passes into the stools, accounting for the unpleasant odor of the stools of formula-fed infants. Not only is it unpleasant for the adults changing those diapers, but the baby will pick up from their negative reaction that he is unpleasant. The breastfed baby gets the message that he's always lovable—the lower fat content and the difference in sugars and bacteria in the stools of a breastfed baby produce a milder, sweeter smell like cheese or buttermilk.

Cholesterol. You might be surprised to hear that human milk is high in cholesterol. The cholesterol issue is an example of how scientists have become confused in their efforts to "humanize" the milk that the Creator designed for cows. We know that adults who have high cholesterol in their blood and diets are more prone to heart and blood vessel diseases; therefore, scientists decided to make baby formulas low in cholesterol in an effort to prevent heart disease. However, common sense dictates that the milk designed and adapted for the survival of our species should not be tampered with.

In studies where some newborn rats were fed diets low in cholesterol and some were fed diets high in cholesterol, the results showed that God was right after all: the newborn rats fed high-cholesterol diets actually had lower amounts of cholesterol in their blood when they reached adulthood. The newborn rats fed low-cholesterol diets had higher blood cholesterol as adult rats. Formula manufacturers are still uncertain what to make of these studies.

Protein. Since cows grow four times faster than humans, the amount of casein protein in cow's milk is four times that of human milk. Human milk contains more whey protein, which produces a smaller and more digestible curd than that of cow's milk or formula, so it takes less time to digest. This is why mothers have observed that formula-fed babies remain "full" longer than breastfed babies. The protein in human milk also includes the amino acid taurine, which stimulates brain growth.

Carbohydrates. The predominant sugar in milk is lactose. Researchers have noted that mammals with larger brains have a larger percentage of lactose in their milk. Human milk contains more lactose than cow's milk; that is why it tastes sweeter. Soy formulas have no lactose at all. To bring the sugar level up to that of breast milk, cane sugar or corn syrup is added to formulas. The problem is that these sugars are not as healthy. Cane and corn sugar is digested more rapidly than lactose, causing blood sugar swings.

Lactose also favors the development of certain beneficial bacteria in your baby's intestines. This is known as the "ecology of the gut." It is interesting that God has designed certain beneficial bacteria that can live in your baby's intestines provided they have the ideal chemical conditions. These bacteria ward off harmful bacteria that cause diarrhea.

Minerals. Cow's milk is high in calcium and phosphorus because cows have a much higher rate of bone growth than humans. These excess mineral salts place an extra load on your infant's immature kidneys. Your milk is lower in mineral salts and therefore is easier on your newborn's kidneys.

Iron. Your baby needs iron to make new red blood cells as she grows. As your baby was developing *in utero,* she stored a lot of the iron she got from your blood through the placenta. She uses up these iron stores within her first six months after birth; after that she needs iron from her diet. The iron in your milk is different from any other kind of iron; it is well absorbed and used very efficiently.

Your baby can absorb only 10 percent of the iron in formula or cow's milk compared to 50 percent of the iron in breast milk. The reason for this difference is that a special protein called "lactoferrin" attaches to the iron in your milk. It helps your baby's intestines absorb the iron, thus protecting your baby against anemia. Babies who are fed human milk very rarely become anemic; babies fed cow's milk or formula without iron often will become anemic between one and two years of age. The excess iron added to formula is excreted in the stools and gives them a greenish color. A baby's stools neither look right nor smell right when her intestines are called upon to handle milk they were not designed to handle. And this excess iron in the intestines allows harmful bacteria to thrive in your baby's intestines.

Vitamins. Breast milk contains all the essential vitamins your baby needs. Vitamin supplements are not necessary in healthy, term, breastfed infants who are getting adequate breast milk, certainly not for the first six months.

The Blessings of Breastfeeding

Breastfeeding helps mothers know their child better. They learn to determine when their child is full by watching for signs of contentment rather than counting ounces of formula. This very early, very basic watching teaches mothers the importance of observing their babies, and they become sensitive to many other things about their babies that need observing, such as what comforts baby best, what causes baby to fuss, and what all those little (and not so little) noises mean. They learn to read their babies rather than read lines on a bottle or hands on a clock. They get tuned into the baby as a unique individual rather than regard him as a project. Not only do the mother and her nursing baby have a greater potential for being in harmony with each other, but they learn to trust in their mother-baby dialogue.

Mothers who breastfeed have much higher prolactin levels in their blood. This helps them handle stress and be more responsive to their babies. This is especially true for mothers who do not restrict their breastfeeding in any way, such as using bottles at night, relying on the use of pacifiers, or sticking to a certain schedule. Breastfeeding mothers spend more time with their babies, and good things happen because of it.

For example, mothers often describe breastfeeding as a time of loving with their babies. Loving comes naturally to mothers, but this is only the beginning. As mothers spend time with their newborns, they learn how to nurture their babies. We learned over our many years of loving our babies that God's design for breastfeeding goes beyond physical and emotional benefits. It is His way of bringing each new child into a love relationship with Himself. Here is an entry from Martha's journal from when Erin was a baby:

> We have been teaching our baby to love. When she hears the word, she responds by placing her head against the person holding her. To her, love means warmth, holding, closeness, gentleness, and a crooning "ah-h-h." This didn't just happen overnight. She has been learning this little by little since day one.
>
> Psalm 22:9 says, "Yet you brought me out of the womb; you made me trust in you even at my mother's breast." Breastfeeding continues the nurturing begun by God in the womb, and it begins the trust relationship that is so vital for a healthy parent-child relationship to develop. A breastfeeding mother is giving herself totally, and the baby gets the message. That message eventually will translate into the concept of love from God: the mother teaches the baby first to trust, then to be loved, then to show love to others, and finally to understand what it means to love God our Father and to be loved by Him. Our baby won't understand all of this for

a long time, but even at age sixteen months when she looks at a picture of Jesus and we say, "Jesus loves you," she smiles. When we say, "Erin loves Jesus," she puts her head down on the book and snuggles. To this growing child, the concept of love will not be abstract, and the concept of love from and for God will be real. It all begins with the kind of love God teaches us about in the Bible. First Corinthians 13:4–7 says, "Love is patient, love is kind. . . . It is not rude, it is not self-seeking, it is not easily angered, it keeps no record of wrongs. . . . It always protects, always trusts, always hopes, always perseveres."

John 3:16 says that "For God so loved the world that he gave his one and only Son"—He gave Himself. John 15:12 says, "My command is this: Love each other as I have loved you." And John 15:13 says, "Greater love has no one than this, that one lay down his life for his friends."

A daily willingness to lay down your life for your baby means *giving of yourself*. This is why God designed mothers to be able to give of themselves—so they could teach their babies about love. Of course, a mother can love her baby and teach him to love whether she breastfeeds or not. Breastfeeding completes the picture, fulfilling God's plan so perfectly for the care and nurturing of His little ones.

THE JOYFUL RELATIONSHIP

Mothers, you become a giving person when you breastfeed, and you enjoy this giving because you notice the peace and joy breastfeeding gives you and your baby. Isaiah 66:11–13 beautifully illustrates this feeling of rightness:

"For you will nurse and be satisfied at her comforting breasts; you will drink deeply and delight in her overflowing abundance." For this is what the LORD says: "I will extend peace like a river, and the wealth of nations like a flooding stream; you will nurse and be carried on her arm and dandled on her knees. As a mother comforts her child, so will I comfort you; and you will be comforted over Jerusalem."

TIPS FOR SUCCESSFUL BREASTFEEDING

Breastfeeding is the natural, biological relationship that God has designed for mothers to nourish their babies with confidence. Being confident is the key to successful breastfeeding, and prayer is the best confidence builder. Another source of confidence is the support a new mother can get from other mothers experienced in the art of breastfeeding. If you have not attended a series of La Leche League meetings during pregnancy, consider doing so now that your little breastfeeder has arrived (see p. 72 for more information). Many mothers appreciate the mother-to-mother support, enough to continue attending monthly meetings long after the birth of their baby.

Getting the Right Start

The following suggestions will help you learn how to breastfeed your baby most comfortably.

ELEMENTS OF SUCCESSFUL BREASTFEEDING

Why are some breastfeeding relationships more successful than others? Here are some features we have noted of the more successful breastfeeding relationships. Put these elements in place and you and your nursing baby will be off to a great start.

- A supportive husband
- Involvement in natural childbirth classes and La Leche League meetings
- A positive birthing experience
- Rooming-in after birth
- Help to ensure baby is latching on correctly and sucking well
- No supplemental feeding unless medically necessary
- Unscheduled feedings
- Sleep-sharing

Get help. Ask for someone trained in breastfeeding to check how the baby is nursing before you go home. Most hospitals have lactation educators on staff, and some offer the service of checking up on you once you have gone home. If there are no lactation services available, you can call your doctor's office for a referral or call La Leche League if you are having any problems. (See "Common Breastfeeding Questions," p. 139.)

Forget the clock. Ignore the outdated advice of "begin with five minutes of nursing and gradually increase the time each day so you won't get sore." In the first few days, every baby has a different suck. Some begin sucking enthusiastically immediately after birth; others only snooze and lick for the first day. It is not how *long* a baby sucks, but *how* he sucks that can cause sore nipples.

Position yourself. Sitting up in an arm chair is usually the best position for nursing, and pillows are a real must. Place one behind your back and one alongside you to support the arm holding baby. Use one or two pillows (or a specially designed nursing pillow) on your lap to bring your baby up to the level of your breasts. Use a foot stool to make your lap higher and to avoid straining your back. You may be more comfortable lying in bed on your side for your first few feedings, especially if you have had a cesarean section.

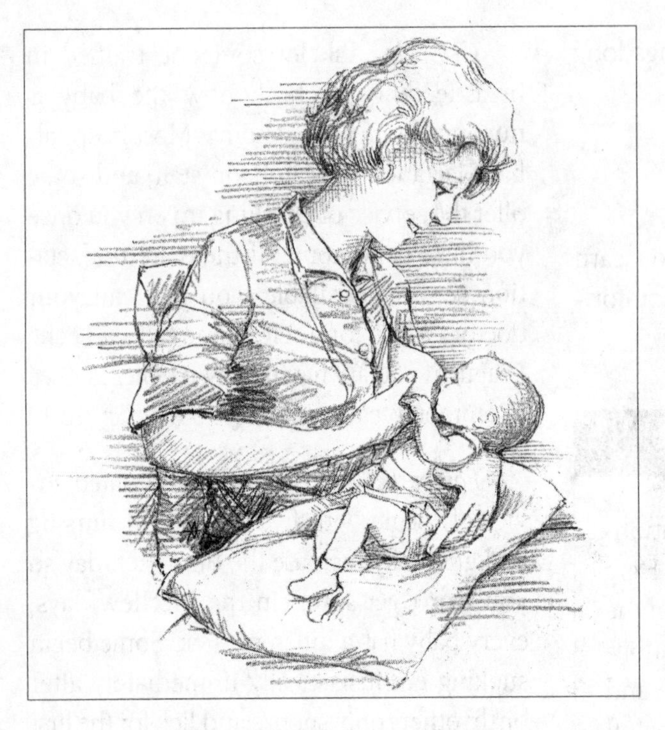

Correct nursing position: Tickle your baby's lips with your nipple until his mouth opens wide.

Then pull him close, keeping his head and body aligned with yours.

Position your baby. First, unwrap your baby so he can snuggle in close to your body. Position him alongside your arm (which is on the pillow on your lap) so that his neck rests in the bend of your elbow, his back along your forearm, and his hips next to your hand. Have him on his side so he is facing you front to front. Keep his head in line with his body. Your baby should not have to turn his head and strain to reach your nipple. (Turn your head to the side or up to the ceiling and try to swallow!) Tuck his lower arm straight alongside his body in the soft pocket of your midriff so that it doesn't get bent or get in the way.

Support your breast. Cup your breast with your free hand, supporting your breast with all four fingers underneath and your thumb on top. Be sure your hand stays way back, clear of the brown area, called the areola. It is important to continue holding your breast throughout the feeding until baby is strong enough to manage the weight of your breast himself. Manually express a few drops of colostrum. (See "How to Manually Express Breast Milk," on p. 149.)

Get correct latch-on. Using your nipple as a teaser, gently tickle your baby's lips so he gets a taste of colostrum, encouraging him to open his mouth widely (babies' mouths often open like little birds' beaks—very wide—and then quickly close). The moment your baby opens his mouth widely, direct your nipple toward the roof of his mouth (to be sure it goes above his tongue), and *quickly* draw him *very close* to you with the arm that is holding him. (If you don't do it quickly enough, the little mouth will close and you'll have to start over.) Don't lean forward, pushing your breast toward your baby. Pull him toward you. Most new mothers do not pull their babies in closely enough.

The key to correct latch-on is for your baby to suck on the areola, the dark area of your breast surrounding your nipple. Under the areola are the milk sinuses that must be compressed for proper milk release. Attempt to get a large part of the areola into his mouth. Pull your baby so close that the tip of his nose touches your breast. Don't be afraid of blocking his nose, since he can breathe quite well from the sides of his nose. If his nose does seem to be blocked, use your thumb to press gently on your breast to unblock his nose or pull his feet in closer to change the angle.

If your baby is latching on correctly, you should not feel painful pressure on your nipple. If you feel that the baby is sucking mostly on your nipple, use your index finger to push down on his lower jaw and lip to open his mouth wider. You should notice an instant relief from the pain. If your baby does not cooperate, detach baby and start again. Some babies do not detach themselves readily. You need to break the suction by sliding your finger into the corner of baby's mouth and between his gums. Never pull your baby off the breast; you can damage your nipple.

Improper latch-on is the most common cause of sore nipples, so it is important that you work with your baby until he learns the right way. Incorrect suck can also cause pain. Both these problems can also mean baby will not get enough milk. If you have sore nipples that are getting worse, seek immediate help from a La Leche League leader or a lactation consultant.

Types of Suck

You will notice that your baby sucks in two different ways: comfort sucking, a weaker suck that involves mainly the lips and tongue; and nutritive sucking, in which the whole jaw moves vigorously. You will notice the muscles of his jaw working so hard that his ears wiggle and the bones of his head move during intense nutritive sucking. This kind of sucking delivers the higher-calorie hindmilk, the creamy milk that comes later in the feeding. The visible contractions of your baby's jaw muscles and the audible swallow sounds (little gulping noises from his throat after every one to three sucks) are two reliable indications that your baby is getting milk.

Alternative Nursing Positions

If you have had a cesarean section, it may be easier for you to nurse your baby lying down.

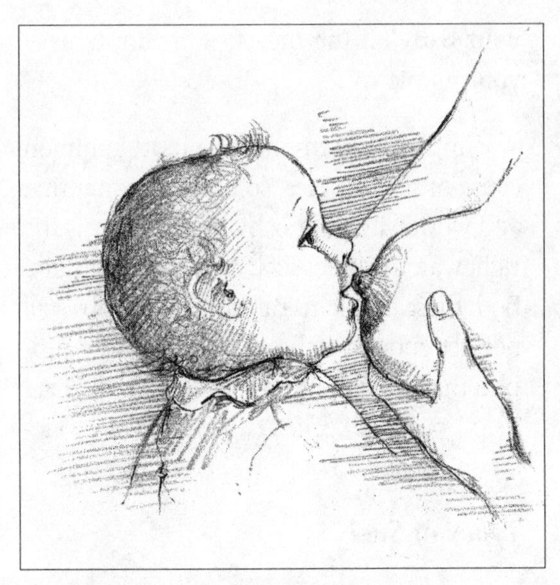

Teasing baby's mouth open wide.

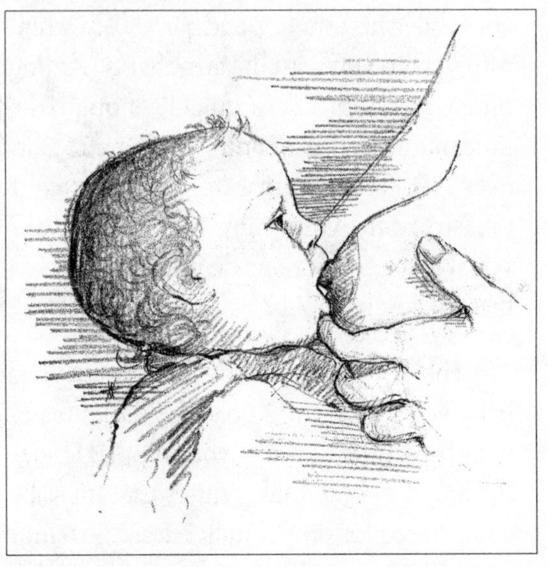

Helping baby open mouth wide enough for proper latch-on: depressing lower jaw and everting lips.

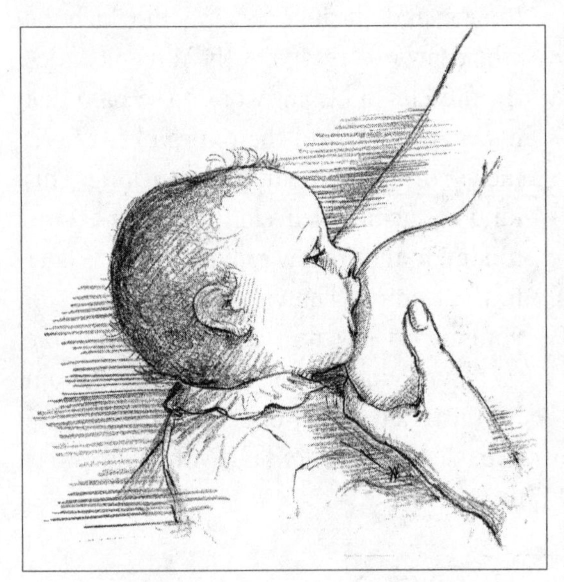

Proper latch-on: Notice baby's lips correctly everted.

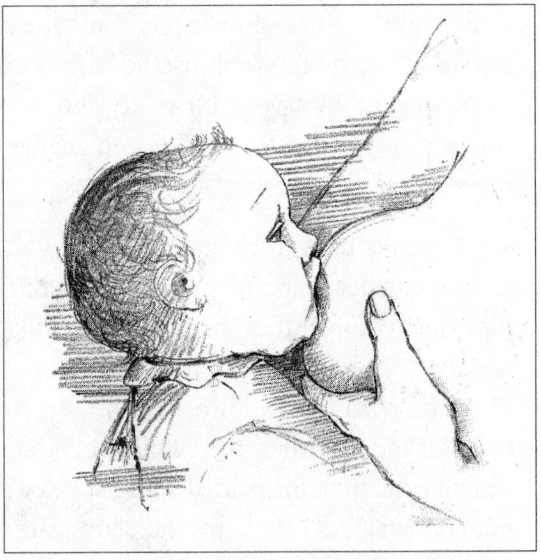

Incorrect latch-on: Notice baby's lower lip is tucked in.

Turn on your side and have someone wedge some pillows behind your back; use another pillow to support your top leg, and try an extra pillow under your head. You may also want a pillow supporting and protecting your lower abdomen. Ask your helper to place your baby on her side facing you, nestled in your arm, and to position her so her mouth lies close to your nipple. Hold and support your breast as described above. Then tickle her mouth open with your nipple. When her mouth opens widely, pull your baby in close as described above, helping her to latch on correctly.

Another alternative nursing arrangement is the "football hold" or clutch hold (see figure on p. 138). This is useful for a mother who is unable to stand the pressure of her baby on her incision after a cesarean, or for a baby who has difficulty latching on. While sitting up, place pillows under your arm at your side, and put your baby on the pillows. Cup the back of his neck in your hand and let his legs rest against the pillow supporting your back. Follow the same procedure for proper latch-on as mentioned above. This position works particularly well for babies who squirm, arch their backs, and frequently detach themselves from the breast.

Some babies latch on to the breast and suck properly within the first day or so; other babies are slow starters and like to suck a little, then snooze a little. These types of nursing babies need to have a little prodding

Improper Nursing Posture: Baby's head and body are not in line. Mother is leaning into baby instead of pulling baby close to her.

FINDING A LACTATION CONSULTANT

Many hospitals now have at least one lactation consultant on staff to help new mothers with breastfeeding. You do need to be aware, however, that there are vast differences in training and in competency to handle more complicated breastfeeding problems among people who bear that title. Some may have attended just a brief, weekend workshop. Others have studied for years and have an IBCLC (International Board of Certified Lactation Consultants) certification for which they have passed a board examination. If you and your baby are experiencing problems that are not being resolved in a day or two with the help of one lactation consultant, you should ask her to refer you to someone with more training or more experience in the particular problem you are having. Another way to find someone with the skills you need is to ask for a referral from La Leche League.

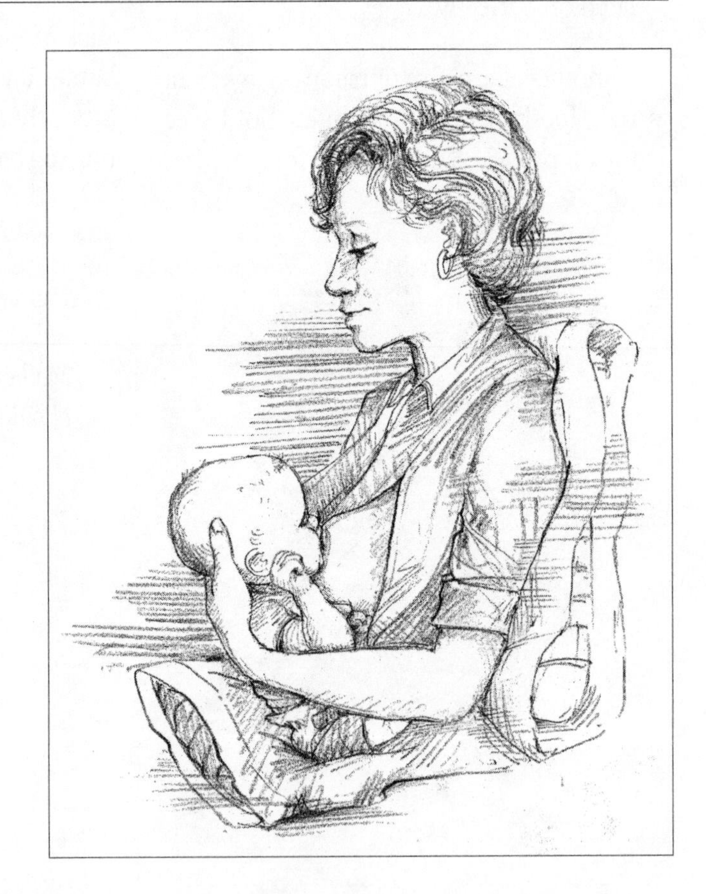

The Clutch Hold: Rest your baby on a pillow beside you and support her neck with your hand.

and need skin-to-skin contact in their mother's arms. With steady encouragement, the sleepy baby gradually will suck longer and more enthusiastically. Have a doctor, nurse, or lactation consultant check on the baby if he is still sleepy after three days.

How to Care for Your Nipples

There is no need for special cleansing of your nipples either before or after nursing. The little bumps on the areola around your nipple are glands that secrete a bacteriostatic and lubricating oil to protect the nipples and resist germs. Daily bathing or showering is all that is necessary to keep your breasts and nipples clean. Avoid using soap on your nipples since it will remove the good oil and can cause dryness and cracking. Water is enough. After nursing, pat your nipples dry before you put your bra flap up.

If your nipples are sore or sensitive, express a few drops of milk after a feeding and massage into the skin to promote healing. If your nipples are red, sore, or cracked, try applying a small amount of pure lanolin after feedings to protect the area and keep the skin moist so that it will heal faster. Pure lanolin (Lansinoh is one brand) is available in drug stores and through La Leche League. A cotton bra, or going without a bra, will allow air to reach sore nipples. You may need to use a breast cup or shell to keep a very sore nipple free of any clothing. Most importantly, realize that red, sore, or cracked nipples are usually caused by incorrect positioning and latch-on. Call La Leche League or a lactation consultant for help.

COMMON BREASTFEEDING QUESTIONS

"When Will My Milk Come In?"

The milk mothers produce immediately after birth is colostrum. It contains high levels of immunities and also has a laxative effect, which helps baby pass the first stools. Your true milk will appear gradually or suddenly sometime between the second and the fifth day after your baby's birth, depending on whether this is your first baby, the fatigue level of your birthing experience, how well your baby learns to latch on to your breast, and how frequently and effectively your baby sucks. Frequent, effective nursing will help this process happen more quickly and can prevent engorgement (painful, swollen breasts).

"What Happens If I Have Too Much Milk?"

When your milk first appears, your breasts may feel very full because of the presence of milk and because of the swelling of the tissues. This feeling is called "engorgement."

HOW BREASTS MAKE MILK

Your milk is produced in tiny milk glands throughout your breast. The milk drains into tiny channels that merge into reservoirs, called sinuses, beneath your areola. Milk empties from these sinuses through approximately twenty openings in your nipple. When your baby sucks, the nerve endings in your nipple stimulate the pituitary gland in your brain, which secretes prolactin. The prolactin stimulates your milk glands to produce more milk and has a calming effect, which also helps. The milk your baby receives first at each feeding is foremilk, which looks watery because of its low fat content.

As your baby continues sucking, the nerve endings stimulate the pituitary gland to secrete another hormone called oxytocin. This hormone causes the tissue around your milk glands to contract like a rubber band and squeeze a larger supply of milk from the milk glands into the sinuses. This is called the "let-down reflex" or "milk-ejection reflex" (MER). This latter milk, or hindmilk, is much higher in fat and slightly higher in protein and, therefore, has greater nutritional value. The hindmilk is the primary nutrient for your infant's growth. Most mothers have a tingling sensation in their breasts as the hindmilk is released from the milk glands into the milk sinuses. They also notice a change in the rhythm of their baby's suck when the milk flows more quickly.

A reliable MER is a key to successful breastfeeding. Sometimes stress or being preoccupied can inhibit this reflex. Baby becomes frustrated and upset, or gives you a look that says, "Come on, Mom!" A few moments of concentrating on your baby, stroking his hair or admiring his feet, will bring your mind and body together again, and your MER will function. Consciously trying to relax, using the deep breathing and releasing you learned for childbirth, will also help. Having a favorite, regular spot for nursing conditions the MER. Actually, you may find that your milk lets down (and leaks) if you just think about your baby or about nursing.

OVERACTIVE MILK-EJECTION REFLEX (MER)

If your breast is quite full at the start of a feeding, the MER can cause milk to spray out quite forcefully even if your baby stops sucking, causing him to gulp and swallow air and even choke. Some breasts just have a more forceful MER, and some babies are less able to handle the sudden gush of milk that comes with the let-down of milk. It helps if you express some milk before starting to nurse, or let the gush of milk spend itself in a towel.

Nursing the baby in a more upright position, so his head is actually higher than the breast, may help him cope with the flow. If you seem to have an overabundance of milk and a strong let-down, try limiting your baby to one breast at a feeding. If he wants to nurse again twenty minutes later, offer the "empty" breast for comfort.

Engorgement is your body's signal to get the milk out. Do not let this engorgement get worse because continued engorgement can lead to a breast infection. Encouraging your baby to suck frequently and effectively is the best way to prevent engorgement. The best way to treat engorgement is to empty your breasts, and nothing does this better than your baby. Standing in a warm shower or immersing your engorged breasts in warm water before feeding can help the baby stimulate your milk-ejection reflex. Or you can apply warm compresses right before feedings. Also, express your milk manually (see p. 149), just enough to soften your areola so baby can latch on more easily. If your breasts become rock hard and very painful, you will have to move to another level of treatment. Stay in bed and apply ice-packs continuously between feedings to take down the swelling enough to allow the milk to flow easily. This should resolve in a day or two.

Engorgement, which can lead to plugged ducts (a red, hard area on the breast), is often due to an upset in the baby's or the family's routine—too many visitors, missed feedings, use of supplemental formulas—that throws the "timer" out of balance. Continued mother-infant attachment and frequent feedings are the best ways to prevent this uncomfortable engorgement. If you still have more milk than baby needs, you can hand express or pump just enough milk to relieve the over-full feeling several times a day. Within a few weeks, your body's supply and baby's needs will even out.

"What If I Get a Breast Infection?"

Sometimes engorgement or plugged ducts can lead to a breast infection (mastitis). Above all, don't stop nursing! The breast will heal faster if you keep the milk flowing. Nurse baby on the affected breast first, until the soreness subsides. If high fever, chills, fatigue, body aches, and increasing soreness and redness of your breasts occur, then you probably need antibiotics. You also need bedrest and lots of water to drink. Call your doctor if you have these symptoms. Your baby still can breastfeed while you are taking antibiotics.

"What If I Don't Have Enough Milk—or Any Milk?"

Most delays in milk production are the result of an interference in mother's and baby's timers. Recovering from cesarean birth, separation due to a medical problem with mother or baby, not rooming-in, giving supplemental bottles, and scheduling feedings are the common causes of delayed lactation. Nurses, not wanting to hear a baby in the nursery cry, will sometimes feed the baby some formula. The formula temporarily satisfies the baby's hunger so that by the time he comes to his mother he is not hungry enough and does not suck enthusiastically. As a result, the mother's milk production is not stimulated.

Scheduling feedings also causes a lag in milk production, especially when the schedule is adhered to despite the baby's cues of hunger. And once again, the reason is that an increase in milk production (for example, during a growth spurt) depends also on the frequency of nipple stimulation and not solely on the total amount of nipple stimulation. If your milk is not appearing, or if it is lagging behind your baby's need, keep your baby close to you for as many hours of the day as possible. Take your baby to bed with you and nurse lying down, having skin- to-skin contact with each other. Look at, caress, massage, and groom your baby while you are nursing to stimulate the milk-producing hormones.

Insufficient milk production during the first month may mean that you are taking on too many outside responsibilities. Reorganize your commitments and priorities and get back into full-time mothering. Pray daily that God will give you the commitment and the milk sufficient to mother your baby in the way He has designed.

Complaints and fears about not having enough milk are very common among new mothers. It is a rare mother whose body cannot produce enough milk for her baby. Don't assume that your milk supply is at fault if your baby is fussy or wants to nurse "all the time." Babies fuss for lots of reasons, and many of them have a period during the day when they want to nurse every half hour or so. This is when confidence becomes important. Rid your house of negative advisors who drop defeating hints such as, "I couldn't breastfeed my baby either"; "She seems hungry all the time"; "Are you sure she's getting enough milk?" You don't need discouragement when you are trying to build up your confidence as a new mother. Surround yourself with supportive people. Call an experienced breastfeeding mother, or go to a La Leche League meeting.

"How Often and for How Long Should My Baby Feed?"

The duration of a feeding varies because babies' sucking techniques and nutritional requirements vary. Many babies will actively suck about ten to fifteen minutes on one breast and five minutes or longer on the other breast. Once your baby gets the hang of it, and if she is an enthusiastic nurser, she can actually get most of her milk in the first five minutes of nursing. During that time you will have experienced a milk-ejection reflex. The remainder of the time is important for meeting her sucking needs. Let your baby decide when she is finished with the first breast before you offer the second. (If she doesn't want the second breast, she'll let you know. If she takes in too much milk on that second breast, she'll spit up.) Less enthusiastic babies require a longer time to get sufficient milk. Also, you may experience a series of small milk-ejection reflexes throughout the feeding rather than one large one. Some babies, especially sleepy babies and small or premature babies, do better with the technique of switch nursing. (See "Why Isn't My Baby Gaining Weight?" p.148).

"How Do I Know My Baby Is Getting Enough Milk?"

After the first month or two, you will know from experience that your baby is getting enough milk. He will feel and look heavier. In the first few weeks it is not as easy to tell that your baby is getting enough milk, especially if you are a first-time mother. Here are some signs that your baby is getting enough milk in the first few weeks. (1) Your baby will have wet diapers often—at least six or eight wet cloth diapers (four to five wet disposables) and two or more substantial bowel movements per day. (2) Your breasts may feel full before feedings, less full after feedings, and leak between feedings. (3) If you feel your baby sucking vigorously, hear him swallowing, feel your milk-ejection reflex, and then see your baby drift contentedly off to sleep, chances are he has gotten enough milk.

"How Can I Get My Sleepy Baby to Nurse?"

Breastfeeding a baby who won't wake up is frustrating. This problem is quite common in small infants and premature babies.

During their first few weeks, these babies continuously fall asleep at the breast before they get enough milk. One of a baby's last systems to mature is the feeding mechanism. So a baby who is three weeks premature may require at least three weeks before she can suck as vigorously as a mature baby and gain weight sufficiently.

Try the following suggestions for breastfeeding your sleepy baby:

1. Undress your baby and yourself to increase the skin-to-skin contact during feeding.

2. Review the positioning techniques described earlier. Be sure to tickle your baby's mouth open wide enough for her to get enough of your areola into her mouth. Sleepy babies are prone to flutter sucking, especially when they are latched on only to the nipple and get very little milk for their sucking efforts.

3. Manually express some of your milk before feeding; this will soften your areola and allow your little snoozer to get more of it into her mouth and thus get more milk.

4. During the feeding, as your baby's sucking intensity and swallowing diminish, gently prod her by stroking her cheeks and pulling her lower jaw down to help her keep her mouth open wide.

5. Small or premature babies tire easily at the breast and do not adjust well to the usual technique of feeding ten or fifteen minutes on each breast. They do better with the switch nursing (see p. 150).

6. If baby's weight gain is lagging, see a lactation consultant. You may need to be using a breastpump to stimulate milk production and to supplement your baby's feedings with more breast milk.

7. Pray for perseverance. Sleepy babies are a real challenge to nurse, but the difficulties usually last only a week or two. Ask God to help you persevere in your breastfeeding relationship until your baby becomes more mature.

"Does My Baby Need a Bottle?"

The breastfed baby does not need supplemental bottles of formula or bottles of water. Formula-fed babies do need the extra water to wash out the formula's excess salts. The use of supplemental bottles can interfere with your milk supply, especially in the early weeks.

"Should My Baby Be on a Feeding Schedule?"

Early in your breastfeeding relationship you will realize that the term *schedule* has very little meaning in breastfeeding a baby. The concept of scheduled feedings did not exist before artificial baby milk (formula) came on the scene. The only schedule your baby will have, and should have, is his own. One of the most beautiful and natural biological negotiations is a mother and a baby working together to get their biological clocks synchronized and the law of supply and demand working comfortably. Listen to your baby's cues and don't clock-watch.

Breastfed babies cannot be scheduled as easily as formula-fed babies because breast milk digests more easily than formula; therefore, breastfed babies feel hungry more often and need to be fed more often. Another reason is that whereas a baby fed by bottle receives a measurable amount at each feeding, the baby fed at breast depends on the storage capacity of his mother's breast (which is not always related to breast size or appearance) to determine, in part, how much milk is available at each feeding. This helps explain why some breastfed babies can consistently go longer between feedings than other breastfed babies. Also, babies have growth spurts during which they need more food for more growth. The only way for breastfed babies to get a higher supply of milk is to increase their demand for it so that the milk production hormones will signal the glands to make more milk. Babies also enjoy periods of non-nutritive sucking in which they are more interested in the comfort they get than in the food. Remember, babies get more than just food at the breast.

Most babies breastfeed eight to twelve times in twenty-four hours during the first few months. These feedings will not be spaced evenly around the clock. Many younger babies nurse very frequently in the late afternoon and evening (a concept called "cluster feeding"), but then sleep much longer stretches at night. Frequent feeding is one of the many realistic expectations you should have about parenting; breastfeeding is more than a mathematical exercise. One nursing mother put it this way, "I don't count the number of feedings any more than I count the number of kisses."

Many breastfed babies do settle into a predictable routine after the first few weeks, once the milk supply is more established. Even then, the key to both mother and baby being content is for mother to stay flexible, free of expectations. If having a routine is important to a mother, she will eventually be able to communicate that need for regularity to her baby, as long as that routine takes into consideration the above-mentioned variables. (See box on p.146, "The 'Happy to Starve' Baby.")

"Why Does My Baby Want to Nurse All the Time?"

In their first few months babies have "frequency days" when all they want to do is nurse. We call this "marathon nursing." These high-demand days are a response to

THE "HAPPY TO STARVE" BABY

There is one situation in which a mother will need to follow a schedule in feeding her baby. Some babies do not communicate hunger reliably. If the mother relied on cues from this baby, he would not get fed enough. Lactation consultants have labeled this baby "happy to starve." Some premature babies need to be placed on a schedule that calls for feeding frequently enough (every two to t hree hours during the day) to accommodate their small stomach capacity, even after they have gone home from the hospital. We experienced this firsthand with our seventh baby, who has Down Syndrome. Even after he had caught up from being born two weeks early, we still had to initiate most of the feedings for many more months. Other very laid-back babies can be like this, even though everything else about them is normal. If your baby is happy to wait for four hours or more on a regular basis, you'll know if he needs more frequent feedings by the weight gain he has at his well-baby check-up. Your baby's healthcare provider will advise you if you need to schedule the feedings and feed him more frequently to increase the amount of milk he receives.

regular growth spurts. Increased nursing is simply a signal that your baby needs more milk to keep up with his sudden growth. By accommodating your baby's need for more frequent breastfeeding, your supply will increase to meet his demand after a few days; and the supply-demand relationship will be reestablished at a higher level of milk production. You may be advised to have someone give baby a bottle while you catch up on sleep; however, supplemental bottles, if used regularly, can actually diminish your milk supply and lead to premature weaning. Some babies may also be going through periods of higher need and they nurse a lot for comfort. You can become exhausted as you try to satisfy your persistent, needy baby. Try the following "survival tips" for new mothers:

Be sure your baby is getting mostly milk at each feeding and not a lot of air. Burp baby frequently if she is an air swallower. Attempt to get more of your hindmilk into your baby to satisfy him longer. (See "Why Isn't My Baby Gaining Weight?", p. 148.)

If your baby is a lazy nurser, one who nurses a little, sleeps a little, and then wants to nurse again, try the following ideas. (1) Undress your newborn to promote skin-to-skin contact. This will help her stay alert. (2) Once or twice a day, crawl into bed with baby and get some rest yourself as she casually feeds. (3) At night sit up in bed at a

CUE (DEMAND) FEEDING VS ROUTINE (SCHEDULE) FEEDING

The term "demand feeding" has been around a long time. It has always been understood to mean that a baby will signal when he is hungry. Some have taken offense at the negative ring to the word "demand," thinking it not right that parents allow a baby to be demanding. This is why we have chosen a different word to describe this kind of feeding. By calling the baby's signal a "cue" we want to take the emphasis off the demand issue (if seen in a negative light) and take note instead of the fact that the baby is communicating hunger. (There are, of course, times when the baby is cueing for other reasons.) For this same reason, the term "routine" is now being used to replace the term "schedule" since it seems to imply a certain amount of flexibility. The dictionary definition for "routine," however, does not include the concept of flexibility. Of course, schedules and routines can be flexible and that's *at the least* what most babies need. Machines run on schedules, babies don't.

From a scientific angle, recent research confirms what lactation experts have always taught: cue feeding improves the quantity and quality of milk. It has been found that the fat content of a mother's milk is directly related to feeding frequency. It addition, it has been shown that prolactin (the milk-producing hormone) is also increased by feeding frequency. In a nutritional nutshell, for most babies cue feeding is biologically correct; scheduled feeding isn't.

Each mother-infant pair must work out a feeding approach that works for them. One example of this would be how to manage the baby who prefers to play during the day and feed at night. The mother would purposely initiate more feedings during the day so baby learns that daytime is more for feeding, nighttime is more for sleeping.

forty-five-degree angle and nurse if your baby is one of those exhausting babies who awaken as soon as they are put down. You both can sleep in this semi-upright position.

Avoid the "filler food" fallacy. You may be advised to give your baby cereal before bedtime or between nursings. This is not good advice for a younger baby, and it seldom works anyway. A suddenly increased demand to feed is often misinterpreted as a need for solid food, which is not necessary until your baby is around six months old. Your baby wants and needs more milk, not filler food.

Exhaustion can interfere with your milk supply, so sleep or catnap when your baby sleeps. This requires delaying or delegating many of the seemingly pressing household chores. If you are blessed with a baby who nurses frequently, you may think, "I don't get anything done." But you are getting something done. You are doing the most important job in the world—mothering your baby. Remember, anyone can clean the house. You are the only one who can make milk.

"Why Isn't My Baby Gaining Weight?"

This section is about the healthy breastfed baby who does not have any underlying illness that would cause him or her not to grow. In the first few weeks, most breastfed babies who are not gaining weight properly are actually getting enough milk, but not enough calories. They are getting plenty of the low-calorie foremilk, but not enough of the high-calorie, creamy hindmilk they need to put on weight. These babies are active and have at least six to eight wet diapers a day, but their little arms and legs look scrawny and their faces look lean instead of filled out. This condition can be caused by problems such as faulty sucking or an inhibited milk-ejection reflex.

Another reason healthy breastfed babies do not gain weight properly is that they are not fed often enough. Some breastfed babies can handle a three-hour feeding schedule, but most will do a lot of crying, using up energy they could use to grow; and there may be less milk available. Remember, feeding a baby on cue is the best way to be sure he is getting his hunger needs met. It is also the best way to increase your milk supply. (See "Should My Baby Be on a Feeding Schedule?" p. 144.)

Usually, if a breastfed baby is not gaining weight, there is something about the baby's nursing habits that needs improvement. The following suggestions are aimed at improving the efficiency of your baby's nursing so that he will get more of the high-fat hindmilk he needs to grow.

Get more rest. This will require reorganizing the household chores and responsibilities that compete with your nursing relationship.

Spend a lot of time in touch with your baby. This includes skin-to-skin contact, eye-to-eye contact, grooming, caressing, and sleeping together. The more you are together, the more likely your baby is to feed, which stimulates your prolactin.

Increase the frequency of feedings. Have *at least* one feeding every two to three hours. Wake your baby during the day if she sleeps longer than two or two and a half hours. Take your baby to bed with you and nurse during the night. Your baby often will nurse very well when nestled in bed with you away from the competition of a busy world. (See chapter 8, "Nighttime Parenting.")

HOW TO MANUALLY EXPRESS BREAST MILK

The simplest way to remove milk from your breasts is to do it by hand. A good way to learn this skill is to try it in the shower. This is often the first place you would need to do it anyway—mothers find the best way to relieve painful engorgement is to stand in the shower with warm water flowing over the breasts and express some milk. Here's how:

> First, massage both breasts gently and stimulate your nipples by brushing across them lightly with your fingertips. Next, position your thumb at the edge of the areola on top of your breast and position your fingers directly under your breast, so your fingers and thumb form the letter "c." (This works better than simply cupping your breast in your hand.) Then move your thumb firmly, in a rolling motion, down toward your nipple while at the same time pressing firmly with your fingers from below your breast, also rolling them toward your nipple. Your milking movements will become rhythmical after you get the hang of it. Do this movement over and over again until the milk begins to drip. As the milk-ejection reflex activates, the milk will begin to spray out. Rotate your thumb and fingers "around the clock" of the areola so that all the ducts are expressed evenly.

La Leche League International publishes a pamphlet entitled "Manual Expression of Breastmilk, Marmet Technique," which you can get from your local La Leche League leader.

Try switch nursing. In the traditional method of nursing, you encourage your baby to nurse as long as he wishes on one breast (usually at least ten minutes) and to complete his feeding on the second breast, reversing the process at the next feeding. This may not work well for babies who fall asleep easily at the breast or who do not suckle enthusiastically for several minutes at a time. Try switch nursing, also called the "burp-and-switch technique," to keep the baby sucking longer. Let your baby nurse on the first breast until the intensity of his suck and his swallow diminishes and his eyes start to close. Remove him from this breast and burp him well; then, switch to the next breast until his sucking diminishes again and burp him to wake him up a second time. Repeat the entire process until the baby has nursed well for a total of at least ten minutes. This burp-and-switch technique keeps the baby interested. It also encourages your body to produce more of the creamier, high-calorie hindmilk because your milk-ejection reflex will occur more frequently.

Try double nursing. After you nurse your baby and she seems to be content, carry her around in the upright position instead of immediately putting her down to sleep. Burp her well, and about ten minutes later breastfeed her a second time and burp her again. If your baby regurgitates this larger volume of milk, either hold her upright or carry her in a sling-type carrier for twenty to thirty minutes after feeding until her stomach empties partially.

Be sure latch-on and suck are correct. Most infants instinctively know how to suck, but some infants have to be taught how to latch on correctly. Two bad habits that newborns tend to develop are flutter sucking, which is sucking in short spurts with little or no jaw action, and nipple chewing. Improving the latch-on will also improve the sucking.

Efficient sucking requires a baby to draw the areola well into his mouth and compress the milk sinuses under the areola with his gums. His tongue should compress the milk sinuses against the roof of his mouth and "milk" the milk out of the sinuses. Some babies do not get enough of the areola into their mouths to effectively compress the sinuses or do not use their tongues correctly on the breast. (The use of supplemental bottles will often cause this problem.) As a result, these babies get only foremilk, and mothers' nipples get sore.

Review the positioning techniques for correct latch-on as described earlier in this chapter. Also, be sure that your breasts are not too full and hard. An engorged breast is difficult to nurse from since your baby is able to suck only on the nub of your nipple and not on a soft and compressible areola. If your breasts are too full, manually express some breast milk prior to each feeding to soften your areola. (See box, "How to Manually

Express Breast Milk,"p. 149.) If you are still experiencing difficulties, see a lactation consultant who is familiar with suck problems.

Avoid supplemental bottles. Introducing bottles too early (within the first four weeks) can cause baby to develop a preference for the artificial nipple, then "forget" how to suck at your breast. Supplements can also interfere with your milk supply and lead you to wean your baby before her time.

Premature babies and babies with weight gain problems as a consequence of faulty sucking may need supplemental formulas (or supplementing with pumped breastmilk) until their own sucking mechanisms mature. If your baby needs supplemental feedings, there are other ways to give it to her besides using a bottle. Cup feeding is a low-tech alternative to bottles. Put an ounce or two of supplement in a soft plastic cup, support your baby upright on your lap, and bring the milk in contact with her mouth so she can sip at it. You can also use an eyedropper or a feeding syringe alongside your finger in baby's mouth.

If you want to give the supplement right at the breast, you can use a supplemental nutrition system (SNS), which is a small container that contains formula or breast milk and hangs around your neck. A thin, plastic tubing runs from the container onto your nipple. As your baby sucks milk from your breast, he also gets supplement from the tubing. When used correctly, this device can train your baby to suck more vigorously at your breast, thereby stimulating you to produce more of your own milk. This system, which can be located through your local La Leche League or from a lactation consultant, can be discontinued gradually as your milk supply and your baby's sucking techniques improve.

Relax, pray, and get consultation. Another cause for poor weight gain, mentioned earlier, is inhibition of the milk-ejection reflex. Baby sucks and cries, sucks and cries, and no milk flows. Stress and the resulting tension are the main reasons for this happening. Pain and emotional distress are two big sources of this kind of stress. If you had a cesarean, be sure you are using your pain relievers. Use the relaxation techniques you learned in childbirth class to consciously relax once you have baby latched on—imagine your milk flowing like a river. Ask someone to stand behind you while you feed baby and rub your back, especially up and down the spine of your upper back. Then pray—turn your mind to the Lord and ask Him to bless the feeding of your baby. Allow yourself to be held in His arms and think on Isaiah 40:11, "He tends his flock like a shepherd; He gathers the lambs in his arms and carries them close to his heart; he gently leads those that have young."

Problems with weight gain can almost always be corrected. The fault does not lie in the mother's body, but in the breastfeeding technique. All too often, a mother is advised to put her baby on a bottle because he is not growing on her milk. This advice is popular because it gets everybody off the hook, and no one has to work hard at finding the real reason a baby is not growing. Obtain consultation from someone who knows a lot about breastfeeding before succumbing to this advice.

"We're Adopting a Baby—Can I Breastfeed?"

We have had both professional and personal experience with this special situation, since our eighth child came into our family by adoption. Yes, you can breastfeed a baby that you adopt, even if you have never breastfed before or even been pregnant. Through the use of the device mentioned above, the supplemental nutrition system (SNS), your baby can be fed at your breast. As baby sucks at your breast, the production of the hormone prolactin is being stimulated in your brain, which in turn stimulates your breasts to start the lactation process. You gradually, over a period of weeks, build up at least a partial supply of milk so baby receives both breast milk and supplement through the tubing. Some women actually achieve a full milk supply for their babies. Most importantly, all these babies and mothers are able to experience the special bonding that occurs with feeding from the breast. This way of breastfeeding is certainly not as easy as bottle feeding, but we wouldn't trade the closeness it has given us with Lauren for anything. La Leche League has excellent material on breastfeeding and adoption, and any lactation consultant can acquaint you with the method involved.

NURSING NUISANCES

As baby gets older, the breastfeeding relationship settles down nicely. By six weeks most mothers find that any earlier problems have been resolved and they can fully enjoy feeding their baby. There are just a few things that you might run into and need help with.

The Distracted Nurser

Between four and six months of age, babies become so interested in their surroundings that they might suck for just a few moments, then stop to look around. This suck-a-little, look-a-little nuisance makes nursing sessions seem to last forever, and constant latching on and pulling off can become unpleasant for your nipples. Take your baby into a quiet, dark, and uninteresting room to nurse him when he is distracted by too much visual or auditory stimulation.

The Biter

When your baby is four to six months old and is feeling pressure in his gums from the early phase of teething, your nipple can become a handy teething object. Toothless gums chomping down on your tender breast can be disturbing enough, but cutting teeth justify a complaint—it hurts! Your surprised reaction to the pain—"OUCH!"—is sometimes enough to startle your baby loose, although he may instead clamp down even harder. Just don't overdo the startle effect; scaring your baby might cause a nursing strike (see below). You can quickly and smoothly disengage your baby's viselike grip by pushing down on his lower jaw with your thumb.

An alternative technique is to quickly pull your baby very close into your breast as soon as you sense he is clamping down. This "reverse psychology" requires him to let go if he wants to breathe. Being removed from your breast and hearing various sounds of disapproval will train your baby out of this pastime. You probably will find that he does this toward the end of a feeding or when he is not really hungry, but just fussy from teething discomfort. Watch for the pre-bite gleam in his eye and take him off the breast. Substitute a less sensitive object (e.g., a rubber teether) if he is desperate to have his gums eased. (See "Teething" in chapter 11.)

The Nursing Strike

A nursing nuisance that commonly occurs between six and twelve months of age is the nursing strike; your baby may lose interest in nursing for a few days. This strike can come at any time. Don't immediately interpret a nursing strike as the time for weaning. This lack of interest in breastfeeding can be the result of any number of occurrences. Your baby may have a cold or may be teething; he may be reacting to a change in his routine, his environment, or your milk; or he may be reacting to a physical or emotional change in you. During this temporary strike, give your baby extra love and security, pump your breasts frequently to keep your milk flowing and spend a lot of time physically together.

Relax, quit watching the clock, avoid bottles and pacifiers. Feed your baby your pumped milk in a cup. Take your baby to bed with you and offer your breast to him while lying down. Many babies will go off strike when they nurse in bed, especially if they are very sleepy. It sometimes helps to walk around as you breastfeed. A last resort may be to nurse your baby while he is sleeping. These nursing strikes seldom last for more than a few days, but plan to spend a lot of your time with your baby as you win him back to the happy relationship you had before the strike.

Spitting Up and Burping

All babies spit up, but some babies spit up more than others. At what point does spitting up go from being just a nuisance to being something medically wrong? If your baby is gaining weight normally and looks happy and healthy, then spitting up is probably just a temporary nuisance rather than a medical problem. If your baby seems to be in pain or is not thriving normally, then you should consult your doctor for further advice on why your baby is spitting up. Spitting up is usually caused by swallowing excessive air or milk, by an allergy, or by gastroesophageal reflux (see p. 233). Some babies spit up several times a day, and the volume of regurgitated milk always seems more than it really is. This problem usually subsides between six and eight months when baby starts sitting up more on his own. He may still spit up occasionally after a feeding if he's jostled or crawls.

There are several ways to lessen this problem:

- Minimize the air baby swallows by burping him more often. If your baby is a gulper, more frequent feedings will help him feed more calmly—he won't be so desperate for milk. If he sleeps too long between feedings, try waking him sooner, and don't wait till he's screaming to take a cue that he's hungry. If you are bottle-feeding, be sure the nipple hole is large enough for milk to pass through it freely. If the holes are too small, your baby will have to suck more vigorously to obtain milk and consequently will swallow more air. Milk should drip out at a rate of at least one drop per second from a full bottle held upside down and not shaken. If the hole seems too small, take a small sewing needle and insert it eye-end into a cork and heat the needle on a stove burner until it is red hot. Poke a hole in the nipple large enough to see through. Collapsible plastic bags that fit into a bottle-holder also may lessen air intake.
- See box, p.141, "Overactive Milk Ejection Reflex (MER)."
- Some babies do not burp easily, and some babies need to burp more frequently. If your baby spits up persistently or seems uncomfortable after a feeding, then your burping techniques may need improving. The key to burping a baby is to place firm pressure on baby's tummy to dislodge the bubble of air. Patting or rubbing her back firmly will also help. This can be done in any of three positions, as long as you maintain pressure against the tummy: (1) With baby seated on your lap, lean her weight forward against the heel of your hand to apply pressure to the area of her stomach. This seems to work best for newborns. (2) Drape baby way up over your shoulder so it is pressing against her tummy. You can walk around using this position. Be sure to grasp baby securely with one hand (the side on which you are holding her), and pat her back with the other hand so you won't worry about dropping her. (3) Lay baby across one leg

of your lap if the first two positions don't work. If after a few minutes no burp occurs, put baby down or carry her upright as you go about your business. She may not need to burp. If she does, she'll let you know by squirming, grimacing, or fussing when you lay her down, or she'll refuse to suck again if she's only part way through her feeding. Babies usually need to burp after a big feeding, less so after a snack. As long as she's uncomfortable, keep trying.

- For nursing at night, lying down, you can prop baby up over your hip if he needs to burp, once he's a little older.
- Feed baby in a more upright position, allowing gravity to hold the milk down and let the air rise to the top of baby's stomach where it can be burped out more easily.
- Keep your baby's nasal passages clear (see p. 250). A stuffy nose forces baby to breathe through his mouth, and mouth-breathing during feedings aggravates air-swallowing.

FORMULA FEEDING

Although we believe that breastfeeding is God's design for infant nutrition, the commercially prepared infant formulas are relatively safe and effective as an alternative source of nutrition for most infants. But formula is only a distant second best. Formulas are prepared using cow's milk or the legume soybean as a protein base. Vitamins, minerals, and processed portions of various nutrients are added in an effort to "humanize" the formula. Artificial baby milk cannot provide the immune factors and live enzymes breast milk contains. You should be aware that studies show that certain diseases in adulthood can be traced to formula feeding.

Commercial formulas are available in three forms: powdered formula with directions on adding water, concentrated liquid formula that should be mixed half and half with water, and ready-to-feed formulas that can be poured directly into a bottle. Your doctor will help you choose which formula will work for your baby. A word of caution: never mix the formula in greater strength than the directions advise. Always add the specified amount of water. Adding too little water makes the formula too concentrated for your baby's immature kidneys and intestines to handle and can make him sick. Babies usually like their formula slightly warmed, like breast milk. Iron-fortified formulas should be used unless your doctor advises otherwise.

The amount of formula your infant will drink will depend upon his weight and his appetite. Use the following rule of thumb for your baby's first six months: two to two-and-a-half ounces of formula per pound per day. For example, if your baby weighs ten pounds, he will take twenty to twenty-five ounces of formula per day. This amount may change from day to day. After six months, the daily volume of formula probably will remain the same or gradually diminish as your baby's intake of solid food increases.

Formula-fed babies can be put on a schedule more easily since the amount taken can be measured and because formula is digested more slowly. However, formula feeding mothers who want to be sensitive to their baby's needs do not adhere rigidly to a schedule. During the first few weeks they wake their babies for feedings during the day, if they sleep more than three hours, to discourage the exhausting feeding pattern of a day sleeper and night feeder. Frequent feedings during the day and bottles at 7:00 P.M. and at 11:00 P.M. (and, of course, one or two night feedings until he's older) seem to be the most comfortable feeding schedule for most parents.

Feeding time should be a time of special closeness. During a feeding, talk to your baby; look at him and caress him during bottle-feeding. In the early weeks we suggest you partially undress yourself and your baby and hold him in close skin-to-skin contact at your breast even though you are bottle-feeding. Remember, not only is the kind of milk your infant gets important, but also how he gets it. Above all, resist the temptation to prop the bottle for your baby to drink alone. Not only is this practice unsafe, it is not nurturing. (Refer also to "Spitting Up and Burping" on page 153.)

"What about Vitamin and Fluoride Supplements?"

Commercial infant formulas contain all the vitamins necessary for your infant, but remember that in order for your baby to receive the daily recommended amount of vitamins, she has to take the recommended amount of formula. Many babies do not consume sufficient amounts of formula to supply the vitamins they need every day until they are a few months old, so vitamin supplements may be recommended by your pediatrician. In later infancy and childhood many children have erratic diets, eating well one day and poorly the next. Your pediatrician will recommend vitamins according to your child's individual needs. Fluoride supplements may or may not be prescribed by your physician, depending upon how much fluoride is in your drinking water, how much water your child drinks, and whether you are using fluoridated water to prepare formula.

Iron is necessary to make new red blood cells and to replenish the stored iron that came from your blood *in utero*. Formula-fed infants should receive iron-fortified formulas from birth on. Parents may feel occasionally that the added iron causes gastrointestinal upsets in their infants, although controlled studies comparing iron-fortified formulas and formulas without iron showed no difference in the number of intestinal problems. If the iron-fortified formula does not agree with your baby, iron-rich foods (meat and iron-fortified cereal) can be offered to your baby at the age of five or six months, according to your pediatrician's suggestion. Iron-fortified formula gives a baby's stools a green color.

"How Long Should My Baby Be on Formula?"

Keep your baby on formula for at least one year. Each species' milk is its ideal baby food (human milk for humans); it is not the ideal food when it crosses species (cow's milk is for cows, not humans). Babies fed cow's milk before they are one year of age often have diarrhea and anemia. Most formulas are based on cow's milk that has been modified for babies, so formula gives babies the nutritional advantages of cow's milk without the problems of drinking it straight.

Generally, we advise mothers to keep their babies on formula until they lose the taste for it. If your pediatrician feels your baby is gaining too much weight on the usual formula (twenty calories per ounce), he or she may suggest you feed him a lower-calorie formula. Low-calorie formula is an imitation of human milk, which naturally decreases in calories as the infant grows older because he needs fewer calories per pound of body weight. Often, mothers are eager to switch from formula to cow's milk, since this switch is considered a sign of the baby's "growing up." Thinking of your baby's formula as "milk" can help you overcome this temptation.

When it is time to switch from formula to cow's milk, you must decide what kind of cow's milk to feed your baby. Milk differs in fat content and, therefore, calorie content. Pediatricians advise against the use of skim milk before a baby is two years old since this lower-calorie milk deprives the baby of a valuable energy source and essential fatty acids and because it contains more salt and protein than a baby's immature kidneys can handle. If your baby is taking whole milk and is overweight, two percent milk is a safe alternative. If your baby is not overweight and is not a compulsive drinker, then use whole milk.

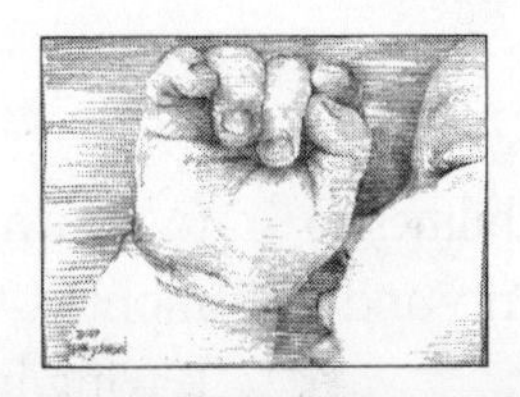

CHAPTER SEVEN

Going Back to **Work?**

Mothers have always worked, even the Proverbs 31 woman, and most have worked outside the home. In cultures with different support systems for the family unit, mothers working outside the home has not posed as great a dilemma as it does in our culture. In those cultures, mothers are commonly able to stay with their babies as long as they are the sole source of nourishment. Then, if mothers do return to the work force, there are family members available to take over with the baby and young child.

CHOICES

In our culture, many mothers have no choice but to return to work outside the home as soon as possible, leaving their weeks-old babies in the hands of day care. Other mothers choose to get back to their jobs quickly simply because they don't understand how disruptive that is to the well-being of their babies. So many babies in our culture are not being cared for in the way God designed, and we as a nation are paying the price.

God's Design for Mothers and Babies

A strong mother-infant attachment is part of God's design for helping the young reach their fullest potential. This attachment is an ongoing maturing process that begins with the mother's strong biological commitment to her baby. Just being close to her baby allows her God-given mothering abilities to develop, and it gives her baby security and a sense of belonging.

A mother learns to read her baby's cues and respond to his needs. The baby is motivated to continue giving cues because he trusts her consistent and appropriate response. Mother in turn becomes more comfortable with her responses because she sees the feedback and appreciation from her baby. This helps her feel confident in her mothering and draws her and baby even closer. This strong mother-infant attachment is especially important for the high-need baby (see chapter 10) and has far-reaching effects later on (see chapters 14–16 on discipline). What a beautiful design! The hormones prolactin and oxytocin are powerful determinants of mothering behavior. Just being close to your baby stimulates these hormones in a breastfeeding mother. God put these chemicals to work in mothers for a purpose—a strong attachment.

Consider the new mother who previously had a high-recognition job and is worried about whether she will be fulfilled by full-time mothering. We advise this mother to practice as early as possible all the principles in the attachment style of parenting. More often than not we notice that mothers who practice these principles from the beginning elect not to return to work. One mother who "discovered" attachment told us: "Because I really liked my job, I had planned to return to work when my baby was three months old. Now, I wouldn't dream of leaving her. I never knew there could be so much joy in being a mother. My friends can't understand how I can stay home all day with my baby, but I love it."

What Are the Effects of Mother-Infant Separation?

When mother and baby are regularly separated, they are both deprived of many of the benefits of mother-baby attachment. In the mother-infant attachment design, the baby must first become attached to one consistent caregiver. When a baby has multiple caregivers, this attachment cannot develop in the same way. If mother goes back to work, someone else needs to be there consistently as the primary caregiver in the first two years.

To what degree attachment is weakened or does not develop depends on several factors:

- The need level of the baby
- How separation-sensitive the baby is
- The substitute caregiver's ability to respond appropriately to the baby's needs
- How much the mother is away from her baby
- What the mother does when she is with her baby

Early in the mother-infant communication process the baby learns to expect a certain response to certain cues. He learns that his needs will be understood and that his cues will be consistently and appropriately met; this process attaches the baby to his primary caregiver. Substitute caregivers, no matter how caring, how loving, do not have a God-given biological attachment to your baby. They do not enjoy the harmonious and "hormoneous" (remember the hormones prolactin and oxytocin) relationship that you do with your baby, and they cannot respond as well. When an infant's cues are not consistently and appropriately met, trust in his caregiving environment is weakened.

The Cycle of Nonattachment

Nonattachment is a subtle problem that creeps into the lives of many mothers and babies. A mother who has many demands on her outside the home or who lacks confidence in her parenting abilities may have difficulty really getting into mothering and forming a close mother-infant attachment. Although this mother sincerely loves her baby, she has ambivalent feelings about attachment mothering and resorts to an increasing use of substitute caregivers. Since the mother is not confident in responding to her baby's cues, she often does not do so appropriately. As a result of this loss of appropriate feedback, the infant does not reward the mother with the kind of appreciation that would stimulate her mothering. Mother and baby gradually drift further apart, the mother into her career outside the home and the baby into dependence on the substitute caregiver. Periodic attempts to get back into mothering are uncomfortable and therefore unsuccessful because the continuum of mother-infant attachment has been interrupted at a very early stage.

How about Quality Time?

The "quality time" concept is an example of adults thinking first of their own needs and finding a way to justify putting others second. The idea has been capitalized upon by the child-care industry. This concept has become popular because it alleviates the guilt a mother sometimes feels when she returns to a full-time job outside the home while her baby is very young.

Actually, the idea of quality time originally developed in reference to fathers working long hours away from home. They had little time to be with their children, but if they made it "quality time," it was considered sufficient. This rationale has now been taken up by working mothers. The child who receives only quality time from both parents is squeezed in between their busy careers at their convenience.

This quality-time concept ignores some basic truths: children are spontaneous; their learning is often mood dependent; and they have unanticipated needs. Although God made children resilient and adaptable, most of their needs cannot be scheduled. One of the common fallacies about child care is that parents always have to be stimulating or giving input to their children when they are with them. The parent does not always have to be leading the parade. Many times the most important role of a parent is simply being available and approachable when "quality" moments occur.

The concept of quality time allows many couples to justify their lifestyles. But the difficulties with the idea are obvious. Why is only the parent-child relationship relegated to a few minutes of quality time? Why can't school teachers dismiss their students after only one hour of quality-time teaching instead of a full day of quantity time? Why not say to your boss, "I am only going to work an hour today, but it will be quality time."? This new math for parents says one hour of quality time equals eight hours of quantity time, but this is simply not true.

In some situations, such as that of a single working mother, quantity time is hard to come by. One Christian mother shared with me: "I have to work all day, so I give up a lot of time I might otherwise spend on entertainment to be with my baby. When I'm not working, I'm fully devoted to him. Besides quality time, I probably give him more quantity time than many nonworking mothers who spend a lot of time each day pursuing their own forms of entertainment." This mother is truly doing the best she can do.

Is There an Answer?

- "I want to work for my own fulfillment."
- "I want to use my education."
- "If I stayed home all day, I would go stir crazy."
- "I am a better mother if I am away from my child for a while and also am fulfilled outside the home."

These are real feelings from real mothers who truly love their children. Again, understanding the dilemma of today's mother is more important than being judgmental. It helps to remember that developing a harmonious mother-infant attachment is the main issue, not whether a mother has to stay at home. While full-time mothering definitely gives this relationship a more stable foundation, there is more to be considered.

To understand better this dilemma, review what has happened historically to the changing roles of women. In past generations, even in biblical times, women were employed in the home. Proverbs 31:10–31 is a beautiful description of the mother working from her home. However—and this is an important consideration—the father also usually worked at or near home. The family business operated out of the home or farm. Parenting and working were integrated, and homes often contained more than just the nuclear family; grandparents, other relatives, or adult children were in the same house or lived close by and shared the work. With the coming of industrialization and urbanization, men began leaving the home to work, and women became increasingly isolated at home. In the first half of the twentieth century, two world wars took women out of their homes into the industrial world to do traditionally "male" jobs, but they were sent back home when the war was over to become consumers rather than producers.

Today's women are given many more options, many more career choices. If you ask a class of high school girls what they are going to be, seldom will you get the response "I want to be a homemaker" or "wife and mother." Although no one actually says it, the subtle message in our culture is that full-time mothering is less desirable and less important than a career. Women have been leaving home just as men did in previous generations. Day care has become the parent. "Get out and work, get fulfilled, buy things" is the message of a society that attaches higher status to paid work than to motherhood.

As a result of this philosophy, many women have come to feel that their careers outside the home should not be affected by motherhood. We have talked with many women who believe they wouldn't be content if they stayed home full time and cared for their children. They would do so resentfully; their children would sense the underlying tensions; and both they and their children would lose. It's important in this situation to look at a variety of options. For example, by pursuing a part-time career outside the home or, *best of all, inside the home,* a mother can maintain her self-image, feel better as a person, and therefore feel better as a mother. Both mother and children profit. Mothers who after much prayer and deliberation have found ways to satisfy both their children's needs and their own truly have the best of both worlds. These usually are the mothers who were able to understand the need to be home with their children when they were young.

If you have these ambivalent feelings concerning the career-motherhood dilemma, the following suggestions may help you to resolve them: (1) During your pregnancy, ask God for the wisdom to see His career plans for you. Be open to His direction. (2) Give full-time mothering a chance. Don't enter your mothering career with expectations that you will go crazy at home. If you do, you will. (3) Practice the mothering styles noted earlier in this book. You may be surprised at how fulfilling mothering can be when God's design for mother-infant attachment is followed. If, after at least several months of mothering experience, your decision is to return to your career, then consider all the available options.

Mother Has to Work

There is a story about a pastor who said to a working mother, "You should be home taking care of your child." The mother replied, "We have no home; that's why I'm working." *Having* a home is a necessity, but *owning* a home is a separate issue. Unfortunately, the American dream of owning a home is beyond the reach of many young couples with children, and a second income may seem the answer to this and other economic struggles. Mothers, before you decide to return to work while your child is an infant, consider these points:

Evaluate your priorities. No material possessions are more valuable to your infant than you yourself. Consider whether you can afford not to give your child your full-time self.

What is your worth at home in dollars and cents? Consider exactly what you will have left over by the time you deduct from your paycheck the costs of clothing, food, transportation, child care, increased taxes, and medical bills (babies in day care centers get more infections). You may be surprised at how little you have left over by the time you deduct these expenses.

Plan ahead. Economize and save as much money as you can during the early years of your marriage and during pregnancy, letting the savings from your second income help your family while you are a full-time mother. Save enough for at least the first three years. Many couples become accustomed to a standard of living that depends on two incomes and then feel they must maintain this lifestyle after the baby is born. Early in your marriage, consider living on one income and saving the other lest you become trapped by your lifestyle and a hefty mortgage payment. Since most of today's married couples didn't do this, you may have to consider other options.

Consider borrowing the extra money you need until your child is approximately three years old and you can return to work. We don't generally encourage debt, but when it is used to allow a mother to nurture a baby, in our opinion, debt is justified. A common example is when the dad is a student. Our first child, James, was born while I (Bill) was a "poor intern." Martha juggled mothering and working part time. Looking back, it's amazing that we didn't even consider alternatives. We could have used her inheritance. Or we could have cut our standard of living even further and then borrowed the rest short term. It is easier to repay money than reparent children. One of the best invest-

ALTERNATIVES FOR MOTHERS ON THE JOB

If working from home is not possible for you, you may want to consider some other alternatives.

Part-time work. There is an ever-expanding market for part-time workers because, according to industrial studies, part-time workers offer employers increased efficiency but require fewer financial obligations and fringe benefits. Part-time work is often more attractive to the woman who *wants* to work than it is to the woman who has to work.

One mother in our practice who switched from full-time to part-time work said, "Full-time work was too much for my toddler; full-time at home was too much for me."

Flex-time work. Flex-time is full- or part-time work with flexible hours. Flex-time allows a woman to adjust her hours to be at home when her child is sick or has a special need. Flex-time may make it possible for Dad to be the baby's caregiver when Mom is gone.

Shared jobs. This type of work arrangement requires the cooperation of two people sharing the work of one full-time job. Sometimes they share child care as well.

ments you can make in your child's future is to give her the commitment of yourself, at least for the first couple of years and longer if possible.

Grandparents are often a willing source if they realize that this is probably one of the most valuable investments they can make in their grandchild's future. Years ago a friend of ours (an investment counselor) was always trying to get us into some sound investments. Shortly after the birth of his first grandchild, his daughter was planning to return to work because they had become used to a second income and they felt they still needed it. After convincing her of the wisdom of staying home with her child for at least two years and borrowing the extra income, we phoned our friend—the child's grandfather—to let him in on this opportunity for "a great long-term investment." This man, wise in financial matters, agreed that helping care for his grandchild would indeed be a good investment.

WORKING AT HOME

Starting a home business may be a realistic answer to the second-income dilemma. Mothers, this works best when you take time to find work that you want to do and have realistic expectations about the time available to do it. Doing work that you dislike will wear thin after a while. Some examples of home businesses are caring for children, word processing, telemarketing, bookkeeping, sewing, doing arts and crafts, giving piano lessons, being a sales distributor. One woman wrote to tell us about her dog obedience business (she loves working with animals). Some professional women bring their businesses into their homes and turn their spare rooms into offices. You may be surprised at the variety of work you can do during the times when your baby is content or sleeping. We know a mother who is an editor and works on her home computer that is tied into the main office. The mother "goes to the office" without leaving her nest. Another mother has a business of delivering fresh, cut flowers that she arranges to homes and offices. Her clients love the service and love seeing her baby every week.

A mother who makes the choice to stay home has lots of company, but none of that company may live on her street or even in her neighborhood. Two places you will find like-minded women is at church, since many Christian mothers try to stay home while their children are small, and La Leche League, since mothers who seek out support for breastfeeding tend to understand the value of full-time mothering. And there is an organization that serves the needs of mothers at home. Contact Mothers At Home, 8310-A Old Courthouse Road, Vienna, VA 22182-3809, (800) 783-4666. They also publish a book entitled *What's a Smart Woman Like You Doing at Home?* (see bibliography).

WORKING OUTSIDE THE HOME

Let's suppose an anxious mother comes in to our office for her baby's three-month checkup. "My husband and I have decided after much prayer about our family situation that it's best for me to return to my job. But I want to be a good mother also. I need help." Or, she's a single mother who has no choice about working outside her home. Both these mothers need to understand that continuing the attachment relationship with her baby is most important, so our advice is geared to helping her find ways to do that.

If you must work outside the home, the following tips will help you continue your good mothering and even indirectly benefit your career. Feeling good about mothering will make you a better employee.

Plan ahead. Organization is the key to combining employment with mothering. Working outside the home does not allow you much time for cooking and housekeeping. Sit down with your husband, or with other family and friend support if you are a single mother, and plan out how the household will run (i.e., chore-sharing) so time for your baby is not wasted on household duties.

Keep it simple. Working and mothering is more than enough for you to handle. Say no to other obligations while your baby is small. Lower your housekeeping standards. Simplify your meals. Concentrate on taking care of yourself and your baby.

You can breastfeed and work. At first glance breastfeeding and working might seem incompatible. But this is not the case. We encourage working mothers to continue breastfeeding because this gives them a special tie to their babies and alleviates some of the disappointment of having to leave the baby to go to work.

Some suggestions for breastfeeding while working include:

1. Encourage your baby to have a long leisurely feeding before you go to work, when you return home, and when you put the baby to sleep. Be available and open to other shorter nursings "on demand" throughout the time you are together. Be prepared for increased night nursing.
2. Pump when you are away from your baby. When your breasts feel full (approximately every three hours), manually or with a pump express your milk to avoid uncomfortable engorgement and possible breast infection, and to provide the next day's feedings. Store the milk in a clean container in a refrigerator or cooler for the next day's use. (Actually, you can keep it unrefrigerated for up to ten hours, if you have to.) You can store your breast milk in the refrigerator up to five days; in your refrigerator's freezer for three to four months; and in a deep freeze (zero degrees Fahrenheit) for many months. You can pump during your coffee break or your lunch period. Try to pump at least once in a four-hour workday, two times if you're gone for eight or nine hours.
3. If it's convenient, have your baby-sitter bring your baby to you a couple of times during the day for breastfeeding, or go to the sitter's at lunchtime. You might want to find a sitter close to your workplace rather than close to home. Some major corporations have quality day-care centers in the building so that mother and baby can be within nursing distance of each other.
4. Expect your baby to nurse several times during the night (see chapter 8) and more frequently on weekends when you resume full-time mothering. This is a realistic expectation, and you will be understandably tired, so remember the above: *keep it simple.*
5. Advise your baby-sitter of your expected time of arrival and ask her to try not to feed your baby during the last hour before that time. In this way your baby will eagerly take your breast as soon as you arrive. The first hour after

you arrive home should be a special time of closeness and breastfeeding, a time to be reunited with your infant without any interference from telephones or pressing household chores. Take the phone off the hook, put your feet up, turn some music on, and settle down to nurse your baby before you think about starting dinner. This is your well-deserved time to unwind from a hard day's work and reconnect with your baby.

FATHER FEELINGS AND WORKING MOTHERS

Fathers, be sensitive to the dilemma facing many of today's mothers. Job satisfaction is as important to them as it is to you. It can be difficult for a woman to give up the world of work to stay at home and be a full-time mother. This change of status is especially difficult for the woman who has had an exciting career outside the home before settling into her career inside the home.

As a sensitive, caring husband, you can be mindful of these feelings that your wife will probably have at some time during her early adjustment to mothering. Give her positive reinforcement. Convey your consistent love for her as a person, a wife, and a mother. Give her the message that you appreciate what she is doing—the most important job in the world.

A good example of what not to do is portrayed in the 1980 movie *Kramer vs. Kramer.* Prior to having a child, both Mr. and Mrs. Kramer had professional careers. After the birth of their first child, as many professional women do, Mrs. Kramer decided to stay home and devote herself to mothering. As Mrs. Kramer became more deeply involved in mothering, Mr. Kramer became less and less involved as a father and more involved in his career. Instead of meeting his wife's emotional needs when he was home, he spent most of his time talking about how exciting his career was. Needless to say, Mrs. Kramer became less and less satisfied as a person, gave up mothering (and the marriage) entirely, and returned to her career outside the home. Only after Mr. Kramer took over the parenting responsibilities did he realize the daily challenges facing a full-time mother. He learned the real value of the term *homemaker.* This is a classic example of what happens when a husband fails to perform his supporting role in God's design for the family.

If a mother is to work outside the home, the father will need to work more inside the home. Shared child care is a realistic fact of life, and especially so when the mother has a job outside the home. The mother also needs some "down time." Nothing in God's order for the family or in the biological makeup of men says men cannot do housework. If the traditional role of the woman is changed somewhat and she is helping to meet the family's economic needs, the traditional role of the man must also change. Remember how Jesus washed the feet of the apostles.

Fathers, pitch in and do your share of housework. Help meet your child's daily needs. Actually, one of the fringe benefits of mothers working has been to bring fathers back into their homes and into knowing their children better. Father-involvement is especially important when a mother continues breastfeeding while working, and we encourage you to encourage her to do that.

CHOOSING A BABY-SITTER

One of today's great paradoxes is that at the very time when research is confirming the wisdom of God's design for mother-infant attachment, the demand for substitute caregiving is increasing. You may be greatly disappointed when you search the marketplace for quality substitute mothering and find that the demand is far greater than the supply. Also, substitute caregiving is just that—a substitute, not a replacement for the mother. The following suggestions discuss different options in child care and how to choose a substitute caregiver.

Baby-sitters Are Mother Substitutes

We don't actually like the term *baby-sitter.* It's too static. Baby care involves a lot more than sitting. Try to find a mother substitute who practices the child-care style you value. Ask questions of her such as, "What do you do when an infant cries?" If you are uncertain about her child-care philosophy, tell her exactly how you want your child mothered in your absence. Be specific: "When he cries, I want you to pick him up. He needs to be 'mothered' to sleep. He should not be left unattended in his crib when he is awake. He needs to be carried around and be in your arms a lot." Show her how to use your baby carrier and let her know how much easier it can make things for her.

Parents should look for specific qualities in an infant caregiver. Watch the prospective caregiver in action and examine her nurturing qualities. Does she look at, touch, and talk to your baby with the message of "I care, I am interested in you as a person with needs, I am sensitive to you"? Does she have a working knowledge of the usual developmental milestones? Does she have realistic expectations of children at various ages? Is she resilient and able to adapt to the ever-changing moods of some toddlers? Does she have a spontaneous sense of humor? This is a real must for coping with toddlers. Watch how she handles a child who has gotten out of control. Is she kind but firm? Most importantly, observe how her Christian values carry over into her work with children.

Children should be present at the interview; see how they relate to the caregiver and vice versa. Children are often the best critics of their own care, but unfortunately they often have no voice in that choice. If a child has a certain sparkle in her eyes as she relates to the caregiver, you can be sure that there is meaningful communication going between them.

Remember, no substitute caregiver has a biological attachment to your child. Don't expect anyone else to have a built-in radar system that intuitively responds to your baby's cues as you do. For this reason you must give your substitute caregiver detailed instructions on how to recognize your baby's cues and how to respond to them. When your baby exercises a newly acquired developmental skill, impress upon your caregiver the importance of acknowledging your baby's accomplishments. If no one responds to a developmental skill, a child may be less motivated to exercise that skill. Mothers, spend time together with your baby and the caregiver so that she can see how you want your baby mothered.

Use the Same Caregiver

A child who has a long string of baby-sitters will have difficulty forming an attachment to any of them. As we have mentioned, developing the ability to form attachments is one of the major accomplishments of early childhood. Children who are deprived of consistency in caregivers may show certain "diseases of nonattachment" that are reflected in aggressive and impulsive or withdrawn behaviors. Be prepared for your baby to love his caregiver. It's important for him to do this.

Options in Child Care

Toddlers are often more comfortable being cared for in their own homes where they are secure than in the caregiver's home. A one-to-one caregiver-to-child relationship is usually the best for the infant under one year. If a one-to-one relationship is not economically feasible, try to find another mother who will care for your child along with her own.

Some mothers open their homes to care for children as a means of supplementing the family's income; some godly mothers even feel that this is their ministry to children. In most cases, home care is preferable to commercial day-care centers, especially for babies and toddlers.

Tips on Selecting a Day-Care Center

If a day-care center is the only feasible option for your family situation, visit the prospective center and look for the following conditions:

1. What is the ratio of caregivers to children? One caregiver to four infants is the maximum you should accept.

2. Examine the credentials of the staff. Determine if they have special training

in child development and have realistic expectations of children at various stages.

3. What is the turnover rate among staff members? (Unfortunately, day-care workers have a very high rate of turnover, so the likelihood of having a consistent caregiver is minimal. For this reason alone, day-care centers are not a good choice for the child under three.)

4. Are they nurturers? Are they genuinely sensitive to a baby's needs? What do they do when a baby cries? How do they guide toddlers?

5. Examine the facility and the equipment. Is it clean, safe, and appropriate for the age and the stage of each child's development?

We are truly sympathetic with mothers who are faced with the dilemma of balancing a career and mothering. We have struggled with this in our own home and have concluded that difficult problems do not have easy solutions. The ideal cannot always be achieved in today's society, but with prayer and support for one another you can try to come close to that ideal.

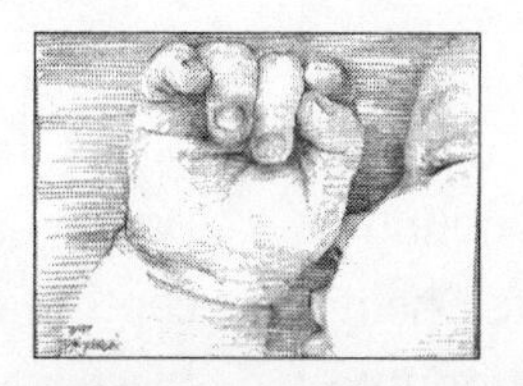

CHAPTER EIGHT

Nighttime **Parenting**

"Lord, please let me have just one full night's sleep." This is a common plea from exhausted new parents, most often mothers. Coping with night waking is one of the most common problems new parents face. We have this problem because in our bottle-feeding culture we've come to expect that babies should sleep through the night as soon as possible and that, in fact, it is good for babies to do so. This expectation is highly influenced by the belief that the baby sleeping through the night as young as possible is good for parents too. Actually, both these "givens" are not based on scientific fact or parenting wisdom, but rather on cultural bias.

Ever since we became a bottle-feeding society early in this century, we have had these misconceptions. You see, artificial baby milk alters babies' physiology. Pediatric journals have reported studies that show breastfed babies naturally awaken more at night. And now we are learning that this level of arousal from sleep has protective benefits for babies, as well as biological advantages for mother. Here's another little-known fact: "sleeping through the night" is defined in medical research as five straight hours of sleep, not eight or ten.

Can we agree that God would not have designed a system of infant feeding that would prove to be the undoing of countless mothers' and babies' nighttime well being? Can we agree that as long as the amount of night waking does not overtake a mother's ability to function, we will discard the notion that eight to ten straight hours of sleep for a baby as young as eight weeks is a desirable thing? When frustrated parents come to us saying, "We've tried everything to get our baby to sleep better and nothing works, at least not consistently," we know we are in for a bit of troubleshooting. A short, easy response like, "Let him cry, he'll just have to learn" would appeal to us as busy professionals. But we've learned from our wealth of experience that difficult problems do not have quick and easy answers. Parents must begin by having an understanding of how babies sleep (or don't sleep) and by having realistic expectations for nighttime parenting.

NEWBORNS' SLEEP PATTERNS

Just as there are wide variations in babies' temperaments, there are wide variations in their sleep patterns. It is important for you to approach parenting without preconceived images of what a baby should be like, especially about how he should sleep. One tired mother shared with us, "Before our baby came, I thought that all newborn babies did was eat and sleep, but all my baby does is eat."

Early in their parenting career, preferably before the birth of their baby, we advise parents to ask God to guide them in accepting whatever temperament their baby is blessed with and to give them the energy to parent according to the needs of their child. Some parents are blessed with easy sleepers; other parents are blessed with frequent wakers. In both cases, the parents are blessed to have their child as he is.

You need to be open to adjusting your parenting style to your baby's needs. If you approach your nighttime parenting with the same openness you bring to answering your baby's needs during the day, you and your baby will eventually sleep well and, more importantly, will feel right about it. If you approach your nighttime parenting determined to make your baby fit into a sleep pattern you feel he or she ought to have, you will either experience a lot of frustration or you will desensitize yourself to your baby's needs.

Have Realistic Expectations of How Babies Sleep (or Don't Sleep)

Babies' sleep patterns differ from those of adults. Babies don't sleep through the night, and they can get their days and nights mixed up for a while. They awaken regularly for feedings. One of the first facts of parenting life that new parents should know is that babies do what they do because God designed them that way.

The first few months the average baby sleeps fourteen to eighteen hours out of twenty-four, but that is not true for every baby. The sleep pattern of tiny babies resembles their feeding patterns—small, frequent feedings and short, frequent naps. In their first three months, babies' sleeping patterns are poorly organized. At that age, the concept of day and night has little meaning to them. Until babies' sleep patterns mature, wise parents organize their lifestyles and sleep styles around their baby's. The mother sleeps during the day when the baby sleeps. In the first months, it is much more realistic for the mother to "sleep like a baby" than to expect the baby to sleep like an adult. As your baby gets older, his developing brain becomes capable of blocking out arousal stimuli. He will gradually be able to sleep more deeply and for longer stretches, and his sleep pattern will resemble an adult's by around two years.

Sleep states. Sleep has stages: light, or active, sleep and deep sleep. Most adults spend the greatest percentage of their sleep time in deep sleep while babies spend most of their time in light sleep. If you watch your baby sleeping, you can identify easily which state of sleep he is in. When babies are in a state of deep sleep, their bodies are quiet and they are not easily aroused. In a state of light, or active, sleep, babies squirm, their breathing movements are somewhat irregular, and sometimes their eyes are only partially closed. If you lifted their eyelids, you would notice that their eyes move often. In fact, this state of light or active sleep is called REM, or rapid eye movement, sleep.

How Babies Fall Asleep

Infants enter sleep differently than adults. We adults can "crash" rather quickly. We can go directly from the awake state into the state of deep sleep. Infants cannot do this. They enter sleep through an initial period of light sleep (lasting about twenty or thirty minutes), then enter a period of transitional sleep, and then drift into deep or non-REM sleep. If an arousal stimulus occurs during the first half hour of sleep, a baby will awaken easily because he has not yet reached the deep-sleep phase. This fact of infant sleep accounts for the baby of whom mothers say, "He has to be fully asleep before he can be put down."

As babies mature, they begin to go more quickly into the state of deep sleep. But even when they are older, most infants and toddlers need to be parented to sleep. If they are just put down they will cry, and most will cry long and hard, until they fall alseep from exhaustion. The presence and support of the parent helps them relax into sleep until they are old enough to do that on their own. In the early months, especially, they need to be nursed, rocked, or walked to sleep and gentled through this initial phase of light sleep. Effective nighttime parenting includes the art of inducing deep sleep in your baby by gentling him through the initial REM period.

Why Your Baby Wakes at Night

Throughout the night, people experience cycles of light and deep sleep. The adult sleep cycle is about twice as long as an infant's, ninety minutes compared to forty-five to fifty minutes. Night waking is most likely to happen during the transition from deep sleep into light sleep. Because their sleep cycles are shorter, babies have more of these transitions, and so they are more likely to wake up frequently during the night. One of the ways to minimize night waking is to gentle your infant during these vulnerable periods. How you can do that as a nighttime parent will be discussed later in this chapter.

Settling

Babies settle more easily as they get older. *Settling* means getting off to sleep easily and staying asleep for longer stretches through the night. The age at which babies settle and the number of hours they sleep without interruption vary tremendously from baby to baby. In sleep studies, settling is defined as sleeping from midnight to 5:00 A.M. Expecting any baby under one year of age to sleep through the night from 8:00 P.M. to 8:00 A.M. is unrealistic. It is a rare baby who will do this, unless he has been subjected to sleep training, being left to cry off to sleep. If you are blessed with a good sleeper, consider this a luxury. If your younger baby wakes frequently at night, count yourself in good company. Most babies wake at night.

As your infant gets older, he or she reaches what is called "sleep maturity" when the percentage of light sleep decreases and deep sleep increases, and the vulnerable periods of night waking lessen. Some studies show that about 70 percent of babies settle by three months and 90 percent by one year. (Remember, settling means they sleep one solid five-hour stretch.) Ten percent of babies never sleep uninterruptedly during the first two years. Even those babies who settle well may continue to have periodic night waking.

Toward the end of the first year, or even sooner, as your baby's brain becomes more capable of blocking arousal stimuli, both you and your baby will probably enjoy periods of uninterrupted nights. However, just as you feel your baby has kicked the night-waking habit, he or she may begin waking up again, but for different reasons. The same low stimulus barrier that can make babies restless during the day makes them restless sleepers as well. The stimulus of teething is a common cause for restlessness, for example. Other causes are discussed on page 191. Some babies will eventually go to sleep easily but do not stay asleep; and some have trouble both going to sleep and staying asleep. Fears, separation anxieties, and disturbing dreams are the main stimuli for night waking of children from one to three years.

Parents, be assured that your baby's sleep pattern is not a reflection of your parenting. A baby's sleep pattern often reflects his basic temperament. This may come as a surprise to some parents, but even-tempered babies enjoy a larger percentage of deep sleep. Children who exhibit very active temperaments during the day seem to carry their waking personalities into their sleep, having shorter periods of deep sleep and more frequent night waking. On the surface this would seem to be a mismatch of temperaments and sleep patterns. You would think that the more active babies would need more sleep (their parents do!).

Why Infants Are Not Easy Sleepers

The longer Bill has practiced pediatrics and the more children we have had, the more we have come to respect the fact that babies do what they do because they are designed that way. Babies do not awaken to annoy or exhaust the parents. God seems to have designed babies to wake frequently at night for two reasons: (1) survival benefits and (2) developmental benefits.

Night waking has health benefits. In the first few months, the infant's needs are high, but her ability to communicate these needs is low. Suppose your baby had your sleep patterns and was subjected to much more deep sleep than light sleep. She would not be easily aroused. If she became hungry and needed food, she might not awaken; if she got cold and needed warmth, she might not awaken; if her nose were plugged and her breathing compromised, she might not awaken. Babies sleep lightly so that they can communicate the needs that are important to their health.

Night waking has developmental benefits. Some prominent sleep researchers theorize that the predominance of light sleep during the first year is important for development of the baby's brain. During the state of light sleep, all of the brain continues to operate; during the state of deep sleep the higher brain centers shut off, and only the lower brain centers continue to operate, controlling breathing and other essential activities. The theory is that during the rapid brain growth in the first year, the higher brain needs to continue functioning during sleep in order to continue developing. As brain development gradually slows down, the infant has less light sleep and more deep sleep.

If tired parents have faith that God has indeed designed babies according to a plan that has both survival and developmental benefits, they can better accept the challenges of nighttime parenting. One day in the office, Bill was offering a tired mother the explanation of why frequent night waking seems to be in accordance with God's design for development of her infant's brain. She responded, "In that case, he's going to be very smart."

Although frequent night waking may be part of God's design for many babies, persistent fatigue in both babies and parents is not divinely ordained. We feel that God has given parents the ability and the tools to help the baby organize his sleep patterns. We firmly believe that God would not have created a baby with a sleep pattern too difficult for the parents to cope with. Exhausted parents and tired babies simply cannot enjoy the relationship God has intended. Here's how to help your baby organize his sleep patterns, and how to widen your acceptance level and be responsive to your baby's nighttime needs.

SHARING SLEEP

One decision that is very important to helping babies organize their sleep patterns concerns where they sleep. Quite honestly, we feel that whatever sleeping arrangement gets all three of you the most sleep and leaves all three of you feeling right is the right sleeping arrangement for your individual family. What works for one family may not work for another.

This section will present reasons why it is good to let your baby sleep with you and why it may in fact be according to God's design. Sharing sleep is an arrangement whereby you welcome your baby into your bed early in infancy and allow him to remain until he can sleep alone comfortably. Many parents are confused about the conflicting opinions on this subject. They ask, "Is it all right for our baby to sleep with us?" Our opinion, one that we have formed after much prayer and experience, both personal and professional, is that God intended babies to sleep in close contact with the mother until they can comfortably sleep independently. We have advocated the concept of sharing sleep for nearly twenty years, and we have practiced this arrangement in our own family. It is beautiful! It works!

Perhaps this sleeping arrangement does not work for all families at all times, but in our experience it works for most families most of the time, especially when it is done with the confidence that God seems to have designed babies this way. Babies sleeping close to or with the parents is a part of a natural continuum babies experience as they go from mother's womb to mother's breasts and parents' bed. The newly-born baby and the young infant are extremely dependent on mother for everything. Mother's presence is the plan God has for the safety and security of His babies. Weaning from places of security should occur only when mother and baby are ready.

The concept of sharing sleep is actually more an attitude than a decision about where your baby sleeps. It is an attitude of acceptance and mutual trust whereby infants trust that their parents will be continually available for support during the night just as they are during the day. It requires trust on the part of parents, too, in that they trust themselves and what seems right in parenting their child rather than accept the cultural norms of society or yield to the dictates of peer pressure. It is often difficult for new parents to listen to and accept the cues of their child about what type of care she needs. This is usually because of the unfounded cultural taboos that have interfered with knowing what babies need (sex takes place in the parents' bed, so children are forbidden) and because of the unreasonable fear their baby will manipulate them (babies are driven by the sin nature, or babies are just plain "out to get" parents).

Be open to accepting whatever sleeping arrangement works for your family. If all three of you sleep better with your baby in your bed and it seems right for your family, this arrangement is best. (Of course, you may not all sleep well at first—it can take some getting used to, as with most things new parents do. Be willing to try it for a while if it doesn't work right away. Some dads, especially, hate it at first, then grow to love it.) This sleeping arrangement is sometimes called "the family bed." We prefer to call it "sharing sleep" because that implies more than just sharing a place to sleep; it also means that parents and babies share sleep cycles and attitudes about sleep.

Babies Sleep Better

Remember that babies have a vulnerable period for waking up as they pass from deep sleep into light sleep. Since they have these sleep-cycle changes every hour (or even less), babies are vulnerable to waking up at least once every hour. Sleeping with a familiar, predictable person helps baby get through this vulnerable period and resettle into the next stage of sleep before he actually awakens fully.

Why do babies need help with staying asleep? In the first year, babies do not understand the concept of object permanency. When something is out of sight, it is out of mind. Most babies less than a year old do not have the ability to think of Mother as existing somewhere else. When babies awaken alone in a crib, their anxiety will keep them from resettling into the next stage of deep sleep without awakening in a state of stress or fright.

Adults wake from sleep in various states of alertness, but they usually can drift into the next state of sleep without becoming fully awake because they know where they are. For a baby, waking up next to a familiar presence can smooth the transition from one state of sleep to the next and keep him from waking fully or at least help him resettle into the next state of sleep without a great deal of fuss.

Babies can be trained to fall back to sleep on their own by being left to cry. The reason this works with some babies is that some babies are less separation sensitive. Most babies who are left to cry learn a very expensive lesson—no one will respond to my call for help, so I will give up. The price babies and parents pay is too high. Trust is undermined and a distance develops that no one may even notice.

When we had babies sleeping in our bed, Bill would sometimes watch, gazing upon the contented face of our baby. He could tell when the baby was passing through the vulnerable period for waking because the baby would often reach out and touch one of us. A smile would appear, and an "I'm OK" expression would radiate from the precious little face, yet the eyes would remain closed, and baby would not fully awaken. Beautiful moments like this in nighttime parenting can only be realized by being open to your child at night.

Mothers Sleep Better

Mothers, you may be surprised to discover that not only does baby sleep better when sharing sleep, but you do too. It goes back to the concept of harmony. Just as it is important to achieve harmony with your child during the day, sleeping with your baby at night allows this harmony to continue so that baby and mother can get their sleep cycles in sync with each other.

When this harmony is achieved, babies awaken their mothers during their mutual light-sleep cycles and sleep during their mutual deep-sleep cycles. Mothers are awakened less often from a state of deep sleep, so they are bothered less by sleep disruptions. Being jolted out of a deep sleep by a hungry baby crying from down the hall is what leads to exhausted mothers, fathers, and babies.

Some mothers have trouble getting comfortable in the side-lying position for nursing, so they develop back and shoulder aches. Side-lying is much more comfortable when you use a pillow under your top leg to support its weight and ease the strain on your back. Also, try having a pillow wedged behind your back to give you something to lean into (unless your husband doesn't mind you using him to lean on).

Helping the "Hormoneous" Relationship

In previous chapters, you've read that the hormone prolactin has a calming effect on mothers. Three situations make prolactin increase in your body: (1) sleeping, (2) breastfeeding, and (3) touching or simply being with your baby. Sleeping with your baby allows all three of these situations to occur throughout the night. When your baby shares sleep with you, his touches and nursing stimulate the release of more prolactin and also ensures a plentiful milk supply. It is noteworthy that it is not nighttime that stimulates prolactin but the act of sleeping itself. Frequent naps with the baby during the day will also boost prolactin levels.

Mothers who share sleep with their babies and have mastered this nighttime harmony often tell us that as time goes on they seem to need less sleep and feel more rested despite their babies' waking and nursing during the night. Their acceptance and tolerance of nighttime mothering seems to broaden. There are, of course, other mothers whose babies wake too much and who become exhausted. We will cover this problem later in the chapter.

There are probably many beneficial effects of sharing sleep that are in the divine design that are not known about yet. Some researchers have even suggested that mothers' and babies' sleep and dream cycles and brain wave patterns are in unison when they sleep and nurse together. Science is just beginning to confirm what God has designed and mothers have known all along—that something good happens when babies and mothers share sleep.

Breastfeeding Is Easier

When baby and mother are in close proximity they can meet each other's needs often without either one becoming fully awake. A mother who had achieved this nighttime nursing harmony with her baby shared the following story with us: "About thirty seconds before my baby wakes for a feeding, my sleep seems to lighten and I almost wake up. [She is entering her phase of light sleep.] By being able to anticipate his feeding, I usually can start breastfeeding him just as he begins to squirm and reach for the nipple. Getting to him immediately keeps him from fully waking up, and then he drifts back into a deep sleep right after nursing."

What happens is that the baby nurses through the vulnerable period of awakening and then reenters the state of deep sleep. If mother and baby had not been near each other, the baby would probably have had to wake up crying to signal his need. By the time the mother reached the baby in another room, both mother and baby would have been wide awake and would have had difficulty settling back to sleep.

"My baby is suddenly wanting to nurse all night," is a common concern of nighttime mothering. This occasional "marathoning" seems also to be in accordance with God's design. Babies have periodic growth spurts during which they need extra nighttime nutrition. It is interesting that one of the oldest medical treatments for the slow weight-gaining baby is the simple advice, "Take your baby to bed and nurse." This is how mother's milk supply gets boosted to accommodate her baby's increase in growth. After a few days and nights of increased nursing, the supply comes up to baby's new need level and baby goes back to his usual amount of nursing.

Sharing Sleep Helps Space Babies

In our experience, depending on breastfeeding as a natural way of child spacing seldom works unless mothers and babies share sleep. And this is not because the baby interferes with mother and father's sexual relationship! The increased prolactin levels suppress ovulation when the baby continues to nurse at night. (For a complete discussion on natural family planning, see page 124.) If you believe in a divine design for child spacing, it follows that the concept of sharing sleep would be part of God's design.

SIDS and Sharing Sleep

No one knows the exact cause of Sudden Infant Death Syndrome (SIDS). One widely accepted theory is that SIDS may be the result of a disorder of arousability in some infants. Researchers feel that SIDS may be due to the loss of ability in some infants to breathe automatically during the state of deep sleep or to arouse from sleep and trigger a self-start mechanism in response to a breathing problem. Our hypothesis is that breastfeeding and sharing sleep can prevent SIDS in certain high-risk infants. Sharing sleep and breastfeeding increase mutual sensitivity between mother and baby. During shared sleep mother acts as a respiratory pacemaker to remind baby to breathe. Sharing sleep also increases the amount of light sleep that acts as a protective state against breathing failure.

The subject of SIDS prevention is finally getting attention from pediatricians and public health officials. While no one knows exactly why some infants become victims of this tragedy, dying suddenly and unexpectedly during sleep, researchers are finding that there is much you can do to decrease your baby's chances of SIDS. This includes not smoking, breastfeeding your baby, and putting your baby down to sleep on her back or on her side, rather than on her tummy. It is interesting to note that mothers who sleep with their babies automatically have the baby either on his side or back because that gives the baby better access to the breast. (For more on SIDS prevention and the fascinating research on sleep sharing and SIDS, see *SIDS: A Parent's Guide to Understanding and Preventing Sudden Infant Death Syndrome* by William Sears, see bibliography.)

DISPELLING MYTHS ABOUT SLEEP SHARING

For years "experts" have advised against babies sharing sleep with parents. No doubt you have heard plenty of pronouncements about babies in bed with parents. There are many popular myths about this subject, and they are repeated by health care providers as well as relatives. It's time to dispel the myths and faulty information so that parents can appreciate the beauty of God's design for infant sleep.

The Dependency Myth

"Doctor, won't she become dependent and never want to sleep alone?" The answer here is yes and no. Yes, your baby will seem dependent temporarily and will not want to leave your bed. This is natural. When you are close to someone you love and you feel right about it, why give up a good thing? But this relationship is better labeled "trust" than dependency. Your infant trusts that you will be there to listen to his cues, and you trust your ability to respond appropriately to these cues.

This means that, no, your baby will not grow up to be more dependent. Your baby will eventually sleep alone. The trust he has in you will eventually become trust in himself and he will feel secure as a separate person. However, the age at which a child goes from oneness to separateness varies from child to child. What is important is that you allow your child to separate from you on the terms that are comfortable for both of you, not according to some preconceived time chart determined by peer pressure or child care advisors. In our experience, children who are given free access to sharing sleep eventually become *more* secure and independent because they reach the stage of separateness when they are ready and are not hurried into separate quarters too soon or with a lot of anxiety.

It is not the parents' responsibility to force a child to be independent. Parents are to create an environment of security that allows the child's independence to develop naturally, in the way that is right for him ("in the way he should go" Prov. 22:6). It is important, however, that the parent not hold a child back from separating because the parent needs the closeness. If you are not sure whether it is your child's need or your need, take your concern to an older, more experienced mother who agrees with your parenting style and ask her to help you discern this.

The Disturbed Marriage Myth

"Having the baby in bed with us will interfere with our sexual relationship." Absolutely not! This may be the bed where your baby was conceived, and this baby is a product of your love. Caring for your baby in a loving way doesn't mean you treat each other less lovingly. We do not think our babies have "come between us" significantly—*and* we have eight children!

Of course, parents want to be discreet about how they show affection in front of their child at any age. When you share your bed with your baby, some ingenuity is required for husband and wife to find a private time to be together. Sleeping baby can be shifted to another spot in your room, or can be put down asleep in another place for the first (or last) part of the night. Or you and your mate can do the shifting. Remember, the master bedroom is not the only place where lovemaking can occur. Couples who have successfully enjoyed the concept of the family bed often discover that every room in the house is a potential love chamber. This attitude, along with a sense of humor, probably leads to more variety in the couple's sexual relations.

As your baby grows into a child, you can teach him about knocking on the door first, and have clear communication about your need for privacy. You can tell your child to go play somewhere else "because Mommy and Daddy want to be alone for a while." It is healthy for a child to get two messages concerning the master bedroom: (1) the door is open to me if I have a strong need to be with my parents, and (2) there are private times when Mommy and Daddy want to be alone and this is okay too. The attitude within the bedroom is what counts to both parents and child, not the actual timing of lovemaking.

The Single Parent Myth

Single mothers (and fathers) worry more about all aspects of parenting. One of their more common worries is whether sleeping with their infant or child is alright. The same principles of nighttime parenting apply to all parents, whether single or not. Since most single mothers have to work outside the home, sleeping with their babies allows them to reconnect with their baby and make up for the missed touch time during the day.

The next concern is how long it is okay to sleep with the child. Again, the answer is the same as for couples who share sleep with their children. Once the child is three or four, he should have his own room, his own bed, so that he knows he is a separate person who has his own space. He should be encouraged to start out the night in his own bed, parented to sleep by you if that's what he needs; then he can come into your room if he needs you. Gradually, he will outgrow his need to come find you. He is in your bed, or your room, only if he needs you. It should never be because you need him, of course. That is not appropriate. Also, wear conservative sleepwear so that boundaries are in place, as discussed in "It's Time to Cover Up," p. 325.

The Smothering Myth

"I might roll over on my baby and smother him." This is one of the oldest myths about sharing sleep, and it does indeed disturb some parents. The subject deserves a thorough explanation. The story of the two women who came to Solomon arguing about whose baby had died in the night has contributed to this myth: "During the night this woman's son died because she lay on him" (1 Kings 3:19).

When there are reports of babies being smothered there are also unusual elements present, such as a drugged or drunk parent or too many persons squeezed into too small a space. In the account in 1 Kings remember that these mothers were prostitutes, so conditions were far from ideal and most likely involved drunkenness, crowding, or some other problem in lifestyle.

The Consumer Product Safety Commission has issued a warning that children should never be allowed in their parents' bed. We feel that this warning is overstated, because most parents are conscientious enough to make their baby's sleep environment safe. Some parents shouldn't sleep with their babies due to safety concerns. See the box on the next page entitled "Sharing Sleep Safely" to learn how to ensure your baby's safety while sharing sleep.

The "Nobody Else Does This" Myth

"Isn't this an odd custom? What will people say?" You might think that sleeping with your baby will make you seem unusual. Just the opposite is true. In most cultures, from biblical times to present times, babies have slept with their parents. Parents have been following this practice for decades but were reluctant to tell their doctors and their in-laws about it. If you want to get a feel for how prevalent sharing sleep really is, join in with a group of young mothers and confide to one of them, "My baby is sleeping with me. What do you think about this arrangement?" Your confidante will probably look around to make sure nobody else is listening and then whisper back, "My baby sleeps with me, too, but don't tell anybody."

Infants sleeping with their mothers is not a recent fad but a return to a traditional practice that time and maternal wisdom have proven to be right. Early medical books recommended that babies sleep with mother. For example, a child-care book written in 1840, *Management of Infancy,* by A. Combe, stated that "there can scarcely be a doubt that at least during the first four weeks and during winter and early spring a child will thrive better if allowed to sleep beside its mother's side and be cherished by her warmth than if placed in a separate bed." An East African tribal chief once said, "At night when there was no sun to warm me, my mother's arms and her body took its place."

We predict that sharing sleep will be practiced more and more until it becomes the usual custom in Western culture, as will many other traditional and time-proven concepts of child care. It is interesting that

SHARING SLEEP SAFELY

- Be sure baby can't roll out of bed, though it is unlikely as long as mother is present. Babies, like heat-seeking missiles, automatically gravitate toward a warm body. To be safe, have baby sleep between mother and a mesh guardrail or wall (see figure on p. 189). Be sure the mattress is flush against the guardrail or wall so there is no crevice baby could sink into.

- Wait until baby is older before he sleeps next to dad. A mother is so beautifully aware of her baby's presence that she simply would not roll over on a baby, unless she were under the influence of any drug that would diminish that awareness or lessen arousability from sleep. A father generally doesn't have this same awareness, so it is possible he might roll over on or throw out an arm onto baby.

- Place baby on his back or on his side with his lower arm extended forward.

- Use a large bed, preferably king-size, or two smaller beds pushed together. Be sure there are no crevices between beds, or between bed and headboard, that baby could get wedged into. (The money you save not buying a crib can be used to treat yourselves to a safe, comfortable sleeping area.)

- Some parents and babies sleep better if baby is still in touching and hearing distance but not actually in the same bed. For them, the sidecar arrangement works well. Push the crib, with one side down, flush up against your mattress, experimenting until you get the mattresses level. You can use clamps to keep it from shifting, or use special tape, available from baby product catalogs, to seal the mattresses together. Lock or remove the crib wheels.

- Use caution if you are very obese or extremely large-breasted. Both present risk of smothering. Use caution if you are exhausted from sleep deprivation, since this lessens your awareness of your baby and your arousability from sleep. Baby-sitters also have less awareness than mothers.

SHARING SLEEP DON'TS

- Don't sleep with baby (or place baby alone) on a free-floating, wavy waterbed. He may be unable to lift his head clear of the depressions that form, or he may get his head wedged between the waterbed mattress and the bed frame. "Waveless" waterbeds (with internal baffles) or those filled to be as firm as a regular mattress may be safer, especially if baby sleeps on a special mat placed on top. Be sure all the crevices between the mattress and frame are filled.
- Don't fall asleep with baby (or place baby) on a beanbag chair or other "sinky" surface on which baby could suffocate.
- Don't fall asleep with baby on a couch. It is particularly unsafe for a parent or older sibling to do this with a tiny baby. Baby can get wedged between the back of the couch and the larger person's body, or baby's head can get buried in cushion crevices or soft cushions.
- Don't allow older siblings to sleep with a baby under nine months, because they don't have the same awareness of tiny babies as parents do, and a too small or too crowded bed space is unsafe.
- Don't overheat or overbundle baby.
- Don't wear lingerie with string ties longer than seven inches or long chains in which baby could be entrapped.
- Don't use strong scents that could irritate and clog baby's tiny nasal passages.
- If your baby is being electronically monitored, check with your doctor or monitor technician before sharing a bed with your baby.

breastfeeding was unusual in the 1950s in the United States, but it has made a remarkable comeback. Other "unusual" customs are also coming back because, in reality, they never left the intuitive hearts of mothers.

The Expert Advice Myth

"But my doctor told me not to let our baby sleep in our bed." Parents shouldn't be asking their doctors about sleep sharing, and doctors shouldn't give definite yes or no answers. This doctor's dictum is a carryover from the days when a new mother felt more comfortable taking her doctor's advice rather than following her own God-given wisdom. The doctor is put on the spot when asked to come up with an answer on a subject in which he has no training. Many doctors elect to join the camp of "separate sleepers" because the detachment and separation philosophy has been so popular and there is always security in numbers.

There are aspects of child care on which you do not need your doctor's advice. Where your baby sleeps and whether or not you should let your baby cry in a particular situation are questions that can be answered only by you. When it comes to maternal-infant attachment, you do well to follow your own God-given sense above the advice of anyone else since no one else has your biological attachment to your infant. When you become parents you are given responsibility for a lot of decision making. That is what makes you mature as individuals and pushes you to educate yourselves about caring for children.

Take heart. Even doctors are now realizing that parents are the best judges of where their baby should sleep and that different families will have different solutions to common problems. Fortunately, many doctors, who are also experienced parents, have already recognized the rightness of God-given maternal intuition concerning sleeping arrangements.

The Psychosexual Disturbance Myth

We are absolutely certain that there are no psychosexual disturbances that are caused by sleep sharing in healthy families. Some psychologists have had this concern, and we can understand why when they see abnormal situations all the time. Yet we are not talking about problem cases, just healthy parents with normal, loving relationships. In connection with any parenting practice there are, of course, guidelines that enable a child to develop his own personal identity and to develop healthy (and moral) sexual boundaries. These concerns are addressed more specifically in "The Single Parent Myth" and "The Disturbed Marriage Myth."

FATHER FEELINGS ABOUT SHARING SLEEP

"I want my baby to sleep next to me, but my husband refuses." Many husbands fall prey to the previously discussed myths. Read this chapter together. Pray together, asking God to guide you on the best sleeping arrangements for your family. Discuss the advantages of sharing sleep and talk about solutions to any concerns you may have. If God's design for the family is followed, your child should never be allowed to divide you as a couple. A fulfilled Christian marriage is the foundation of the family. It is vital to God's order for the family that both husband and wife agree on where the baby sleeps.

Dads, if you have ambivalent feelings about your baby sleeping in your bed, trust your wife's leading. This is one instance in which mother knows best. Having the baby sleep between parents concerns some fathers. If this bothers you, let us suggest the sleeping arrangement shown in the illustration below; baby can sleep between mother and a guardrail or wall, and you and your wife still have your snuggling time.

Actually, once reluctant fathers get used to sleep sharing, most of them enjoy it. It is an occasion for wonderful closeness. When you consider how little time you may have to be physically close to your baby during the day, you may decide that nighttime fathering provides a boost to your father-infant relationship. Again, whatever sleeping

arrangement gets all three of you the most quality sleep is the right sleeping arrangement for your family. King-size beds are a wise investment for all new families and are actually cheaper than buying a lot of unnecessary baby furniture that your baby will probably not use or outgrow quickly.

Be prepared for a few good laughs, such as the one we experienced when one of our babies got her directions mixed up and rolled over to nurse from Bill instead of Martha. Then there was a time when one of our babies was enjoying one of her many middle-of-the-night meals. We had a rather large Labrador retriever who had a habit of drinking out of her water bowl on the back porch with an exceptionally loud slurp. Bill is a very light sleeper and easily awakened by unusual sounds. One night this sound occurred and Bill jumped out of bed determined to put an end to our dog's disturbing nighttime thirst quenching. Martha was quick to inform him that it was not the dog at all, but our little nursing baby who was making these sloppy, slurping noises. God has given us a sense of humor so that we can survive parenting and so our children can not just survive but thrive.

You might also enjoy the experience one father related to us. When he awakes because of some worry, instead of letting his worry keep him from going back to sleep, he looks over and sees the face of his child sleeping soundly within the security of those who love him. He finds that the sight of a peaceful child usually will dispel any worry of the world since it keeps his priorities in perspective. It also reminds him that he can be safe in his Father's care, just as his child is worry-free and feeling safe in his.

ARE THERE ANY DISADVANTAGES TO THE FAMILY BED?

Occasionally parents complain that they cannot sleep well with their baby in their bed. There are several explanations for this.

When parents have not welcomed their baby into their bed early on, neither parents nor baby are used to the arrangement. It does take some getting used to, so be willing to try it for a while. Most parents find that the size of the bed makes a big difference. If you have a double bed, try putting a twin bed next to it for a larger sleep space. Older babies who squirm a lot can learn to respect other family members' space. Ask a squirmy toddler to please lie still or he has to leave. He'll soon get the idea that squirming is an unacceptable nocturnal habit. (Or, there could be a physical cause for the squirming, especially in a younger baby, see p. 197, "Allergies and Sleep.")

Parents may try the family bed reluctantly. They may accept their baby into their bed out of desperation: "We'll try any arrangement so we can get some sleep, but we really don't like this idea." A baby senses when he is an unwelcome guest in the family bed. He doesn't feel secure and doesn't sleep well.

Some parents enjoy having their babies and young toddlers sleep with them, but worry about how long it should continue. Of course, every child has a different timetable for weaning from the parents' bed, and every family situation is different. It is easier to wean a child from your bed when there is an older sibling to share sleep with. Most children wean themselves from the family bed by two to three years of age and into their own rooms by three to four years of age. Thereafter they sleep comfortably and independently, although they may return to the comfort of the parents' bed or bedroom during particularly stressful times. Weaning from the parents' bed to sleeping alone usually requires intermediate steps, such as using a mattress next to your bed for a while. Some parents have an older toddler start out the night in his own room, parenting him off to sleep with stories if he no longer nurses off to sleep. Then when he wakes up he can come quietly into the parents' room and bunk down on his mattress on the floor.

COMMON SLEEP PROBLEMS

Sleep problems occur at various ages and fall into one of two classes: (1) child not going to sleep and (2) child not staying asleep. Remember, difficult problems do not have easy solutions. Sleep problems are highly individual. You may have to give them a lot of thought and try several approaches to find something that works.

Night Waking

At the beginning of this chapter we described how children have different sleep cycles from adults. They are aroused from sleep more easily and sometimes have difficulty resettling. Nighttime is scary for little people because they don't yet know how to manage on their own, even in the daytime. The following are the most common reasons for children awakening:

- Physical discomforts—hunger, thirst, wet diaper, teething, stuffy nose, ear infection, pinworms, uncomfortable sleeping position, gas pains and stomach aches, allergies, kidney infection, food intolerance, gastroesophageal reflux.
- Environmental causes—loud noises, wet sheets, too hot, too cold.
- Emotional disturbances—dreams, fears, separation anxieties.

Here are some common sleep scenarios that occur in the early years, along with possible solutions. In none of these cases is letting baby cry it out appropriate, and in fact

NIGHTTIME TIPS FOR NEWBORNS

Many babies come into the world with an established sleep-wake cycle the reverse of what we want because *in utero* they came awake when Mom went to sleep. By day they were lulled by the movement of mother's body. When she went to sleep, the movement stopped and they would "go to town!" You need to teach your newborn that daytime is for feeding and interaction with her new world and nighttime is for sleeping. Here's how: During the day, wake your baby for feedings so that she does not sleep longer than three hours at a stretch. Play with her after each feeding for as long as she can stay awake, and keep her with you in a mildly stimulating environment. At night, keep things calm and quiet—low lights, quiet music, soft voices. When your baby awakes at night, respond to her quickly but in a no-nonsense mode (keep talking to a minimum and use a nightlight to see by). The message you want to communicate is that you expect your baby to fall back asleep. In normal sleep development, you will find that as the weeks progress, your baby's stretches of daytime sleep automatically shorten and nighttime sleep stretches will lengthen. Parent your baby to sleep; don't just put your baby to sleep. A breast (or bottle) and a rocking chair make a winning combination for the tiny infant.

Make sure your baby is dressed comfortably. Use 100 percent cotton clothing and receiving blankets. Some babies settle better in loose coverings that allow them more freedom of movement, but others settle better when they are securely swaddled, so experiment to see which works best.

Lie down with your baby and snuggle, cradling your baby in your arms. We call this ritual "nestle nursing."

Once baby drifts off, if you place baby in his crib, lay one hand firmly on your baby's side (if side-lying) or tummy (if back-lying) and rhythmically pat him with the other hand. Very gradually lessen the pressure of your hands as you notice your baby drift off into deeper sleep. Remember, deep sleep doesn't come for at least twenty minutes.

Monitor baby's sleeping position. In their first few weeks, tiny infants sleep best on their side. Place a rolled-up towel or a specially designed wedge behind baby's back, taking care to have baby's lower arm extended out. Babies should sleep on their back after one month to lower the risk of SIDS.

NIGHTTIME TIPS FOR NEWBORNS (CONT.)

Play soothing sounds—tape recordings of running water or ocean sounds, classical music, a metronome, or a ticking clock if baby needs extra help settling.

Provide a warm fuzzy. Falling asleep on Dad's chest is a warm fuzzy. Tiny babies enjoy this sleeping arrangement when they are small enough not to wiggle off easily, usually during their first two months. A lambskin mat is also a warm fuzzy that babies can get used to and that will condition them to sleep wherever the mat is placed.

that approach could actually be physically harmful in some situations.

Marathon Nighttime Nursing

"My baby is six weeks old. She used to awaken only once or twice and then resettle after nursing. Now she awakens every two hours for a feeding and doesn't resettle quickly. I'm exhausted." Your baby is probably going through a growth spurt and needs to nurse more frequently for a few days. Redefining your daytime priorities is necessary during this time—you need to catnap during the day to recharge your nocturnal parenting battery. This is one instance when it would be wise to welcome your baby into your bed and enjoy nursing there. This will give her more milk during a growth spurt and she should interrupt your sleep less.

Difficulty Resettling

"My baby is six months old, waking more often and resettling less well, yet he doesn't seem hungry." Between four and six months of age babies start being awakened by the physical discomforts of teething—painful gums, referred pain to the ears, and the collection of profuse saliva in the back of the throat that usually accompanies teething. If these irritations occur during the light phase of sleep, babies usually awaken. Babies who are teething are somewhat reluctant to feed because of the pain in their gums. Ask your doctor to recommend the correct dose of acetaminophen, based on baby's weight, to dull the pain. (See p. 260.)

Six-month-old babies who sleep alone often do not resettle easily for two reasons. First, they are intensely interested in their environment and want to look around. For this reason, try to keep the lights off and use quiet, soothing words. Second, anxiety about being away from the mother he feels and touches all day long may also keep baby from resettling. Remember that your six- to nine-month-old baby might be suffering separation anxiety because he lacks the ability to call up a mental image of you being elsewhere.

Middle-of-the-Night Playtime

"My baby is one and a half years old and awakens happily at 4:00 A.M. ready to get up and play, but I am not." Your baby's sleep may need some repatterning. Many mothers confess, "She's not ready for bed at 7:00 P.M., but I'm ready for her to go to bed." But it is unrealistic to put babies down at 7:00 P.M. and expect them to sleep until 7:00 A.M. Repattern your baby's sleep by delaying her nap until later in the afternoon, keeping her up later in the evening, and getting her to sleep later. This is especially important if baby's father doesn't get home until 6:00 P.M. Children who are put to bed early will miss evening time with their fathers.

The eighteen-month-old to two-year-old child is verbal enough to understand that nighttime is not playtime. Give your child a loving hug, tell her firmly that Mommy and Daddy are going back to sleep and that you expect her to do the same. You may offer to lie down with your child or let her lie on a mattress next to your bed, or you can convey in some other way that this is not playtime. Then you pretend to sleep.

Separation Anxiety

"My two-year-old is awakening more and more frequently and generally will not stay in his crib. Sometimes when I get up in the morning, I find him asleep outside our bedroom door. He's becoming increasingly more difficult to resettle in the middle of the night unless I stay with him." This child is exhibiting separation anxiety and may even be having nightmares. By two years of age most toddlers have achieved object permanency and can feel comfortable with mother in another room. Yet, the child who falls asleep outside the parents' door obviously wants to be near them.

If a child is continuously standing up in her crib, rattling her cage, or climbing out, the message is clear—there's something about sleeping in the crib that is not right for this child. The parent can insist that she will sleep in the crib, but this leads to unending nighttime struggles in which nobody wins. The wise parent will listen to what the child is actually saying and offer the child alternative sleeping arrangements. This is not manipulation. This is communication; this is trust. It is trusting your child to recognize where she feels right sleeping; it is trusting yourself to confidently and appropriately respond to your child's cues. Welcome your child into your bedroom, and if sleeping with you is not an option with which you feel comfortable, give your child a mattress or a sleeping bag next to your bed. At this point, you can tell him firmly that if he wishes to sleep in your bedroom, you expect him to sleep quietly until the morning and not disturb you. Tell him, "If you wake up, you know we're right here and you can go back to sleep."

Making the Transition to Sleep

"My two-year-old just doesn't know when to give up. I know she's tired by her droopy eyelids and her yawning, but she fights going to bed." Some children do not want to put away the excitement of the daytime world. In this case, you should know best, and oftentimes a child is waiting for someone in authority to override her lack of wisdom. She also may be fighting bed because she does not want to go to sleep alone.

Have a quiet hour before a realistic bedtime; instead of energetic activities, try wind-down activities, such as reading stories, rocking in a rocking chair, or listening to soft music. A warm, calming bath, a story, and a good-night lullaby make a winning combination to help heavy eyelids overcome busy minds. Help her to relax enough to fall asleep and stay with her until she does. Fathers can often assume the major role in the bedtime ritual, especially if there is a younger baby.

Drawn-Out Bedtime

"It takes my husband too long to get our two-year-old to sleep. We have a large family, and we run out of time." Prolonged bedtime is a common ploy of young children in a large family. Sometimes the only time a child gets one-on-one attention from Dad is at bedtime, and he is going to play this special time for all he can get. Parents need to accept this as a normal attachment phase, and be thankful that their children want to be with them. Do the best you can. One of the realistic expectations of fathering a large family is that you can't give enough time to all your children all the time. Your children and your God will understand this dilemma.

Nightmares

"My three-year-old is afraid to go to bed alone and often wakes with scary nightmares." Children from two to four years of age develop vivid imaginations and often distort reality in their dreams; a dog turns into a dinosaur in a dream. Attempt to find out what the scary thing is. It may be something your child saw on TV that day. Encourage your child to talk about the nightmare as you lay with her. Make the connection for her if you identify the source of her fear. Talk about it the next day, too, so she can learn to replay her scary dreams in the light of day and begin to understand how dreams work. Let her have a light on in her room until she falls asleep, and even keep it on all night if need be.

We pray with our children each night that Jesus will give them nice dreams, and we thank Him for always being with us. Still, some children will need a parent's continued presence for the "dragon" to be gone. This is one of the best reasons we know for parents having an open door policy during the night. A sleeping bag next to your bed provides sanctuary when troubles hit.

Nighttime Nursing

"My six-month-old baby wants to nurse a lot at night." Some infants need to nurse at night and you should not discourage it. God designed breastfed infants to nurse more frequently at night than their formula-fed counterparts. It is normal for babies under one year of age to need a feeding two (and occasionally three) times during the night.

One way to cut down on the number of times you have to wake up is to wake your baby for a long nursing before you go to bed. Then make sure he really feeds when he wakes up at night, rather than having a series of wakings in which he sucks just long enough to lull himself back to sleep but not deal with his hunger. You may have to actually sit up in bed and pick the baby up so he will actively feed long enough to get a full tummy.

Some babies want or need to breastfeed during the night because they are easily distracted during daytime nursing. Between two and three months babies become very interested in the visual delights of the world around them. They suck a little and look a little, constantly interrupting their feeding because something more interesting comes along.

During the day there is often more competition for the baby's and the mother's interest. However, at night the baby has the mother all to himself so that there are fewer distractions for both of them. Lots of nighttime nursing is especially common in busy households or in those with breastfeeding mothers who work outside the home during the day. Twice during the day take your baby to a quiet spot and encourage her to have a nice long feeding. If she can get more sucking in during the day, she'll need less at night.

Babies learn at a very early age how to get what they need. Some child psychologists consider night nursing a manipulative behavior, a habit, a want rather than a need. In our opinion, babies nurse at night from need rather than habit. Of course, what they need may be more contact with mother, not just more milk.

Allergies and Sleep

"My five-month-old daughter cannot sleep longer than an hour at night, even though she sleeps in our bed. When she wakes she screams or fights and insists on staying awake. Then when she goes back to sleep she tosses and turns. And she can't nap unless I lie down with her the whole time."

Environmental allergies or dietary sensitivities can greatly disturb sleep. The baby may be showing no other signs of allergy, or the fitful sleep may also be accompanied by rashes, colic (or history of colic), fussiness, chronic ear infections, and/or persistent runny nose and puffy, reddened eyes. The profile of this type of nightwaking includes fitful tossing and turning, crying out, waking every forty-five to ninety minutes, crib rocking, or head bumping. Often this baby cannot nap for longer than twenty minutes, and the mother is exhausted.

Cow's milk protein in the mother's diet (or directly in the baby's diet if on formula or eating dairy products) is often the culprit. Bovine beta-lactoglobulin has been shown in studies to enter human milk, causing a sensitive baby to have sleep problems. Other protein foods, such as egg, shellfish, soy, peanuts, wheat, and corn may also be implicated. The problem food sets up an internal irritation that can cause a baby to wake up when she is in one of the vulnerable periods for night waking. If she is breastfeeding, the mother must eliminate the offending food from her diet and also from her baby's diet. Start with cow's milk and all cow's milk products (read labels to detect whey or casein). Improvement is usually seen within one or two days, although often the symptoms will reappear temporarily. The food should be eliminated for at least two weeks to tell if that food is a problem. There may be several offending foods (see list above) that need to be eliminated simultaneously and then gradually reintroduced. (See the box on p. 233 for more information.) Keep notes on what you are eating each day so you can correlate your diet with any further night waking as you reintroduce these foods.

Testing for food allergy or sensitivity can be uncertain, so most of the determination will be on a trial and error basis. Consulting a nutritionist or food allergist may be necessary if the mother becomes confused or feels she needs help pinpointing the problem foods. (*Detecting Your Hidden Allergies*, by William Crook, M.D., is a helpful book, see bibliography.) She may also need a calcium supplement to be sure she gets the recommended daily allowance (RDA) of 1,500 mg for a lactating woman. Environmental irritants such as smoke, feather pillows, molds, mildew, certain laundry products, polyester sleepwear, and even some bedroom furniture made with particleboard can also be responsible.

A Hurting Baby

"I have a two-month-old baby whose colic is not getting better and who spits up a lot after feedings. The worst part, though, is the way she wakes with painful cries at night. She seems OK as soon as I nurse her, and she goes back to sleep well, but then the whole things starts all over again. We have tried everything, and there is no relief."

A newly recognized cause of night waking is gastroesophageal reflux (GER). The acidic stomach juices are regurgitated up into the esophagus causing a painful, burning sensation. This problem usually causes frequent spitting up and a baby who cries a lot and awakens frequently. Breastfeeding upon night waking relieves the pain momentarily. Occasionally, babies with this problem do not actually spit up so that the regurgitation is not observed, and the diagnosis may be missed. Special abdominal x-rays confirm the diagnosis, and treatment is with medications. In some cases, GER is accompanied by food sensitivities, as discussed above. (See p. 233 for a more thorough discussion of GER.)

DON'T LET 'EM CRY

You've probably heard it said, "If you don't respond to your baby's cries, she'll learn to stop crying." This sounds logical—if you believe that crying is negative behavior. In many cases this is not true, and it's certainly not true for babies. Crying is baby's language for communicating needs. If a baby's language is responded to during the day but not during the night, the baby will be terrified—a feeling that certainly goes against the goal of helping your child feel right. But, you say, "This waking up could be a habit, not a real need." Yes, we agree, this may be the case. How do you tell the difference? Habits are negotiable; needs are not.

If your baby's cries are intensifying and your inner parenting voice says this is a need you must satisfy, then listen to yourself first and not a book or an advisor. If your baby's cries wind down shortly after they begin and your inner parenting sensor says baby is okay, then this is probably a habit. Habits are easily broken; needs are not. But the difference is often difficult to discern. If you're not certain whether to answer a baby's nighttime cries, we feel it's better to err on the side of needs. (See chapter 9 for more discussion of why babies cry.)

Psalm 5:1–2: *"Give ear to my words, O LORD, consider my sighing. Listen to my cry for help, my King and my God, for to you I pray."*

THE EXHAUSTED-MOTHER SYNDROME

You may gather from this discussion that we favor parenting through the night. We do. It's part of the investment you make in building a trusting relationship with your child and in her emerging sense of feeling right about herself. However, mothers do sometimes reach a point where their maternal reserves run out. When giving of herself at night compromises a woman's effectiveness as a mother during the day, the entire mother-child relationship suffers a net loss. The marriage may be strained too. If you are a mother who has reached the point of exhaustion, your need for sleep must become a priority. Along with the following suggestions, begin implementing your search for the physical cause of baby's waking, (These are listed on page 191 under "Common Sleep Problems.")

Find more time to sleep. If you are not getting enough sleep at night, you need to sleep during the day. Lie down with the baby when she naps; don't read, don't think, just sleep. Nurse the baby and doze off on the couch while your preschooler watches a video. If baby wakes up cheerful and ready to play at sunrise, have Dad get up and take baby for a walk while you sleep in. Or go to bed early while Dad gives baby a bath and winds her down for the night. If baby goes to bed an hour or two before you do, wake her and nurse her again when you're ready to sleep so you won't be awakened shortly after you drift off.

Shift work. For a couple of nights the father gets up with the baby, rocks the baby, walks with the baby, gives a bottle if bottle-fed, and if nothing else works, takes the baby for a car ride. Meanwhile, the mother sleeps (or tries to). For breastfeeding mothers, the father can burp, walk, or rock baby while the mother goes back to sleep. Certainly, if the mother has a job outside the home during the day, both parents should share these nocturnal interruptions.

Redesign your sleep sharing. An occasional baby will actually sleep better in his own sleeping space. Some mothers have found that their older babies seem to be stimulated by the mother's closeness and have gotten better sleep with baby still in the same room but not right next to her. Try having baby next to dad, or in a sidecar arrangement (crib with side down up against your bed).

It's okay to say no to your toddler. Once babies are past the age of eighteen months, they can handle this at night. We experienced this with our seventh baby, Stephen, who had been sleeping well, waking usually only twice at night to be nursed. When he was twenty months old, he began waking three or four times at night. He was not sick, so we were puzzled by this. It went on for two or three nights and Martha was getting worn out. We decided Stephen had to be taught that she would not nurse him so often. Bill picked Stephen up when he woke and walked with him. He cried angrily on and off for an hour the first time. When he fell back to sleep, Bill put him down again next to Martha. She only nursed him once that night. The other times Bill walked with him. After four nights, each night having less and less crying, he was back to only waking once or twice, and he didn't return to that exhaustive pattern of waking again. Yes, he did some crying, but he was not alone. We felt right about how we helped Stephen change.

TWO TESTIMONIES ON SHARING SLEEP

There were many reasons why we decided to have our baby sleep with us. Although there were some problems, we have been able to overcome them. My husband was afraid that he would roll over on her, but he never did. Friends told me that the romance would go out of our marriage if we had a baby sleep with us. If anything, I think it has made us more loving. We know she is safe and she has us there if she needs us.

We did run out of room as she got older. That problem was solved by attaching a crib to our bed. We removed one side of the crib and adjusted the mattress to the level of our mattress. Now she loves to go to her "bed" and get tucked in. She can still see us and crawl to us if she needs to. Having her with us has made nursing a breeze.

She almost never cries at night or, for that matter, during the day. She and her father are very close. Occasionally, she still will fall asleep on his stomach. All in all, having her with us has been great. We feel good knowing she is secure and not lonely. More importantly, she knows we are there for her if she needs us. We will miss her when she goes to her own bed.

* * * * * * * *

After meeting our six-month-old son, his grandfather was impressed that John seemed so secure and well-adjusted. This made us feel that our parenting principles were on the right track.

Our pregnancy was entirely positive, with my husband participating in every way possible. Childbirth classes were taken seriously . . . homework included. A number of people had "prepared" us for the "terrible" experience labor was to be; consequently we were happily surprised to have a very positive birth. As a couple, those hours during labor and birth brought us the closest we had ever been, and I felt I was literally watching the three of us become a family.

Our baby roomed-in with me in the hospital, creating a special two-day private family time for us. The first weeks of parenting did not bring the tension between us that we had been warned about. The baby was someone we both had planned for and wanted very much, and we were ready to pour ourselves into his little life.

Totally breastfeeding and nursing our son on demand encouraged us to try the family bed; a big plus is not getting out of a warm bed several times a night to feed the baby, and we have fine-tuned our nursing techniques so that now neither Mom nor baby fully wakes for a feeding.

My husband was to be the barometer in this relationship. Wanting to respect his feelings, we decided that if he thought it was not working out, we would get a crib. We don't have one yet. All three of us enjoy the closeness, and we rest secure knowing John is OK—warm, right next to us, and easy to find in the dark. In anticipation of a large family we are making plans for a larger bed. John rarely wakes up crying in the morning. He is content and happy, a nice way to start each day.

On particularly demanding days, I appreciate nursing, knowing that if John were bottlefed I would tend to bottle propping. This way I must sit down and spend some time touching and holding him. I cannot compromise my responsibilities.

We travel together almost everywhere. As a twosome my husband and I were very devoted, and bringing our son with us now is the natural extension of our loyalty. We find we like to be together and have not as yet wished for the proverbial weekend away.

When someone suggests that "we must let our baby know where he stands" and "make certain he is not running our lives" it does lead to self-doubt. Until it is brought to my attention, it doesn't even occur to me that I may be taken advantage of. If I don't feel right about leaving him in certain situations and he doesn't like to be left, are we both wrong? If I leave him at someone else's recommendation and we're both miserable, who benefits?

Ultimately, I know that the wisdom that we parents need must come from the Lord. Though people may err in offering damaging advice, I too err in putting so much stake in their words. Perhaps God allows this to teach me to trust Him and to underscore the importance of having His Word dwell richly in my heart. As I continue to grow in Him, my confidence will be increasingly in Him, and when questions arise regarding parenting, I'll know who to ask.

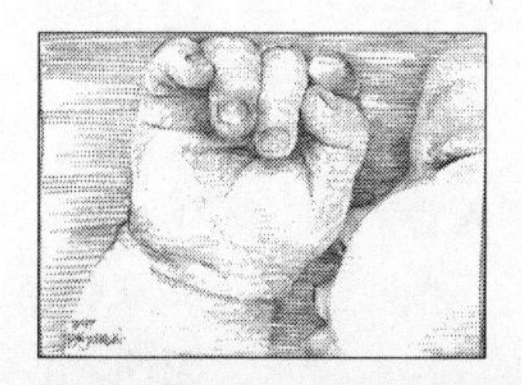

CHAPTER NINE

Responding to Your Baby's Cries

"Should I let my baby cry?" is one of the most common questions new parents ask. More wrong advice is given about this question than about any other aspect of parenting. To illustrate the confusion, let us share the responses to a questionnaire we sent to a group of parents.

The questionnaire pertained to parenting styles. One of the questions was, "What advice do friends and relatives give you about what to do when your baby cries?" Most of the parents answered that often they were told to be unresponsive: "Let him cry it out"; "She must learn to be independent"; "Don't pick her up every time she cries or you will spoil her"; "You are creating a bad habit if you come every time he cries."

In response to the question, "How do you feel about the 'let your baby cry' type of advice?" we received the following statements: "I can't let her cry when I know that I have the means to comfort her"; "It goes against my instinct"; "It just doesn't feel right to me"; "It would drive me nuts to do that"; "I feel so guilty if I leave her to cry." There is a big difference between what parents hear and what they know in their hearts. In this chapter, we will present what we feel is God's design for this special type of communication.

A BABY'S CRY IS A BABY'S LANGUAGE

Throughout the Old Testament there are more than one hundred references to how people communicate with God through crying. Psalm 72:12, for example, says, "He will deliver the needy who cry out." In these biblical passages crying conveys need and the speaker trusts that his crying will be heard.

The crying communication between a mother and her baby is very similar to the cries throughout Scripture. There is a hymn (based on Acts 16:31) whose refrain has these words: "Only trust Him, only trust Him, only trust Him now; He will save you, He will save you, He will save you now!" A baby has genuine needs. When he calls out to someone whom he trusts, he confidently expects an appropriate, sensitive response. This section will show you how to develop this communication network so that an appropriate response to your baby's cry benefits both you and your baby. You will also find that being a sensitive parent will help you be a more sensitive Christian. And it will help your baby learn about the character of God. You can model your behavior as a parent on Jesus' own compassionate responses to those in need around Him.

A mother once said to Bill, "If only my baby could talk, I would know what she wants." He responded, "Your baby can talk, you just have to learn how to listen." From the day she is born, regard your baby's crying as communication, not as a habit to be broken. This starts your parent-baby communication network off on the right "ear." Be open to your baby; take a risk. With time, interpreting your baby's cries will get easier and easier because you have allowed this communication network to develop in the way God designed it to work. A baby's cry is her own unique language. No two people talk the same; no two babies cry the same; no two mother-baby units are wired the same.

In their first few months, babies cry a lot because they need a lot. Their needs are high, but they don't have a lot of ways other than crying to communicate these needs. During the first three to four months, babies are attempting to adjust to their new environments. During this adjustment period, they are very sensitive; some are more sensitive than others. They signal their normal biological needs and their sensitivities by crying. The key to guiding their behavior is for parents and other caregivers to respond to their needs.

How to Develop a Sensitivity to Your Baby's Cries

Every new mother has a built-in receiver to her baby's cries. The more she allows herself to respond spontaneously and promptly to her baby's cries, the more attuned she becomes to her baby. And the more attuned she becomes, the more appropriately she can respond. When a mother says, "I can't stand to let him cry," we know she has not desensitized herself.

The physiological changes that occur in a new mother's body when she hears her baby cry illustrates that it is God's design for her to respond promptly to her baby's cries. In response to her baby's cries, the blood flow to a mother's breasts increases, often accompanied by the urge to nurse or by activation of the milk-ejection reflex. This is a biological clue that God designed a mother to pick up her baby (and usually nurse him) when he cries. Considering that a cry is baby's best way of getting food when he's hungry or getting picked up when he's insecure, this urge of the mother to pick him up and bring him to her breast is God's way of being sure babies thrive. We've had enough "mama cats" in our family over the years to see that it is not only human mothers who have this propensity. (There may be some who would say we can't look to the animal kingdom for parenting lessons. We disagree. Jesus pointed us to birds in the sky, sparrows, and sheep to teach us things we need to know.)

How to Trust Your Response to Your Baby's Cries

How a mother and baby develop their crying communication network is a forerunner to building an important aspect of their relationship—trust. Mother's and baby's trust is interdependent: the baby trusts his mother to respond to his cries, and the mother trusts her baby to communicate his needs; she learns to trust her ability to meet his needs and he learns to trust his inner sense of right and not right.

The more you exercise a skill, the more skillful you become; the more promptly and appropriately you respond to your baby's cries, the more confident you become in your ability to comfort your baby. When a mother picks up and nurses her crying baby, she will observe the peaceful feeling her prompt response gives her baby. This immediate calming in response to her efforts creates a sense of rightness within her. This further increases her confidence and trust in herself.

Some babies are not as easily consoled as others, not because of their parents' abilities (though this could be a factor), but because of their own sensitive temperaments. Babies who have difficulty adjusting to their new environments are called "fussy babies," "colicky babies," or as we like to call them, "high-need babies." If a baby does not stop crying when she is picked up and consoled, a new parent will find it hard to gain confidence. Some very sensitive babies cry a couple of hours each day of their first few months, no matter how experienced their caregivers are. If you have been blessed with

INSTINCT, INTUITION, DISCERNMENT

These are three tools God has given us, and we as parents call on them constantly. Each has its own purpose and each can even be seen as part of a continuum in the area of parental responses. Let's look at definitions.*

Instinct:	The innate aspect of behavior that is unlearned, complex, and normally adaptive; a powerful motivator or impulse; an innate aptitude.
Intuition:	The act or faculty of knowing without the use of rational processes; immediate cognition; a capacity for guessing accurately.
Discernment:	The act or process of being astute or perceptive or discriminating.

We use the word "instinct" when talking about meeting a baby's basic need immediately. For instance, when a baby is crying, picking him up is an instinct on the part of the mother that should not be ignored. Breastfeeding the baby may also be an instinctive response at that time, depending on the situation. This is not something a mother has to learn. She just knows that she should pick her baby up when he is crying.

We use the word "discernment" when there are several issues to think about and time is not an issue. For example, when developing an appropriate consequence to give for a certain type of misbehavior that occurs frequently, we can think over all the points and options and perceive which one is appropriate for us or our children.

We see the meaning of the term "intuition" as falling between the meanings of these other two. It is less rational than discernment, but involves more thought than instinct. Instinct is immediate and sure. Discernment considers a variety of options, then carefully and perceptively chooses the best. The use of intuition implies there are at least two choices to consider (the definition mentions "guessing accurately") but that it really is a guess for the most part and less rational than the use of discernment. An example would be how a mother knows why her baby is crying, or how she knows whether or not her child is telling the truth.

*Definitions taken from *The American Heritage Dictionary.*

a baby whose cries are not easily consoled, developing your crying communication network will be more challenging, but God will give you the strength and patience you need, providing you do not interfere with His design. If you remain open to your baby and promptly respond to his cries, eventually the two of you will get your cry-and-response system working, so that you can supply the comforting measures necessary to meet your baby's needs.

Parents who persevere through this process and rely on prayer for patience do learn to comfort their babies, and their babies become better at receiving the help they need. One mother of a high-need baby shared with us, "When he becomes unglued, I now feel I can help him pull himself back together. It has been a long, tough struggle, but I feel I am finally beginning to cash in on all my efforts." This mother is saying that she trusts herself because she has let herself be open to the conditions that allowed her trust to develop.

As the mother and father are learning to trust their parenting abilities, the baby is learning to trust also. Trust contributes to harmony in the parent-child relationship. The more you trust your infant's signals, the more he learns to trust himself. When you believe that your baby cries because he has a need and you respond to that need, he feels that you trust his cues. The more you respond to his cues, the more he trusts his developing ability to signal his needs. That trust is the forerunner of a healthy self-image. Put yourself in your baby's place. When his cries are answered, he probably feels, "I am a special person. When I cry, someone listens and helps me."

The After-Cry Feeling

Imagine that you are living on a deserted island—just the three of you. There are no "experts," no mothers-in-law, no books to tell you what to do. Your newborn baby cries and you know exactly what to do. It doesn't even occur to you to doubt for one instant that you are to pick your baby up. If he continues to cry, you offer your breast. Over a period of days and weeks you and baby figure it out. The important thing is that you are open to listening to your baby tell you what he needs. And you are rewarded by the feeling of confidence that comes from knowing what he needs. So when your newborn cries, respond spontaneously, instinctively, and freely to the first little blip that comes in on your radar screen. If you think you have to analyze your response to your baby's cry, analyze your response after and not before you respond. Don't waste a lot of time thinking while your baby is crying. (Who can think under those circumstances?) Too much intellectualizing takes this beautiful communication network out of the realm of an intuitive art and turns it into a series of mental gymnastics.

After you have responded instinctively to your baby's cries, examine your feelings. If you feel right, then you probably made the right decision and responded appropriately. If you have not responded appropriately, you will not feel right. Either way, you can learn from the situation and fine-tune your maturing intuition for the next time. We feel that God puts this crying-consciousness into a mother for the survival of the baby and the development of the mother. Being unable or unwilling to listen to this crying-consciousness gets new parents in trouble.

Different Cries Call for Different Responses

Think of your crying-consciousness as an inner computer in which the stimulus of a particular cry is matched with a response of a particular type and speed. Picture yourself with several response buttons that are labeled (1) red alert, respond immediately; (2) hold off a bit; and (3) sit tight, grin, and bear it. When all the circuits are working correctly, the response button that matches your baby's crying signal and your feeling of rightness is like an "OK" message that comes on your screen. If the cue-response network does not match up according to the program, a feeling of unrightness is the result and a "guilt" message appears on the screen. This is a healthy guilt that means you have developed an inner sensitivity, a crying-consciousness that tells you your response was not appropriate and you should respond differently next time.

How you respond to your baby's cries in the middle of the night is an example of this crying-consciousness at work. Suppose your baby awakens from a very deep sleep. This usually means that the stimulus that is waking him is very strong. As a result, he cries a piercing "I need immediate attention" kind of cry. Your "red alert" or wake-up-and-respond light goes on. You wake, you attend to your baby, and everybody feels right about it.

Another type of middle-of-the-night cry is the settling cry a baby makes when he is in transition from one state of sleep to another or when he is adjusting his sleeping position. This fretful cry is usually of low intensity and is only mildly unsettling to your baby and not alarming to you. The cry lasts a minute or two and quickly diminishes. This type of crying usually matches well with your "hold off" button, and your baby often settles himself back to sleep without any outside help. Because your cue-response network was in harmony, your "OK" message goes on and a feeling of rightness results.

If, however, your baby emits a persistent, high-intensity cry and you press the "grin-

and-bear-it" button, the stimulus and the response won't match. If you have not desensitized yourself already, you will be left with a sense of unrightness and the "guilt" message will appear. If this happens, listen to and learn from that inner voice; and then the next time a similar cry is heard, you will push the right button.

If you continue to push the wrong button, the circuits eventually burn up and insensitivity results. When it comes to responding appropriately to your baby's cries, no third-party advisor can push the right button for you. Your baby's crying circuitry is wired into your computer, nobody else's.

The Ultimate in Harmony

One intuitive mother who had developed a very sensitive crying-consciousness said to us, "Isn't it a shame that some babies *always* have to cry to get what they need?" The ultimate design for harmony between you and your baby is for you to be so tuned in to your baby's cues that he does not necessarily have to cry to get attention. The more you follow the attachment style of parenting, the more likely that you will have this sensitivity.

Parents who have their radar systems tuned in toward their babies often can sense when they are hungry just by the looks on their faces or by how they act. Attached parents are also on the lookout for stress indicators and often will respond before their babies start crying. For example, when Erin was a baby, she would look up at Bill with raised arms signaling, "Daddy, pick me up." If he picked her up, she wouldn't cry. If he missed her opening cue, a cry would follow. We have never had a particularly high tolerance for babies' cries, so in our home we have found it much more pleasant to create an atmosphere in which our babies usually do not have to cry to get what they need.

Some advisors might object and say if you pick up a baby every time she lifts her arms to you, you are spoiling the baby. Let us offer an alternative viewpoint. If you respond to your baby's signals before your baby has to cry, you are reinforcing those signals instead; you are teaching the baby to "ask nicely." If you let your baby cry, you are teaching her that only hard, desperate crying gets results. Babies who are responded to promptly learn there are other ways to get help besides crying, or at least they learn that they don't have to resort to wailing. Best of all, they learn their cries are listened to and responded to.

EXCUSES FOR NOT RESPONDING TO CRIES

The suggestion that babies should be left to cry comes from people who spend a lot of time worrying that children will run parents' lives, manipulate them, and never learn to respect authority. Schedules, dictums, and checklists also are popular with these parenting advisors. Parents who want quick and easy solutions to difficult child-rearing problems are often tempted by this advice.

One of the most popular and, unfortunately, still prevalent pieces of advice concerning the baby who wakes up during the night says: "Let your baby cry for three nights and by the fourth (or fifth or sixth or . . .) night he will sleep." The advice comes complete with crying schedules and rules for parents about offering comfort. This advice often does not work; quick-result parenting is an unrealistic expectation. More importantly, not responding to a baby's cries interferes with the development of trust between parent and child.

Unfortunately, this other point of view is common, especially in Christian circles. We want to address the issue of letting babies cry point by point for the benefit of all those new parents who hear so much conflicting advice.

"You Might Spoil Him"

Spoiling is a word that has crept into baby books over the years, but never should have. Spoiling implies something has not been attended to properly; it was left alone, put on a shelf to rot. Actually, leaving a baby to cry, holding back, is more apt to spoil babies than responsive attachment parenting.

"Hold back" parenting teaches that if you respond to your child's cries when he is an infant, you will create a whiny child who cries when he doesn't get his way. This is simply not true. Several studies (and personal experience) have confirmed that infants whose cries are promptly responded to actually cry less when they are older.

"You Must Discipline Your Baby"

Discipline is another goal of the "let your baby cry" advice, but these advisors are confusing discipline with control. They suggest that if you respond promptly to your baby, your baby is controlling you, and you are losing your authority as a parent.

Many Christian parents are drawn to this concept of control. They want to have well-behaved children who grow up to adopt their parents' values and avoid the temptations around them. These concerns are valid. There is much to worry over when you are raising children in today's world. However, control is not the same thing as discipline. Control is something imposed from the outside. Discipline's goal is to teach a child to behave appropriately and have the motivation for that behavior come from within. The next step, freely choosing to please God, can then more easily come from within. Parents cry, "I don't know how to discipline my child." What they really are saying is "I don't know my child." Parents who hold back from responding to their babies' cries hinder the process of attachment and getting to know their baby.

"It's Good for a Baby's Lungs"

Another piece of erroneous advice is that crying is physiologically good for baby's lungs. Studies have shown that excessive crying can be harmful to a baby's cardiovascular and respiratory systems. It can increase a baby's heart rate to dangerous levels (over two hundred beats per minute) and decrease the oxygen level in baby's blood.

WHAT'S WRONG WITH BEING UNRESPONSIVE

Sensitivity to a baby's cry seems to be universal. Even two-year-olds know that the cries of their younger siblings need a response. For example, a mother brought her twenty-two-month-old daughter and her one-month-old baby to Bill's office for a well-baby exam. As soon as the baby began to cry, the older child pleaded, "Quick, Mommy, pick baby up." The mother then said, "She always feels this way. I can't get to her baby sister fast enough."

The advice to turn a deaf ear goes against a mother's intuition. A mother is not designed to let her baby cry, and a baby is not designed to be left to cry. When God's design for this crying communication network is not followed, the result is disharmony in the mother-baby relationship, which can lead to serious struggles in that child's life. Mothers, have faith in your God-given instinct. If any advice runs counter to your inner sense of rightness, don't follow it.

The Advice Is Based on Presumption

When parents are advised to let their baby cry, the advisors are presuming that they know why the baby is crying. But they don't. They may say that the baby is crying to manipulate or to annoy. This is unfair and untrue. Or they may be just presuming that nothing is really wrong with the baby, but they do not have the facts to warrant such a conclusion. They are also presuming that the mother would be better off if she let the baby cry, which is also untrue. Most of all, they are

SHOW ME THE STUDIES

For those parents who are interested in following up on the scientific data available, all the studies we have cited here, along with more detailed descriptions of these studies, are annotated in William Sears's book *SIDS: A Parent's Guide to Understanding and Preventing Sudden Infant Death Syndrome* (See bibliography.) The majority of these 250 studies show the effect of parenting styles on the infant's overall physiology and well being.

presuming to know better than the parents why the baby is crying. How can they know better? They have no biological attachment to that baby and are not near him at 3:00 A.M. when he cries. Outsiders have neither a harmonious nor a "hormoneous" relationship with that baby. So they do not qualify as baby advisors. This kind of advice is unfair to the baby, unconstructive to the parents, and basically unchristian. "Be kind and compassionate to one another" (Eph. 4:32).

We do not wish to offend the new parents' friends or relatives who may be reading this section. We are sure you mean well and sincerely care about the well-being of both mother and baby, but please consider the effects of your advice before offering it. Keep in mind that the new parents, especially the new mothers, are vulnerable to any child-care advice because they love their child so deeply. Their love is coupled with natural concern that they do not do anything harmful to their baby. Even though allowing their baby to cry goes against their inner wisdom, they may feel unsettled and think: *We will not be good parents if we don't follow this advice*, or *Our baby may be affected harmfully if we don't let her cry.*

The "let your baby cry" advice is probably the most counterproductive advice in childrearing. It creates a dilemma within the mother and a conflict between what she hears and what she feels. It undermines her own very personal knowledge of her child, which should be one of her most valuable tools as a parent. The writers and preachers who continue to teach unresponsiveness should reassess whether or not their doctrine is in accordance with God's design.

The Advice to Hold Back Desensitizes the New Parent

We sympathize with parents who fall prey to restraint advice. One day Bill was sitting in our backyard reading a psychology book on reinforcement of negative behavior (which is a valid concept as long as one uses discernment in deciding what is negative behavior and what is normal behavior). While he was reading this book, he was generally in a negative mood toward any childish behavior because this was the topic of the book. Erin, a year old at the time, cruised by on her riding toy and tumbled off into the soft grass. She certainly did not appear to be hurt, but she started whimpering a bit. Her whimper steadily increased to an all-out cry. Because of the book he was reading, Bill was heavily involved in mental gymnastics: *Is she crying because of habit or need? Will I be reinforcing negative behavior? Will she be manipulating me?* As he was thinking these fruitless thoughts, Erin looked over at him as only a toddler can do, with a look on her face that said, "Dad, cut the psychology. Follow your instincts, come over here, and pick me up." He eventually did, and they both felt better. Perhaps Erin was telling Bill to quit doing so much reading and start doing more intuitive fathering.

Unresponsive Parenting Discourages Trust

When you trust that your baby is crying because she has a need, your baby learns to trust her ability to give cues and to trust that her cues will be appropriately and consistently responded to. When you use a nonresponsive approach to your baby's cries, you are using the principle of nonreinforcement: if you do not reinforce the behavior, the behavior soon stops.

There are two problems with this approach: (1) it assumes the baby's crying is negative behavior, which is a false assumption, and (2) it may have a damaging effect on the baby's emerging sense of self-worth. If a baby's action elicits a positive reaction, he feels good about his ability to communicate and have his needs met. He is further motivated to develop better communication skills with his responder, meaning that he is motivated to communicate with his caregiver in a noncrying way. When his action fails to elicit a response, he remains in his state of need and confusion and does not learn positive ways to control himself. We have questioned several hundred parents about how they respond to crying, and for the majority, the restraint approach does not work. But occasionally a parent will report, "It works—he stopped crying." Let's analyze the possible effects on the babies for whom this approach "works."

By not responding to your baby when he cries in the night, you are not really teaching your baby to sleep; you are teaching him that his form of communication is ineffective. He may fall back to sleep, but he has to withdraw from the disappointment (anger) of not being listened to. By not giving in to your baby, you are teaching your baby to give up. Is this a lesson you want your tiny child to learn?

Parents who have held themselves back from responding to their babies' cries often report that when they later pick up their babies, they feel the infants withdraw from them. They sense a feeling of "baby anger." What the babies are exhibiting and the parents are feeling is the disharmony that results when God's design for parent-infant response is ignored. (See "What Would Jesus Do?" box on page 37.)

RESPONDING AS A ROLE MODEL

Responding to your crying baby models a parenting style for your older children. How they see you parent a new baby has a great effect on their own future parenting styles.

The importance of modeling became evident to us one day many years ago. We were in the kitchen and heard our nine-month-old daughter, Erin, crying from our bedroom. As we started toward the bedroom, we heard her crying stop. When we reached the bedroom, we saw a beautiful sight: our sixteen-year-old son, Jim, was lying next to Erin, gentling and consoling her. Why was Jim doing this? Because he had learned from us that when a baby cries, someone listens. Now that he is a parent himself, he is able to sensitively respond to his little daughter without worrying that it might be the wrong thing to do. Through his openness to his child he has been able to learn appropriate ways of responding to her from infancy through her preschool years.

FATHER FEELINGS AND MOTHER-INFANT ATTACHMENT

Occasionally, fathers of infants share these feelings with Bill about their wives: "She's too attached"; "All she does is nurse"; "I feel left out"; "We need to get away alone." These are real feelings from real fathers who sincerely love their children but feel displaced by them. If you are a father who is feeling pushed aside, let us assure you that your feelings and your wife's attachment to your baby are very usual and very normal. Perhaps an understanding of God's design for mother-infant attachment and the changes that happen in your wife after birth will help you appreciate her apparent (and temporary) focus on your baby.

After a woman gives birth, her maternal hormones increase and stay at high levels for at least six months, during which time a woman's maternal urges take priority over her sexual interests. This shift of hormones is part of the divine design to ensure that the young get mothered. In addition, a new mother is often kept very busy by her responsibilities, and experiences the fatigue that comes with child care. On some days, she may feel drained by the incessant needs of her baby, so that by the time the baby is asleep, she just wants to be left alone. Mothers commonly describe this feeling as being "all touched out."

A new mother is programmed to be attached to her baby physically, chemically, and emotionally. This should not mean that the father is being displaced by his baby, but, rather, that much of the energy previously directed toward him is now being directed toward his infant. In time, this energy will be redirected toward the father. Let me (Bill) share with you something I have learned in my practice and in my own family: if you are a caring, involved, and supportive husband during this early attachment period, the sexual energy will return to you at a much higher level.

We call the early attachment period a "season" of the marriage, a season to nurture a new life. If the growth of this season is mutually tended with care, the season to be sexual will return with even more fulfillment in store. Wives need their husbands to be sensitive to these low energy times. Even though sexual intercourse may be the last thing your wife wants, "emotional intercourse" is very high on her list. What she really needs is to be held in your arms, with no pressure to go further. This must be genuine and you must be patient, loving, and kind, as only the Holy Spirit can enable. And husbands need their wives to remember that their sexual drive has not changed one bit. In fact, if anything it has increased. Seeing his wife go through childbirth increases a man's love for his wife, and that love for a man is expressed sexually. What he really needs is to be able to express his love and feel that you really want it. Be gracious enough to receive it, even though you can't find the energy to be as sexually responsive as you were before.

THE OVERATTACHMENT SYNDROME

God designed the family to function as a father-mother-child unit, not as a mother-child unit separate from the father. You should not have to choose between your marriage and your child. If both relationships are kept in perspective, both will operate on a higher level. A child should not divide a marriage; a child will be a catalyst to bring husband and wife closer together, if their marriage is God centered. And both relationships should benefit.

Here is a story about what we call the "overattachment syndrome." Mary and Tom had a reasonably good marriage, but as with most young couples, their relationship still needed a lot of maturing and a stronger foundation on Christ. After their baby arrived, Mary tried very hard to be a good mother. Tom was somewhat uncomfortable about handling babies, but he loved his little daughter very much. Mary sensed Tom's uneasy father feelings and was afraid to trust him to comfort the baby when she cried for fear he might upset the baby more. Tom felt more and more left out, and gradually they drifted down separate paths, Mary into her mothering and Tom into his work.

As Mary became more attached to the baby, Tom became more attached to his job and eventually made a few "attachments" of his own. Finally, Mary found herself in her pediatrician's office wondering why her marriage was disintegrating. "But I tried to be such a good mother," she said. "My baby needed me. I thought Tom was a big boy and could take care of himself." This scenario occurs when there is a breakdown in God's order for the family.

Watch out for "red flags" in the attachment relationship: Is there too much stress and is it causing a division in your marriage? Are you spending less and less time with each other? Is Dad working more and enjoying fathering less? Now is the time to do some "damage control"—come together and talk about the needs of each other that are going unmet. Don't discuss feelings; be concrete. Find out exactly what you each need, and decide how to deal with expectations. Remember, unmet expectations can get you into a deadly spiral of resentment and bitterness. Realize that what your baby needs most is two happy parents. Figure out how you can both stay happy and stay together. You may need a professional to help you do this.

FROM ONENESS TO SEPARATENESS

Timely separation is a very important concept. A child must be filled with a sense of oneness with the mother before he can develop separateness. A baby must first learn attachment before he can handle detachment. A baby must first have a strong identity with his mother before he can take on his own self-identity. The age at which babies go from oneness to separateness varies tremendously from baby to baby.

Going from oneness to separateness according to God's design enhances child development. When a baby is securely attached at one stage of development, he more easily progresses to the next stage of development. Eventually the natural desire for individuation stimulates the baby to begin to detach gradually from the mother. *It is important that the baby detach from the mother, not the mother from the baby.* For example, a toddler who is just learning to walk cruises farther and farther from his mother but periodically turns toward home base to check in. He feels secure as long as mother is there. However, if mother leaves during this separation-sensitive stage, the toddler might become less secure in exploring because homebase is gone. Dependence actually fosters independence as long as it happens according to the child's own timetable.

Realizing that healthy attachment makes separation easier is good protection against those who insist attachment parenting makes babies too dependent. Exactly the opposite is true. The baby who is the product of attachment parenting is actually less dependent later. Over the past twenty years, research has confirmed what mothers have intuitively known—that early attachment fosters later independence. (These scientific studies are summarized in the book *Growing Together.* See bibliography.) The way in which babies go from oneness to separateness has long been appreciated by writers of secular books on child care. Unfortunately, it has not been understood by many writers of Christian child care books.

If you are an attached mother, you will think very carefully about leaving your baby. You will probably experience some withdrawal symptoms the first time you leave your baby. How often and at what age a mother leaves her baby depend on many variables, including her own need to get away. You may honestly feel you need occasional relief. If you feel a need to be refilled by some outside interest, follow your desire—an empty mother is no good to anyone, especially her baby. Oftentimes your restlessness will not really mean you need to get away from your baby, but that you need a change of scenery. You may feel you're not the stay-at-home type. Consider taking your baby along. "Home" to a tiny baby is where her mother is; take your baby to church, to the mall, to adult parties. God's design is a bond, not bondage. When planning a time to be apart from your baby, ask yourself the following questions:

How separation-sensitive is your baby? Some babies separate more easily than others because of their individual temperaments (although it can also be because a close bond is lacking).

What is your baby's need level? High-need babies separate with difficulty; they are designed that way.

Who is the substitute caregiver? When you leave your baby, be sure to give explicit instructions on how you want your baby mothered in your absence. For example, tell the caregiver, "When she cries, I want you to pick her up immediately and comfort her." Show her how to use your baby carrier and ask her to use it rather than leave baby sitting in a swing or lying alone in a crib. If possible, try to leave your baby during her prime time,

WHICH URGE IS HEALTHY?

You see new mothers peering through the window the first time they've left their babies in the church nursery. They are not being overly possessive, which means keeping a baby from doing what he needs to do because of some personal need. They are simply being attached. If you are a new mother and you feel a continual urge to get away from your baby, we advise you to pray and seek counsel because very often this desire implies some departure from God's design. It is OK to enjoy being with your baby so much that you really have difficulty being away from him—although an occasional outing can be refreshing.

which is the mornings for most babies. Do not leave your baby during fussy times when she needs your nurturing. Use the same caregiver so that your baby can learn to trust just one other person.

THE REWARDS OF RESPONDING

Responding to your baby's needs is how your attachment grows. The sensitivity God gives you for responding helps your attachment unfold according to His design. Mothers grow more confident and babies grow more delightful. They both benefit as the attachment grows and then changes. The following is a description of Martha's experience with attachment.

> *Before birth, a mother and an infant are completely attached to each other. Birth brings a drastic change to their physical attachment, but in every other way the attachment only changes subtly and gradually over a period of two to three years. In some ways, such as emotionally and intellectually, the attachment actually increases. In other ways—functionally and biologically—the attachment takes new forms and gradually lessens.*
>
> *After birth, baby and mother need to remain physically together. Although the physical link between them is severed, the necessity for closeness is intense. The baby needs to be surrounded by familiarity, to be warmed, held, and suckled. The mother needs to be assured that the kicks she had become accustomed to on the inside are still there, and that the pregnancy she has "lost" is very surely "found" in the squirming newborn placed on her abdomen. She needs to envelop with her arms and drink in with her senses the feel, sight, sound, and smell of her newly-born child. She needs to marvel at the miracle God has wrought.*
>
> *In the first days after birth, the attachment shows itself in new ways. The slightest whimper, the subtlest change in breathing rhythm, or the least shifting of the little body brings the mother to immediate attention. She very quickly responds by drawing her baby close to her, and she feels a rightness flood over her body and mind. She sleeps with "one eye open" in case her baby needs her. If her baby is in a separate room for the night, she wakes often to listen. She finds she sleeps better when they stay together.*
>
> *As she goes about her daily routine, she keeps her baby on her body in a baby carrier. When one time she finds her week-old baby crying, she is disturbed that she was not right there when the baby needed her. This increases her vigilance and her desire that it not happen again while her baby is so small and needy. She learns to stay near baby when*

he naps, and that napping is what she needs to do anyway.

As the weeks pass, a pattern of attachment develops that is custom-made for this mother and her baby; it is a secret code known and trusted only by the two of them. The father knows and understands this attachment only in part by watching it unfold before him. He develops an attachment of his own to the baby, but it doesn't seem to ease the feeling he has sometimes of being left out of the inner circle around mother and baby. How good it is when he feels secure enough not to interfere with their closeness and not to feel threatened by it.

The father eventually becomes intrigued with the fine tuning he sees between his wife and their baby. "How did you know?" he'll ask, incredulous that such a subtle clue from the baby (indiscernible to himself) could be so completely and accurately understood by the baby's mother. The mother herself is amazed by her sixth sense about what her baby needs. He doesn't have to cry to let her know he wants to nurse or be picked up or shifted for a change of scene. The baby has a language of gestures, glances, and tiny noises that communicates his needs. The mother and baby are so close, so attached, that the baby seldom cries. The mother has learned to read her baby.

The attachment brings daily discoveries to the mother about herself and about her baby. For instance, she finds that if her baby takes an unusually long nap, she begins to yearn for her baby to wake up. She tingles with excitement when she finally notices that her baby is stirring awake; she has missed her baby and discovers how good it is to be reunited.

She makes another discovery in the church nursery, debating with herself whether or not to leave her baby for the first time. She watches other babies being handed over to the nursery workers and put into their assigned slots—one in a swing, one in a crib, one in an infant seat. She pictures herself handing her baby over and considers what instructions she will give. But it doesn't feel right. She watches for a while longer and feels a growing conviction that she should keep her baby with her. As she leaves the nursery with her baby still in her arms, she is relieved the separation hasn't happened.

More weeks go by, and she discovers that her baby has a finely developed sense of attachment in terms of measuring acceptable distances. As long as she is within touching distance or within seeing or hearing distance, the baby feels OK. The baby can tolerate lesser or greater amounts of distance between himself and mother, depending on the needs of the moment. Mother's constant availability enables her baby to develop a trusting nature.

As the baby gets older, the mother feels less urgency in responding to her baby's expressions of need. She feels OK about hurrying through a task, calling "Mama's coming," rather than dropping her work instantly to tend to the baby. Their attachment is now strong enough to handle a slight delay; the mother knows just how long the baby is able to wait before he pushes the panic button. And these panics rarely occur now that she has learned so much about her baby and about herself as a mother.

A major milestone has been reached, and there will be many others. The attachment that started out to be so total and so intense has changed and will change even more, but there will be one constant thread throughout: the mother and child have a bond that will last a lifetime; it will serve the divine order for both their lives. The mother will have nurtured and the baby will one day nurture others. Their attachment has given birth to human love for generations to come and has guaranteed the fulfillment of God's design for His children.

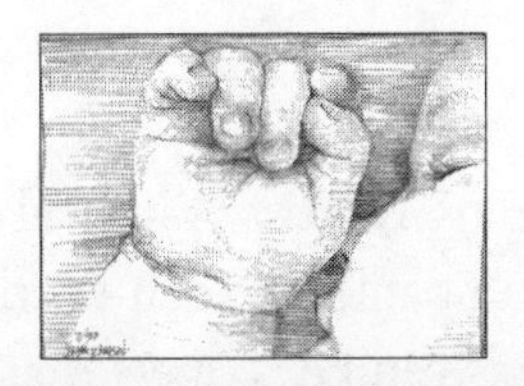

CHAPTER TEN

The Fussy **Baby**

(Alias the High-Need Child)

God blesses some parents with babies who are more difficult than others. These children are known by various titles, such as "fussy," "demanding," or "exhausting." As they grow older they acquire additional labels, such as "hyperactive" or "strong-willed." We prefer to call this kind of baby "the high-need child." This is not only a more positive term, but it more accurately describes what these children are like and the kind of parenting they need. You will know beyond a doubt if you have this kind of child. High-need babies challenge their parents' patience from morning to night. Since understanding increases acceptance, it is important to learn about why high-need babies fuss and why you react the way you do.

There is a wide range of temperaments among babies—happy, laid-back, busy, serious. Each baby comes not only with her unique temperament, but each has her own unique needs. Having parented eight very individual children, we have been intrigued with how God works so specifically in each one's life, depending on each one's temperaments and needs. Every baby, in one sense, is "high need" relative to other ages and stages in life. Yet some babies seem more highly needful than others, or at least they are able to express their needs more intensely. At any rate, each temperament is accompanied by specific needs. When these needs can be met, the rough edges of that temperament will be smoothed out and the child's entire personality enhanced. This is just as true for the quiet, "low-need" baby who needs to be held and stimulated as it is for the fussy, high-need baby who needs to be held and quieted. The variations are endless, just as God's creation is endlessly varied.

PROFILE OF A HIGH-NEED BABY

We have pulled from our gallery of high-need babies the following personality traits that mothers have shared with us about their babies.

"She is supersensitive." High-need babies are keenly aware of changes in their environments. Babies are endowed with stimulus barriers that allow them to filter out disturbing stimuli and receive pleasant experiences selectively. This process helps them adapt to their environment. In sensitive babies, the stimulus barrier is more permeable, and more sounds, sights, and touches bother them. They startle easily during the day and settle with difficulty at night. These babies need their parents to provide the security and stimulus barriers they cannot provide for themselves.

"I just can't put him down; he wants to be held all the time." High-need babies crave physical contact and are not known for their self-soothing abilities. New parents often expect that their babies will lie quietly in their cribs, amuse themselves with dangling mobiles, and gaze with interest at whatever comes into view. Realistically, few babies are like this, and this is certainly not the play profile of the high-need baby. These babies are often content only in their parents' arms and at their mothers' breasts.

"She is so intense." Fussy babies put a lot of energy into their behavior. They feel things more intensely and express their feelings more forcefully. They cry with gusto and are quick to protest if their needs are not met. They seem to have tightly wound springs connecting all their parts.

"He wants to nurse all the time." The term "feeding schedule" is not in this baby's vocabulary. He needs prolonged periods of comfort sucking and he does not wean easily.

"She is stiff and uncuddly." While most babies mold easily into the arms of caregivers, some high-need babies arch their backs and stiffen their arms and legs in protest at any attempt to cuddle them. Their muscles are tight (hypertonic), and they need help getting their bodies under control.

"He awakens frequently." A tired mother lamented, "Why do high-need babies need more of everything but sleep?" These babies carry their general sensitivity into their

naptime and nighttime. They seem to be constantly on the alert, as if they never turn their lights off, even during sleep. Parents often describe their special babies as "tiring, but bright." This brightness keeps high-need babies awake.

"She is unpredictable." Unpredictability is another behavior trait of these special babies. High-need babies are hard to appease. What works one day often does not work the next. One exhausted father exclaimed, "Just as I think I have the game won, she ups the ante."

"He is demanding." High-need babies are certainly demanding. Their signals have a sense of urgency. "Red alerts" dominate their crying vocabulary. They cannot wait and do not readily accept alternatives. They are quick to protest if their needs are not met or if their cues have been misread. Their incessant demands lead to a common complaint from their parents: "I feel drained."

This profile of the high-need baby may appear to be predominantly negative, but it is only part of the story of parenting these special babies. Parents who practice the attachment style of parenting and who seek out the support of like-minded parents struggling with similar difficulties gradually begin to see their babies in a different light and use more positive descriptions such as "challenging," "interesting," and "bright." Parents of high-need babies need to realize that the qualities that at first seem to be liabilities are likely to become assets for their children. The intense baby may become the creative child; the sensitive infant becomes the compassionate child; and the little "taker" becomes a big "giver."

THE NEED-LEVEL CONCEPT

A high-need baby can bring out the best and the worst in a parent. Part of the divine design for the parent-child relationship is what we call the "need-level concept," a way of understanding how parent and child are designed to fit. High-need babies call for a high level of parenting—a level that these parents may have to stretch themselves to provide.

Every baby comes wired with a certain temperament that is determined in large part by genetics and is influenced somewhat by the womb environment. That temperament will go on to be influenced by the caregiving environment. The child needs a level of care that is matched to his temperament in order to fit well into his environment. Some babies need a higher level of care than others. To get the level of care he needs, a baby has the ability to give cues to signal his needs. Some babies are able to give stronger cues than other babies. In the divine design, high-need babies come wired with the ability to extract from their caregiving environments the kind of care that will satisfy their needs.

For example, a baby who needs to be carried all the time will cry if he is not carried enough. He is demanding the care he needs.

Parents can view the term *demanding* as a positive character trait that will benefit their baby's development. If a baby were endowed with high needs yet lacked the corresponding ability to communicate her needs, her developmental potential would be threatened and her emerging self-image would be in jeopardy. We feel that God made high-need babies demanding so that they will get the level of care needed to reach their maximum potential.

How does a parent handle the incessant demands from a high-need baby? In God's design for this need-level concept, the baby's signals bring out the nurturing responses of his parents. As babies come wired with certain temperaments, mothers also possess certain nurturing abilities. For some mothers, nurturing proportionate to their babies' needs develops easily. For others, nurturing is not so automatic and the response needs time to mature. We do not believe God would give parents a baby with greater needs than they can meet, with His help. The Scripture verse that comes to mind here is 1 Corinthians 10:13. We like the way Eugene Peterson says it in *The Message:* "No test or temptation that comes your way is beyond the course of what others have had to face. All you need to remember is that God will never let you down; he'll never let you be pushed past your limit; he'll always be there to help you come through it."

WISDOM FOR PARENTING THE FUSSY BABY

Whole books have been written on this subject. There is much to learn, and we heartily suggest you read at least one (see bibliography). The kernels of wisdom that follow can make the difference between "barely surviving" and thriving.

Don't Feel Guilty

Many new mothers think, "What am I doing wrong?" or "I'm not a good mother" when their babies are fussy. Babies fuss because of their own temperaments, not because of their mothers' abilities. Of course, there is more than temperament that will cause a baby to fuss. We will discuss physical causes in the baby, and explore ways that an inexperienced mother can learn to help her fussy baby manage life.

Your fussy baby can shake your confidence as a new mother and absolutely destroy many of the rewarding aspects of parenting. The less confident you are, the less effective you are at comforting your baby, and the more inconsolable he becomes. This can leave you feeling like you want to escape, a normal reaction as an attempt to relieve your guilt and preserve your sanity. But "escape mothering" breaks the need-response continuum of parenting and will prevent you from getting in harmony with your baby. You need a more effective way to deal with your feelings.

Remember, your responsibility is not to make your baby stop crying—your responsibility is to comfort him to the best of your ability, seeking any means that can help until things get better. Your baby may still cry, but you are responding and you are not leaving him to cry alone. You can feel good about yourself for sticking it out when the going gets tough. Your baby needs you to be strong and to be there for him while he learns how to accept comfort. He doesn't need you to hush him frantically just because his crying is aggravating or upsetting you or making you feel ineffective as a parent.

Try to pinpoint how your baby's crying makes you feel—desperate, helpless, panicky, or angry. Try to discover why you are feeling this way. Your anguish of heart may be rooted in very early pain you experienced when you might have been left alone a lot, to "cry it out." Or, it may have something to do with your feelings about yourself right now. Take a deep breath, pray, and ask the Lord to heal the hurt inside of you. Then, carry on with comforting.

Our hearts go out to mothers who hang tough in the compassionate care of their fussy babies. Their rewards will be great both on earth and in heaven.

Learn to Accept Your Blessing

Parents of fussy babies need to develop a high level of acceptance. In counseling parents of fussy babies, we often start with, "You have been blessed with . . ." Quite frankly, by the time many parents come in for counseling they feel anything but blessed and truly wish that God had blessed someone else.

Parents, you have been blessed if you have a high-need baby. God has blessed you with a special child, and He will help you become special parents. In many instances, our Creator matches the temperaments of mothers and babies so that a fussy baby has a mother with a high level of acceptance. Occasionally, a family may have a fussy baby and a mother with a low level of acceptance. This tough situation needs much prayer and consultation in order for mother and baby to find a way to fit. Your level of giving will increase when you pray for strength to fulfill the conditions that allow God's design to work, using the attachment style of parenting, and being responsive to your baby's cries. Remember, you wouldn't have this baby if God didn't know you could rise to the challenge. One mother said to us, "Yes, sometimes God matches a high-need baby with a mother with a high level of acceptance. And sometimes He matches one with a mother in whom He wants to develop it. I genuinely believe that was the case with me."

Have Realistic Expectations

Fussiness is often in the eyes of the beholder. We often refer new parents who feel they have a fussy baby to parents who have coped successfully with a fussy child. After meeting with these parents, the new parents often exclaim, "Praise the Lord, we don't have a fussy baby after all." Prenatal expectations of what babies are like are often not realistic. When parents understand more about infant behavior and let go of their preconceptions about parenting, they can better accept their own baby.

Parents of fussy babies often feel disappointed that they don't enjoy their babies. Parents can resort to prayer, support, and counseling to help them adjust, but babies have no recourse but their parents. They need their parents to accept them, enjoy them, and focus on them, not the problem.

Don't compare babies. A mother of a high-need baby may feel something like this: "Why can't I handle my baby? Other mothers seem more in control of their babies. They can leave them and get other things done; I can't." We advise this mother not to compare her baby with other babies. Those other mothers may not share her views on attachment parenting. And high-need babies are not "better" or "worse" than other babies—just *different.* Besides, many people tend to exaggerate the goodness of their babies. Comparing babies contributes nothing to your relationship with your baby and will contribute to frustration and burnout. It is common to have both easy and high-need babies in the same family. Our first three babies were relatively easy, our fourth was high-need. We had to "throw out the books" and start fresh—in fact, this baby inspired Bill to write a book on the subject: *The Fussy Baby.* (See bibliography. See also our newer book: *Parenting the Fussy Baby and High-Need Child.)*

Don't Let Your Baby Cry

One of the most common dilemmas of parents, especially parents of fussy babies, is whether or not to let their babies cry. This problem is thoroughly explored in chapter 9, but let us remind you of a few points right here: Young babies do not cry to annoy, to manipulate, or to take advantage of their parents. They cry because they have needs. To ignore their cries is to ignore their needs.

A fussy baby is endowed with a high-need level and a low stimulus barrier. He needs help with learning to fit into his environment. Whether or not he learns to trust in his environment is one of the prime determinants of his eventual personality. An infant who does not receive a predictable response to his signals soon learns not to trust himself and not to trust his caregivers. He may eventually become less motivated to cry and will stop, but at what expense to his self-image and his relationship with his parents? In this situation, a high-need baby completely resigns himself to a lower level of care.

Yes, babies are adaptable and resilient. Praise the Lord for having made them so; otherwise neither babies nor parents would survive childrearing. Yet babies whose cries fall upon deaf ears turn their outward anxieties inward and experience behavior problems or emotional difficulties later on. Not being responded to causes terror, whereas response is experienced as love. Babies who are left to cry become insecure, angry babies and even angrier children who can't feel loved, no matter how much the parents may have love for them. Parents tend to think the child should know he is loved, but they have to communicate in a way that makes sure the child knows it.

Gentle Your Fussy Baby

Our first fussy baby was not fussy—as long as someone was holding her. She was, in fact, a delightful baby—as long as she didn't feel alone. Most fussy babies are calmed in two ways: with motion and with physical contact. These forms of behavior modification use the "principle of competing behavior." When you gentle your fussy baby, you try to override your baby's tense behavior with your gentle behavior. To comfort the fussy baby you must determine what type of motion and physical contact she likes and needs and how much of this you can give without exhausting your parental energy. (Call in the reserves if you need to.)

Experiment to find out what comforts your baby the most. Most babies prefer bare skin-to-skin contact. Some babies need almost constant stroking and patting, and they enjoy being left undressed. Other babies enjoy the security of being swaddled and held firmly but quietly. Others need swaddling and bouncing. Experiment with which position your baby likes to be held in: bent over your shoulder; upright against your chest; tummy down across your knee; held up facing you, one hand on her back and the other hand on her bottom looking into her eyes while you sing to her and move rhythmically; or draped (stomach down) over your arm, your hand firmly under her pelvis and her head nestled snugly by the bend of your elbow.

After a while you will develop your own type of "colic carry." Our fussy babies liked Bill to hold them in the "neck nestle": firmly up against his chest, with head turned to one side and nestled under dad's chin, while he swayed rhythmically from side to side, singing a low-pitched lullaby.

The combination of skin-to-skin contact, the baby's ear over your heart, your breathing movements, and your total body rhythm often will soothe a fussy baby. A mechanical baby swing can be useful, but be careful not to overuse it and let it become a parent substitute.

During the first few months of comforting your fussy baby, you will log many miles of walking, rocking, floor pacing, dancing, pram pushing, and so on. When all else fails, place your baby in a car seat and take a ride. This often works. But there are some babies who cannot tolerate being in a car seat for very long.

Baby carriers are ideal for calming a fussy baby, especially the sling-type carrier in which you can hold your baby facing forward and bent at the hips, which helps relax his tense abdomen (see "Babywearing," p. 243). Within a few tiring weeks or months, your baby will have told you what mode of transportation he likes best. Another "soother" is a sound and rhythm that mimics mother's heartbeat, something he was accustomed to *in utero,* such as a metronome set at seventy-five beats per minute, a recording of a heartbeat (available commercially), or the ticktock of an old alarm clock. Water sounds help babies relax. Try letting your faucet or the shower run. If it works, get a tape recording of running water. The sounds of water fountains are the best.

Relax the Mother and the Baby

A fussy baby can shatter the nerves of even the most shatterproof mother. Relax by whatever method works. Here are some relaxation tips:

1. *Breastfeeding will usually soothe a fussy baby,* but sometimes even that doesn't work. If your baby refuses your breast and does not stop fussing, your baby may be signaling that he wants to lie down with you in bed and nurse, snuggled in your arms. In our family this has been a successful technique.

2. *Take a warm bath with your baby.* Recline in the bathtub and fill the tub to just below breast level. Let your baby partially float while he is nursing; this ritual can sooth you both.

3. *Get outdoor exercise.* A long, brisk walk with your baby in a carrier or pushed in a springy carriage can be a daily calming ritual for a tense mother and fussy baby. One therapist recommends a brisk two-hour walk in the morning and another one in the afternoon, for as long as baby is difficult to manage.

4. *Find time for yourself.* Sometimes when your baby sleeps, take the phone off the hook and have a private, relaxing time doing something just for you. Spending time reading God's Word is a real lift. All

give with no refilling wears very thin after a while, even for the most caring and giving parent. You can't give when your own energy and emotional reserves are depleted. Remember, what your baby needs most is a happy, rested mother.

Plan Ahead

You will spend a lot of time with baby at your breast since high-need babies have a high need for sucking. Comfort sucking is what gets a lot of young babies (and their mothers) through the day. Have one or two comfortable places set up in your home where you will enjoy sitting with your baby for long stretches of time. Have pillows and a footrest, a good book and the Good Book, the telephone, some nutritious snacks, a beverage, and some water (you'll get thirsty), and the things you'll need for baby if he spits up. Have some relaxing music on, perhaps some praise and worship songs. Avoid watching TV—there is very little on that will nurture you. Choose some of your favorite old videos that you know are not stressful. Humor is a wonderful companion; put on something that will make you laugh. Enjoy this time of sitting in your nest. Your baby will pick up on your good mood and you'll both be happier.

Most babies have their best and their worst times of day, although being unpredictable is one of the hallmarks of a fussy baby. Most babies have some pattern of daily fussiness. Plan ahead and use your baby's best time for fun activities and giving attention to your other children, to yourself, and to your spouse. Some mothers use quiet time in the morning to prepare the evening meal. Most babies have their main fussy periods from 4:00 P.M. to 8:00 P.M. If you've accomplished most of your daily duties by this time, you can settle down during the fussy period and devote most of your energy to comforting your baby. And make sure you haven't taken on too many daily duties while baby is very young.

Lean on Your Support Groups

You may reach a point in caring for your fussy baby when you need more support than advice. Surround yourself with supportive people and avoid the advice of the "let your baby cry" and "you're getting too attached" crowd. To get the most out of your support group you must honestly share your feelings. Parenting is a guilt-producing profession. Nearly all parents at some time have the feeling of "I am not doing a good job." If you have a low acceptance level of your baby's crying and have reached the end of your rope, say so.

Many sincere and caring mothers have had momentary thoughts of *I hate my baby,* or *I feel like I am being had.* If you confide these normal feelings to other parents who have survived and thrived with fussy babies, you will probably receive the following comments: "It's OK to have these feelings"; "You are not being taken advantage of"; "You are not spoiling him"; "You are doing the most important job in the world—raising a human being." Finding these like-minded parents to talk with is worth the effort you may have to make. One mother in our practice put a notice up on our bulletin board announcing her desire to find women to talk with. La Leche League meetings are a good place to meet women who are supportive of attachment parenting. *The Nurturing Parent* is a journal published "to encourage healthy parent-child relationships through attachment parenting practices." Not only are the articles supportive to parents of a high-need

JOIN A CHRISTIAN SUPPORT GROUP

A mother in Bill's practice started a small morning Bible study in her home for mothers of high-need babies. (The babies attended too of course. Martha attended with Erin, baby number five.) Our support group was based on the theory that if we remained in harmony with God, we would remain in harmony with our children. The following verses were our favorite ones to commit to memory.

2 Chronicles 15:7	"But as for you, be strong and do not give up, for your work will be rewarded."
Proverbs 3:5–6	"Trust in the LORD with all your heart and lean not on your own understanding; in all your ways acknowledge him, and he will make your paths straight."
Philippians 4:13	"I can do everything through him who gives me strength."
Isaiah 40:31	"But those who hope in the LORD will renew their strength. They will soar on wings like eagles; they will run and not grow weary, they will walk and not be faint."
1 Thessalonians 5:16–18	"Be joyful always; pray continually; give thanks in all circumstances, for this is God's will for you in Christ Jesus."
1 Peter 5:7	"Cast all your anxiety on him because he cares for you."

child, *The Nurturing Parent* also helps families network by having a list of parents available who are interested in meeting one another to support and encourage. Contact *The Nurturing Parent,* 303 E. Gurley St., Suite 260, Prescott, AZ 86301, (800) 810-8401, e-mail: letters@TheNurturingParent.com or www.TheNurturingParent.com.

SOME PHYSICAL CAUSES OF YOUR BABY'S FUSSINESS

Although some babies fuss primarily because of their own temperaments and not because of any physical problems, pain-producing problems or disturbing stimuli in a baby's environment often account for fussiness. Discovering these takes a lot of detective work by the baby's parents and a physical examination by his pediatrician. If your baby's doctor can't find a cause, you should get more opinions. Some of the more common causes of pain or discomfort in young babies are listed here.

1. *Is your baby hungry?* See chapter 6 to troubleshoot this cause.

2. *Is your environment too busy?* Birth is a social event that often brings a long line of well-wishers into the home of tired parents and a baby who may not be ready to be a socialite. Some babies fuss because of overstimulation: too many people, noise from the TV, overly-excited older siblings. Surprisingly, some babies actually enjoy a busy environment and settle better when there is a lot of noise.

3. *Check for environmental irritants,* such as cigarette smoke, perfumes, hairsprays, cleaning products that give off a strong odor, or irritating noises.

4. *Does your baby have an illness?* Ear infection, throat infection, eye irritation, constipation, hernia, and irritating rash are things that would cause a previously comfortable baby to have pain. (See chapter 11, "Common Concerns of Infancy.")

5. *Does your baby have colic?* If you're wondering if baby's fussiness is colic, it's probably not. The gut-wrenching, agonized outbursts of prolonged, inconsolable crying leave no doubt. Around 20 percent of babies have some almost daily bouts of crying during the early months. A medical rule of three's says that a baby has colic if the crying:

   - lasts at least three hours a day, occurs at least three days of the week, and continues for at least three weeks;
   - begins within three weeks after birth;
   - seldom lasts longer than three months;
   - occurs in an otherwise healthy, thriving baby.

The typical colicky baby cries from intense physical discomfort, draws his legs up onto a tense, gas-filled abdomen, and clenches his fists as if he were angry about the spasms of pain racking his small body. Parents often feel helpless. What to do?

First, do everything you can to find the cause of your baby's hurting (see next section). Once you understand the possible cause, it is easier to understand how to help your baby. Review the earlier sections in this chapter entitled: "Gentle Your Fussing Baby" and "Relax the Mother and the Baby."

Massaging your hurting baby's abdomen can help move the gas through or relax the spasms. Start by warming her tummy with warm washcloths or a heating pad set on low. Then use your flattened hand to stroke in the direction of the large intestine, starting at the lower right of the abdomen, massaging up, over, and down, over and over again. Using baby oil or unscented massage oil will help your hand move more smoothly. Use a firm stroke and do it rhythmically. This is only effective if it helps baby relax. One unorthodox way we've heard of to get a screaming baby to stop long enough for you to do this is to play back a tape recording of your baby's screaming. He hears it, stops to listen, and then may be able to let you massage or cuddle.

Causes of colic. There are two physical causes and one other cause of colic to consider:

1. *Your baby could be intolerant of a substance in your milk or the formula.* Suspect a digestive problem when your baby's fussiness is accompanied by a hard, tense abdomen, legs drawn up in pain, or screaming and pulling back from the breast or bottle. If you are formula feeding, ask your doctor to recommend a less allergenic formula. If you're breastfeeding, the following items in your diet could cause baby's fussiness (in order of frequency):

a. milk and milk products

b. caffeine-containing substances taken in excess—coffee, tea, colas, and chocolate, and some medicines

c. gas-producing raw vegetables—broccoli, cabbage, onions, green peppers, and beans

d. citrus fruits or juice, or even too much apple juice

e. eggs

f. medicines

g. decongestants, cold remedies, and prenatal vitamins containing iron

Anything in your diet could be causing trouble. Consider wheat, corn, nuts, shellfish, tomatoes. Keep a record of what you are eating to help track down the offending foods. If you suspect any of these offenders, eliminate the suspected foods for a period of at least two weeks. Sometimes it is a

AN ELIMINATION DIET

Another approach to tracking down problem foods is to restrict your diet to the foods most easily tolerated in each food group. For two weeks you eat only the following foods: range-fed turkey, lamb, rice, millet, plain potato or yam, green and yellow squash, pears, and pear juice. These foods are rarely the cause of sensitivity. Use a rice-based beverage instead of milk and use a calcium supplement. If your baby's behavior improves while you are on this restricted diet, you have reason to believe that sensitivity to something in your diet is the problem. After baby improves, reintroduce foods one at a time into your diet, watching your baby's reaction.

It helps if you keep a written record of what you eat and baby's behavior. If certain foods seem to provoke fussiness, eliminate them from your diet for the next several months. This is based on work done by Dr. William Crook. Read his book *Detecting Your Hidden Allergies* (see bibliography) if you want more help. We have personal experience with the effectiveness of this diet. Both our sixth baby, Matthew, and our granddaughter, Lea, responded to it within a day or two when they were just a few weeks old and suffering from colic. A word of caution, however, when you need this diet in the early weeks postpartum—there is not enough fiber, so if you have hemorrhoids, use a bulk-forming product like psyllium husk to keep your stools soft but which won't get into your breastmilk to bother baby. Drinking lots of water also helps avoid constipation.

combination of several foods that is causing problems. Consider following the "Elimination Diet" (see box, above).

2. *Your baby could have gastroesophageal reflux (GER).* This occurs when the angle between the stomach and the esophagus is shallow or the valve is floppy, allowing milk to be pushed back up and regurgitated. This is what happens when babies spit up, but it usually doesn't cause pain. Sometimes GER is more serious; irritating stomach acids are regurgitated into the esophagus, causing heartburn-like pain. This occurs more in the horizontal position, accounting for greater pain when baby is laying flat. This is why babies feel better when upright, and why they need to be held constantly.

Symptoms of GER include: frequent bouts of painful crying; spitting up after feeding, sometimes forcefully through the nose (but some refluxing only comes partway up); painful night waking (but some babies are exhausted from crying all day, so they sleep well at night); in pain after feeding—legs drawn up, arching, or writhing; less pain when held upright and when sleeping prone (on stomach) on a thirty-degree incline; frequent colds, wheezing, chest infections; stop-breathing episodes.

GER can be diagnosed by testing the pH levels in baby's esophagus. If GER is evident from baby's symptoms, your doctor may choose to begin treatment without doing the test. In most babies, it lessens by six months and subsides by one year. Some children continue to need treatment, or are not even diagnosed, until later.

Treatment for GER is as follows:

- Place baby stomach down on a thirty degree incline for thirty minutes after feeding and while sleeping. A special sling is available for this purpose from Tucker Designs Ltd., P. O. Box 641117, Kenner, LA 70064, (504) 464-7479. Or hold baby upright for 30 minutes after feeding.
- Feed rice cereal during or after breastfeeding, or add it to the formula, to thicken what's in the stomach.
- Offer smaller, more frequent feeds (milk acts as an antacid).
- Use medication to neutralize stomach acids or accelerate their passing from the stomach.
- Wear your baby to decrease crying (see p. 243). Babies reflux more when crying.

3. *Your baby's colic could be caused by a combination of disorganized biorhythms and a very sensitive temperament.* This would be a neuro-developmental problem rather than an intestinal problem. Babies who have a supersensitive, intense, disorganized, slow-to-adapt temperament have what we term a *colic tendency.* Whether or not this tendency escalates into colicky behavior depends, to some extent, on the caregiving environment baby meets.

Biorhythms are internal master clocks that automatically secrete regulating hormones and govern our daily changes of body temperature and sleep-wake cycles. Some babies enter the world organized and expect their caregiving environment to keep them organized. Other babies enter the world with disorganized biorhythms; we say they are unsettled. Failure to become organized or stay organized results in a behavior change we call "colic." Instead of fussing all the time, babies can store up a day's worth of tension and release it in one long evening blast. New research is just beginning to uncover a hormonal basis for colic behavior in babies. Until we have more answers, we simply have to continue giving babies what they need, lots of holding and nurturing.

THE FUSSY FAMILY

Having a fussy baby can become a problem for the whole family. You will expend so much energy comforting your baby that you may have little energy left for the needs of your spouse or other children. It is difficult to be a loving spouse or parent to your older children when you are emotionally and physically drained day after day.

The next statement will not set well with some mothers: most Christian writers agree that God's order of priorities is God, marriage, children, job, and church activities. It is difficult for many devoted mothers to put their marriage relationship before their children, especially when a baby has so many needs.

With prayer and consultation this does not have to be an either/or decision. Parenting a fussy baby is a family affair. Both parents must work together to convey love and comfort to their baby and to each other. The fussy baby demands shared parenting. If a mother finds she has no time left for her husband, she can look closely at what other things (besides the baby) take her time and then make some changes. Time with her husband is more important than housework. It is easy for parents of a fussy baby to experience burnout early in their parenting profession and in their marriage. Wives, keep a few channels of your communication network open for your husbands. Husbands, be sensitive to your wives. The single best support system for a fussy baby is a healthy Christian marriage.

HOW TO AVOID MOTHER BURNOUT

"I feel trapped"; "I can't cope, but I have to"; "I can't handle this any longer"; "I'm not enjoying motherhood." These are quotes from Christian mothers who have shared their mothering difficulties and feel they are burning out.

What Is Burnout?

Burnout is a collection of symptoms very much like those discussed in the section on postpartum depression (see chapter 5). It happens when a mother's reserves are totally exhausted and she is experiencing an increasing lack of fulfillment in the mothering profession. Burnout also stems from chronic disenchantment, a feeling that motherhood is not all it is cracked up to be. In fact, some mothers think they are cracking up just being mothers. Throughout Scripture, children are presented as being a joy to parents, not a burden. When a mother reaches burnout, there has been some fundamental breakdown in God's design for the joy in the parent-child relationship.

What Causes Mother Burnout?

The most common cause of mother burnout is the isolation that plagues today's mothers. Never before in history have mothers been required or expected to do so much alone with little or no support. Today's society is caught up in the supermom myth. Shortly after giving birth, the new mother is expected to resume her previous roles as impeccable housekeeper, loving and giving wife, gourmet cook, gracious hostess, and contributor to the family income. Few mothers today are allowed the luxury in the first few weeks and months after birth of following God's design—mothering as a first priority and all else following when time and energy permit. Today's women often enter motherhood with confusing role models, inadequate prenatal preparation, unrealistic expectations of what babies are like, a lack of coping skills to handle the babies they get, and very little support from experienced mothers.

Mothers burn out when too many demands are placed on them that divert their energy away from the baby, or when they do not have a supportive environment that allows intuitive mothering to flourish.

Are babies to blame for mother burnout? It is true that a high-need baby places more strain on the mother. However, the causes of burnout can usually be found in some other interfering influence that has thrown off God's law of supply and demand, so that the mother is not supplied with the energy she needs to cope with her high-need baby.

Mothers who experience burnout shouldn't feel guilty or feel they are not good mothers. In fact, burnout is more likely to occur in highly motivated mothers. Women who strive to be good mothers or who have expectations for themselves in many roles are most likely to burn out. Mothers who are attracted to attachment parenting are good candidates for burnout. A person first has to be on fire in order to be burned out.

WHAT TO DO TO AVOID BURNOUT

Have Realistic Expectations

During your pregnancy, become involved in a support group that can help you develop realistic expectations of what babies are like. La Leche is good for this, and we recommend that mothers attend a series of four meetings prenatally. Most new parents do not realize how a new baby will absolutely dominate their lives and completely change their previously predictable and organized schedules. A common complaint pediatricians hear when tired couples come for their babies' two-week checkup is, "Nobody prepared me for this."

Encourage Father Involvement

We have rarely seen a case of early mother burnout in a home in which the father (or someone) "mothered" the mother and created an atmosphere in the home to allow God's design of attachment parenting to flourish. In most homes suffering from later mother burnout, the mothers did not recognize the signs of burnout and did not call for help, and the fathers were insensitive to their wives' impending trouble.

Fathers, be sensitive to early warning signs and risk factors. Don't wait for your wife to tell you she hates motherhood, since wives do not usually confide these negative feelings to their husbands, perhaps because they do not want to shatter their husband's image of them as the perfect mother. As one exhausted mother complained, "I'd have to pass out in front of my husband before he would realize how tired I really am."

Burnout is common when things get out of balance. Mother immerses herself in meeting the needs of her child and tries her best to mother according to God's design. Father, because he feels shaky handling his baby (and also feels his wife is becoming too attached) withdraws and retreats to interests away from home that he can control more easily.

A high-need child, a burning-out mother, and a withdrawing father make up the situation with the highest potential for a total family burnout. It is also the situation with the highest potential for a marriage burnout. If mother shuts father out, father may form outside attachments of his own, and the whole family eventually may fall apart.

Practice Attachment Parenting

With time and commitment, attachment parenting helps you develop harmony with your baby, increases your perseverance level, helps you know and have more realistic expectations of your baby's behavior, and generally helps you enjoy your baby more. Enjoying your baby is important because it seems to have a snowballing effect on your acceptance level and your self-confidence. A detached style of parenting, on the other hand, often leads to chronic disenchantment with the whole parenting role, mainly because of the distance that develops between parents and children.

Many mothers facing burnout are encouraged to start letting their babies cry, to get away from their babies, not to be so involved. In our experience, this may bring short-term gain, but it produces a long-term loss. It is usually not separation from the baby that the mother needs; it is a complete overhaul of her support system to minimize the competing influences that drain her energy. She also needs to find other ways to boost her sense of self-worth.

Know Your Tolerance Levels

Just as there are wide variations in temperaments of babies, there are wide variations in the tolerance levels of mothers. Some mothers seem to have high acceptance levels that allow them to parent a bunch of kids and function like a human gymnasium all day long. Other mothers have lower acceptance levels and have more difficulty coping with the constant demands of small children, especially in the toddler age group. As one mother of a newborn and a two-year-old put it, "I feel like I'm still pregnant with our two-year-old." If you already have a high-need baby and are having difficulty coping, pray about the spacing of your children. Ask God for His wisdom in this area of your life. He knows your limits even better than you do.

Many mothers continue to operate on their energy reserves too long before seeking help. If you find you are reaching the upper limits of your tolerance level, seek counseling now. Then you can make some necessary changes in your family situation to bring the demands on you in line with what you can tolerate. One mother of a high-need child, frustrated by not measuring up to all that was expected of her, gave this illustration: "My life is a circle revolving around my child, but I need a square around it with some corners left just for me."

It's important to find a counselor who understands and supports attachment parenting. If you can't find one in your area whom you can work with in person, you can locate one through a referral service offered by *The Nurturing Parent* (see "Lean on Your Support Groups," p. 229). Call their order line (1-800-810-8401) and request the free counselor referral sheet, leaving your name and address on the voice mail. They will include names of both Christian and secular counselors who do phone work.

Join Forces

One way you can carve out a little space for yourself, and keep your baby with you as you accomplish this, is to join forces with another woman who has a baby close in age to your baby, and perhaps is also high need. Start spending time together in each other's home (two, three, even four times a week) doing things you enjoy or things you want to get done. Cook together, clean together, do projects, pray, relax, play with your babies. Go out shopping together, to the park, to the movies (babies usually nurse off to sleep when they are little). Spend time on weekends as couples if your husbands enjoy one another. The friendship you will build, and the relationship your babies will have as they grow together, will be a priceless gift you may not have had if it were not for your "fussy babies." Most importantly, you will not be getting through this challenging time alone. You will have a sister you can count on to understand when things get rough and who can help out if you need her. And once the babies are a little older they will be so attached to each other's moms that she and you will be able to baby-sit for one another. Run, do not walk, to find this woman.

Define Priorities

Mothers of high-need children often say, "But I get nothing done." You *are* getting something done, something important. You just don't receive the gratification of seeing instant results. One day a mother looked at her kitchen floor and woke up: "That floor doesn't have feelings. No one's life is going to be affected if that floor is not scrubbed every day. My baby is a baby for a very short time, and she has feelings." A wise mother determines just what needs to be done. And many days what really needs to be done is to stay peaceful and pleasant so that you can accurately reflect God to your little one.

RISK FACTORS FOR BURNOUT

The following checklist can help mothers avoid burnout. Mothers, can you identify any risk factors you may have that predispose you to mother burnout?

1. Do you have a history of difficulty coping with combined stresses? (This is discussed in the section on risk factors for postpartum depression, chapter 5.)
2. During your pregnancy, did you have ambivalent feelings about how your child would interfere with your current lifestyle?
3. Were you involved in a high-recognition career before you became a mother?
4. Did you have poor mothering role models from your own mother?
5. Did you make inadequate prenatal preparation, or did you have unrealistic expectations about how easy it is to care for babies?
6. Did fear and pain predominate during your labor and delivery? Did you have a generally negative birthing experience that was not what you expected?
7. Were you and your baby separated for several hours after birth?
8. Is yours a high-need baby?

RISK FACTORS FOR BURNOUT (CONT.)

9. Is there a mismatch of temperaments? You have a high-need baby, but you have a low level of acceptance.
10. Is there a lack of harmony in your marriage? Did you hope that a baby might solve your marital problems?
11. Does your baby have an uninvolved father?
12. Are you highly motivated and compulsive? Do you strive to be the perfect mother?
13. Are you an overcommitted mother with too many outside priorities?
14. Have there been too many changes too fast, such as moving, extensive remodeling, or redecorating, to upset your nesting instinct?
15. Is there a medical illness in mother, father, or baby?
16. Do you have financial pressures?
17. Are you becoming confused by conflicting parenting advice?
18. Are your babies closely spaced, that is, less than two years apart?

If you answer yes to several of these questions, you should take steps to guard against burnout and be ready to recognize it if it happens. When Bill sees a mother in his office whom he feels is at risk for burnout, he places a red star at the top of her baby's chart, signifying a red alert that this mother is on her way to burning out unless preventive steps are taken. We urge husbands, pastors, friends, relatives, and health care professionals to also be on the lookout for these red flags.

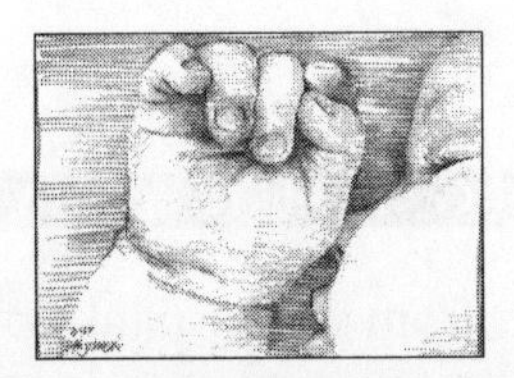

CHAPTER ELEVEN

Common Concerns of **Infancy**

Love for your baby will generate a long list of concerns for your baby's welfare. In this chapter we have addressed all the nuts and bolts of infant care, from what you have to buy to what you may worry about. You'll turn here first when you can't remember what they told you in the hospital about bathing baby or diaper rash. This will be the chapter you turn to most often in the middle of the night when baby seems sick and you wonder if you should call your doctor. First-time parents will find this chapter hard to put down. It will be intriguing to read and tempting to memorize. Enjoy learning how to care for your precious little charge.

YOUR BABY'S BELONGINGS

Parents are often preoccupied with the preparation of their baby's room; they take a lot of time and go to great expense to fix it the way they want it. Perhaps the least important factor in caring for an infant is having her room equipped with all the latest baby paraphernalia. God has already endowed mothers with the most important things needed to care for babies: arms, hands, breasts, eyes, ears, and a heart. (Fathers have most of these things too.) Have a good time feathering your nest, but remember: it is more important to spend time and money preparing yourselves than fixing up a nursery.

OUTFITTING YOUR BABY'S LAYETTE

Before you bring your baby home from the hospital, you will need to prepare his layette. The following chart will help you know what kinds of items and how many of them to have.

Supplies:	• mild bath soap and shampoo • mild laundry soap • diaper pins (if using cloth diapers), 3 pairs • diaper pail • cotton balls	• diaper cream or zinc oxide • cotton-tipped applicators • rubbing alcohol for cord care • nasal aspirator with 2-inch bulb • thermometer • baby bathtub or molded bath aid
Equipment:	• bassinet, cradle, or crib (optional) • storage chest for clothing • infant car seat • baby sling • changing table or padded work area	• portable bed (optional) • diaper bag • rocking chair (optional) • vaporizer-humidifier • night-light
Linens:	• flannel-backed rubber pads, 4 • crib or bassinet sheets, 2 • washcloths, 3	• baby blankets, 2–4 • hooded baby towels, 2 • cotton receiving blankets, 6
Clothing:	• diapers (cloth), 3 dozen • diapers (disposable) • loose fitting plastic pants (if using cloth diapers), 4 • sweaters, 2 • undershirts (3–6 month size), 6 • bunting or snowsuit (depending on where you live and the season)	• booties, 3 pairs • sunhats, 2 • warm hats, 2 • lightweight tops (sacques and/or kimonos), 8 • terrycloth sleepers and/or heavyweight sacques, 8

Cradles and Rocking Chairs

Babies are accustomed to motion because they have been carried around for nine months. If you choose to have a separate sleeping place for your baby, we advise using a cradle instead of a crib for the first five or six months. When your baby shifts his weight, the cradle will sway and sometimes lull him back to sleep. Many mothers find that they themselves become their newborns' "cradles." Most babies need to be put to sleep before they are put down, rather than being put down to go to sleep. Being in motion becomes a habit for mothers of infants. A mother who had been her baby's human cradle for many months told us this story: "I was standing at a party by myself, holding a glass of ginger ale. I didn't realize it, but I was swaying back and forth from the habit of rocking my baby. A friend came up to me and asked if I had had too much to drink."

The human cradle wears out after a while, so rocking chairs are a real must. A rocking chair is a useful purchase, but before buying one, try it out. Be sure the arms are at the right height to support your arms comfortably while nursing or holding your baby. The breast and the rocking chair are a winning combination for mothering a baby to sleep.

Babywearing

We advise parents to use a sling-type carrier, such as The Original Baby Sling, to "wear" their babies during much of the time the baby is awake. It makes life easier for the parents and keeps babies more content. Baby carriers bring your baby much closer to you than plastic infant seats and strollers. Plastic infant seats were originally designed for sick babies with heart problems who needed to be kept upright. They were not designed to be a substitute for a parent's arms. Although

CARRIED BABIES CRY LESS

In 1986 a team of pediatricians in Montreal reported on a study of ninety-nine mother-infant pairs, half of whom were assigned to a group that was asked to carry their babies for at least three extra hours a day and were provided with baby carriers. The parents in this group were encouraged to carry their infants throughout the day, regardless of the state of the infant, not just in response to crying or fussing. Parents in the control group were given no instructions on carrying. After six weeks, the infants in the first group cried and fussed 43 percent less than the second group.

they are useful for some situations (such as eating in a restaurant with a small infant), they are certainly second best to a sling or front/back carrier.

Babywearing gets your parenting career off to a great start. When you wear your baby, you learn his cues more quickly. You also have a happier baby, since babies who are carried tend to cry less. This means your baby has more energy left over for development. Being close to you and your voice is stimulating for your baby, and the constantly changing view from the baby sling is certainly more interesting than a fancy mobile hanging over the crib.

Babywearing is practiced in many cultures where mothers work in the household or outdoors and simply keep their babies with them. In Western culture, with its cribs, cradles, infant swings, bouncers, and seats, we've lost touch with the idea that the best place for baby is in mother's arms. But once you get a babywearing mindset, you'll discover that you don't need all that other equipment.

Will babywearing "spoil" your baby? Of course not, no matter what all those advisors from that school of parenting have to say. Babywearing teaches your baby to be happy, content, and secure—qualities that will eventually make him more, rather than less,

Babywearing: Mother holds baby in a sling with baby facing forward.

independent. He'll learn to communicate with you in subtle ways, rather than having to cry, and your mind will be at peace because your baby is close by, no matter where you are and what you are doing.

When you choose a baby carrier, look for one that is safe, versatile, and easy to use. We have found that sling-type carriers meet all these requirements, and we have used slings with our last three children. (Note to fathers: babywearing is not just for women.) We recommend slings regularly in our practice, and most mothers, once they learn to use them, find a baby sling to be their most used piece of baby equipment.

Swings and Other Things

Wind-up baby swings are often useful for soothing a fussy baby when the "human swing" wears out. Babies more than three months old usually have enough head control to adapt to the swing, or their heads can be propped up with a head support. Some babies don't like swings, so you might want to borrow one to try it out before you buy one. Some babies like the swing so well that a word of caution is needed: don't allow the swing to become a mother substitute. You and baby need to be together most of the time. You want him bonded to you and your husband—to people, not to a swing or a crib.

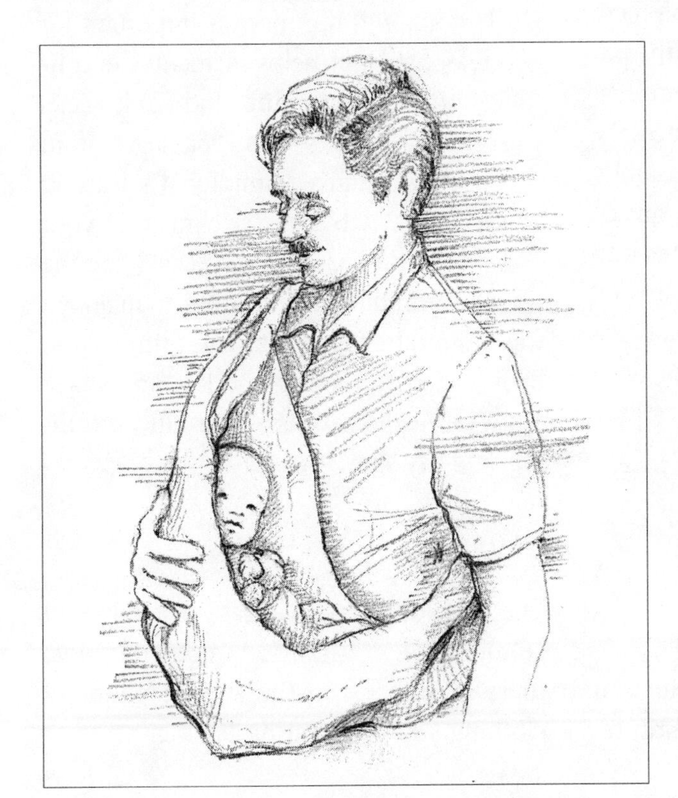

Babywearing—Cradle Hold: For newborns, use the shoulder pad of the sling to provide more support for baby's head. Note that the sling is worn backwards for the cradle hold.

Use all of these "things" wisely, as a way of giving yourself a break or to get something done for yourself that can't wait.

Mobiles to watch and rattles to grab are good toys to occupy and stimulate babies. Tiny babies are more attracted to the colors of red and yellow, and they like light and dark contrasts such as black and white patterns. Use the marvels of nature to attract and hold your baby's interest. Place your baby in front of a window facing a garden, trees, rain, or anything that is moving. These are God's mobiles and they are thoroughly enjoyed by the curious infant.

Walkers are one piece of baby equipment we caution parents about because of the potential for injury. In fact, the American Academy of Pediatrics specifically discourages the use of walkers unless the baby is constantly supervised. Too many babies have "walked" themselves over the edge of a staircase or into some other danger. There is nothing about a walker your baby needs. Developmentally inappropriate, a walker will keep him from being busy practicing his own motor skills.

CARING FOR YOUR NEWBORN

Temperature of Your Baby's Environment

The smaller the baby, the more careful you need to be about changes in temperature. Premature babies and babies weighing less than five pounds have immature temperature-regulating systems for the first few weeks; therefore they need to be kept warm. Term, healthy newborns, especially large ones weighing more than eight pounds, have body fat and mature temperature-regulating systems to adapt easily to an environmental temperature comfortable to an adult. A room temperature of about seventy degrees Fahrenheit is adequate for a term, healthy baby. What is more important than the actual temperature is its stability. Babies do not adjust well to marked temperature swings for their first few weeks.

Humidity in the room is important for two reasons: (1) it helps maintain the constancy of the temperature, and (2) it keeps your baby's narrow nasal passages from drying out. A relative humidity of at least 50 percent is advisable. A dry climate or your home's central heating may necessitate the use of a humidifier or vaporizer to maintain this humidity. Signs that the humidity in baby's sleeping room is too low are persistently clogged nasal passages, sniffily breathing, and dry skin.

Clothing

The way you dress your baby is a matter of culture and temperature. As a general guide, dress your baby in the same amount of clothing you are wearing for a given temperature, plus one more layer. Cotton clothing is preferable because it absorbs body moisture, allows air to circulate freely, and is not irritating. Also, be sure the clothing is loose enough to allow your baby to move freely.

Taking Baby Outside

If you live in a climate where the temperature inside and outside the house is similar, then a term baby weighing more than six pounds can be taken outside right away. By the time your baby weighs about eight pounds, he has enough body fat and his temperature-regulating system is mature enough to tolerate some exposure to temperature swings. Babies less than six pounds do not tolerate marked changes in temperature; therefore, it is necessary to maintain consistency of temperature, for example, by traveling from heated building to a heated car.

Smoking around Baby

Cigarette smoke is the most commonly overlooked irritant to a baby's tiny respiratory passages. Studies have shown that babies of smoking parents have three times more ear and respiratory infections. (They are also two to three times more likely to die of SIDS—Sudden Infant Death Syndrome.) Persistent nasal stuffiness and hacking coughs are the usual signs of irritation from cigarette smoke. We strongly advise parents to have a strict no-smoking rule in closed spaces, such as a house or car, especially around children less than two years old.

Bathing Your Baby

The items you need to bathe your baby are a small plastic tub or sponge form, several thick towels, a washcloth, cotton balls, cotton-tipped applicators, and a mild soap. A sponge bath is recommended until the umbilical cord falls off.

Babies rarely get dirty enough to require a daily all-over bath for cleanliness. It is usually enough to bathe your baby twice a week and wash her hair no more than once a week. Place a towel in the bottom of the tub to keep your baby from slipping, or use a specially designed sponge form. You can use a washcloth, or try using cotton gloves to make it easier for you to hold your slippery baby. Put a little mild soap on the wet gloves, and use your gloved hands as a washcloth. Cotton-tipped applicators are handy for cleaning the creases in and behind the ears (never inside the ear canal) and the crevices of the navel. Use the cotton balls and plain water to wipe baby's face. After your baby's bath, wrap her in a thick towel to dry her off, keeping her head covered to avoid chilling. Handle baby firmly and avoid sudden movements to be sure she feels secure during this procedure.

Babies startle easily and can wind up crying through the whole bath if they become frightened. It is not necessary to proceed with bathing if your baby is protesting. Wrap her up to calm her and try again later to see if you can correct what distressed her. Or, just give her a brief sponging and call it a bath.

Another way to bathe a baby is to take her into the bath with you. A baby loves the closeness of taking baths with Mom in the tub. Draw the warm water (around body temperature, 98°F) to just below your breast level, and allow your baby to float slightly, nestled in your arms. Nurse her if she wants. This water ritual is relaxing for both of you, especially during a baby's fussy periods. Place your baby in a baby seat lined with a towel on the floor next to the tub while you get in and out. This is a wonderful way for Dad to spend some "skin time" with baby too.

We discourage using powders and oils on a baby's skin because it is already naturally oily, and excess oil can attract bacteria. Powders, if inhaled, can be irritating to a baby's sensitive lungs. If you find that your baby's skin is becoming excessively dry, you may be washing her too often, thus removing the natural oils from her skin. Scented oils and powders mask the natural baby scent mothers find so appealing. Babies do love an oil massage before the bath. The wonderful ritual of massaging babies is described in Vimala Schneider McClure's *Infant Massage* (see bibliography). Use an unscented, pure plant oil.

Care of the Navel

Your baby's umbilical cord will fall off sometime between one and three weeks of age. Twice a day, clean around the cord, swabbing deep into the crevices with a cotton-tipped applicator. Use alcohol or the antiseptic solution your doctor recommends. It is normal to notice a few drops of blood when the cord falls off. Continue applying the antiseptic solution for a few days until the scabbed area is healed.

COMMON MEDICAL CONCERNS OF BABY'S FIRST YEAR

The well-baby care system in North America is very effective and will guard your baby's health in the early years. In this system, your child is examined by your physician at periodic intervals: at birth; two weeks; two, four, six, nine, twelve, fifteen, eighteen, and twenty-four months; two and a half and three years; and once a year thereafter.

This schedule may vary according to the parents' needs and the baby's general health. The purposes of these periodic exams are:

- to check for actual or potential abnormalities in growth and development

- to note your child's nutritional requirements at various ages
- to discuss developmental and emotional changes
- to point out specific age- and stage-related needs
- to discuss your questions or adjustment problems
- to help your doctor get to know you and your child during the child's well state, which serves as a reference point for medical judgment when your child is ill
- to treat any conditions that may be detected during examination
- to administer necessary immunizations

Just as parents are developing their intuition about their child in the early stages of parenting, the pediatrician also is developing insight about your child and about you as parents. It is very important for your doctor to know your child. Nothing is more frustrating for a doctor than to see a child only when he is ill. The doctor will feel he or she does not know the total child and is therefore at a disadvantage in making appropriate medical decisions. Scheduling periodic exams is the best preventive medicine, and it is also an economically wise investment in the long run.

Getting the most out of your visits with your doctor can be summed up in one word: communication. Shortly before your appointment, make a list of your concerns. Put this list in a place where you cannot forget it—the diaper bag, your coat pocket—in the rush to get out the door. Being well prepared when you visit your doctor conveys that these visits are important to you and your child. When possible, both parents can attend these well-child visits since this also conveys the message of commitment.

Another kind of doctor's visit is for a specific problem. Because illnesses cannot be conveniently scheduled, your doctor will usually reserve some time during each office day for treating sudden illnesses. Limit your discussion to the specific problem for which you brought your child to the office since your doctor is probably fitting your child in between patients already scheduled.

A behavioral or psychological problem may require a visit to your doctor. Since these visits usually require more time, request a long appointment and indicate to the receptionist the purpose of your appointment.

Sniffles

Sometime in his first few weeks you may think your baby has his first cold. These noisy, gurgling sounds are usually not colds (meaning a viral infection), but they certainly may sound like a cold and can be a source of concern. Babies do not breathe the way adults do. Adults breathe through either their

PRAYING FOR YOUR CHILD

If you have a Christian physician, you can ask him or her to pray with you for your child when your child is sick. This practice gives your child total Christian medical care. We are given clear instructions on how to pray for the sick in James 5:14–15. If there is a particularly disturbing medical problem, we recommend you call the elders of the church and ask them to come and pray over your child, perhaps even anointing with oil, for healing.

noses or their mouths, and their air passages are relatively large. Babies are predominantly nose breathers, and their air passages are relatively small. For these reasons, even a slight amount of congestion in the nose or throat can bother them. Sniffles in tiny babies are more often caused by environmental irritants than by infections. The most common irritants are lint from blankets and clothing, dust, chemical fumes, and cigarette smoke. In fact, children of smoking parents do have more colds than children of nonsmoking parents.

Another cause of clogged nasal passages is very dry air, especially during the months when homes are heated. As a general guide, when the heat goes on, so should a humidifier. A baby cannot blow his own nose; you must do it for him. Here's how:

Clearing your baby's nose. Use saline nasal drops or spray (available without prescription) for each nostril. This solution will loosen the secretions and stimulate your baby to sneeze them toward the front part of his nose. Next, take a rubber-bulb syringe, called a "nasal aspirator," or a rubber ear syringe and gently suck out the loosened secretions. Babies do not enjoy having their noses cleared, but sometimes it's necessary.

When to clear your baby's nose. Signs of a baby's obstructed nasal passages include frequent waking up, inability to sustain nursing (he needs his mouth to breathe), and breathing with his mouth open. If your baby sleeps comfortably with his mouth closed and he has not changed his nursing pattern, you do not need to clean out his nose even though he may sound noisy.

Sometime around his first or second month, your baby may experience what is called the "two-month cold." Again, this is probably not a cold. Babies often make more saliva than they are able to handle initially. As a result, the saliva collects in the back of their throats, causing noisy, gurgly breathing. You also may hear and feel a "rattle" in his chest, but the problem is not really in his chest. What you hear and feel is the air moving past the vibrating mucous in the back of his throat, producing sounds and vibrations like a musical instrument. These secretions are often too far back to get with a nasal aspirator, and the baby's problem is usually not in his nose anyway. Keeping a vaporizer running when he is sleeping can thin these secretions. These throaty noises occur less when your baby is sleeping since saliva production usually lessens with sleep. These noises may continue during the first six months and can become more noticeable during times of teething. As soon as your baby begins to spend more of his time in an upright position and learns how to swallow the excess saliva, these noises gradually disappear. (See the section on colds later in this chapter for ways to recognize and treat actual infection.)

Eye Discharges

In a baby's first few months, discharge from the eyes is usually caused by blocked tear ducts. Most infants begin tearing by three weeks of age, and these tears should drain from the nasal corners of the eyes through the tear ducts. At birth, the nasal ends of these ducts are closed by a thin membrane that usually breaks open shortly after birth allowing the proper drainage of the tears. Often this membrane does not open fully, the tear ducts remain plugged, and tears accumulate in one or both eyes. There is a general principle of the human body that if fluid does not drain properly, it soon will become infected. The discharge from your baby's eyes may become persistently yellow, indicating that there is an infection in the region of the blocked tear ducts.

Treating blocked tear ducts. Gently massage the tear duct, which is located beneath the tiny "bump" in the nasal corner of each eye. Massage in an upward direction (toward the eye) about six times. Do this as frequently as you think of it during the day, for example, before each diaper change. If you properly massage the tear duct, this pressure on the fluid trapped within the ducts should pop open the membrane and clear the tear ducts. If you notice persistent tearing or yellow discharge from one or both eyes, mention this to your doctor during your baby's checkup, and your doctor will instruct you in the proper treatment of this condition. Blocked tear ducts usually clear up by six months of age. Occasionally, it is necessary for an eye doctor to open these ducts by inserting a tiny probe into them, but this should not be done until a period of treatment using massage and eye drops has been attempted.

Thrush

Thrush is a common yeast infection in the baby's mouth that looks like white patches on the inner cheeks, inner lips, tongue, and roof of the mouth. This fungus infection seldom bothers the baby unless it goes untreated. The treatment is an antifungal prescription which is painted on the white patches. The baby also may have a raised, red, bumpy diaper rash that will need prescription medication. A breastfeeding baby can transfer the infection to his mother's nipples, which can make nursing painful, so that a prescription cream will be necessary to treat her too. Sore nipples that appear after weeks of pain-free nursing are often a sign of a thrush infection that may not be apparent in the baby's mouth.

Birthmarks

Most newborn babies have smooth, reddish pink marks on the back of the neck, on the forehead, between the eyes, and on the upper eyelids. These "stork bites" are areas of skin where the blood vessels are prominent and show through baby's thin skin. These marks often become more noticeable when the baby cries. As your baby grows and accumulates more fat beneath her skin, her reddish areas become less noticeable and probably will disappear well before her first birthday.

The most common kind of birthmark looks like a small strawberry and is called a "hemangioma." It is caused by the proliferation of tiny blood vessels within the skin. It may not be present at birth but can appear within a baby's first few months. Hemangiomas gradually grow larger, begin to dry up by turning a grayish color in the center, and usually disappear within several years. Five percent of these hemangiomas are "rapid growing" and need to be watched carefully—they may require laser surgery.

Non-Caucasian babies often have bluish birthmarks on the skin of the lower back that look like bruises. These normal spots usually disappear with time but can remain until adulthood.

Rashes

Milia. These tiny, whitish, pin-head-sized bumps are most prominent on the face, especially on the skin of the nose. This rash is caused by oily sections plugging the pores of the skin and disappears as the pores open up. You can help it along by gently washing with warm water and mild soap.

Newborn "acne." Newborns usually develop a pimply, oily rash on the face resembling acne, which appears several weeks after birth. The increased hormone levels at birth cause the oil glands of the face to swell. The acne-like rash can be improved easily with gentle washings with warm water and a mild soap. If the condition worsens, begins to look infected, or spreads up into the scalp and down onto the neck, shoulders, and chest, consult your doctor. This spreading can be the first sign that baby is allergic to something in your milk (usually dairy products) or to the formula.

Seborrhea. Sometimes a crusty, oily rash will appear behind the ears and on the scalp. In addition to washing with warm water, a prescription cream may be needed.

Cradle cap. A crusty, oily, plaque-like rash that appears on the baby's scalp, it is most common over the soft spot. Cradle cap is best treated by massaging vegetable oil into the crusty areas and gently removing the softened scales with a washcloth or a fine-toothed comb or facial brush. If this rash persists, a special shampoo and a prescription cream may be needed.

Prickly heat. These rashes are tiny pimples with red bases and clear centers. Prickly heat usually appears in areas of the skin where there is excessive moisture retention, such as behind the ears, between the neck folds, in the groin, and in areas where clothing fits tightly. The rash is treated by gently washing the area with plain, cold water or with a solution of baking soda (one teaspoon to a cup of water). Dressing your baby in lightweight, loose-fitting cotton clothing also should soothe this rash.

Diaper rash. Human skin, especially the sensitive skin of a newborn baby, was not designed to be in prolonged contact with wet cloth. Diaper rashes are caused by the chemical irritation of acids in the stool and ammonia formed by the urine and also by the mechanical rubbing of wet cloth on sensitive skin. Bacteria and yeast can attack the weakened skin and irritate the area even more. The following suggestions are for the prevention and treatment of your baby's diaper rash.

1. Experiment with both cloth diapers and disposable diapers to see which one causes fewer rashes in your baby. If you use disposable diapers, be sure to fold the edge of the diaper down so the plastic lining does not touch your baby's skin.

2. Change wet diapers as quickly as possible. If diaper rash is a persistent problem, change your baby when he wakes during the night also, or use double or triple cloth diapers.

3. After each diaper change, wash your baby's diaper area with plain water or mild soap, rinse well, and gently blot dry. Avoid strong soaps and excessive rubbing on already sensitive skin.

4. Soak your baby's bottom in a baking soda bath (a tablespoon of baking soda in two quarts of water in his tub). After soaking the baby's bottom, give a "sniff test" to detect any smell of ammonia.

5. Allow the diaper area to "breathe." Avoid tight-fitting diapers and plastic pants that retain moisture. Reserve plastic pants for occasions where a leaky diaper may not be socially acceptable. Place flannel backed rubber pads underneath your baby to protect his bedding. Expose your baby's diaper areas as much as possible to the air. While he is sleeping, unfold the diaper and lay it beneath him. In warm weather, let your baby nap outside in the shade with his bare bottom exposed to fresh air.
6. Creams are usually not necessary when your baby's skin is not irritated, but at the first sign of a reddened, irritated bottom, apply a barrier cream such as zinc oxide. Treat the diaper rash early before the skin breaks down and becomes infected. Barrier creams also should be used during times when your baby has diarrhea, such as when he is teething or has an intestinal infection. Avoid cornstarch on the diaper area because it encourages the growth of yeast.
7. Yeast or fungal diaper rashes are red, raised, rough, sore-looking rashes that have tiny pustules and are resistant to simple forms of treatment. This kind of diaper rash needs a prescription cream along with the measures noted here.

Teething

Six months is the average age for a baby's-first tooth to appear, but this is quite variable. Some babies have teething symptoms starting as early as two months. They include drooling, irritability, chomping on objects, discomfort with sucking, diaper rash and looser stools, and night waking. Even a low fever and a cough can develop. Of course, all of these things can be caused by things other than teething too. So you never really know a tooth is on its way until you see the gums swelling. Some babies make their eager parents wait several months longer, and that is hard to do when everybody else's baby has already gotten their first tooth. It's even harder when baby has enough of the symptoms to make him rather miserable. Try to empathize and be patient—remember, if you can, what it felt like when your wisdom teeth were erupting.

The best thing for aching gums is to have something cold and hard to gnaw on. Offer your baby any or all of these surefire cures: mom's hand, mom's shoulder, dad's knee (all fine before the tooth breaks through), sock with an ice cube inside, frozen banana, juice popsicle, teething ring toy, and frozen teething biscuit. Teething preparations that numb the gums are available, but we hesitate to recommend them. They often don't work as well as the commercials imply and there is no research to validate their safety. Some mothers tell us that homeopathic teething remedies help their babies when the above sure-cures wear out their effectiveness.

One thing that usually helps a baby who is in obvious pain from teething is to give acetaminophen. (Check the chart on p. 260 to be sure you are giving enough to be effective.) This is especially helpful when a baby can't sleep due to teething pain. Give one dose at bedtime and another four hours later if needed. A one-time double dose is best if baby is in severe pain.

Now is a good time to get baby used to oral hygiene. Use a piece of gauze wrapped around your finger to gently wipe baby's gums and newly erupting teeth every day. A toothbrush makes a good toy for a toddler to play with during a diaper change. Eventually, he'll want to imitate you in brushing his teeth.

Fever

What constitutes a fever? A rectal temperature greater than 100.5 degrees Fahrenheit (38 degrees Celsius) is considered a fever. Most children have a normal oral body temperature of 98.6 degrees Fahrenheit (37.5 degrees Celsius), but normal temperature varies among children from 97 to 100 degrees Fahrenheit (36.1 to 37.8 degrees Celsius). *Rectal temperature registers about one degree higher than oral temperature.* Many children show normal daily fluctuations in body temperature. It can be lower in the morning and during rest and a degree higher in the late afternoon or during strenuous exercise.

What causes fever? Fever is a symptom of an underlying illness, but it is not an illness itself. A fever occurs when more heat is produced in the body than can be released, thus raising your child's temperature. Germs from infection within your child's body release substances into the bloodstream called pyrogens, which cause the fever.

Normal body temperature is maintained by a thermostat in a tiny organ of the brain called the hypothalamus, which regulates the balance between the heat produced and the heat lost in the body. Anytime there is a change from normal body temperature, the thermostat reacts to help the body bring that temperature back to normal; for example, when your child is cold, he shivers to produce heat. When your child has a fever, the blood vessels of his skin become larger (as evidenced by his flushed cheeks), and his heart beats faster. These mechanisms cause more blood to reach the surface of the skin to release the excess body heat. A child with fever also sweats to cool his body by evaporation and breathes faster to get rid of heat through the warm air he exhales. In addition to having these general signs of fever, a child may have headaches and fatigue.

How to take your child's temperature. Practice "feeling" your child's temperature by placing the palm of your hand on her forehead or by kissing her forehead so that you are used to telling when she has a fever. Then confirm it by taking her temperature with a thermometer.

When your child is running a fever, keep a temperature chart by writing down the time, your child's temperature, and the methods you have used to treat the fever. You can take your child's temperature in four places: the rectum (rectal), the armpit (axillary), the mouth (oral), and the ear. Rectal temperature is one-half to one degree higher than oral temperature, and axillary temperature is usually one degree lower than oral. Follow these steps to take your child's rectal temperature:

1. Use a rectal thermometer (one with a rounded, stubby end that is marked "rectal").
2. Shake down the thermometer with a wrist-snapping motion until the mercury column is below 95 degrees Fahrenheit.
3. Lubricate the bulb end with a petroleum jelly.
4. Lay your child face down across your lap and get him to relax. Reassure him that you won't hurt him. If he's old enough to understand, tell him to take big breaths through his mouth. (Demonstrate this ahead of time.)
5. Gently insert the thermometer bulb only about one inch into the rectum, allowing the thermometer to seeks its own path. Don't force it.
6. Hold the thermometer in place between your index and middle fingers with the palm of your hand and your fingers grasping your child's buttocks. By holding your child in this position you can hold the thermometer and keep your child from moving. Never leave a child alone with a thermometer in place.
7. Try to keep the thermometer in place for three minutes. Sing a little song or recite something familiar to keep your child relaxed. The rectal reading will be within a degree of the true temperature after one minute.

A child more than five years of age will usually cooperate with having his temperature taken orally. Follow these three steps:

1. Use an oral thermometer (the oral thermometer has a longer, thinner bulb than the rectal thermometer and is marked "oral"). Shake down the thermometer as described in the paragraph on rectal thermometers.
2. Have your child lie or sit quietly and place the mercury end of the thermometer under her tongue, slightly to one side. Instruct her to keep her mouth closed and to close her lips firmly, but not hold the thermometer with her teeth. Allowing the child to open her mouth to breathe with the thermometer in place will make the temperature reading

inaccurate. If she can't breathe through her nose, take a rectal or axillary temperature.

3. Try to keep the thermometer in place with mouth closed for two to three minutes.

If your child resists having her temperature taken rectally or orally, you can take an axillary reading. An oral thermometer should be used for taking an axillary temperature, but four minutes are required to achieve an accurate temperature reading. Simply place the bulb right in the center of the armpit and secure it there by holding your child's arm across her chest as she sits on your lap. The newer electronic thermometers are easier to read because of the digital display, but some are not accurate. The ear thermometers are quite expensive, but they are very easy and quick to use.

When to worry about fever. Both viral and bacterial infections cause fever. Viral infections are usually less worrisome and show the following features: (1) the fever comes on suddenly in a previously well child; (2) the fever is usually very high (103 to 105 degrees Fahrenheit orally); (3) the fever is easily brought down for a while using the methods listed in the section below on how to treat your child's fever; and (4) the child seems to feel better when the temperature is brought down. When their children have viral infections, parents often say, "I am surprised the fever was so high because my child does not look or act sick." The most common viral infection in the first year of life is called "roseola"; it produces a very high temperature (103 to 105 degrees Fahrenheit) for about three days, but there are no other symptoms and the child does not appear as ill as the high fever would indicate. After the fever breaks, a faint, generalized, reddish pink rash appears and lasts for less than twenty-four hours.

In a bacterial infection the temperature may not be as high as that of a viral infection, but the fever does not come down as easily with the methods recommended for treating your child's fever. Also, when your child has a bacterial infection, he acts sicker.

When to call your doctor about fever. If your child does not act particularly sick, administer all the recommended methods to lower your child's temperature (see below) before calling your doctor. Remember, your doctor is more interested in how sick your child looks and acts rather than how high the temperature is. How your child responds to temperature-lowering methods is one of the main concerns your doctor will have. The younger the infant, the more worrisome the fever. (Note: Any fever in an infant less than four months old should be reported *immediately* to your doctor.) If your child's temperature cannot be lowered by using the methods suggested in the next section, and if he is becoming more ill, call your doctor. Also, call your doctor if obvious signs and symptoms are associated with the fever, such as ear pain, severe cough, sore throat, or any problems associated with urination.

When examining your feverish child, your doctor is attempting to determine whether the fever is caused by a virus or a bacteria. Bacterial infections need antibiotics; viral infections usually do not and the fever is treated as indicated in the following section. Sometimes it is difficult to determine the kind of infection, and your doctor may perform some laboratory tests to help make this decision. Or your doctor may elect to wait a day or so before making a definite decision and request that you notify him of your child's progress. It is important to keep the use of antibiotics to a minimum since they are not without side effects and the overuse of antibiotics leads to resistant strains of bacteria.

Because of the common difficulty of determining the kind of infection, it is very important for you to report to your doctor if your child's general condition worsens; your doctor may have to revise his diagnosis. Viral infections usually last three to five days and gradually subside. Bacterial infections, however, usually worsen if untreated.

How to treat your child's fever. You lower your child's temperature by two basic mechanisms: (1) giving your child fever-reducing medications such as acetaminophen which reset her thermostat, and (2) using methods that get rid of excess body heat. It is necessary to lower your child's thermostat with medications before using heat removal procedures. Your child's thermostat is set so that if her body temperature is lowered, her body is programmed to produce more heat and therefore raise her body temperature again. For example, removing a child's clothing and placing her in a bath with water cooler than her body temperature will cause her to lose heat. But her thermostat will respond, causing her to shiver to produce more heat and constricting her blood vessels to conserve heat. Fever-lowering medications can reset the thermostat so that when the child's temperature is lowered by cooling, her body will not react to produce more heat. An example of this mechanism is evident in the way heat is regulated in your house. If your house is too warm, you lower the thermostat and then open the windows. If you open the windows first without resetting the thermostat, heat production continues and your house remains warm.

The most commonly used medication to lower a temperature is acetaminophen (Tylenol, Tempra, Liquiprin). It lowers fever and helps relieve some of the general aches and pains that often accompany childhood illnesses. Aspirin has fallen out of favor for treating children's fevers. Aspirin use during certain viral illnesses, such as chicken pox or flu, has been linked to a serious brain and liver disease called Reye's Syndrome.

Acetaminophen is generally recommended instead of aspirin for the young child for the following reasons: (1) it is not linked with Reye's Syndrome; (2) it is available in liquid form and therefore is easier to administer to the young child; and (3) it does not keep building up in your child's blood with prolonged usage and so is less likely than aspirin to produce a toxicity with routine use.

Acetaminophen is available in the following forms: (1) drops: 0.8 milliliters equals 80 milligrams; (2) elixir: 5 milliliters or one teaspoon equals 160 milligrams; (3) tablets (chewable): one tablet equals 80 milligrams; and (4) adult tablets (regular strength): one tablet equals 325 milligrams.

The dosage schedule of acetaminophen (on p. 260) will help you determine the proper dosage for your child.

Doses should be administered four or five times daily—but do not exceed five doses in twenty-four hours. It is not usually necessary to awaken a child to give fever-lowering medication.

Other ways to lower your child's fever. In addition to using acetaminophen to reset your child's thermostat, the following methods will help remove the excess heat from your child's system.

1. *Undress your child completely,* or at most, dress him in light, loose-fitting cotton clothing. This allows the excess heat to radiate out of his body into the cooler environment. Avoid the tendency to bundle up your child when he has a fever because this will only cause his body to retain heat.

2. *Keep your child's environment cool.* Decrease the temperature in his room, open a window slightly, use an air conditioner or a nearby fan. A "draft" will not bother your child. This cool air helps remove the heat that is radiating out of his body. Yes, your child may go outside when he has a fever. The fresh, circulating air is good for him.

3. *Give your child a lot of extra fluids* when he has a fever because excess body heat causes him to lose fluids. Give him cool, clear liquids in small, frequent amounts.

4. *Give your child a cooling bath.* If in spite of these other measures your child's temperature remains over 103 degrees Fahrenheit orally (39.5 degrees Celsius), or if she continues to be uncomfortable

ACETAMINOPHEN								
AGE GROUP	0–3 mos.	4–11 mos.	12–23 mos.	2–3 yrs.	4–5 yrs.	6–8 yrs.	9–10 yrs.	11–12 yrs.
WEIGHT (lbs.)	6–11	12–17	18–23	24–35	36–47	48–59	60–71	72–95
Dose of Acetaminophen in milligrams	40	80	120	160	240	320	400	480
Drops (ip mg/0.8 ml) in droppersful	½	1	1½	2	3	4	5	—
Elixir (160 mg/5 ml) in teaspoons	—	½	¾	1	1½	2	2½	3
Chewable tablets (80 mg each)	—	—	1½	2	3	4	5	6

with the fever, place her in a tub of water and run the water all the way up to her neck. The water temperature should be warm enough not to be uncomfortable but cooler than her body temperature. If the young child protests this tub bath and begins to cry, sit in the bathtub with her and amuse her with her favorite floating toys. Crying and struggling will only increase her temperature. Keeping your child in the cooling bath for twenty to thirty minutes should bring her temperature down a couple of degrees. During the bath, rub her with a washcloth to stimulate more circulation to the skin and increase heat loss. After the bath, gently pat your child dry, leaving a slight excess of water on her skin, which will evaporate and produce a further cooling effect. Do not use alcohol rubs because they can produce shivering and toxic vapors. If your child's temperature zooms back up again, it may be necessary to repeat the tub bath.

Can fever be dangerous? In most children, the fever itself is not dangerous. Fever does make children very uncomfortable, creating a headache and muscle aches and pains. The main reason for controlling high temperatures in young children is the danger of convulsions. The young child's brain does not tolerate sudden temperature fluctuations and may react with a convulsion. It is not so much how high the fever is, but how fast the temperature rises that causes convulsions. Most febrile convulsions can be prevented by using all the methods to control temperature just described. Febrile convulsions, while alarming to parents, seldom harm the child. The frequency and severity of these convulsions lessen as your child gets older and seldom occur in a child more than five years old.

Because a child with a fever is often uncomfortable, keep his body quiet. Breastfeeding is very comforting to a child, and this may be the only nourishment he will want. Pray for your child, asking God to relieve the fever and the illness producing his discomfort.

Colds

What is a cold? In medical terms, colds are called "upper respiratory infections" (URI), which means an infection of the lining of the air passages: nose, sinuses, throat, ears, and larynx. Germs, either viruses or bacteria, infect the lining of these air passages, and the tissue of this lining reacts by swelling and secreting mucous. Runny nose and postnasal drip are caused by the accumulation of mucous. Your child may then sneeze and cough, which is his way of automatically clearing this mucous. Swelling of the tissues accounts for many of the signs of a cold: swelling of the nasal membranes causes a child to breathe noisily through his mouth; swelling of the veins and tissues beneath the eyelids causes a bluish discoloration; swelling of the tonsils and adenoids causes the throaty noises most commonly heard at night; swelling of the larynx causes the croupy, seal-bark cough. Most children have several colds per year. The school-age child is a very social being and "shares" her cold germs with other children. As the child grows, her immunity to various germs increases, and the number and severity of colds gradually decreases.

Although colds are, strictly speaking, caused by infections, allergies may also account for swelling and mucous secretion. The germs can then settle in these secretions resulting in an infection. It is common for young children to have both allergy colds and infection colds.

When is a cold more than a cold? The "common cold," as it is often called, is usually caused by a virus and subsides with the general measures mentioned here. However, it is important for parents to recognize when a cold needs a consultation with the doctor.

The following general guidelines will help you decide when to take your child to a doctor for a cold.

1. Determine how much the cold is bothering your child. If your child is happy and playful, eats well, sleeps well, and is not particularly bothered by the cold, then it is most likely a viral infection. This cold is simply a noisy nuisance and probably will subside with simple supportive care.
2. Check the mucous coming from his nose. If the secretions are clear and watery and your child is generally happy, his cold is most likely caused by a virus. If the discharge from his nose becomes thick and yellow or green and persists that way throughout the day, and if your child becomes increasingly cranky and awakens more at night, he probably has a bacterial infection. Medical advice should be obtained. The eyes are often the mirror of the cold's severity. If your child has a persistently yellow drainage from his eyes, most likely he has an underlying sinus or ear infection and should be examined by your doctor.

When is a cold contagious? If your child has a fever, snotty nose, and cough, consider him contagious and keep him away from other children and out of the church nursery. Children are most contagious the first few days of the cold. It is not necessary to quarantine a child who has no fever, is not sick, and has only a clear-running nose or slight cough.

DR. BILL'S RULE

If your child's nose progresses from runny to snotty and his behavior progresses from happy to cranky, your child should be examined by a doctor.

How should you treat a cold? General treatment of the simple cold is aimed at keeping the nasal discharge thin and moving. Secretions that become stagnant are likely to result in a worsening infection. Use a vaporizer while your child is sleeping. Do not add anything to the water in the vaporizer since an additive could irritate a young child's respiratory passages. Give your child a lot of fluids to drink. Clear the nasal passages (see p. 250). Encourage the older child to blow her nose well and not to sniff the secretions back up into her sinuses. Most children need extra sleep when recovering from a cold. If a cough is not bothering your child or disturbing his sleep, he doesn't need cough medicine. Some viral colds will cause a cough that can persist for up to six weeks.

Over-the-counter medications for colds are called decongestants. They are designed to dry up the secretions and shrink the swelling of the lining of the respiratory passages. In our experience, these medications have limited usefulness for children. If a child is given a high enough dosage of a decongestant to help the cold, he may experience the undesirable side effects of drowsiness or hyperexcitability, rapid heart beat, or nightmares. Dosages recommended on the package inserts are often so low as to be ineffective.

Decongestants are more effective for colds produced by allergies than for those produced by infections. Overuse of decongestants may, in fact, dry up the secretions to the extent that the child cannot cough up the secretions. Thus the cold worsens. Nose drops for a persistently runny nose that is really bothering the child may be effective, but they should not be used more than twice a day or for more than three days at a time. Most of these over-the-counter remedies are used in desperation to give the child some relief. It is best to check with your doctor before using any over-the-counter medication.

Antibiotics for colds. Viral infections generally do not need antibiotics, but bacterial infections do. This is the judgment your doctor tries to make when examining your child for a cold. Your doctor listens to your child's chest and looks into his nose, throat, and ears to determine if there are any signs of bacterial infection. If there are not, your doctor may say to you, "This is a viral infection, which does not need an antibiotic, and your child should get better by simply giving him fluids and cleaning out his nose. But call if he gets worse." Keep in mind that you are going to your doctor primarily for consultation, not necessarily for medication. Do not be disappointed if your doctor "doesn't find anything." It often requires more judgment *not* to treat an illness with antibiotics than to treat one with them. Remember your doctor's closing statement to call if your child gets worse, since viral infections can progress to bacterial infections and a change of treatment would be necessary. If your doctor suspects your child's cold is caused by a bacterial infection, an appropriate antibiotic will be prescribed. Be sure to complete the entire course of the prescribed antibiotic.

Ear Infections

Because of the frequency and severity of ear infections in young children, you should have a full understanding of their causes and treatment. Children harbor germs in the secretions of the nose and throat to which they have not yet become immune. Because of the proximity of the nose and throat to the ears, germs commonly travel up the eustachian tube into the ear during a cold.

The eustachian tube in younger children often functions inadequately. The eustachian tube has two main functions: (1) to equalize the air pressure on both sides of the eardrum, which allows the eardrum to vibrate freely and produce a sound; and (2) to drain the middle ear of fluid and germs that collect during a cold. A child's eustachian tube is short, wide, straight, and at a horizontal angle, all of which allow germs to travel more easily from the throat up into the middle ear. As your child grows, the eustachian tube becomes longer, narrower, and more angled, thus making it more difficult for germs and fluid to collect in the middle ear.

During a cold (or allergy) fluid accumulates in the middle ears. If the eustachian tube does not function properly and the fluid remains trapped, germs can cause an infection of the fluid within the cavity of the middle ear. The infected fluid accumulates behind the eardrum, presses on the eardrum, and produces intense pain. If the pressure from the trapped fluid builds up too much, this fluid can rupture the eardrum, and you may notice drainage of fluid outside the ear canal. This fluid resembles the secretions of a runny nose.

It is important for parents to be vigilant about recognizing the signs of a ruptured eardrum. Once the eardrum ruptures, the pressure is released, and the child feels better. But this is actually a false improvement; the infection still should be treated to allow the perforated area of the eardrum to heal. Repeated scarring of the eardrum can result in permanent hearing loss.

Ear infections often bother a child more at night. When she is lying down, the fluid presses more on her eardrum. A parent will often notice that the baby feels better when held in an upright position or when she stands up in her crib.

How to recognize an ear infection in your child. The older child can tell you when his ear hurts, but it is often difficult for a parent to identify an ear infection in a preverbal child. While some infants give no easily identifiable signs of ear infections, most show the following signs: your baby starts off with a clear, runny nose but is reasonably happy, the nasal discharge progresses from runny to thick, and your child's behavior moves from happy to increasingly cranky and irritable. Teething may be confused with ear infections, but when teething, your child should look generally well and his throat and nose secretions should not be persistently yellow or green. The combination of a discharging nose, with or without yellow drainage from the eyes, and increasing crankiness in the child should alert parents to the possibility of an ear infection, and a doctor should be consulted. Ear infections by themselves are not contagious. The child is contagious if he has a cold along with the ear infection.

HOW TO PREVENT EAR INFECTIONS

Most children, because of the eustachian tube structure, will have occasional ear infections. The following suggestions may help lessen the frequency and severity of these infections.

1. Breastfeed your infant as long as possible. Breastfed infants have fewer ear infec tions.
2. Control allergies. Allergies often cause fluid to build up in the middle ear, which can get infected. Food allergies, especially those caused by dairy products, and inhalant allergies, especially those caused by cigarette smoke and dust (such as that caused by stuffed animals in the bedroom), are the most common.
3. Observe your child's "cold pattern" and treat these colds early and appropriately. If your child has had previous ear infections and the usual sequence of events is first a runny nose, then a snotty nose, then crankiness, it may be wise to seek medical attention at the snotty-nose stage before the cold settles in your child's ears.
4. Some medications can be used to prevent the frequent occurrence of ear infection. Your doctor can recommend what is best for your child. (See section on recurrent ear infections, p. 266.)

Sometimes the fluid that builds up in the middle ears does not become infected and may not produce significant pain (this is called "serous otitis media"). This fluid will restrict the movement of the eardrum, thus diminishing your child's hearing. Even if only fluid is in the middle ear and there is no infection, most children show some change in behavior as a result of their diminished hearing. This altered behavior may be the only sign to alert you of a middle ear problem.

Treating ear infections. Most children can be grouped according to their type of ear infection: those with an occasional infection that clears up well with treatment; those with recurrent infections that need long-term treatment; and those with recurrent infections that do not respond to medical treatment but require surgical procedures.

The child with an occasional ear infection. After your doctor diagnoses an ear infection (otitis media), he or she will usually prescribe an antibiotic. The strength of the antibiotic and how long it is to be taken will depend upon the severity of the infection and your child's past history of response to treatment.

The healing of an ear infection usually goes through two phases. In the first phase your child should feel better within one or two days, and may seem perfectly well within two or three days. During this time most of the germs have been killed by the antibiotic and the pressure of the fluid lessened somewhat so that your child's pain is nearly gone in the first few days. The second phase is a gradual resolution of the fluid or drainage of this fluid from the middle ear through the eustachian tube. This takes longer. For this reason it is important to complete the prescribed duration of treatment. If you stop the antibiotics as soon as your child feels better, the remaining fluid in the middle ear can become reinfected, and the whole process must start again. It is also extremely important for your doctor to recheck your child's ears as soon as the prescribed antibiotic is finished. Your doctor may elect to continue a milder medication for a while longer if the infection is not completely gone. Partially treated ear infections are a common cause of permanent hearing deficits; therefore, follow-up checks are extremely important.

What can you do if your child awakens in the middle of the night with an earache? It is usually not necessary to phone your doctor immediately since antibiotics take as long as twelve hours to have any effect and will not immediately relieve the pain. Try the following pain-relieving measures. Seat your child upright, and try to rock or soothe her back to sleep in that position. This often takes the pressure of the infected fluid off the eardrum and eases the pain. Warm some oil (slightly warmer than body temperature), such as olive oil, and squirt a few drops into the sore ear. Encourage your child to lie with the sore ear up, and pull gently on the auricle to move slightly the outer edge of the canal, trying to move the drops down toward the eardrum so it can relieve the pain. You can see air bubbles rise to the top of the oil if you do this right. If your child has had infections before, it is wise to keep an anesthetic ear drop on hand for these middle-of-the-night earaches. Give him acetaminophen to lessen the pain (see chart, p. 260). These measures will tide your child over until morning. Be sure to consult your doctor then, even though the child may seem to feel better by morning.

The child with recurrent ear infections. Some children have one ear infection after another, occurring every few weeks. Parents are usually frustrated by the continued medical expense. Although children are usually resilient, children with recurrent ear infections often begin to show deteriorating behavior, such as chronic irritability. The "ear personality" is common in children with recurrent ear infections simply because they do not feel well or hear well. One of the main changes parents notice after these recurrent ear infections are treated appropriately is that their children act better. Remember, a child who feels right is better able to act right.

Parents, take heart. There are ways to prevent these recurrent ear infections. The usual reason children have them is that a previous infection has never completely cleared up and the fluid remains behind the eardrum even though the germs have been treated appropriately with antibiotics. What usually happens is that the child has one ear infection and is treated for seven or ten days; he feels better, and then three or four weeks later he is back in the doctor's office with another ear infection because the fluid remained in the middle ear (or it built up again) and became reinfected.

Preventative regimen for ear infections. If your child's ear infections are occurring more frequently and lasting longer, your doctor may suggest a prevention regimen aimed at preventing the fluid from reaccumulating in the middle ear and at preventing the fluid which does accumulate from becoming infected. One such regimen consists of the following measures:

1. Strict allergy control. Your doctor should take a history to determine what possible allergens, such as dairy products, cigarette smoke, animal dander, or dust from dust-collecting stuffed animals, could be affecting your child. These allergens should be removed from your child's environment. If respiratory allergies are bothersome, consult your doctor about using an air filter.
2. Eustachian tube exercises, such as blowing up balloons, are designed to pop open the eustachian tubes, allowing the accumulated fluid to drain. This is similar to the yawning you do to clear your ears during air travel. Eustachian tube exercises and strict allergy control are designed to keep the fluid from accumulating in the middle ear.
3. Daily medication. Your doctor may prescribe a mild antibiotic to keep the fluid from constantly becoming reinfected. These daily small doses of mild antibiotic are often easier on a child's system than the periodic strong antibiotics.

This prevention regimen is extremely effective for the majority of children. Keeping a child's eustachian tubes free of infection for several months allows them to function properly; repeated infections hinder the eustachian tube from functioning, which results in more infections, and the cycle continues. These prevention regimens are used for periods of three to six months, and thereafter your child is taken off the medications to see if the infection recurs. Most children outgrow these recurrent ear infections by age five.

Surgical treatment. Occasionally a child will not respond to medical treatment of an ear infection. His middle ear will continue to have persistent fluid until it eventually becomes thick and gluelike, and the fluid can be removed only by opening up the eardrum (called a "myringotomy") and draining out the fluid. Tiny plastic tubes are then inserted surgically through the eardrums to allow accumulating fluids to drain out, thus lessening the frequency of middle-ear infections and giving an immediate improvement in the child's hearing. Most children who have had their infections treated appropriately, who have been followed up appropriately, and who have been put on prevention regimens early and long enough have avoided surgical treatment.

We want to caution parents against a common mistake in using the medical system. A child has a few ear infections, and a well-meaning friend or relative says, "Why don't you take your child to an ear specialist?" It is unwise to rush off to a specialist on your own. A better use of the current medical system is to stick with your child's pediatrician, who is trained primarily in the medical treatment of ear infections, is more familiar with childhood ear infections, and is less likely to recommend a surgical remedy. If your child has gone through the nonsurgical steps of treatment and the ear infections continue, your pediatrician then will refer you to an ear specialist. In this case, the decision to administer surgical treatment for your child's ear infections is a combined decision between parent, pediatrician, and ear specialist, and your child will ultimately profit from this communication between his caretakers.

We cannot overemphasize the importance of being vigilant in treating your child's ear infections. Problems with recurrent ear infections usually occur during a time that is very important for language development in the young child. If a child's hearing is diminished periodically during these formative years, the child may show some speech delay as well as some permanent hearing loss. Even more noticeable are the chronic behavioral problems that occur with chronic ear infections. Poor school performance is also a common result of chronic ear infections in the older child.

Common Intestinal Problems

Some variations in children's stools are normal. The first stools of a newly born baby are called meconium and are dark green with a sticky, tar-like consistency. After a few days the stools change to greenish-brown for the next week or two, and then to a normal yellowish-brown color. The stools of breastfed babies tend to be mustard yellow, seedy, and quite soft (even runny) with a buttermilk-like, nonoffensive odor. It is normal for stools to show an occasional green color. They can be persistently green if the child's formula contains added iron. A sick child with a persistently green stool, which is extremely runny and mucousy, may have an intestinal infection. Intestinal problems in a child are nearly always manifested by some outward sign, such as paleness, pain, or poor weight gain. If your child is generally well, it is unlikely that she has any serious underlying intestinal problem, even though her stools may seem unusual.

A change in diet is often accompanied by a change in stool consistency. Some formulas are more constipating than others. Rice and bananas tend to be constipating foods; food that loosen the stools are corn syrup and most fruits and fruit juices, especially prunes or prune juice. It is common for stools to be loose during any condition that produces a lot of mucous in the throat, such as teething or a cold. Because antibiotics often change the kind of bacteria that normally reside in the intestines, a few weeks of loose stools often follow a course of antibiotics. We advise parents to give an acidophilus culture, either liquid, tablets, or powder mixed in water, when a child is taking an antibiotic to help replenish the intestines with helpful bacteria that may have been killed by the antibiotic. Buy the kind sold in nutrition stores that is kept under refrigeration.

Constipation refers to the consistency of the child's stools and difficulty in passing them, not to the frequency of stools. Some infants and small children have bowel movements once every three to five days, and if they do not appear uncomfortable, they are not constipated. A constipated baby draws his legs up onto a distended abdomen, strains, and becomes red in the face; he passes hard, pellet-like stools with much difficulty. Since the infant's rectum is often small, the passage of a hard stool can cause a small tear in the wall of the rectum called a rectal fissure. This fissure can produce a few streaks of fresh blood on the stool or a few drops of blood on the diaper. It can also cause bowel movements to hurt so that an older baby will become reluctant to let his stools pass.

Treatment of constipation. To help your constipated infant pass a stool, use child-size glycerin suppositories. These are available at drugstores without prescription. They look like little rocket ships, and for the tiny baby, you may need to cut the suppository in half and insert the pointed top end. Insert the suppository high into his rectum, and hold his buttocks together for a few minutes so that the suppository can dissolve.

If one formula appears to be constipating, try a change of formula, and give your baby extra water. Adding a tablespoon of corn syrup to eight ounces of formula also may soften your infant's stools, but do not add it more than once or twice a day without first checking with your doctor. By three months of age a bottlefed baby may need some dietary laxative and is old enough to add some pureed prunes or prune juice to his diet.

Constipation in the breastfeeding baby is seldom a problem. Occasionally, breastfed babies older than two months may have a bowel movement only once every three to seven days; when the stool finally comes, it is not hard at all, but more like a major mudslide! Unless the baby is uncomfortable (most are not), you don't need to worry. If the stool is hard, or baby is uncomfortable, follow the advice given on the use of suppositories, prunes, and/or extra water.

Constipation in the older child commonly causes recurrent abdominal pain. Busy children often ignore the urge to defecate, and they allow the stool to remain in the rectum until it gets hard. Because a hard stool is usually a painful stool to pass, children choose to ignore their urges and their constipation worsens. The longer a child continues this pattern, the weaker the rectal muscles become. This weakens the urge to defecate, creating a vicious and long-standing cycle of constipation. Older children (ages five to ten) who are chronically constipated often will soil their pants. This embarrassing problem presents itself as a "diarrhea" problem, but is in reality due to the leaking of stools from lower intestinal muscles that have been weakened by chronic constipation. Paradoxically, treating the child with soiled pants as a constipated child can resolve this embarrassing problem.

You can treat constipation in the older child by following these suggestions. Teach your child to respond immediately to her urge-to-go signal, not to hold on to her stools. Explain to her that not following this signal weakens the "donut muscle" around the rectum (draw her a simple sketch), causing the constipation to get worse, and will eventually cause her to have pain when she has a bowel movement.

Your doctor may prescribe stool softeners or laxatives before bedtime to encourage your child to have a bowel movement the next morning. Some naturally laxative foods include fruit, prune juice, corn syrup, vegetable roughage, and bran cereal. Encourage your constipated child to drink lots of water as well. Potentially constipating foods are rice, cheese, bananas, and chocolate. Remember that it takes four to six weeks to treat chronic constipation. The stools need to remain soft for that length of time in order for the intestinal muscles to regain their strength.

Diarrhea, meaning "liquid stools," refers more to the consistency of the stools than to the frequency. Infants and children normally have prolonged periods of loose stools due to some conditions already mentioned above. When should you worry about diarrhea? The most frequent cause of problem diarrhea in childhood is the intestinal infection gastroenteritis, usually caused by a virus. If the intestinal lining becomes infected, it heals very slowly. During the healing process, the enzymes in the intestinal lining that help digest and absorb food do not function properly. This results in stools that are very frequent, watery, explosive, green, mucousy, and foul smelling. This kind of diarrhea is usually accompanied by cold symptoms and a generally unwell child.

Diarrhea becomes a worrisome problem when it leads to dehydration, a condition in which your child loses more water and body salts than he takes in. Signs of dehydration in your child are: obvious weight loss; dry eyes, dry skin, and dry mouth; diminishing urine output; and often fever. No matter how frequent and loose your child's stools seem to be, if he is happy, bright-eyed, has wet eyes and mouth, is urinating well, and has not lost weight, you do not have to worry.

Treatment of diarrhea. Your main goal in treating your child for diarrhea is to avoid dehydration. Decrease those foods that cannot be absorbed by infected intestines, and increase solutions containing extra salt and water to replenish what your child loses in the diarrhea. The following suggestions will help you accomplish these goals.

Weigh your baby (without her clothes) on the most accurate scale you can obtain. This is her baseline weight. Weigh her daily, preferably each morning before you feed her. If she has no significant weight loss, she is not becoming dehydrated. As a rough guide, if your child loses up to 5 percent of her baseline body weight (for example, a twenty-pound child loses one pound), she has experienced a significant amount of dehydration, and you should call your doctor. Rapid weight loss should concern you more than slow and gradual weight loss. A twenty-pound infant's losing a pound of body weight over a period of two days is a much greater concern than his losing the same amount of weight over a period of a week or two. Infants usually appear very sick with a rapid weight loss, but do not usually appear that sick if the weight loss has been slow and gradual.

Stop all solid food, dairy products, and formulas made with cow's milk. If you are breastfeeding, continue, since human milk is not nearly as irritating to infected intestines as cow's milk products. This is true also if your child is vomiting. Breast milk is easy on the stomach and will help fight the infection. Meanwhile, nursing is comforting to your child.

If you are bottlefeeding or if your child is weaned from the breast, give him a clear fluid diet. These fluids should contain simple sugars, which are easy to digest in order to provide calories, and salts, which your child is losing in the diarrhea fluid. Make a sugar solution by adding one level tablespoon of ordinary table sugar to eight ounces of boiled water (do not boil the sugar solution, as that can cause it to be too strong). Flat ginger ale and colas (left open so the fizz is gone) are ready, available sources of sugar. Fluids that contain the right balance of salts are called "oral electrolyte solutions" (Pedialyte and Infalyte are available at your pharmacy or grocery store without prescription). Do not continue these electrolyte solutions for more than twenty-four hours without checking with your physician. The sips-and-chips method of administering fluids provides your child small, frequent feedings (two ounces at a time) rather than a large feeding. In the older infant this is accomplished best by frequent sips of fluid along with ice chips or juice popsicles. A clear fluid diet alone should not be continued more than forty-eight hours without checking with your physician, since this kind of diet continued too long may itself produce diarrhea, called "starvation stools."

After twenty-four to forty-eight hours, if your child is not losing weight and the diarrhea has lessened somewhat, add semi-solid foods such as rice cereal, without milk, and mashed bananas. Continue the regimen of small, frequent fluid feedings. As the stools continue to improve, gradually add applesauce, saltine crackers, gelatin, and yogurt. As your child's stools become more solid, so can his diet.

Resume milk or formula very gradually and only after you have seen much improvement in your child's condition. At first, dilute the milk or formula at half its regular strength. Gradually return to the regular strength over the next several days. Do not boil milk or give undiluted skim milk to a child who is recovering from diarrhea since these solutions are too concentrated and may worsen the dehydration.

If the diarrhea worsens after you have gone back to dairy products, go back a few steps and begin the regimen all over again. For a formula-fed child who is recovering from diarrhea, a soybean-based formula is often tolerated better than a formula made with cow's milk. Following an intestinal infection, it is normal to have a prolonged period of loose stools ("nuisance diarrhea"), which may last for several weeks or months. This is because the intestinal lining is very slow to heal in most children. If your child has persistent diarrhea, it is important to assess the total child rather than only his stools. If your child appears generally well and is not continuing to lose weight, you do not need to worry even though his stools remain loose.

When to call your doctor about diarrhea. If you have followed these steps and your child

INFECTIOUS CHILDHOOD DISEASES

Since children are social creatures, they tend to share infectious diseases. The following chart will help you identify these illnesses and treat them appropriately.

	CHARACTERISTIC FEATURES	TREATMENT AND PRECAUTIONS
Measles (red measles)	• begins like common cold: runny nose; severe cough; reddened eyes, sensitive to light • high fever (104 degrees), lasts five days • rash: purplish-red, raised, begins on face, spreads to entire body, begins at height of fever, lasts five days	• contagious from onset of symptoms until end of rash • preventable by vaccine • treatment: fever control, comforting measures
German measles (rubella)	• low fever (101 degrees), mild cold • rash: pinkish-red, faint, disappears by third day • swollen glands behind neck • differs from red measles: child not very sick, lower fever, fainter rash, less cough	• contagious from a week before rash to five days after rash gone • preventable by vaccine • avoid exposure to pregnant women • treatment: comforting measures
Mumps	• begins as flu-like illness • neck glands beneath earlobe markedly swollen and tender • low fever (101 degrees), headache, nausea	• contagious from onset of symptoms until swelling gone • preventable by vaccine • treatment: comforting measures
Roseola	• usually affects babies between nine and eighteen months of age • sudden onset of high fever (103–105 degrees) in previously-well baby • lasts three days • baby "not very sick" • rash: rose-pink, faint, appears after fever gone, lasts twenty-four hours	• not considered a serious illness • no vaccine • not highly contagious • treatment: comforting measures
Chicken pox	• low fever (101–102 degrees), generally unwell feeling • rash: initially may appear on trunk as tiny dots resembling bites, rapidly progresses to blister-like vesicles on red bases; new crops appear rapidly as old ones form a crust	• contagious from two days before rash until all vesicles crusted over • preventable by vaccine • treatment: comforting measures, try to limit scratching
Scarlet fever	• sunburn-like, red rash • fever (103 degrees) and sick child • sore throat, swollen neck glands • tongue white-coated or strawberry red, same as strep throat with a rash • rash: rose-pink, faint	• cause: streptococcus • contagious for twenty-four to forty-eight hours after antibiotics begun • treatment: antibiotics

continues to lose weight, shows signs of dehydration, is in increasing pain, or looks increasingly ill, call your doctor for more advice. Before making your call, have the following information available: the frequency and characteristics of the stools; the degree of weight loss and over what period of time; details about any associated symptoms such as vomiting, fever, signs of a cold or increasing pain, and any signs of dehydration; and what kind of treatment you have been giving. Parents, do not be disappointed if your doctor decides not to administer medication to attempt to stop your child's diarrhea. Most diarrhea in childhood is best treated by dietary restrictions and time. Narcotic medications, which are often used to control diarrhea in adults, are generally not safe for children.

Besides these methods of treatment, much patience and prayer are needed to cope with diarrhea in a young child because this problem is usually a long-term nuisance. Vomiting and diarrhea occurring together are more worrisome than if one occurs without the other.

Vomiting in the young infant. Most vomiting in the first few months is simply regurgitation (spitting up) resulting from a temporary feeding problem, such as air-swallowing or overfeeding (see also GER, p. 233). This vomiting is not usually a medical problem and usually subsides when the infant sits upright, when he is between six and eight months. Milk allergy is also a cause of vomiting in the young infant.

Vomiting in the older infant is caused most often by an infection or an irritation of the stomach, called "gastritis." This condition is often accompanied by nausea, stomachache, and retching (dry heaves).

There are more serious causes of vomiting. In the tiny infant, projectile vomiting (vomitus propelled under great force for several feet) that persists with nearly every feeding and is accompanied by signs of weight loss may indicate a condition called pyloric stenosis. This condition occurs primarily in male infants under two months of age and is due to the lower end of the stomach being too narrow for food to pass through. The sudden onset of vomiting in a generally ill-appearing child, persistent green bile vomitus, accompanied by severe abdominal pain, are signs that the intestines are twisted and obstructed. These conditions are surgical emergencies and require immediate medical attention.

How to assess and treat the vomiting child. If your child's vomiting is associated with other symptoms, such as moderate abdominal pain, signs of cold, high fever, headaches, or increasing drowsiness, it is probably due to a temporary intestinal infection that can be treated by methods similar to those described in the section on diarrhea. Prevent dehydration by replacing the fluids he loses in his vomitus. Use the sips-and-chips method of fluid replacement. Popsicles made with frozen apple juice, flat (no fizz) ginger ale, flat cola, or ice chips are the best means of getting fluids into an infant or a child very slowly. Popsicles also can be made with the oral electrolyte solutions described earlier. The sips-and-chips method gives the small, frequent feedings necessary if the lining of the stomach is infected. Allowing larger amounts of fluid intake can cause rebound vomiting, resulting in more electrolyte loss. Breastfeeding can continue; express some of your milk before offering the partially empty breast to your baby if larger amounts of milk come back up too quickly.

Follow the same guidelines described under the section on diarrhea for noting signs of dehydration and for knowing when to call your doctor. Anti-vomiting medications are usually not effective in children. As with the treatment of diarrhea, diet restriction and fluid replacement will prevent dehydration in the vomiting child.

COMMON CHILDHOOD EMERGENCIES

Because children are active and curious, they are subject to bumps and scrapes. Be familiar with the following information to respond effectively in the event of a medical emergency.

Poisoning

If your child swallows a potentially poisonous substance, the following emergency steps should be followed:

1. Encourage your child to drink lots of water to dilute the poison.

2. Call your local poison control center. Their phone number may be found by consulting your local hospital or in the yellow pages. It would be wise to display the phone number of the poison control center in a conspicuous place, such as on your telephone. Or, call the operator.

3. Keep *syrup of ipecac* in your medicine cabinet. This syrup is very effective for inducing vomiting, thereby removing the potentially harmful substance. If advised to induce vomiting by your poison control center, give your child one tablespoon (three teaspoons) of syrup of ipecac in eight ounces of water or noncarbonated fruit juice. If vomiting does not occur within twenty minutes, give one more tablespoon of ipecac in juice or water. Be prepared for the vomiting by keeping your child in the bathroom for forty-five minutes after the first dose of ipecac. It is important not to give ipecac or induce vomiting before consulting the poison control center because certain poisons may be harmful if

vomiting is induced, and some substances may not require vomiting at all.

Head Injuries

God anticipated busy children would sustain many falls and knocks to the head during the normal process of growing up. For this reason, He provided the skull as a helmet to protect the brain so that most falls on the head hurt the scalp but do not injure the brain. Because the scalp is very rich in blood vessels, even a small cut on the scalp bleeds profusely. Blows to the scalp may break the underlying blood vessels, producing the large swelling known as a "goose-egg."

First-aid steps for head injuries: (1) If your child has a cut or swelling, apply an ice pack and pressure for at least twenty minutes. This usually stops the bleeding and will reduce the size of the eventual goose egg. (2) Lay your child down in a comfortable place and begin a period of observation. If there is an underlying brain injury, it takes time for the swelling or bleeding in the brain to produce signs of internal pressure. The signs of a brain injury may not develop for several hours. Observe your child for the following signs:

1. *Is your child alert?* Is he responding to simple questions? Does he seem aware of his name, where he is, where he lives, the names of Mommy and Daddy and brothers and sisters? Be prepared for your child's wanting to go to sleep after a head injury since sleep is the usual refuge of consolation for an injured child. Let your child fall asleep, but observe him every couple of hours for any change in breathing patterns or skin color.

2. *Can your child look at you straight in the eye?* The eyes are the mirror of the brain, especially in a head injury. If your child looks at you straight in the eye, if his pupils are the same size in both eyes, and if he can see objects clearly, he is not likely to have an underlying brain injury. Ask your child to cover one eye and count how many fingers he sees. If he complains of seeing double, you have cause for concern.

3. *Is your child vomiting persistently?* It is normal for children to vomit once or twice after a blow to the head; therefore, it is wise to feed your child only clear fluids following the injury. If your child shows persistent vomiting, even of clear fluids, call your doctor.

4. *Is your child walking steadily?* If your child is off balance, especially if he is exhibiting weakness in one arm or leg, contact your doctor.

5. *Does your child have headaches?* Some headaches are to be expected after a blow

to the head, and they usually subside within a few hours. If your child's headaches increase in severity—especially if they are accompanied by increasing disorientation and persistent vomiting—call your doctor. Do not give aspirin for head injuries since it may increase the bleeding. Acetaminophen is the preferred pain-reliever.

When should you call your doctor? If any of the above five concerns occur, call your doctor immediately or take your child to the hospital. If none of the signs are apparent, you may wish to check with your doctor shortly after the accident for further instructions. If signs of brain injury are not present, you do not need to rush your child to a hospital for x-rays. A period of careful observation and a medical examination are more useful than x-rays. Your doctor will advise you as to whether x-rays are necessary.

Choking

Infants and small children like to "mouth" small objects, which can get caught in their throats and obstruct their breathing. Try the following procedure if your child starts choking:

1. If your child can talk, cry, or cough, her airway is not obstructed and you should not interfere with her own efforts to dislodge the material. If your child is breathing normally and is not panicky, give her emotional support and allow her cough reflex to expel the object.
2. If your child cannot speak or cry, is having difficulty getting air, is blue, or is losing consciousness, position her head-down and apply four hard blows to her back between the shoulder blades. If the blows to the back do not dislodge the object, administer four chest thrusts: with your child lying on her back on the floor, place your hands alongside the lower rib cage on both sides and quickly compress the chest inward and upward with the thrusts of your arms. If the chest-thrust procedure does not dislodge the object, repeat the four back blows.
3. While administering step 2, call to someone to summon the paramedics. It is wise to have your local paramedics' number displayed conspicuously on every phone in the house. In most metropolitan cities the paramedic system is now tied in with a simple 911, making it unnecessary to take time to look up a number. In many cities, the 911 system is automatically tied into a computer that gives the paramedics the name and location of the dialing phone. It is wise to check periodically to see if the 911 emergency system is operating in your community.

The Heimlich maneuver is another procedure for dislodging an object caught in the airway of a choking person. Most authorities recommend the combination of back blows and chest thrusts in infants up to three-year-olds because of the possible damage to abdominal organs with the Heimlich maneuver. For children over three years of age the Heimlich maneuver is preferable and is performed as follows: stand behind the choking child and wrap your arms around her waist, making a fist with one hand and grasping the fist with the other. Place the thumb side of your fist toward the upper abdomen and compress with a quick upward thrust, repeating several times if necessary. This abdominal pressure is transmitted to the lungs, and pushes the object up out of the airway.

It is not wise to use your finger to dislodge the object from the back of the child's throat unless you can see the object and are certain you can get your finger around it. Inserting a large finger in a child's small throat may push the object farther back into the throat or may cause the child to panic and suck the object into her lungs.

Interrupted Breathing

If your child is still not breathing after any foreign object is expelled (see "Choking," above, and be sure someone has summoned the paramedics), employ mouth-to-mouth breathing. Place your child on his back and slightly bend his neck forward and his head backward in the so-called sniffing position. This is best attempted by kneeling alongside your child and placing one hand under his neck and the other on his forehead.

Fit your mouth snugly around your child's lips and nose. If your child is too large for you to make a good seal over his mouth and nose, pinch his nose and seal his mouth only. For a tiny baby, give four quick, gentle puffs (a puff is about the amount of air you can hold in your cheeks). For an older child, give enough air to make his chest rise. Apply a breath every two to three seconds. Continue the mouth-to-mouth breathing until your child resumes breathing himself or until trained help arrives.

We strongly advise all parents and expectant parents to take a CPR course from their local Red Cross.

Swallowed Objects

Children are prone to swallow small objects such as coins. Most of these pass through the intestines and are eliminated in twenty-four to forty-eight hours without causing harm. Occasionally, objects such as a coin or hard candy may lodge in the child's esophagus, causing excessive drooling (because the child cannot swallow his saliva) and pain in the area where the object has become stuck. If these signs occur in your child, take him to the hospital or call your doctor for advice.

Convulsions

Most convulsions in a previously well child less than five years old are caused by fever and are called febrile convulsions. These convulsions usually stop when you lower the fever (see p. 258-260) for ways to lower your child's fever). As long as he is breathing well and is not blue during these febrile convulsions, your child's shaking arms and legs do not harm him, and the shaking will gradually subside as the fever is lowered.

If your child stops breathing during a convulsion, is foaming at the mouth, or turning blue, place him on his stomach with his head turned to one side, allowing the secretions to drain out of his throat and his tongue to fall forward. This clears your child's airway, allowing him to breathe during the convulsion. If your child is showing signs of breathing difficulty during the convulsion, paramedics should be called immediately.

Burns

If your child is burned, the following emergency steps will lessen the pain and severity of the burn:

1. Immediately submerge the burned area in cold water for at least twenty minutes. Do not use ice packs or bare ice cubes on the burn since these may increase the damage to the tissue caused by the burn.
2. Cover the burned area with a clean cloth and run cold water over it until the pain of the burn subsides. Do not apply butter or oils.
3. Take your child to the hospital or call your doctor for advice on continued care of the burn.

Besides the above first-aid measures to alleviate the pain and minimize skin damage, the following suggestions will lessen the cosmetic scarring of the burned area:

1. Keep the burn covered with an appropriate antibiotic ointment, such as silvadene, prescribed by your doctor.
2. Do not break the blisters without your doctor's advice.
3. Wash the burned area twice a day under a jet of water, such as a tap or shower, and pat it dry thoroughly with a clean cloth.
4. To prevent contracture of the burned area if the burn is over a place where the skin must flex (such as the palm of the hand or the wrist), frequent stretching of the burned area should be encouraged.
5. As the burned area is healing, your doctor may need to remove some of the dead tissue to minimize infection. Some burns heal better with the open method (washed frequently and covered with an

appropriate antibiotic ointment but without a dressing), and others need to be covered with a dressing. Your doctor will advise you which method of treatment is necessary.

Nosebleeds

Most nosebleeds in children are due to nose picking or drying of the tiny blood vessels lining the inside of the nostrils. They are more common in the wintertime, especially in homes with central heating, because the low humidity causes the inside of the nose to dry. If your child is prone to nosebleeds, running a humidifier or vaporizer during the months requiring central heating may be necessary.

Apply the following first-aid measures during a nosebleed. Push a ball of wet cotton into the bleeding nostril and pinch the nostrils together for ten minutes. At the same time, apply pressure to the upper lip just below the nostrils. This compresses the major blood vessel supplying the nose. Seat your child leaning slightly forward. After the nosebleed stops, leave the piece of cotton lodged in your child's nostril for several hours and then remove it very gently, being careful not to dislodge the clot and cause bleeding to recur. If using these measures does not stop your child's nosebleed, call your doctor or take your child to the hospital.

Nose Injuries

The nose contains tiny, soft bones and acts like a shock absorber that protects against jarring of the underlying brain. Nasal bones are easily fractured, and the following emergency measures will minimize cosmetic and functional impairment from a blow to the nose. Apply an ice pack to the area of swelling for at least a half hour following the trauma. After this, if your child can breathe easily through both nostrils and the nose is not crooked, it is likely to heal well without the fracture having to be set. If signs of breathing obstruction or cosmetic distortion are present, consult your doctor immediately.

Eye Injuries

The two most common eye injuries in childhood are irritations from chemicals splashed into the eye and foreign bodies lodged in the eye. If your child splashes an irritant into her eye, immediately rinse out the eye for ten minutes. This is best accomplished by pouring a gentle stream of lukewarm water over your child's eyes from a pitcher. Foreign bodies (such as an eyelash or a speck of dirt) are most safely removed by a twist of moist cotton cloth. If the foreign bodies are not easily removed by this method, seek medical advice.

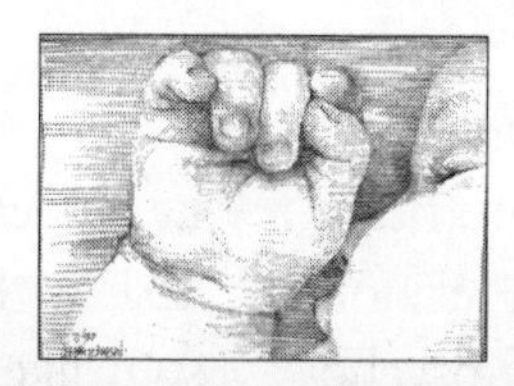

CHAPTER TWELVE

Weaning, Starting Solids, and **Nutrition Concerns**

By the middle of the first year, many babies are ready to try solid foods. As children's diets become more varied, parents must make decisions about nutrition, and the choices you make now set the pattern for your child's eating habits (and your own) for years to come. This chapter gives you the information you need to help your child learn to eat wisely.

Breastfeeding remains an important part of good nutrition well after the time babies get their first taste of mashed bananas and pureed carrots. It is also an important mothering tool, so if you are wondering if it's time to wean, think again. Nursing a baby into toddlerhood may be a bit unusual in our culture, but it has many benefits for your child and for you.

THE BLESSINGS OF A TIMELY WEANING

We do not recommend weaning for infants. Rather, we believe that western culture's custom of weaning from the breast by six or eight months of age is not in accordance with God's design for mother-infant attachment. Weaning an infant before his time breaks the nurturing continuum and deprives him of an important comforting resource. Our culture thinks of breastfeeding in terms of months and considers it only as a form of nutrition. It is much more; breastfeeding is a relationship. It is both physiologically and psychologically correct to think of breastfeeding in terms of years. Former Surgeon General Antonio Novello put it well when she said, "It's the lucky baby, I feel, who continues to nurse until he's two."

There are several major weanings throughout a child's life—from the womb, from the breast, from home to school—and many minor ones. The pace at which children make these transitions and attain these milestones needs to be respected. La Leche League's term for nursing toddlers, "little nursing persons," demonstrates this respect. Even a baby who is not breastfed, or who is weaned from breast to bottle, deserves this consideration. There is no need to be in a hurry to end a baby's access to sucking until he is ready (perhaps with some encouragement) to leave it behind.

The Biblical Approach to Weaning

Weaning took place very late among the Israelites, at least by today's standards. Hebrew mothers breastfed their little ones for at least three years. When weaning was complete, it was ceremonially a festive occasion, not the end of a struggle that produced a feeling of loss or detachment for the child: "On the day that Isaac was weaned Abraham held a great feast" (Gen. 21:8). The peace and contentment a child should have by the time he is weaned is stated beautifully in Psalm 131:2: "But I have stilled and quieted my soul; like a weaned child with its mother; like a weaned child is my soul within me." And it is a child, no longer a baby, who is now able to comfort himself.

The biblical story of Hannah and her son Samuel is an early account of mother-infant attachment and priority mothering:

> *When the man Elkanah went up with all his family to offer the annual sacrifice to the LORD and to fulfill his vow, Hannah did not go. She said to her husband, "After the boy is weaned, I will take him and present him before the LORD, and he will live there always." "Do what seems best to you," Elkanah her husband told her. "Stay here until you have weaned him. . . ." So the woman stayed at home and nursed her son until she had weaned him. (1 Sam. 1:22–23)*

Bible commentators feel that Samuel's weaning occurred when he was around three years of age. This would have been typical for the Hebrew culture of the time. "Do what seems best to you" is a clear indication that Elkanah supported Hannah's God-given intuition. The Scripture itself doesn't state the age of weaning, but we can safely assume Hannah was not asking Eli, the high priest, to baby-sit. The Scripture says, "After he was weaned, she took the boy, young as he was . . . and brought him to the house of the LORD at Shiloh" (1 Sam. 1:24). After they made the sacrifices, they presented young Samuel to Eli, and Hannah told how God had given Samuel to her. Then she said, "So now I give him to the LORD. For his whole life he will be given over to the LORD." And, the Scripture says, "He worshipped the LORD there" (vv. 25–28).

Chapter 2 opens with Hannah's prayer of praise to God, then tells us that they went home, "but the boy ministered before the LORD under Eli the priest." Hannah's weaning Samuel is an example of God's design for weaning a child from his mother to his God. He was weaned at an age when he would be of service to Eli and be able to minister before the Lord and worship the Lord. Samuel became a great and wise prophet in Israel. He first learned about God from the instructions and then from the actions of his mother, a woman of faith and courage. In the years before he was weaned, he was able to learn all these things. Hannah did not wean him before his time!

The Hebrew word for *weaned* in the above passages is *gamal,* which means "to ripen." The term implies a state of readiness. Weaning should not mean the loss of a relationship or a sudden detachment from mother, but rather a state in which a child feels so full and so right that he is ready to take on other relationships. This kind of weaning implies a smooth continuum from the security and guidance of mother to security and guidance from other relationships, from within, and from God. Weaning before his time can leave a child unfulfilled, his sense of trust violated. A child who is weaned before his time from any childhood need and hurried into independence may rebel both inwardly and outwardly and show what we call "diseases of premature weaning." Many of the usual behaviors of infancy and childhood, such as aggression, excessive clinginess, frequent mood swings, and aloofness may, in fact, be diseases of premature weaning.

Advantages of Extended Breastfeeding

Breastfeeding provides both nutritional and emotional nourishment. We (and the Academy of Pediatrics) advise mothers to breastfeed *at least* one year for nutrition. Many infants who are weaned before their first birthday experience medical illnesses, such as ear infections, diarrhea, and allergies shortly after weaning. Babies weaned this young will need to go onto formula, unless they are past one year and can tolerate cow's milk. In the second year, breastfeeding still provides excellent nourishment and also begins to provide the security toddlers are so in need of, a pick-me-up during times of stress, and a time mother and toddler can relax and have their special dialogue.

You may ask, "Won't prolonged nursing make my baby too dependent on me?" The answer is an unreserved no! Mothers who nurse for several years find their children are secure and confident. When the closeness of breastfeeding continues through toddlerhood, mothers find that they have a good handle on what makes their child tick (part of really knowing your child). They also have an excellent tool for helping their fledglings manage the intricacies and difficulties of early growing up. All of this adds up to giving breastfeeding mothers an edge when it comes to discipline.

Guidelines for Weaning

As your child grows older, her needs do not lessen, they only change. The American Heritage Dictionary defines weaning: "to withhold mother's milk and substitute other nourishment." There are two parts to weaning: withholding and substitution. As a baby is gradually shifted from the nutritional nourishment of mother's milk and solid food is substituted, other forms of emotional nourishment should be substituted for mother's breast.

Don't set an arbitrary date at which you are going to wean. As in many aspects of childrearing, the clock and the calendar have no place in the breastfeeding relationship. You may decide during pregnancy that you're going to breastfeed for six months, nine months, or a year, but you may feel differently about your goal as the preordained time approaches.

The best approach to weaning for both you and your child is to allow the process to unfold gradually according to your child's own developmental timetable. An abrupt or rushed weaning should only happen in emergencies, and then the baby or toddler would need to have a very strong and familiar support system in place to help him through it and maintain his sense of security and attachment. The mother would also need support. A very few babies have weaned on their own as early as nine months, usually because they discover walking and also have satisfied their need for sucking by then. Most often, if a baby under the age of one refuses to breastfeed, it does not mean he is ready to wean. This is actually fairly common and is known as a nursing strike, something you help your baby get through and continue breastfeeding for many more months. (See "Nursing Nuisances" in chapter 6.)

Your baby probably will start to skip one feeding time a day as he becomes busy with other pursuits. After several weeks or months of skipping this nursing, you may find he will be equally willing to miss another feeding. As the weeks and months pass, he eventually will be nursing only for naps and bedtime, maybe in the early morning when he wakes up, or in emergencies like "owies."

Be prepared to have him nurse more during times of stress such as illness, new developmental stages, changes in environment, and so on. A good way to state this guideline is one we have borrowed from La Leche

League: Don't offer, don't refuse. And while, of course, you would not refuse a toddler who is sick, you can certainly take the lead as he gets older and distract, postpone, or offer a substitute snack. Often a toddler asks to nurse because he is bored. He'd much rather be outside playing or helping Mom "wash dishes," or be read to. (Beware the toddler who figures out Mom could nurse and read at the same time!) Watch for signs that you may be rushing the process: clinginess, negativity, withdrawal, excessive crying. You may need to ease off a bit and give your toddler a little more time to mature.

You may be willing, even eager, to continue nursing for quite a while longer. It can be an easy way to get a child to sleep or help her over the rough spots of toddlerhood. If there is a definite reason, however, that you need to encourage an end to nursing, be careful to consider your child's needs too. An important part of the weaning process is substituting not only alternative nourishment, but also alternative attachment. There is no shortcut in this process—you are still committed to filling your little one's needs, one way or another. If you must discontinue the bedtime nursing, for example,

WEANING IN PREGNANCY

If you become pregnant when your baby is under one year of age, and he is not eating much or enough solid food yet, you will probably need to supplement your breastfeeding with formula. The reason for this is that pregnancy causes your milk supply to decrease naturally. Also, your nipples may become too sensitive to allow for the same amount of breastfeeding your baby is accustomed to. Pregnancy is a naturally-induced time for at least partial weaning, even from baby's point of view, because the taste of the milk changes and some babies don't like it. (Of course, other babies couldn't care less.)

Many mothers do continue to nurse during their pregnancy, at least long enough to allow for a gradual weaning. This is completely safe as long as you do not have any risk for preterm labor, and even then it is safe until the oxytocin receptors in the uterus become active around twenty weeks. Some mothers choose to continue nursing through their entire pregnancy and then tandem nurse both baby and toddler. This is a very personal decision that you will want to pray about. In some ways it makes life easier to be able to still have breastfeeding as a comforting tool and a source of security for the older one, as long as you can do it without resentment and are able to set limits. It helps to talk with other mothers who have done this for reassurance and support when you need it.

try substituting a snack, stories, and a cuddle, but you may have to cuddle in positions other than the familiar nursing position. Let your husband take over at these times if possible, and spend more one-on-one time together throughout the day to reassure your child of your availability and commitment.

It is normal to have ambivalent feelings about continued breastfeeding, especially if you are the only person you know who is nursing an eighteen-month-old. Pray to God for the wisdom to know when and how to wean your child and for the perseverance toward toddler-led weaning. Find support for yourself by attending La Leche League toddler meetings or by reading books about toddler nursing and weaning (see bibliography). The weaning period should be a time of contentment for both mother and child. Remember, moving toward other relationships should bring a sense of completion, not detachment and loss.

INTRODUCING SOLID FOODS—WHEN, WHAT, AND HOW MUCH?

Infants under six months of age do not need solid food. Your baby may show signs around four months that make you think he is interested in solid foods. Remember, though, that baby's intestines may not be mature enough yet. And it could just be the activity of eating he's interested in. Proceed with caution if you do feed him, and watch for signs that baby is not ready. If the food goes through into the diapers mostly undigested, if baby becomes constipated, or if he has abdominal pain, hold off and try again when he's older.

Adding solid foods to baby's diet will change the character of his bowel movements. The stool of breastfed babies will lose the almost pleasant "ripe buttermilk" odor (one reason breastfeeding mothers hesitate to start solids). Some babies will get runny stools; other babies will get firmer stools. If your baby becomes constipated, see "Common Intestinal Problems," in chapter 11.

One sign of readiness for solids is a shortened interval between feedings. Your intuition may tell you your baby is less satisfied even after three or four days of increased nursing. The nutritional needs of most infants can be met fully by breastfeeding or by an iron-fortified formula alone for nine months, but mothers are advised to start solids when milk feedings no longer seem sufficient. Solids are usually started for breastfed infants later because breastfeeding mothers respond to a growth spurt by increasing the frequency of feedings for several days, and once the supply equals the new demand level, baby nurses less often. Bottle-feeding mothers are more likely to want to begin solids than to increase the number of formula feedings. And since breast milk is a more complete food, baby benefits more from receiving a larger amount of milk than from having solid food added to his diet.

Your baby's need to chew and bite becomes obvious when she starts getting teeth, which is usually around six months. Her tongue and mouth muscles are getting ready for the new skill of taking in solid food and swallowing it. She watches you eat with great interest, and since the best way to explore any unknown is to grab it and put it in her mouth, that's what she tries to do with the food she sees you eating.

When you find yourself competing with your baby for your own dinner, the time is right to let her discover this new way of eating. With baby in a highchair or on your lap, simply offer her a tiny taste on the tip of your finger. She will grab your finger and eagerly suck on it to experience this new material. If you use a spoon, fill just the very tip of it because she may grab the spoon (be prepared for a mess). Your baby may get a pleased and excited expression on her face, or she may frown and let the offered food slide right back out. Most babies like ripe, mashed bananas or pureed yellow vegetables, like squash or sweet potatoes, or rice cereal mixed with a little breast milk or water. Mashed bananas or a small amount of rice cereal are good test foods for solid feedings because they are most like milk in taste and texture.

TIPS FOR STARTING SOLIDS

- Since infants have no concept of breakfast, lunch, and dinner food, it really makes no difference whether they get fruit for breakfast or cereal for dinner.
- Morning is usually the best time to offer solid foods to formula-fed infants because it is usually the time of day when mothers have the most time to prepare their infants' food.
- Breastfed infants should be offered solids when mother's milk supply is lowest, usually toward the end of the day.
- Begin with a small amount of solid food (possibly a quarter teaspoon), since your initial goal is to introduce your baby gradually to a variety of foods, not to fill him up.
- Never force-feed your baby; this introduces a negative experience into his early eating habits. When baby is satisfied, he will turn his head away or refuse the food.
- Introduce only one food at a time, and wait a few days before adding another food. This will allow you to determine what food is at fault if your baby has a reaction.

Babies have built-in protective mechanisms that enable them to push foreign objects out of their mouths with their tongues. They have to outgrow this tongue-thrust reflex before they are ready for solid foods. If your baby eagerly and easily swallows her first dose of solids, then she has demonstrated her readiness. If the banana comes back at you rather quickly or if your baby demonstrates difficulty in swallowing or a lack of desire, then she is not ready.

Introducing solid food is much easier when your baby has the developmental skills she needs to handle the eating process: sitting up with support, and reaching out and touching food and bringing it to her mouth. Babies often show these abilities by six months.

Infant feeders (or nipples with extra large holes) that allow babies to suck baby food through a nipple are not acceptable. Babies need to learn to use different muscle actions for managing solid foods than for sucking. A baby who is too young to use the correct eating muscles is too young to be given solid food. If it is the mess you are worried about, here is a hint for less messy feeding times: put baby in a high chair facing you and gently hold his hands in your nondominant hand while you feed him with your other hand.

Once he resists your hand holding, just undress him and let him dig in. Older babies should be allowed to feed themselves as much as possible with their hands. The goal here is not how much food you can shovel in, but how well baby learns to explore and enjoy his food. As with breastfeeding, there is more going on at mealtime than just taking in calories. Baby is taking in a new experience with taste and textures, and part of how he learns this is with his God-given instinct for hand-to-mouth movements. His hands need to explore what then goes into his mouth to explore. That process is actually more appropriate developmentally than any lessons in neatness or deportment. Another important part of mealtime is socialization and modeling. Baby will naturally want to imitate your actions. So try to relax about whatever mess may occur. Cover the floor with newspapers or get a dog.

Feed solid food after breast or bottle-feeding. Milk should be your baby's primary food during the first year, since it is the most complete source of balanced nutrition. Solid foods should complement the milk feedings, not interfere with them. The interval between breast or bottle and the solid food is a matter of convenience.

The following suggestions on when and what kind of solid foods to introduce are only general guidelines and should be modified to fit your baby's specific needs and desires, and your family's food choices.

Fruits

First introduce the fruits that are less allergenic and that have less citric acid, such as bananas, pears, and applesauce. Bananas are a good first food. Ripe, mashed bananas are accepted by many babies because they are sweet and have a smooth consistency. Don't be surprised if your baby refuses banana, though. It seems to bother some babies, and it can be constipating. One of the main benefits of fruits is that they mix well with other foods and can be used to increase the acceptance of more nutritious, but less palatable, foods. For example, your baby may take cereal more readily if it is covered with bananas. Stay away from strawberries, since many babies have an allergic reaction to them. Avocados are a good early food for babies; their high fat content means a lot of nutrition is packed into a small amount.

Juice

Do not offer infants less than a year old large volumes of fruit juice. Undiluted fruit juice has almost as many calories as milk but is much less nutritious, and juice is less nutritious than the fruit itself because the pulp has been removed. Because juice is less filling than milk, infants can take lots of juice without feeling full. Consuming large quantities of juice causes obesity in some infants.

When you offer your child juice, dilute it with an equal quantity of water, especially for the compulsive juice drinker. To avoid juice-bottle caries (dental cavities resulting from giving a baby a bottle of juice at naptime), dentists recommend that feeding a baby juice be delayed until he can drink from a cup.

Cereal

Cereal, like bananas, is one of the first solid foods a baby readily accepts. One problem with rice cereal is that it can be constipating. Cereal is often used as a "filler food" to lengthen the intervals between bottles or breastfeedings, or to encourage an older baby to sleep through the night. This filler-food concept usually does not work, and it can contribute to obesity if overused. A baby is more comfortable when fed small amounts of solid foods more frequently. But if you are an exhausted mother who is not enjoying the feeding relationship because you have to feed your baby too often, especially at night, then give cereal for filler a try.

Begin with rice or barley cereal, which are the least allergenic. Avoid mixed cereals until your baby has experienced each cereal made with those grains and has proved not to be allergic to them. Wheat cereal should wait until after one year because it is more allergenic. Mix a teaspoon of rice cereal with formula or breast milk to the desired consistency. Adding fruits such as bananas or pears to the cereal will overcome its blandness and may increase your baby's acceptance of it.

Meats

Meat is an excellent source of iron and protein. Meats and iron-fortified cereals are the prime sources of iron for infants who do not receive iron-fortified formulas. Avoid purchasing meat dinners or meat mixtures. The protein and iron content of these mixtures is lower than that of plain meat since these mixtures are very high in starch. Liver and beef are the meats that are highest in iron, but they may not be accepted as easily by your infant as lamb, poultry, and veal.

Vegetables

Vegetables are a good source of carbohydrates and vitamins. The yellow vegetables, such as squash and carrots, are usually accepted better by young infants because of their milder taste and smoother consistency. In theory, vegetables should be introduced before fruits since they are a much better source of balanced nutrition than fruits; however, because of fruits' sweetness, infants usually accept them better than vegetables.

Egg Yolks

Egg yolks are a good source of protein and fat. Although egg yolks are rich in iron, the kind of iron contained in them is not absorbed easily by human intestines. A baby can be given cooked egg yolk anytime after she is six months old, and one egg yolk every other day is sufficient. Delay feeding her egg whites until she is a year old since egg whites tend to be more allergenic than yolks. If your baby is generally allergic or if you have a strong family history of allergies, delay introducing yolks until she is at least one year of age, and whites until eighteen months.

Dairy Products

It is wise to avoid cow's milk as a beverage until your infant is at least one year of age because younger infants often do not tolerate cow's milk proteins. Yogurts and cheeses, however, are tolerated better than milk because the allergenic proteins have been modified in the culturing process. Yogurt and cheese give all the nutritional benefits of milk without the potential problems and can be introduced into your infant's diet when he is around nine months old.

GIVE YOUR BABY A BALANCED DIET

Giving your baby proper nutrition involves two basic requirements: the right amount of calories and the proper distribution of calories. The calories your toddler consumes should be distributed in the following proportions: 30 percent fats, 50 to 55 percent carbohydrates, and 15 to 20 percent proteins. Your baby uses these calories for the following needs: 50 percent for his basic metabolism (the number of calories he needs simply to keep his body going), 30 percent for the energy he expends during activity, and 20 percent for continued growth. The percentage of calories he needs for growth is greatest during his first few months, 30 percent, and gradually decreases to 5–10 percent by one year of age. For this reason, the sooner nutritional deficiency occurs, the more it affects your infant's growth.

Breast milk and formula contain the appropriate proportions of carbohydrates, fats, and proteins. By one year of age, most infants receive about 50 percent of their nutrients from solid food. Between six months and a year, most infants need twenty-five to thirty-two ounces of breast milk or formula per day, depending on the amount of solid food they are eating.

Your goal is to balance the proportions of carbohydrates, fats, and proteins in your infant's solid feedings as you have in her milk. A one-year-old baby who consumes about twenty ounces of breast milk or formula a day and a large amount of fruits and fruit juices but refuses other food has a nutritional deficiency since the extra, nonmilk calories she receives are almost all carbohydrates, no fats, and no proteins. Another one-year-old consumes about forty ounces of breast milk or formula per day but simply refuses solid foods. If he is receiving the proper iron-fortified formula, then no nutritional deficiency exists. (The baby receiving only breast milk may need to have his diet fortified with iron also. Part of the well-baby checkup at nine months or one year is to check baby's iron count.) This baby has chosen to retain milk as his prime source of nutrition and has a balanced diet. A baby who consumes a variety of solid food (four ounces of meat, vegetables, fruits, cereals, and egg yolk) and only takes eight to ten ounces of milk a day also has a balanced diet but has chosen a feeding pattern based predominantly on solid foods. As long as your baby is receiving a proper supply and distribution of nutrients, the source is not important.

HOW TO PREPARE YOUR OWN BABY FOOD

Baby food companies try to keep quality up and costs down while satisfying babies and their parents. They have tried to use additives to keep food from spoiling and make it more palatable, but parental pressure has prompted them to eliminate monosodium glutamate, sugar, salt, and other chemicals from baby food. Advertising and marketing strategies often leave parents very confused when they read labels. The current labels seem to emphasize more what foods do not contain than what they do contain, and you had better be sure to read the fine print if you want to know what's really in the jar.

Commercial baby food is convenient, but a steady diet of convenience foods has no place in infant nutrition. Making your own baby food from fresh, lean meat and fresh, in-season vegetables and fruits is nutritionally superior to commercially processed baby foods. The process can be as simple as setting aside food from family meals and mashing it with a fork. Or you can prepare special foods for your baby and have fun doing it. The following are tips on how to prepare your own baby food at home:

- You will need a blender or baby food grinder, ice cube trays with individual one-ounce cube sections, small freezer bags, and a pinch of creativity. Puree the cooked food (vegetables should be cooked by steaming rather than boiling to preserve the many nutrients) through the baby food grinder or blender and spoon it into the ice cube tray; then freeze the entire tray full of cube-size baby food. After freezing, remove the cubes and store them in plastic bags. Each time a feeding is needed, simply thaw one or more of these frozen cubes by placing it in a dish in a pan of hot water and you will have instant, nutritious baby food.
- Teething biscuits and nutritious cookies and crackers can be prepared from whole-grain recipes found in a number

EASY, MADE-AT-HOME BABY FOODS

- Mashed or scraped ripe banana. Use a spoon to scrape small amounts off a ripe banana. This saves using a dish.
- Cooled mashed potato or sweet potato. Quick-cook the potato in the microwave, peel it, mash it, serve some, freeze the leftovers. The microwave cooks hard-shell squash in a hurry too.
- Chicken or beef. Save a bit of meat from the family dinner (before the seasonings go in). Grind it in the baby food grinder, or cut into tiny bits with a knife and fork.
- Small chunks of ripe avocado.
- Scraped apple. Take a raw apple, cut it open, scrape with a spoon.
- Cooled, steamed, grated carrots. Lots of fun as a finger food.

of cookbooks on the market. Wheat products should be delayed until at least one year of age.

- Your infant can drink the same fruit juice as the rest of the family, but dilute the juice to half strength with water.
- It is never necessary to add sugar, salt, or any artificial preservatives to any baby food made at home. Lemon juice is often recommended as a natural preservative.

At about nine months, finger foods become fun; and self-feeding is good for baby's fine motor development, even though he may make a jolly mess. The following ideas for finger foods are both appealing and safe: pieces of soft, peeled fruit, small cheese or tofu cubes, cooked carrot pieces, tiny cooked broccoli "trees," pieces of rice cake, whole grain cereal shapes, flakes of tuna or baked fish (check for bones), or bits of chicken.

FEEDING YOUR TODDLER—THE PICKY EATER

"My baby won't eat" is a common complaint about the one- to two-year-old, and periodic disinterest in foods earns the toddler the title of "picky eater." This is normal eating behavior for a busy toddler. During his first year you grew accustomed to feeding him a lot because he grew a lot. However, his growth rate is not nearly as rapid during his second year, so he eats less.

Feeding a toddler is a combination of basic nutrition and creative marketing. Here is a feeding tip compatible with toddler behavior: prepare a "nibble tray" with nutritious bits of several kinds of food—raisins, cheese cubes, avocado wedges, whole wheat bread sticks or strips of toast, orange wedges, apple slices with peanut butter, slices of meat, broccoli trees, hard-boiled egg wedges, and so on. Place this well-displayed "rainbow lunch" on your toddler's table, a table from which he can eat at his own pace. You will notice that your toddler will cruise by the tray and nibble at least ten times a day as he makes his rounds around the house. Teach him to eat the food there—as a safety precaution, he should learn not to walk around the house with it or run around with food in his mouth.

Right now, sitting down at the table can be primarily a time for communication, and as your child grows older, it can be a time for eating a whole meal. The concept of nibbling between meals may not agree with some parents who are used to mealtime discipline and three square meals a day. However, there is a good medical reason for this suggestion: your child will have blood-sugar swings when he is hungry. This is why most children's behavior deteriorates in late morning and mid-afternoon, or just before the next meal. The practice of nibbling nutritiously throughout the day prevents these blood-sugar swings and can be beneficial for your toddler's behavior. Patternless eating is normal for your toddler. He may "eat well" one day and "eat nothing" the next. If you average out his intake throughout the week, you will be surprised how balanced his diet is.

JUNK FOOD

"If you love me, don't feed me junk." This was printed on a T-shirt we bought for our daughter, Hayden, when she was a toddler. It could have come with the scriptural reminder that our bodies are temples of the Holy Spirit. Parents have a responsibility to teach their children to respect and care for these "temples" God gave us.

Two types of food rightfully earn the title "junk food": foods that have artificial preservatives and food colorings (mainly, red and yellow dyes) and foods that are high in fat and/or sugar and low in other nutrients. "Table sugar" is processed so heavily that the few nutrients found in natural sugar are removed. This refined sugar is absorbed more rapidly from the intestines than other kinds of sugar and reaches a high concentration in the blood. This triggers the release of insulin which rapidly lowers the blood sugar, causing behavioral changes and often stimulating the person to eat again.

The child's developing brain is very dependent on a steady blood sugar as its prime source of energy. Fluctuations in blood sugar can cause hyperactivity, fainting, irritability, depression, and aggression. Children with marked blood-sugar swings frequently have difficulty concentrating, and their learning is often compromised. Headaches, visual disturbances, and a tired feeling are symptoms also associated with low blood sugar.

Not all sugar should be considered junk food since our bodies derive about 45 percent of their necessary calories from sugars, including the sugars that occur in the form of fruits, grains, and vegetables. Refined cane sugar or corn syrup, also called dextrose or sucrose on some labels, is what we mean by "junk sugar." Nutritious sugars are the natural sugars such as the lactose in milk and the fructose in fruits. These sugars are absorbed and utilized within the body differently from the way junk sugar is used. They cause fewer swings in blood sugar and, therefore, do not adversely affect a child's behavior.

How can you know whether a food contains a lot of junk sugar? Current label laws require contents to be listed in order of volume. If sugar is high on the list of contents, the food is very high in sugar. If the label says "corn syrup," "sugar," or "dextrose," the food is high in junk sugars. If the label lists several kinds of sugar, junk sugar is probably the food's main ingredient. Some breakfast cereals fit this description.

Highly colored and highly sugared fruit drinks, soft drinks, and sports drinks rank high among junk foods. Besides containing food colorings (which also may trigger behavior problems in some children) and junk sugar, these drinks contain very little, if any, actual juice, have limited nutritional value, and definitely should not be given to children.

FOOD ALLERGIES

Food allergies ("food intolerance" may be a more medically correct term) often are called the "great masqueraders" because they create a variety of symptoms in children that often go undetected. The most common symptoms of food allergies are eczema-like rashes (especially on the face), puffy eyelids, a persistently stuffy nose, wheezing, and chronic diarrhea and abdominal pain. Sometimes the symptoms of food allergies may be very subtle: a pale, tired, or droopy child; a child with headaches, abdominal pain, or muscle aches; or a child with recurrent colds and ear infections. Night waking may be the only symptom in younger children.

Some common food allergens are milk and other dairy products, eggs, soy, nuts, wheat products, corn, citrus fruits, berries, chocolate, and food colorings and additives. If you suspect your child is allergic to any of these foods, you may have to do a bit of detective work. Eliminate the suspected food allergens one by one from your child's diet until the most obvious symptoms disappear. Then reintroduce them to see if the symptoms reappear. If you strongly suspect your child has food allergies, you may want to consult a nutritionist for help.

If you have a strong family history of allergies, the following suggestions may help you prevent allergies in your child: (1) breastfeed your infant for at least one year; (2) delay introducing solid foods until your infant shows definite signs of wanting solid foods; (3) withhold potentially allergenic foods on the above list until your child is more than one year old.

A child who will not drink her milk may, in fact, be sensitive to milk. Withhold milk and dairy products from her diet for at least three to four weeks to see if her symptoms disappear. Then reintroduce the milk and dairy products to see if the symptoms reappear. Repeat the process. If your child has improved on the dairy-free diet in two successive trials, then she probably is sensitive to cow's milk.

If your child cannot tolerate milk, try feeding your child yogurt and hard cheeses; she may be able to tolerate these because the proteins are changed in the processing. Other sources of calcium include fish, tofu, rhubarb, blackstrap molasses, and calcium-enriched soy or rice beverage.

CHILDHOOD OBESITY

At what point should you worry that your child is becoming too fat? If your child's weight is 10 percent greater than the average weight for his sex, height, and age, then he is overweight and potentially obese. If your child weighs 20 percent more than his ideal weight, he is fat or obese. Ten to 20 percent of all children are obese, making them candidates for health problems as adults. A much higher percentage of children are overweight.

The amount of excess fat your child has is a better indicator of obesity than his actual weight. This fat is called "skin-fold thickness" and it is measured at different places on your child's body. The changes in these figures can be used as a measure of weight loss or gain.

The fat-cell theory postulates that the early years are important in determining whether a child will have weight problems in adulthood. Fat tissue is gained either by increasing the size or number of fat cells. During the first two years—the critical period for fat cell development—a child's fat cells increase in number. Lesser spurts in fat cell numbers occur at seven years of age and again during adolescence. After growth is finished and a person has reached adulthood, fat cells do not increase significantly in number, and any increase in fat tissue results from a change in the size of these cells.

If a child is overfed during infancy (or middle childhood or adolescence), the excess calories he ingests may produce an excess number of fat cells. Continued overfeeding will cause these fat cells to get larger. This results in a tendency toward obesity, because there are more fat cells to store fat. Once a child has too many fat cells it is more difficult for him to lose them. Weight reduction can occur only by decreasing the size of these cells. According to this theory, a child who has an excess number of fat cells may have to watch his weight all of his life.

Factors Contributing to Childhood Obesity

Heredity plays a very important part in the tendency toward obesity. Perhaps the most important determinant of childhood obesity is the body type of the parents. There are three body types: ectomorphic, mesomorphic, and endomorphic. Ectomorphs are lean and lanky; they can "eat everything and not get fat." Ectomorphs are better able to match their food intake and their activity level. Mesomorphs have a medium build and usually medium height. They have more of a tendency toward obesity, carry any excess fat much less attractively, and have some difficulty balancing their food intake and their activity level. Endomorphs have a short, fat body type and are most likely to have obese children.

According to statistics, overweight parents do produce overweight children. If both parents are obese, the probability of their having an obese child can be as high as 80 percent. If one parent is obese, there is a 40 percent chance of the child's being obese; and if neither parent is obese, they have only a 7 percent chance of having an obese child. Studies of children who are adopted show that they tend to follow the weight trends of their biological parents more than their adoptive parents, indicating that heredity plays a greater role in obesity than environment. Because of these hereditary factors, some children have a higher obesity potential than others, but whether or not they become obese depends also on other factors in their environment.

Calorie balance. Weight control requires a balance of the number of calories a child takes in and the number of calories the child burns off. Children need calories for three basic purposes: to maintain their bodily functions, to grow, and to obtain fuel for exercise. Adult caloric requirements vary only with exercise (and pregnancy); children's caloric requirements are greatest during their periods of rapid growth spurts. But if a child consumes more calories than he needs for growth and exercise, the excess calories are deposited as excess fat.

"Appestat." Appetite control means that a child consumes just the right number of calories for her needs and that her appetite adjusts to her changing needs. There are many factors (including psychological ones) that affect a child's appetite control, or her "appestat," and it is not completely known why the system works better in some children than others.

Early feeding practices. It is quite likely that infant feeding choices can affect a child's proneness to obesity. One of the early feeding practices that can affect adult health is breastfeeding. Whether or not breastfed infants are less likely to become obese than formula-fed infants is controversial and difficult to study because of the many variables that contribute to obesity.

However, we feel that breastfeeding does lower the risk of obesity, mainly because of the way breast milk changes to accommodate the changing needs of the growing infant. The fat content of breast milk changes during each feeding, and it also changes at various times of the day, usually being higher in the morning and lower in the evening. The breastfeeding infant gets foremilk initially, which is low in fat, and with continued sucking she is rewarded with the creamier hindmilk that is high in fat and calories. When the infant has obtained sufficient hindmilk, the high-calorie milk signals her "appestat" that she is full, and she stops sucking when both her sucking needs and her appetite are completely satisfied. When breastfed babies are thirsty, they suck a shorter period of time and obtain the foremilk. The bottle-fed baby, however, does not enjoy the advantages of different calorie counts for different needs. He gets the same milk whether he is thirsty or hungry and the same milk at each feeding.

As the infant grows older he needs fewer calories per pound of body weight, and we know breast milk gradually decreases in fat and calories over time. Since there is general agreement that obesity is not healthy, it seems logical that the changes in the caloric content of milk are part of God's design for providing just the right nourishment for His children.

Researchers who have studied the skin-fold thickness of breastfed babies and of formula-fed babies have noted a difference in the feel of the fat. It is more difficult to measure the skin-fold thickness of breastfed babies since they have a less well-defined line between their muscle and fat than formula-fed babies do. Some breastfed babies do indeed appear to be very fat during the first year, especially babies who nurse "all day and all night." Nearly all of these babies lose their excess fat by the time they are two years old.

Temperament. The child's temperament is also a factor in obesity. Children with quiet, placid personalities who enjoy more sedentary activities have a higher potential to become obese. A vicious cycle develops; the less active a child is, the fatter he becomes and the less interested he becomes in physical activities. Fat children do not always eat more than lean children and some may even eat less, but fat children do eat more than they need for their level of activity. Children with normal weight and appetite control strike a balance between activity and appetite. As they move around less, they eat less, and vice versa. Obese children, however, do not achieve this balance. When they are inactive, they do not eat proportionally less. This imbalance between calories and activity is a central concept about weight control. More childhood obesity is caused by too little activity than by too much eating.

Preventing Obesity

You can lessen your child's potential for obesity by following these suggestions:

Breastfeed for as long as possible. This gives your child the best nutritional start.

Determine if your child is at risk for childhood obesity. Are one or both parents obese? Is your child overweight now and does he tend to overeat and under exercise?

Introduce solid food only when you are sure your baby needs solid food. Introduce solids wisely and use these foods for nutrition only, not as fillers to hold your child through the night or to lengthen the interval between feedings. Let the child tell you when he's had enough. Choose foods that are high in nutrition for the number of calories. These are called nutrient-dense foods.

Avoid the "clean plate syndrome." Many mothers feel responsible for how much their children eat. They often equate clean plates with effective mothering. You are responsible for what foods you offer your child, but allow her to be responsible for how much she eats so that she can develop her own appetite control.

Discourage your child from eating to alleviate boredom. Children often turn to the refrigerator for satisfaction, but their appetites really crave more meaningful activities or interaction with other people. It is tempting for a parent or a baby-sitter to bribe a child with food rather than devote time and energy to nurturing the whole child. Discourage your child from eating alone or nibbling in front of a television, and encourage him in activities that boost his self-esteem.

Encourage impulse control and delayed gratification, since "each of you should learn to control his own body in a way that is holy and honorable" (1 Thess. 4:4). The context of that verse is avoiding sexual immorality, but self-control needs to start at an earlier age than that concerned with sexual appetites. We believe a child can be taught self-control early on in regard to eating. Children can give up that second scoop of ice cream, for example. Teach your child the difference between "food that helps you grow" and "special treat" foods. Help him learn to limit his treats.

Model good habits. As is true for all forms of discipline, modeling is very important for disciplining the appetite. If your child sees you overindulge, she most likely will overindulge. It is much easier for you to teach your child to discipline her appetite when she sees you eating appropriate amounts of healthy food. Children are very quick to pick up on the ways parents use food for gratification.

Choose foods wisely. Become a label reader. Look for the protein content, the fiber content, the fat content. One simple rule of thumb we have helps us to be discriminating about prepared foods, especially about the percentage of total calories derived from fat. We have a limit of 30 percent. If it's more than that, we don't buy it. When you check the percentage of calories derived from fat in a certain brand of fish sticks, you would see that it is over 50 percent—250 calories per serving, but 130 of those calories is from fat. You either pass on the fish sticks or decide to serve them with applesauce and carrots instead of creamed peas and scalloped potatoes.

Offer alternatives. Eating for enjoyment is one of the blessings God has given us, but overindulging this pleasure is wrong. If your child turns mainly to food for pleasure and satisfaction, offer alternative forms of enjoyment, such as arts and crafts, games, and staying busy outdoors. Encourage any attractive activity that gets his mind off his stomach.

Recognize the power of television commercials. Television commercials for junk food have contributed greatly to childhood obesity. Unfortunately, many children actually believe that commercials are true, especially when they see their parents eating or drinking what is advertised. These commercials teach children that food should be a source of fun and entertainment rather than a source of balanced nutrition. Teach your child the real purpose God intended for food. While you're at it, teach them we don't believe something just because it's on television.

Encourage a lot of physical activity for your child. Remember that if your child has a sedentary temperament, she is prone to obesity, especially if she has a high-risk body type. Exercise is very important for the sedentary child, especially if she is bored easily. Set limits on television and video games, and attach conditions to the privilege, such as two hours of outdoor play before the one hour of viewing.

Avoid blaming medical problems for your child's obesity. In the great majority of obese children, there are no underlying medical reasons for their excess weight. They simply eat too much of the wrong food or exercise too little, or both. If your child generally seems well and is not unusually short, then a medical problem is unlikely. A short, heavy child should always have a complete medical evaluation.

A Sample Healthy Eating Program

A very important principle of behavior modification is called "shaping," and it is the tool you will use to help your whole family eat right. Shaping is most effective when attempted gradually, moving step-by-step toward a final goal. Sudden, drastic changes in behavior—diets and making too many changes too fast—are usually less effective than small but consistent changes. Ask your pediatrician to oversee your child's progress. For adults, group therapy and individual counseling are often very helpful shaping strategies for weight control, if this is the emphasis needed. These services are found in most major medical centers.

Although obesity is an individual problem requiring an individual solution, there are key elements common to nearly all healthy eating programs. Try the following suggestions to encourage healthy eating in your children.

Determine whether your child is overweight. For example, a child who is five years old and is of average height (44 inches) should weigh around 45 pounds. If your child weighs 60 pounds, he is 15 pounds or 25 percent overweight; therefore, he is classified as obese. Your doctor may measure your child's skin folds on the back of his arm or around his waist. These measurements help determine that the excess weight is primarily fat. They also serve as a basis for monitoring your child's body fat, even if his weight increases as he grows.

Determine why your child is overweight. By reviewing the factors contributing to obesity as outlined in the preceding pages, determine if she is overweight because she eats too much of the wrong food, exercises too little, or both. Review her eating habits, her cravings, her level of physical activity, her hobbies, and her basic temperament. Review your family history. Are there many obese family members? Review the eating habits of the whole family.

Get professional counseling. For a child who is 20 percent or more overweight, a safe and effective weight-control program must be supervised by the child's doctor and a qualified dietitian. Above all, avoid crash diets that may affect the normal health and optimal growth of the child. Remember, we are concerned with *fat loss* and not necessarily weight loss. A child on any weight-control program who is undernourished runs the danger of losing muscle tissue in addition to excess fat. For this reason, in the weight-control program we use in our office, we pay more attention to how trim the child is becoming rather than what the scales show. We use special calipers (called an adiposometer) to measure fat folds in the child's arms and abdomen. A decrease in the size of these fat folds is a more meaningful measure of fat loss than what the scales show. Despite its unappealing ring, it's more nutritionally correct to talk about "fat loss" rather than "weight loss." (Weight loss from crash diets and undernutrition programs is often reflected in the scales as loss of water and/or loss of muscle tissue and not fat loss—which is really the ultimate goal.)

Count calories in various foods. To help you understand which foods provide the most nutrition for the least number of calories, study the following food facts:

- *Vegetables.* Vegetables are your best friend because they are relatively high in nutritional value but low in calories. Some vegetables are more nutritious than others; broccoli contains more protein per calories than most vegetables. Corn, lima beans, and potatoes are high in starch, and therefore contain more calories than the same weight of other vegetables, but they are good sources of complex carbohydrates when prepared with little or no added fat. Lightly steamed vegetables are more nutritious than boiled ones because more vitamins are preserved in the cooking. Generally, the more natural and unprocessed a food is, the higher its nutritional value. Raw vegetables should be emphasized once a child is old enough to chew them thoroughly. Low calorie vegetables like celery and lettuce are free foods, meaning your child can eat as much of these as he likes. Lettuce and celery are very low in calories because of the very high water content. They also provide excellent fiber. A large lettuce and tomato salad (with low-calorie dressing) is a good way to begin a meal. Celery spread thin with peanut butter is a good snack.

- *Dairy products.* The caloric content of milk and other dairy products is determined by the amount of fat they contain. (One gram of fat contains twice the number of calories in a gram of protein or carbohydrate.) Whole milk contains around 3½ percent butterfat; low-fat milk contains 1 or 2 percent; and skim milk has had most of the fat removed. Looking at the percentage of fat derived from calories, though, you see a different story. Whole milk has 150 calories per serving, 80 calories from fat (53%); 2% milk has 130 calories per serving, 45 from fat (34%); 1% milk has 120 calories per serving, 20 calories from fat (17%). Choose reduced-fat cheese. Lowfat, unsweetened yogurt is a wise choice of dairy products. Stir in fresh fruit and a dab of honey to make it attractive to the taste buds.
- *Meats.* The caloric content of meat also depends upon its fat content. Choose lean meat or remove all the fat. Because lean meat has a high amount of nutrition for its calories, it is also a wise choice of nutrition.
- *Poultry.* Poultry has fewer calories than meats such as beef or pork because it has less fat, if you remove the skin. Broiling or baking it (instead of frying) lowers calories the most.
- *Fish.* Fish is a very nutritious food because it has relatively little fat. The fat it does have is nutritionally superior to the fat of other animals.
- *Fruits and juices.* Fruit juices have more calories and far less nutritional value than the same volume of vegetable juice. The fruit itself is nutritionally superior to fruit juice because the pulp offers additional nutrition and fiber. Fruit juice is not very filling, so some children drink an excessive amount of fruit juice, which can be a subtle cause of obesity. If your child is a compulsive drinker, dilute the juice with water to the limits of what he'll accept.
- *Cereals and grains.* Avoid the "junk cereals" that are very high in sugars and calories but low in nutrition. Whole grain cereals and breads are nutritionally superior to processed cereals and enriched white bread.

- *Soft drinks and sweets.* Avoid these junk foods.
- *Oils and dressings.* Avoid breading and frying foods in oil since this greatly increases the caloric content of the food without adding to the nutrition (as we found out when we read the label on the fish sticks!). Use low-calorie dressings. Oils and dressings are very high in fat and calories; one tablespoon of mayonnaise may contain one hundred calories, which is often more than the caloric content of the entire salad.

Cut back on fat in the packaged food you buy. Excess fat in the diet is the source of many health woes, besides obesity. Reducing fat means reducing calories. Read labels carefully to learn about a food's fat content. Look for snack foods that are naturally low in fat, (i.e., pretzels instead of potato chips). Frozen yogurt is generally lower in fat than ice cream. When preparing foods, avoid adding fat. Many recipes can simply have the oil or butter cut in half.

Encourage exercise. It is safer to increase a growing child's activity level than to impose a strict diet. For adults, one hour of sustained exercise—running, swimming, fast walking—will burn off between three hundred and five hundred calories a day, which will reduce body fat by nearly a pound a week. A supervised exercise program will be necessary for sedentary children until they build up their stamina and enjoyment of activity. Sign your child up for soccer or swimming lessons. Go to the park and play chasing games with him.

Change your child's basic eating patterns. Buffet dinners are a no-no for the compulsive eater. Use smaller plates and have the family bring them to the table already filled (the out-of-sight-out-of-mind approach). Cut food into smaller pieces and encourage your child to eat more slowly. Start each meal with a large salad with low-calorie dressing. Have your child eat in only one room, the kitchen or dining room, and discourage the habit of nibbling in front of the TV.

Help your child improve his self-image. More important than scales or growth charts is what the mirror shows and how your child feels about his body. Feeling good about himself is an absolute necessity for any successful, healthy eating program. Junk food is the most readily available source of gratification for a person with a poor self-image. Urge your child to become involved in meaningful activities with his peer group. Help the older child emphasize academic achievements. Promote sports and team play. Take inventory of emotional stresses that contribute to your child's view of himself, and thereby to his eating habits. Seek professional counseling if you are not sure how to do this, or if you yourself have difficulties in this area.

Enlist the school's help. Prompt your school to devote class time to teaching good nutrition to children at the entry level, before the preadolescent and adolescent obesity stages. The menus in school cafeterias should emphasize low-fat foods. Vending machines should contain nutritious snacks and fruit juices rather than candies and soda. There should be as many athletic programs for girls as there are for boys. School-age children need nourishing mid-morning and mid-afternoon snacks to prevent low blood-sugar periods and to improve their learning and concentration.

Set goals if your child is seriously overweight. How many pounds your child should lose and how fast she should lose them depend upon her degree of motivation and upon how overweight she is. A safe and achievable goal for a growing child who is highly motivated is a loss of one pound per week until the ideal weight is reached. This means a deficit of thirty-five hundred calories per week. A steady weight loss is not only safer for growing children but is likely to be more consistent. Slight modification in eating habits are more likely to succeed than drastic changes in behavior patterns.

The cut-out-one-thing-a-day method is very successful for the slightly overweight child. Help your child pick out one hundred calories' worth of junk food in her present diet that she can live without. If your child does nothing but eliminate these calories each day, she will avoid ten unnecessary pounds in one year. Since most children ingest only a slight excess of daily calories, this small change in eating habits may be enough to control their weight. Give the slightly overweight child a realistic goal, "You don't have to lose any weight, but don't gain any weight for one year." If your child continues to lose excess body fat as she gets taller, she really is losing weight, even though the scale stays the same.

If your child who is about 10 percent overweight cuts out one hundred empty calories daily (for example, one cola or two cookies), and does at least a half hour of sustained exercises each day, she will burn off more than five hundred calories per day. This would result in a gradual fat loss of three quarters of a pound per week. The maximum weight loss a growing child should be allowed is one pound per week and this should not be attempted without professional dietary counseling.

Recognize your role. Parents, please do not feel that your child's weight loss is your responsibility. This may be true for the infant and young child, but not for the older child and teenager. Your responsibility is to help your child improve her self-image and to create an atmosphere that is conducive for healthy eating habits. Also, you must model and teach good nutrition by your own example at home. Prayer and support will do much more for your child's weight problem than nagging and probing. The best policy when it comes to parental involvement in weight control is "zip your lip."

Conflicts often arise when parents take a heavy role in their children's weight control programs. Leave the responsibility of weight control to your child and the direction of her program to her physician or dietary counselor. Direct your energies to your child's emotional needs.

BREAKFAST FOR GROWING BRAINS

New research on feeding school-age children has revealed an exciting connection between what children eat and how well they learn. Here's some tips on giving your young student a healthy breakfast.

If your hectic household is like morning rush hour in our home, sleepy kids and hurried parents don't have time for healthy breakfasts. Yet, studies show that children who begin their day with a balanced breakfast do better in school than those who don't. Breakfast eaters are likely to have better behavior, pay closer attention, participate more in class, and are able to do better problem solving. Breakfast skippers, on the other hand, are more likely to be inattentive, sluggish, and make lower grades. Also, the type of breakfast a child eats can influence learning and behavior. Studies show that school children perform best when they eat a breakfast containing both protein and complex carbohydrates, such as yogurt and granola or eggs and toast. For a sweet touch, add some fresh fruits to these combinations.

Your child's growing brain contains trillions of nerves. At the end of each nerve are tiny feelers that are trying to reach out and connect with other nerves. The better these connections, the better your child learns. Throughout the brain, biochemical messengers, called neurotransmitters, help the developing brain make the right connections. Food influences these neurotransmitters—a meal of proteins and carbohydrates seems to be the most brain-friendly food for thought. Why this food-mood connection? Complex carbohydrates, such as healthy cereals, are like time-release packets of energy that fuel the brain. Adding protein to complex carbohydrates (such as dairy and grains) help the neurotransmitters in the brain work better. Sugars such as icings and syrups for breakfast are not friendly to learning, since they cause a rollercoaster effect. The blood sugar skyrockets and then plummets mid- or late-morning, causing the child's attention to wander and behavior to deteriorate. Healthy breakfast foods, like dairy, grains, and fruits provide a more steady supply of energy for the young student's brain. Of course, it's what you eat, not what you say, that impresses a child. By treating yourself to a healthy breakfast you model to your children that eating a healthy breakfast gives the whole family a smart nutritional start.

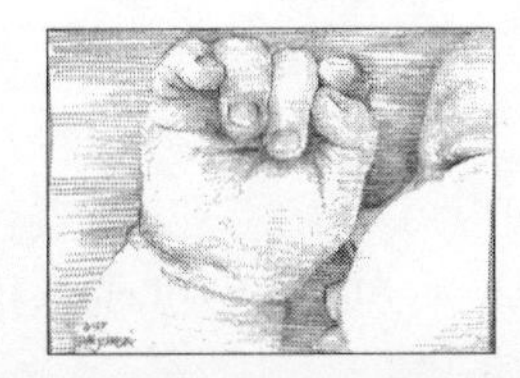

CHAPTER THIRTEEN

Toilet Training, Sibling Rivalry, **and Emerging Sexuality**

Three events occur in a young child's life that set him apart from babyhood. Once a child is out of diapers, parents feel they've passed a big milestone on their parenting journey. Becoming a big brother or big sister makes a clear statement that a child must move on in his journey toward growing up. We discuss these two events in this chapter. (The third event, weaning from the breast or bottle, which we discussed in chapter 12, is even mentioned in Scripture as a measure of maturity!) Another concern that surfaces now is how to address the issue of sexuality with your growing child.

TOILET TRAINING—A CHILD-CONSIDERED APPROACH

There was a time when parents took pride in how fast they could hurry their baby through the developmental stages of infancy and into childhood. This is not healthy. Each stage has its own tasks that must be mastered in their own good time. Hurrying a child into independence can create anger and conflict between parent and child and can cause a child to feel less secure or have a poor self-image. The age at which children achieve awareness of their bladder and bowel functions varies tremendously. Rather than consider toilet training as your task, something you want to get accomplished, take cues from your child. Don't ask, "When should I begin his toilet training?" but rather, "When is he ready to use the toilet?"

Signs That Your Child Is Ready

Most children, especially boys, do not show consistent signs of bladder or bowel awareness until well after they are eighteen months old. This is the age at which the nerves controlling urination and defecation become more mature. Between one and two years of age most children are so overjoyed at having acquired the skill of locomotion that they are too busy to sit still for anything, especially sitting on a hard potty seat. Discerning parents will help their children gradually learn about their bodily functions and will pick up on signs of toilet-training readiness.

The usual indications of toilet-training readiness in a child between two and two-and-a-half years include: (1) a desire to imitate Mommy's or Daddy's toilet functions; (2) signs that he is about to relieve himself—squatting down, grunting, a "quiet look in a quiet place" such as a corner; (3) the after-the-fact telling ("Me poopy").

Many toddlers go through a stage when they resist any outside suggestions about modifying their behavior, especially toilet habits. Toddler negativity, a highly overrated phenomenon, is experienced less often as a negative thing in homes where parents practice the principles of attachment parenting. It is best to respect a negative phase rather than frustrate everyone in attempts to toilet train in the middle of one.

In general, children are mood dependent when it comes to learning. If your intuition or your first attempts tell you your child is not at a stage in his development when he is particularly receptive to toilet training, back off a while. When you sense that your toddler is ready (and willing) for toilet training, you may follow these suggestions on how to begin:

Give your child her own place to go. Around two years of age, most children begin to exhibit a desire for order. They like their own shelves for their toys, their own drawers for their clothes, their own tables and chairs, and so on. They also like their own places for their toilet functions. Place a potty chair on the floor next to one of your toilets. Rather than place your toddler on her potty chair, simply place the chair alongside your toilet and wait for your child to accompany you when you go. When your child is in a "just like Mommy and Daddy" stage, she may sit on her potty chair when you sit on yours without any urging from you. Most children adapt better to a child-size potty chair than to an adapter on a "giant-size" adult toilet seat. Another advantage of the potty chair is that it can be moved from place to place in the house or can be taken along in a car.

Initially, your child may approach the potty chair with her clothes on. Allow your child to sit on the potty chair with her clothes on, sometimes reading a book or simply using the chair as a place to sit. Since imitation is a powerful motivator at this age, a child often will pull off her diaper and sit bare-bottomed on the potty chair as she sees her older siblings or parents do. This approach capitalizes on the internal motivation of the "I did it all by myself" stage.

Remove his diapers. Although diapers seem necessary to protect apparel and furnishings from a baby's being a baby, diapers do diminish bladder and bowel awareness. Uncovered, children learn better how their bodies work—diapers prolong toilet training in some children. This is why toilet training is often more effective in the summertime when your child can be encouraged to run around the yard without diapers. Most children are not afraid when they see their excrement coming out, although some children may worry about losing something that belongs to them. For the child who does not like to be completely undressed, remove his diapers and cover the rest of him with a long T-shirt.

Teach your child words for her actions. Being able to talk about a skill helps a child develop that skill. Teach your child appropriate words for toilet functions; this is actually an early form of sex education. If you are uncomfortable talking about genitalia or toilet functions, the young child will pick up on your feelings. It is amazing how many different terms have been used to avoid addressing toilet functions and genitalia by their proper terms. Give your child appropriate names for his or her genitalia: penis and vulva. However, the terms *urination* and *defecation* may be beyond a child. (These are probably not the words you'd be comfortable using in a department store anyway.) Phrases like "go pee" or "go potty" are much easier. When you notice that your child is exhibiting any of the before-mentioned signs that she is about to go, say to her, "Let's go potty." In that way your child learns to associate the feelings in her body with the phrase "go potty." Words make toilet training much easier, which is good reason to delay toilet training until your child is verbal.

Encourage a toilet routine. Some children readily accept being placed on the toilet at certain times during the day. After breakfast in the morning is usually the best time to encourage a bowel movement. A full stomach stimulates the colon to empty itself. Encouraging a child to have a bowel movement early in the morning also starts his day off with a clean slate, and avoids the tendency to ignore his bowel signals later on in the day when he is preoccupied with other activities.

When your child is verbal enough to understand toilet-training instructions, encourage him to respond immediately to his urge to urinate or defecate. Not following these urges predisposes children, especially girls, to urinary tract infections. Girls should be taught to wipe themselves from front to back after a bowel movement; they should not wipe from the rectum toward the vagina, as this can transfer bacteria from the stools into the vagina and increase the likelihood of urinary tract infections.

Put your child in training pants. After your child has achieved daytime dryness for a few days, she can graduate to training pants. They resemble ordinary underwear but are heavily padded in order to absorb the occasional "accidents" which are certainly to be expected as your child is mastering her newly-acquired skill. Never punish or reprimand her for these occasional accidents. Teach her to wipe up her own little puddles, not as a punishment, but to encourage her sense of responsibility for taking care of her body. Little boys often take great delight in spraying their environment, so they may need a little target practice to hit the toilet.

Parents Can Relax

In our experience, bladder training is completed before bowel training, usually between two and a half and three, but this is very individual. More and more parents are comfortable with late training—they find that once a child decides to do it, it happens easily. This is especially true about bowel compliance. Some children are simply not comfortable stooling without the security of a diaper. They will ask to have one on when they need to go. Even though this can be frustrating to parents, it's wise to stay cool. Any anger or move to take over in this area from you will only delay the day your child discovers he can do it. (Tip: using diaper wipes makes clean-ups easier and the child can often manage this himself.) On the other hand, if you simply run out of diapers one day and decide not to rush right out for more, your child will probably figure out the "big kid" way is easier. Unless, of course, there's a new baby in the house. Once your child discovers the "big kid" way, it may need to be reinforced for a while with a small treat.

Bed-Wetting

Why does a child wet the bed? For the great majority of children, bed-wetting is not due to a psychological disturbance. For most children, the problem is due to immaturity of the bladder, not of the mind. To understand why some children wet their beds, let's first discuss how children normally achieve bladder control.

Infants usually empty their bladders by a reflex called the "bladder-emptying reflex." When the bladder reaches a certain fullness and the bladder muscles have stretched to a certain point, these muscles automatically contract and empty the bladder. Sometime between the ages of eighteen months and two years, most children become aware of this sensation of bladder fullness, which is their first step toward daytime bladder control. The child next becomes aware that he can consciously inhibit the bladder-emptying reflex and hold onto his urine. As a result of this conscious effort, the child's bladder-emptying reflex weakens, and the functional capacity of his bladder increases. When his conscious efforts overcome the bladder-emptying reflex, he achieves daytime bladder control, usually by two-and-a-half or three years of age. Nighttime control occurs when the child's bladder capacity increases and the bladder-emptying reflex becomes so weak that it is able to be overcome by unconscious inhibition of urination. Delay in bladder control, either during the daytime or nighttime, is the result of a delay in awareness of bladder fullness, a small functional bladder capacity, or a prolonged activity of the bladder-emptying reflex. Just as children mature at different rates, these components of bladder control also mature at different rates.

There is often a hereditary basis for bed-wetting, and this supports the theory that bed-wetting is simply a developmental delay. If both parents were bed wetters, the child has a 70 percent chance of being a bed wetter; if one parent was a bed wetter, the child has a 40 percent chance.

Parents of bed wetters mention that their children are very sound sleepers. In some children the messages from the bladder do not reach the mind because of deep sleep. In some children, bed-wetting may actually be a sleep disorder in which the loss of bladder control occurs as the child passes from one sleep stage to another. It is a known anatomical fact that children who wet their beds sometimes have functionally small bladders and must void more frequently. This fact plus the hereditary basis gives strong support to the theory that bed-wetting is not due to a psychological disturbance. In the majority of children, bed-wetting should be considered a developmental delay in one or more of the components of bladder control.

At what age should parents be concerned about bed-wetting? There is tremendous variation in the age at which children remain dry throughout the night. By three years of age, many children are dry at night. At six years of age 92 percent of girls and 85 to 90 percent of boys enjoy nighttime dryness. By fifteen years of age approximately 1 to 2 percent of teenagers still wet their beds. Pediatricians usually consider bed-wetting after the age of six a condition meriting correction. Most children sincerely want to learn how to control their bodily functions and welcome suggestions from parents and physicians on how to remain dry at night. If your five-year-old child is still wetting the bed, here are several ways to help:

Avoid focusing on bed-wetting as a psychological problem since for the vast majority of children this is simply not the cause. Understand the development of bladder maturity, and regard bed-wetting as a temporary developmental delay, a problem that you must understand, support, and parent as you did the challenges during other developmental stages. It is important for you to develop this attitude since your child is likely to pick up on your thoughts and feel as you feel about his bed-wetting. If a child's bladder control mechanisms are simply not mature, outside pressure is doomed to failure.

Early toilet-training habits can affect bed-wetting. If a child is forced into early toilet training according to the norms of the neighborhood rather than her own developmental timetable, she will have a greater chance of prolonged bed-wetting. Children who are toilet trained according to their own developmental readiness tend to achieve nighttime dryness at an earlier age. This is another example of the basic principle mentioned throughout this book: a child hurried through any developmental milestone often will regress later.

Teach your child the principles of bladder control. Your child does not want to wet his bed. He dislikes waking up in a wet, odorous bed as much as you dislike constantly changing his bed and washing his sheets. Older children are painfully aware of the social stigma accompanying bed-wetting, and they do not need further negative attitudes from their parents. Explain to your child how his bladder mechanism works. Draw a simple diagram of a baseball as a bladder, and at the bottom of that ball show a donut muscle that opens and closes to help him hold onto his urine. Tell him that he is not a baby now, but his bladder and his donut muscle have not grown up yet. Assure him that you will help him learn to keep his donut muscle closed at night.

We are not suggesting you ignore bed-wetting, especially in the child older than five or six, since it is a source of social embarrassment and certainly does nothing to help his emerging self-image. But it is important that your child does not feel he is a "baby" in everything. As you should do with other childish behaviors, convey an accepting attitude toward your child as a person.

A child needs motivation. Encourage overnights at a friend's house. He can take along his own overnight pad and sleeping bag to relieve any embarrassment. It helps to prepare the parents at his friend's house, so that they can be understanding and supportive. Chances are, they also have parented a bed wetter.

If your child is a prolonged bed wetter, make a special effort to encourage success in other areas of development such as academics or athletics. A bed wetter should be required to strip his own bed and assist with the laundry, not as a punishment, but as a means to convey to him a sense of responsibility for his bodily functions. Placing a large rubber-backed flannel pad on top of his regular sheet will cut down on the number of wet sheets.

A positive reward system encourages nighttime dryness. Daily rewards are more effective than a long-term reward such as a bicycle if a child is dry for a year. A calendar with a gold star or a coin for each day of dryness is often successful. There is a fine line between motivation and pressure. Try to sense how motivated your child is to stop her bed-wetting and how her bed-wetting affects her self-image. Then gauge your own support level accordingly. Oftentimes a child who wets her bed is more motivated if she is accountable to a third person such as a pediatrician. A child can call the doctor at monthly intervals to report on the number of dry nights on her calendar. You can discuss this approach with your pediatrician.

Restricting fluids after supper is one of the oldest recommended practices for discouraging bed-wetting. This seldom does any good and is a bit uncomfortable for the persistently thirsty child. Food and drinks that contain caffeine should be avoided since caffeine acts as a diuretic and actually contributes to bed-wetting. Teach your child to empty his bladder before going to bed. Little children in a hurry or tired often go to the toilet, dribble a little, and run off to resume play or go to bed. To encourage your child to empty his bladder fully before going to bed, encourage a triple voiding technique. Tell your child to grunt and empty himself three times, waiting a few seconds between grunts. This technique tends to minimize the residual urine left in the bladder when children void only once.

Stop using diapers at night. By age four, most children (and their parents) are eager to be rid of nighttime diapers, but the prospect of wet sheets most nights is not fun. Yet, the longer the diapers are used, the longer the child will feel free to urinate when in a half-awake state when morning comes. A good solution is to discontinue using diapers and have the child sleep with a flannel-backed rubber pad over the sheet. Then, before you go to bed you can more easily carry her to the bathroom to empty her bladder, giving her a better chance of making it dry through the rest of the night. Without a diaper, when morning comes, she'll be able to catch herself in the act of wetting more quickly and be able to stop herself and get to the bathroom. This also keeps the burden of laundry from becoming a source of irritation for you.

The shake-and-wake method is the custom of waking your child before you go to bed so that she can urinate. If you go to the trouble to get your child out of bed, be sure you waken her completely so she can walk to the toilet on her own power. In order to clarify to your child that you are not taking the primary responsibility for her nocturnal toileting, ask her if she wants you to wake her up before you go to bed. If she is willing, then this practice may be worth a try.

A bladder-conditioning device is most successful for helping your child achieve nighttime bladder control. Several of these devices on the market are safe, effective, and inexpensive. The device consists of a pad that the child wears inside his or her underwear at night. The pad is connected by a wire to a tiny beeper that fastens to the child's night garment. When one or two drops of urine hit the moisture-sensitive pad, a beep sounds and wakes the child so that urination can be completed on a nearby toilet.

The device operates on the idea that even if the stimulus of the child's own bladder-fullness sensor is not sufficient to awaken him fully, the stimulus of the beep alarm is. The beep reinforces the intensity of the bladder-fullness stimulus. By repeatedly awakening when the stronger signal occurs, the child eventually becomes conditioned to awaken to the stimulus of his own bladder-fullness sensor. The device is well accepted by the child because it is his own device for his own problem, for which he takes responsibility. Some children try to play a "beat the beeper" game, attempting to get out of bed before the beeper goes off or with less and less urine reaching the pad. Relapses are common after this device is discontinued, and a second course of treatment may be necessary to achieve permanent success. Discuss the use of these bladder-conditioning devices with your doctor.

Medications for control of bed-wetting may be given to a child a half-hour before bedtime. No one is certain about how these medications work, but scientists believe they improve bladder muscle control and affect the state of sleep, allowing a child to be more aware of his bladder fullness. For most children, medications are less safe and less effective than bladder-conditioning devices. Relapses are also more common after the medications are stopped. Medication should not be used to control bed-wetting until all other methods discussed here have been tried and you and your doctor make the decision that your child's bedwetting problem is seriously affecting his general sense of well-being.

SIBLING RIVALRY

Nothing good comes from comparing one's fortunes with another's. Consider yourself. You rate yourself physically in comparison to the physical attractiveness of others; you have monetary worth in comparison to that of others. Even in school you were graded on a "curve," and you had a rank in class. Comparisons often result in feelings of inferiority because no matter what parameter you measure yourself by, there is always someone who has something that you don't. Accepting one's self and situation is an adult goal, which requires years of maturing—a

goal that some adults may never reach. Self-acceptance can be even more difficult for a child.

Sibling rivalry is a particularly sensitive problem because a child not only compares himself to siblings, but he also evaluates how his parents treat him in relation to his brothers and sisters. This can be a heavy load for children to carry. If there is a lot of anger between your children, you need to assess how much anger controls relationships in your family. You also need to look at what you may be doing to contribute to your child's insecurity. Much of the sibling rivalry you are experiencing could be generated by anger in dealings between parents and children or by not having enough balance in the way you favor each child.

Another emotion that underlies sibling rivalry, jealousy, is the fear of losing the parents' love. Children cannot grasp that parents have unlimited, unconditional love for each child. When your second child comes along, your first child may imagine that some of your love for him is transferred to the baby. Instead of understanding that each child gets "one bag full" of love, he fears he has to share his own bag, leaving it only half full (or less!).

Although sibling rivalry is a normal fact of family life, there are ways of minimizing it. There is no guarantee that your child will not get this "disease" at some point despite your immunizing her with preventive "medicine" early. But you can lower the risk and the severity of the disease. The following suggestions will help you lessen the feelings of rivalry between your children.

Preparing for a New Baby

Children seldom regard a new sibling as an unadulterated blessing. Mommy and Daddy may be very excited at the prospect of a new addition to the family, but the current queen of the roost may feel threatened and anxious. Dealing with these emotions will help a child have positive feelings toward her sibling.

Consider wise child spacing. Parents often ask how close together they should have their children. This very personal decision depends on your individual family situation. Sibling rivalry seems to occur less when children are spaced at least three years apart (or around one year apart!). By three years of age a child is probably weaned from the breast and has received a large dose of parental care that makes her feel good about herself and her growing independence. The child is better able to sense her parents' unconditional love by this time (if they have been able to demonstrate it), and is reassured by it, even when her parents are not physically present. The three-year-old is also able to verbalize negative feelings about the new baby, whereas a younger child can express his feelings only by his actions. A three-year-old can even become involved in the care of the new baby. Temperament is an obvious factor in child spacing—a high-need child may need more time before his space is invaded by a sibling.

Concerning child spacing, parents can take a tip from nature and from God's design. Most (but not all) women who are exclusively breastfeeding do not ovulate. In cultures in which babies are breastfed for several years, siblings are naturally spaced three to four years apart.

Spacing a year apart is hard on the parents, especially the mother, but doesn't seem to bother the older child so much, at least not at first, probably because the mother simply realizes she now has two babies and parents accordingly. Although it is true that having children close together is exhausting for the mother and may encourage more sibling rivalry at certain stages, some parents find that this problem is outweighed by the children's having the constant companionship of a sibling near in age. They choose (or manage) to accept more work and supervision in return for a closer relationship between children. Children who are spaced four to five years apart tend to squabble less, but they also may relate less to each other because they have fewer common interests. Children spaced one to two years apart may be more exhausting to parents and may fight more, but they also tend to relate more to each other in positive ways as well. Much also depends on the focus of the parents—how committed they intend to be in their relationship with their children.

Avoid weaning your child before his time. Although nursing during pregnancy can be challenging, it may not be wise to hurry a toddler into weaning just because a sibling is on the way. Some children wean naturally during a pregnancy; others are more persistent. Even a weaned child may show a renewed interest in nursing when the new baby arrives. Allowing the child to "just try it" is all it takes to defuse jealousy. When our fourth baby arrived, our nearly three-year-old tried nursing, quickly became tired of it, and then satisfied himself by walking around sucking on two bottles for a few weeks. Nursing two is called "tandem nursing" and requires a loving, accepting attitude and a bit of humor. If you find yourself facing the challenges of nursing two, call the La Leche League, or someone you know who has done it, for support. Talking with someone who understands what you're going through will help you sort out your own feelings and make wise choices.

Practice attachment parenting. Sibling rivalry is less likely in families where parents have practiced the principles of attachment parenting. There are several reasons for this. First, the child feels right. A child who is secure in her love attachment with her parents will feel less threatened by a new arrival. Second, you know your child. Your intuition has been developed so well with your first child that you are more sensitive to the feelings that lead to conflict between your children. You can anticipate problems and avoid or minimize them. Third, you are role models. By practicing the parenting styles advocated in the early chapters of this book, you have modeled the behavior you expect of your child—similar to how Christ modeled for His disciples. By modeling love, gentleness, and a caring touch, you have taught your child how big people treat little people, and that this is how she is expected to treat someone younger than herself. Many children do not know what behavior is expected of them because their parents do not tell them clearly.

If a child feels inwardly angry, she is apt to act angrily toward the new baby, who comes along and changes everything. She won't know how to manage her insecurity if she doesn't have a solid sense of who she is from healthy, balanced, empathetic parenting. A child whose emotional tank is full, who had her needs fulfilled when she was a baby, will be fine. Of course, no child ever gets perfect parenting, so you will see problems. But that is okay; you will help your child learn from every circumstance in life.

Pray with your child. If your child is old enough to understand, have him place his hands on your pregnant abdomen, and invite him to pray for his brother or sister inside, reminding him that God listens to his prayers. By teaching your child to pray for his sibling-to-be, you are beginning to shape the relationship you expect in your family, that is, siblings praying for each other. The value of encouraging your child to participate in your "pregnancy prayers" hit home to us after the birth of our fifth child. Within minutes after the birth, our four-year-old daughter, Hayden, put her hand upon the head of our newborn daughter, Erin, and exclaimed, "Praise the Lord, Praise Him!" Hayden simply carried over her prayer for the inside baby to the outside baby.

Prepare your child for the new baby as soon as your "bulge" becomes obvious or when she is able to pick up on what is happening from your conversations with friends and family. Let her feel the baby kick. By telling her this is just like she was when she was a baby, you help her identify with the baby inside you. Picture books help clarify misconceptions. Baby is not in Mommy's tummy, where the food is; he is in Mommy's uterus. Show your child baby pictures of herself when she was a tiny baby being held by you, nursed by you, cuddled, played with, and so on, so she can be aware not only of what babies need a lot of, but that she got the royal treatment herself.

Be sure to prepare your child for the time when you go into the hospital. She will be more interested in what is going to happen to her while you are gone rather than in what's going on in the hospital. Tell her where she is going and who will take care of her. Market the whole idea of separation from you not as a loss, but as something special: "Grandma will read you lots of books and do some special things with you." Let her help you plan what these will be. It is usually better to have a substitute caregiver take care of your child in your own home rather than to have someone care for her elsewhere. This will help alleviate her mounting worries about being displaced. If a bedroom shuffle is needed to make room for the new baby, do this during mid-pregnancy, well in advance of bringing the new baby home. Have her caregiver hold to the child's routine as much as possible when you are gone. While you are in the hospital, communicate with your child often by phone. Have her come to the hospital often to see you and the new baby.

As birthing becomes more homelike in the hospital, siblings are being welcomed into birthing rooms. We realize that while some families are comfortable with this idea, others are not. Allow us to share with you our professional discernment. When the older child participates in the birth of the baby, she feels a bond of love and protection for her younger brother or sister, and this bond will have lasting effects on the sibling relationship. Most children can handle the birth experience by age three and sometimes even younger. Be sure there are trusted adults there whose only job is caring for each child and who will be sensitive to allowing the children the freedom to come and go as they are comfortable. They should also be prepared for how hard you will be working to give birth. Let them know, for example, that you will be intensely preoccupied and even rehearse for them some of the sounds you will be making.

When the New Baby Arrives

Although careful preparation during pregnancy may minimize sibling rivalry, you can expect some ambivalent feelings in your child. First, understand your child's position. Just when your toddler/preschooler has achieved a comfortable position in the family, someone else comes along to threaten it. It's very hard to sit back and watch a "stranger" become the focus of love from your parents when you still want that kind of attention yourself. It hurts, especially if you feel unloved as a result of losing that attention.

Here are some things you can do to make baby's entry into the family less threatening. When your older child sees the baby for the first time, have a gift exchange. Receiving a gift "from baby" and giving a gift can be very reassuring. When you bring baby home, have Dad carry the "little bundle" so you can greet your older child with wide open arms, just for him, to get a welcome-home hug. And ask a number of your visitors to bring a small gift for "big brother" or "big sister" so your child doesn't conclude that he or she is not special.

What Behavior Can You Expect from Your Child?

Children vary widely in their reactions to new siblings. These emotions range from a "no hard feelings" acceptance to overt hostility and aggression. Some children sulk and retreat; other children lash out with biting and hitting in an all-out attempt to evict their new siblings; others show ambivalent behavior, one day hugging and kissing the new baby (perhaps a bit "too hard"), the next day hitting him. Children seldom verbalize their feelings about new babies; they usually express them by their actions. Two days after our fourth child was born, the three-year-old shot back "I hate that baby" when Martha told him he'd have to wait for his juice until the baby was finished nursing. We are glad he was able to share his feelings, and we didn't try to convince him otherwise. Looking back, we can see we needed to have a *doula* there to help out in those early days for just such a situation. Of course, Peter did eventually learn how to wait.

The preverbal child is especially prone to physical aggression toward a new baby. Never leave your children alone in the same room together, even if you think she would never hurt the baby. When a child is able to act out her wishes (get rid of that baby), she is extremely frightened by the amount of power she thinks she has. "Murder in the heart" becomes a troubling and destructive burden for such a young child. Also, expect the older sibling to show regressive behavior, for example, the previously dry three-year-old may need to go back to diapers for a while. This is okay. Don't worry, your child will leave these things behind once she can get her solid footing.

After the Baby Arrives

In managing sibling rivalry, remember you can control only your children's actions, not their feelings. Here are some suggestions for handling sibling rivalry after the new baby arrives.

Get your child involved with the new baby. Involvement is one key to helping the young child with ambivalent feelings. Encourage him to be Mommy's and Daddy's little helper, and involve him in comforting the baby, bathing the baby, or running to get a diaper. This role of helper gradually can evolve to the role of teacher. Encourage the older child to teach the younger child. This will profit both of them. The older child will feel older and wiser as he "teaches" his little sister something. The older child can certainly be a source of developmental stimulation for the younger child. Babies often respond more to the sounds and faces of children than they do to those of adults. Using your older child as a teaching model is a real boost to his self-image and encourages responsible behavior toward his younger siblings.

If the new baby is fussy and you're having difficulty coping with her fussiness, bring in the reserve troops of older children. Let them assist you in trying various gentling maneuvers. An older child's ability to calm a fussy baby fosters a healthy, protective attitude and is a great preparation for his own eventual role as a parent.

Help your older child feel important too. Besides having visitors include him in gift giving, include your older child in the visiting and oohing and ahhhing. Let her feel that she is part of center stage, right there with you to show off the new baby. Let her hold the baby under your supervision and have the camera ready for lots of "together" pictures. Consider giving your older child a baby doll that wets, has diapers, and can be bathed. When breastfeeding, "lose" the bottle the doll comes with—you'll be pleased to see how readily your older child (boy or girl) will figure out how to "nurse" the baby doll.

Wear the baby in a baby carrier. This gives your toddler or young preschooler an important message. It tells him that while baby has a lot of special needs, you still have two hands free for him. This body language will speak louder than any words could; and it will be like having an extra pair of hands for all those times when no one else is available to help you out.

Get father involved. Father, take time to give special attention to the older child. Remember your older child is probably feeling she's lost a lot of Mommy's prime time. This is a realistic fact of family life because babies need more physical maintenance than older children. Dad can compensate for this feeling of loss by getting involved more with the older child and doing fun things with her so she feels what she has "lost" from Mom she has gained from Dad.

As the size of your family increases, each child continues to strive for his or her own identity but may have increasing difficulty finding it because of all the competition from within the family. Take some time out every day or every few days to do something special with each child individually. This special time helps satisfy each child's bid for equal time and gives each the feeling of individual worth.

Encourage your older child to verbalize negative feelings. The more he can express in words, the less he will act out. If he says, "I hate that baby," don't say, "No, you don't." If you deny his feelings, you're denying his right to feel emotions. It is better to express your understanding of these negative feelings. ("You're mad because Mommy can't play right now.") Try to turn them into more positive feelings. ("Let's read a story while the baby nurses.") Allow your child much time and space to accept the new baby.

Intervene swiftly if there is an attempt at aggression. Any overture suggesting an older child would try to hurt the younger should be dealt with immediately to convey the message that you will not allow it. Remove the child from the situation and let him know how serious this offense is. The safest place to keep the new baby when you can't be supervising your older one is on your body in your baby carrier.

Rivalry among Children

Squabbles among siblings are inevitable. Part of the realistic expectations of parenting is that parents often will be called upon to referee squabbles among their children, to judge who is at fault, to give direction, and to administer appropriate correction. The following behavior modifiers are designed to minimize rivalry among siblings.

Encourage the older children to model for the younger ones. It is a fact of life in families that older children are expected to care for, teach, and model for the younger children. For example, our six-year-old Peter was having a problem with patience. He was quick to lose his temper and give up on a task if it became too difficult for him. We elicited the help of our twelve-year-old Bobby to go over to Peter at those times of stress, lay his hand on Peter's shoulder, and say, "Peter, let me help you." Another time we asked one of the older children to engage in some brother-to-brother Bible study to model the importance of daily Scripture reading. Not only does the younger child profit from the modeling, it teaches family members to be concerned and aware of the needs of others. If this level of concern for one another's needs does not come easily to your children, a little parental guidance will be necessary.

Pray for one another. A major part of your family devotions can be to encourage your children to pray for one another. One child may have the privilege of praying for the prayer requests of his brothers and sisters, or each one could pray for the one next to him.

Encourage expressions of love for one another. The concept of love for one another can be another focus of your family devotions. You may say, "I'm encouraging you to show acts of love for one another because this is what Jesus asks His disciples to do." Ask each of your children to show at least one act of love for another sibling each day. Try recording these acts in your prayer calendar during family devotions. With encouragement, this can evolve into a pattern of living, a powerful behavior modifier toward developing good feelings among siblings. One night years ago, as we had prayer time, our five-year-old shared that she felt no one in the family (except Mom and Dad) really loved her. We had a beautiful time together as we explored with her and her siblings how life had been going lately and why she had come to feel this way. We all made a commitment that night to find ways for each of us to help this little girl feel our love. We were glad she was able to express her need.

Minimize comparisons among your children. This is often the basis for feelings of inferiority, which can turn into undesirable behavior among siblings. Praise a child for his accomplishments in relation to himself, not in comparison to a sibling. Each child should feel he is equally special in the eyes of his parents.

An excellent book on this subject is *Siblings without Rivalry: How to Help Your Children Live Together So You Can Live Too* by Adele Faber and Elaine Mazlish (see bibliography).

GROWING A SEXUALLY-HEALTHY CHILD

When it comes to teaching children about sex, parents often have difficulty knowing what to say and when to say it. We prefer to use the term "sexuality," meaning developing healthy gender attitudes in addition to teaching the child about sex or the "facts of life." Here are the important messages to teach the child in the preschool years.

Be a Touching Family

The attachment philosophy of child care we advocate throughout this book is the earliest form of sexuality education. The infant who spends much of her early years in your arms, at your breasts, and on your lap receives an early and lifelong sexual message: being comfortable giving and receiving affection.

Model Healthy Sexuality

How husband and wife show affection to one another is another way of teaching sexuality. You are always on stage in front of your children. Not only do children learn from how Mom and Dad care for them, they also witness how mom and dad care for each other. Dad is the first "male" and Mom the first "female" that your child learns from. How parents treat each other is the first lesson on how males treat females and visa versa. If your child grows up in an atmosphere of sensitivity and caring, she files this away as "the sexual norm." This is the healthy way that males and females relate. If, on the other hand, your children habitually see one parent putting down the other, or even worse, abusing one another or using his or her gender as a tool to control the other person, they file in their growing memory bank a picture like "that's the way men (or women) are." How Mom and Dad treat each other strongly influences the gender characteristics that children later choose in a mate. At a time when children see families broken or breaking up all around them, they need to know that their parents love and honor one another and care about how each other feels.

Foster Healthy Gender Identity

Gender identity becomes apparent by age three when children begin calling other children "boys" and "girls." Little girls and boys become aware that they urinate differently and little girls wonder why they have no penis. It's important to reassure a girl that God made her body to be special too. Help a little girl be satisfied about how her body works, explaining where the urine comes from. Help her look with a mirror to see her body parts better if she's interested. You want your children to be comfortable with the gender that God has given them.

Call It What It Is

Don't contribute to congenital confusion by using inappropriate terms for genitalia. Not only are these slang terms confusing to your child, but they also convey the subtle message that you are embarrassed about these body parts. The terms "penis," "scrotum," "vagina," and "vulva" can be spoken and understood by a three-year-old.

Show and Tell

Sometime during the preschool years your child may raise the long-anticipated question, "Where do babies come from?" You will be called upon to begin your child's formal sexuality education. Don't plan on delivering one big lecture; be sure to answer only the questions your child is asking. Girls are much more interested in these things than boys are. Watch for openers. A child may be curious about a friend's pregnant mother or show interest in the new baby a friend's mommy just brought home. Take advantage of teachable opportunities, such as when the family dog or cat has puppies or kittens. These are openers to talk about how babies grow inside mommies and are then born. Use correct terms and facts: babies grow in mommy's uterus, not in her tummy. Use books and visual aids to enhance your own explanations, but not to substitute for them. A helpful book to teach four- to ten-year-olds is: *How Babies are Made,* by Andry and Shepp. Another one is *The Wonderful Way That Babies Are Made,* by Larry Christenson. (See bibliography for descriptions.) Several of our children have participated in the birth of a sibling when they were as young as three years of age (see p. 318, "Prepare Your Child for the New Baby," for ways to prepare children to be present at a birth).

Guide Curious Little Hands

Now and then, in our pediatric practice, we get a call from a distraught parent who has gone ballistic upon opening a bedroom door and discovering two little naked bodies playing "doctor." In preschool children, this is innocent sexual curiosity and not deviant sexual behavior. Try to handle this situation calmly and resist the impulse to tell the children that they have done something "dirty" or "sinful." In a nonangry, but instructive, way convey to your child the concept of "private parts." By the age of four, your child can understand the concept of not touching another child's private areas nor letting other persons touch his without your permission. Private parts are any place that your swimming suit covers. Be sure your child understands that these parts are not "bad" or "dirty," they are just private. Your body language can speak louder than your words. When a child grabs his penis or pokes at her vagina never say "stop that," but rather "Yes, that's your penis (or vagina)," with the same attitude you would talk about his arm or his leg. Minimize opportunities that foster genital play. Don't allow children to be unsupervised behind closed doors. We have a rule in our house that bedroom doors must always be open when friends are over—at all ages.

To a child, massaging his or her genitals is a pleasurable experience; it is not "wrong" or "dirty." To children, genital massage is a discovery that feels good and is a usual stage that children go through as they discover the workings of their body. Using the above concept of "private parts," three- to four-year-old children can be taught that genital play is not appropriate in public, such as when Aunt Nancy is visiting. Above all, avoid scare tactics: "Stop that! It'll make you sick!" Genital play can become more than just a passing curiosity and evolve into masturbation which, again, is a normal stage when a young child discovers that parts of his or her body bring pleasurable feelings. You simply tell your child that touching his or her private parts needs to be done in private because it makes other people (including you) uncomfortable. When you give these clear boundaries, your child will understand, and will most likely choose to stay in your company rather than take himself off to the privacy of his or her room.

It's Time To Cover Up

When your toddler runs into the bathroom as you step out of the shower in your birthday suit, there is no need to dive for cover. Yet, there reaches an age when parental nudity in the home is no longer appropriate. By age four, most children have developed a sense of modesty. Take cues from your child that he or she is developing a sense of modesty. When your child begins to cover up, it's time for you to cover up too.

Between ages three and six, children sexualize their parents in their minds; they are enchanted with their parents' bodies and like to watch them. So by three, you would, for example, wear conservative pajamas for sleeping in, even if your child does not sleep with you. This is important so that the boundaries are in place to safeguard your child's psychosexual development.

Help your child be comfortable with intimacy, his or her body, and have a healthy gender identity, and you have given your child the tools to grow up as a sexually-healthy adult.

CHAPTER FOURTEEN

Discipline and Spiritual Training Birth to Age Three

Parents have become accustomed to thinking about discipline as punishment—some external force that is applied to a child to keep him or her in line. Punishment is indeed a part of Christian discipline, but a minor part. If as Christian parents you sincerely want to discipline your child, your most effective discipline is to create such an attitude within your child and atmosphere within your home that punishment seldom becomes necessary. But when punishment does become necessary, you will want to administer it appropriately. This may mean changing your attitude toward discipline so that your focus is on how to avoid the need for punishment rather than on how to punish. (Right up front we want to say that we have a different way of understanding "the rod" verses, which we will discuss in chapter 16.) In the following section, discipline is understood to be a process of instilling a positive direction within the child rather than imposing external forces on a child's behavior. This is a truly Christian approach to directing behavior and building healthy relationships. It is also a practical way of life.

LAYING THE FOUNDATION

Four basic building blocks form the foundation for discipline and spiritual training of the child: basing discipline on Scripture, providing a spiritual model, knowing your child, and helping your child feel right. God, our Father, has directed parents to do two things for their children: to teach and to discipline. Teaching and disciplining, as used in the Bible, are similar terms, but they differ in degree. *Teaching* means to impart God's Word to your children. *Disciplining* goes one step further—it imparts God's Word to such a degree that His Word becomes part of each child's inner self, his inner controls, his base of operations. In short, to discipline a child means to instill a sense of direction.

Biblical Guidance for Discipline

Today's parents are bombarded with many different theories and books on how to discipline. As a result, many sincere parents flounder in a sea of uncertainty. There is only one way for Christian parents to discipline their children: go to His Word and analyze His specific instructions on how to discipline your children.

Proverbs 22:6 is the master verse of Christian discipline: "Train a child in the way he should go, and when he is old he will not turn from it." The Book of Proverbs is noted for short verses with deep meaning. Dig into this verse and discover what God is saying to you. God is reminding you of your awe-inspiring responsibility to discipline your children. What you do now will affect your child's whole life. These words of authority should inspire commitment to get in there and work at it. In essence, God is saying: "Parents, you must take charge of your children. It's important!" The instruction is the same for all ages, infancy through adolescence; discipline is a constant commitment until your child is ready to leave home.

There are various interpretations of the phrase "in the way he should go." Does God mean a child should follow the general plan He has for all children to keep His commandments and follow His teaching? Or does God imply a more specific plan, one that is according to your child's inherent temperament and characteristics? Biblical scholars suggest the latter interpretation. Each child has an individual bent or "way" and therefore an individual plan. What God is saying to you is to know your child, be tuned in to his individual bent, keep your radar system attuned to the direction he should take, and keep him focused in that direction (which may not necessarily be the direction you want for him). This concept may be hard for parents to understand: "How do we know what direction God has for our child?" If you have parented your child in a way that has helped you to really know him, this question is much less difficult to answer.

Some parents are disappointed when after years of careful training their children seem to depart from the way they have been raised, especially during their teens and twenties when they are deciding whether or not to accept their parents' values as their own. Parents, don't despair. For some children, there may be a longer time gap between the two parts of the proverb. Some children temporarily stray from the way they should go, but because of a strong sense of God's direction, they eventually find their way again and do not turn from it once they are older.

The next biblical concept, and one which is very difficult for many parents to understand, is that within the child's nature is a bent toward good and a bent toward evil. The following scriptures make this concept very clear: "I have been a sinner from birth, sinful from the time my mother conceived me" (Ps. 51:5); "Folly is bound up in the heart of a child, but the rod of discipline will drive it far from him" (Prov. 22:15); "The rod of correction imparts wisdom, but a child left to himself disgraces his mother" (Prov. 29:15). This concept is not in keeping with the secular view that children come into the world in perfection and that a child's personality should be allowed to unfold with little interference from adults. A child left without direction will run into trouble. He will take many wrong turns, will stumble, get hurt, and may have difficulty finding the true path. Even Adam and Eve, who truly were perfect children, took that route because God gave them free will. That original sin is our heritage, along with the free will to choose good over evil.

Provide a Spiritual Model

You cannot give to your children what you do not have yourselves. It is impossible to impart a sense of direction to your children if you do not have direction. Your library may be filled with books about discipline, and you may preach many "sermons" to your children, but your example, what you are through the eyes of your children, will always be their best teacher.

Make a commitment that Christian discipline is a top priority in your own life as well as in your relationship with your children. We stress this term *commitment* because it forms the basis of all of parenting. You are well on your way to effective Christian discipline of your child if you love and fear your God and walk in His ways.

Know Your Child

To discipline your child, you must know your child. To train a child in the way she should go, you must know which way *she* should go. Almost all parents truly love their children; however, parents vary in the degree to which they *know* their children. The attachment style of parenting helps you to know your child better. For review, the essentials of attachment parenting for Christians are prenatal bonding, bonding and rooming-in at birth, a strong mother-infant attachment, father's involvement and spiritual leadership, breastfeeding on cue, timely weaning, nighttime parenting, gentling the high-need baby, compassionate response to baby's cries, and daily prayer for wisdom to know your child.

What do parenting styles have to do with discipline? We have noticed that parents who have practiced attachment parenting do indeed have fewer discipline problems with their children. Attachment parenting provides the best conditions for parents to really know their children, and thus be able to guide them.

Parents who practice these attachment tips have the following characteristics as "disciplinarians":

- They are observant of their child's actions.
- They are confident in the appropriateness of their responses.
- The fathers are involved in parenting.
- Parents are sensitive to the feelings and circumstances that promote misbehavior.
- They know how to convey their expectations to their children.
- They have realistic expectations of childhood behavior in general.
- They have a wide understanding of what is normal for *their* children's behavior and are not often provoked to anger.
- They seek prayer and counsel when the going gets tough.
- They learn the true meaning of giving of themselves.
- They enjoy their children.

The family functions as a father-mother-baby *unit.* It is easier to discipline someone who is part of yourself because you know this "part of yourself" (your baby) so well. It's so beautiful to watch a mother, father, and baby who are in harmony with one another. We know that surely this is God's design for the parent-child relationship. God designed discipline to flow naturally from this inner harmony. Childrearing techniques from some third party advisor will never take the place of this kind of connectedness.

Help Your Child Feel Right

Children who are the products of attachment parenting are easier to discipline because even as infants they learn what it is to feel right, and children who feel right are more likely to act right. This inner feeling of rightness, of being able to trust others, is the beginning of a baby's sense of self-worth, and children's behavior usually mirrors their feelings about themselves. Attachment parenting also allows a mutual trust to develop between caregiver and child. This trust helps the parent know how to direct the child and makes the child willing to follow the parent's lead. Admittedly, the ease with which you can discipline your child is to a great extent determined by his or her temperament. However, a baby who has this inner sense of rightness seems to be able to recognize discipline that helps him maintain this inner rightness. This keeps struggles with stubbornness to a minimum. A sense of "unrightness" within a child makes him less receptive to direction. He does not know what it is to feel right, so he continues to struggle. This accounts for the frustration of parents who state, "We just can't get through to him."

Parents usually begin to think about the how-tos of discipline when their children are between one and two years old, because that is when power struggles between parent and child begin. During their babies' fifteen-month checkup, parents may ask, "Can we discuss discipline now?" Bill replies, "You began disciplining your child from the moment of birth." In reality, discipline is not one isolated part of the total package of childrearing. Everything you do with your child from the moment of his or her birth will play a part in discipline. All the previous chapters of this book have directly or indirectly led up to discipline.

This next statement may surprise you, but we feel that the most important stage of discipline is the period from birth to one year of age. Every little interaction you have with your baby carries over into discipline. During this period you are developing sensitivity to your baby, getting to know him, maturing your God-given intuition, and helping your baby feel right. This is the period in which you are forming your attitudes toward the whole of childrearing. Being open to your baby during the first year prepares you to guide his behavior appropriately during the second year. Before you can discipline your child (in the biblical sense of guiding him), you must first be open to him. Your influence over his behavior will flow from that foundation of trust and openness. In the first few months you will find that being open to your baby means that you anticipate and respond to his needs promptly and totally. You are there for your baby unreservedly, giving him what he needs when he needs it, building love and trust.

Around the fourth month there is a slight shift in the balance. Your baby can now become bored because developmentally she is ready to do more than just be held and fed; she becomes frustrated because her mind drives her to do things her body isn't ready to do yet. The cry that your baby uses to signal her boredom or frustration will be different from the hunger, pain, or "need to be held" cry. You will still respond, but gradually you will learn that these cries don't require the "red alert" response from you. You don't have to drop everything the instant she signals; you find you can buy a little time (half a minute, then one or two) by using your voice to reassure her that you are nearby and you are coming. Your baby knows she can count on you and learns she can wait, and you both learn just how long. When you do respond, you offer stimulation rather than food for comfort—a toy, a book, conversation, or a change of scenery. This all happens gradually, without any calculation, but one day, when she's six months old, you realize that your responses are considerably slower now than they were at six days or six weeks. It would simply not be healthy if you were still trying to be so promptly and totally "there" for your six- to nine-month-old as you were for your newborn.

Knowing your infant, helping him feel right, and seeing that he securely trusts you builds a strong foundation for discipline in the years to come. Without this foundation, discipline will evolve into a science of methods. With this foundation, you naturally and intuitively will guide your child instead of reacting emotionally to his actions.

GIVE SPIRITUAL TRAINING

Parents often ask, "At what stage of my child's development do I introduce the concept of God into discipline?" It is much easier to bring God into discipline at this stage if God is already at the center of your life, your marriage, and your family. If you have already made this commitment, you are well on your way to helping your child experience God's presence in his life. Remember that you cannot feed your child spiritually if your own spiritual commitment is undernourished. Without the foundation of spiritual commitment—Bible study and prayer—you will be less comfortable talking about God with your child. If you learn to recognize God's work in your own life, you will be better equipped to teach your child about God. Wanting your child to know Christ can be a powerful motivation for strengthening your own commitment to your Lord.

A child's concept of God is very simplistic, and it is probably limited to a feeling: "Mom and Dad talk about Him all the time, He must be a very important person; He loves me; He is a big Person." Such primitive concepts are vital to laying the foundation of the child's regard for God, not only as authority figure but also caring Father, at a later age. One of the characteristics of toddlers' language skills is that they receive and understand much more than they say. Your child will understand better the concept of God if she has been saturated with hearing about God from birth. By the time your child is two years old, she hears the words *God* and *Jesus* spoken in association with love and protection. By the time she is three years old, she feels God's presence.

The following are some specific examples of how you can introduce God to your child.

Pray for your child. Thank God for your child every day. Ask God to watch over your child's development and to give you wisdom in rearing him in the way he should go. Daily prayer is vital to Christian family discipline. It becomes a discipline, a persistent spiritual habit by which the parent continuously prays, "Father, I invite You into our family; You are a trusted and vital family member (head of the family, in fact), and my day is not complete unless we talk to each other." By the time your child is two years old, a spiritual feeding of daily prayer becomes as natural a part of child care as food for the body does.

Sing with your infant. Babies can mimic the gestures of songs. As early as nine months, our daughter Erin would lift up her arms at the cue of "praise Jesus." Following our evening meal prayer we had for a while a custom of singing a certain praise song, lifting our hands when the words indicated.

Initially, Erin would simply watch this family praise. Eventually, she began raising her hands when we did. By fifteen months, as soon as the mealtime grace was finished, in anticipation of the praise song to follow she would raise her hands right on cue (sometimes reminding us to sing). Praising the Lord was being imprinted upon her heart even before she could grasp intellectually the meaning of what was being sung. As we all joined hands, bowed our heads, and became quiet for prayer, she did the same. At seventeen months she was able to remind us to say the blessing by reaching for Dad's hand on one side and Mom's hand on the other side. She knew we were

A FATHER'S PRAYER

From the day of the birth of our fifth child, each night before retiring I (Bill) would lay my hands on my little daughter and spend a few moments in prayer. (Actually, this practice had begun months earlier when we prayed as a couple over the baby in Martha's womb.) A few nights I went to sleep having forgotten to do this, but I would soon awaken with the feeling that I had forgotten something. I then performed my duty as spiritual leader of my home and put my hands on my little daughter, thanking God for the blessings of her day and asking Him to be with her during the night. I could then retire with a comfortable feeling that we both would sleep better, because in the quiet of the night Someone who never goes off duty is watching over us. This baby taught me to pray for the three who came after her, as well as the children we already had. I finally learned how to really pray for my children.

supposed to do something special before we ate.

Your Jesus songs don't have to be fancy or formal. You can take a nursery rhyme tune, put simple repetitive words to it, include your child's name, and she'll have her own special song. By four or five she'll probably be making up songs herself.

Read to your child about God. Two-year-olds are fascinated with books. A Bible picture book and a loving parent's arms are a winning combination for teaching a child about God's love. Two-year-olds are able to understand simple Bible story books by looking at the pictures. By reading to your child about Jesus (or telling the story yourself in simple words), you are teaching him a vital message. He learns: "A man in my picture book does all kinds of nice things, and my mommy and daddy talk about this same man all the time. He's a special person, and He loves me." If you can convey to your two-year-old that one message, that Jesus is a special person who loves him, you have laid the foundation for his deeper understanding of Christ and God in subsequent stages.

DISCIPLINING THE CHILD: ONE TO TWO YEARS OLD

By the time a child is twelve months old the roles of both infant and parent take on a new direction. In the first year, your role is primarily that of caregiver. This role certainly continues, but in the second year your parent role broadens to include the roles of authority figure and designer of your child's environment. In this second year, your child's environment widens as he acquires two new abilities: locomotion and speech. As the roles of parent and child take on a broader perspective, so does the concept of discipline. In the first year, discipline means primarily conveying love and security to your infant and learning to know him. You are guiding the development of his inner life. In the second year, discipline also means guidance in the outside world. The following discussion will center on two main features of guiding your child: (1) how to develop realistic expectations and knowledge of normal or usual toddler behavior in general, and of your child's behavior in particular; and (2) how to modify your toddler's bent toward undesirable behavior and channel his energies toward desirable behavior.

At this point, take inventory of what your one-year-old is like as a person. When I (Bill) ask parents to tell me about their child at the one-year checkup, they may say, "He is beginning to walk, he plays with blocks, he feeds himself," and so on. This is not the kind of answer I am hoping for. They have told me what the child *does*, not what he *is*. Other parents may say, "He likes to be held a lot; he is most happy when we go exploring; his favorite toy is his blocks; he loves to roll on his daddy's chest; his mood is generally pleasant, but he has his fussy times at the end of the day. I guess he just gets tired. I've learned to handle these fussy moments. Oh, and he's walking!" Those are the cue words I'm looking for: "he likes," "he feels," "I've learned," "I know when he . . ." These parents have a head start toward effective discipline because they know their child from the inside out. They can see the world through his eyes.

Since discipline begins with knowing your child, use the following checklist to take inventory of how well you know your one-year-old:

- What makes your baby most happy? What makes him laugh and chatter?
- What makes your baby unhappy?
- What parent-child play activity does he like best?
- What are your baby's most noticeable cues that she needs something?
- How do you respond to your baby's cues, such as fussing, crying, gesturing, signs of tiredness?
- What behaviors annoy you?
- How does your baby feel most of the time? Does he feel right?
- Do you enjoy being with your baby most of the time?
- Generally speaking, do you enjoy being a parent?
- Do you pray for your child daily?

This inventory is a general measure of how finely turned your communication network is with your baby. If your answers are more negative than positive, please pray and seek counsel at this stage of your parent-child relationship so that you can have a more positive relationship with your child in the years to come.

Have Realistic Expectations of Normal Toddler Behavior

Many first-time parents have no way of knowing what is usual toddler behavior, and they may therefore label certain normal behaviors as "bad." Not understanding normal toddler behavior may lead you to be harsh when you should be gentle, or restrictive when you should be channeling your child's energy into more appropriate adventures. Learning to distinguish between childish behavior that needs correcting and childlike behavior you must learn to live with is part of attaining maturity as a parent. It is also necessary for effective discipline. The more children you have, the broader your concept of "normal" will become. Your acceptance level will widen, and you won't sweat the small stuff anymore. As parents of eight, this is our first survival tip to you.

Toddlerhood begins when locomotion expands your child's environment, sometime around age one. A characteristic of child development, especially during the toddler stage, is that the acquisition of a new skill compels the child to master that skill and use it to achieve other skills. Until your infant learned to crawl, she was a passive observer of the world around her and mostly dependent upon other people for stimulation and pleasure. Walking now opens up new horizons for her and gives her an insatiable appetite to explore and uncover the secrets of the wide world. She sees that doors are to be opened, drawers pulled out, buttons pushed, knobs turned, and objects taken apart. She is on the go from dawn till dusk, stopping briefly to refuel on food and love, only to jump up again and continue her independent research on the world around her. She does succumb to a daily nap, but does not easily yield to the enemy of all toddlers—sleep.

Many little navigators do not chart their courses carefully. A toddler's explorations are directed more by impulse and trial and error than by calculation and reasoning, though some toddlers are more careful than others by temperament. The challenge of disciplining a toddler is arriving at a healthy balance, exerting just the right amount of guidance without hampering the toddler's desire to learn.

Between twelve and eighteen months of age most of the conflicts that occur are between the child and his environment rather than between the child and his parent. Therefore, most of your authority and discipline are directed toward taking charge of your child's environment and thus indirectly setting limits for him. Even before your toddler has begun walking, you have covered electric outlets, locked your cupboards, moved the plants, removed breakable objects, covered sharp table corners, and put away small objects that can be swallowed. Taking charge of a child's environment is an important part of disciplining him.

Frustration and ambivalence are very characteristic of toddlers. When their desire to explore matches their locomotor capabilities, they are in balance and basically happy. But when the desire to explore is greater than the capabilities for getting around, frustrations will be manifested in tantrum-like behavior. This imbalance between desire and capability also contributes to ambivalence, one of the most normal and noticeable characteristics of toddlers. At one moment they are purposefully exploring their world. A few minutes later you are reminded that in many ways your growing child is still a baby. Watch young toddlers in a room with their mothers. A few will wander off to check out the toys. A few others will cling to Mommy because they seem threatened. Others will move away a short distance, but will look back periodically to home base to be sure Mommy is still there.

Be available on an as-needed basis. Your toddler needs your support while he works out the anxiety that is created by his internal ambivalence. You are still the pivotal point in his widening universe. As he makes his daily rounds throughout the house, he periodically checks on your whereabouts, and he feels more secure knowing you are there.

Be observant of your toddler's behavior. Watch for his cues that he needs you, but also be willing to accept his need for his own space and for some control over his own life. Part of achieving parental maturity and becoming an effective disciplinarian is having your radar system finely tuned so that you pick up his signals on your screen and store each bit of information. A child who has a consistently available and observant caregiver intuitively feels that someone he loves is in tune with him. Consider for a moment your relationship with your heavenly Father; what a feeling of strength and security to know that He is available and observant of your behavior and of your needs.

Adopt the "why" principle. When you don't like what your young child is doing, ask yourself, "Why is he doing that?" Is he tired, bored, hungry, or sick? Is he simply trying to get attention? Is he engaging in a power struggle, trying to gain more control over his life? If you approach your child's behavior by first asking *why* he is doing something rather than reacting to what he is doing, you will focus first on the child and second on the act. This is where knowing your child begins to pay off. When you can understand the drive behind the child's behavior, it is easier to take effective steps to channel that energy elsewhere. Here's an example from our family. Sixteen-month-old Lauren would playfully and gleefully hit her mother on the head or face. Martha would express displeasure and ask her to stop. But usually this was not enough to get Lauren to change her behavior. She was having fun experiencing cause and effect and didn't understand that this game was very irritating to Martha. Time to change the situation. Martha would hold out her hand and say, "Gimme five." The hitting would continue with great gusto, with both parties in the game enjoying it. Focusing on the why is a good habit to get into; when your child is older you will be able to "get behind his eyeballs" and understand what causes certain behaviors.

Provide Good Nutrition

It may seem unusual to talk about good nutrition in regard to childhood discipline. However you are on the offensive—you are considering what you can do to encourage desirable behavior. Good nutrition (or the lack of it) can have a profound effect on behavior. There are three feeding practices that can improve your child's behavior and contribute positively to your discipline relationship.

First, *breastfeed* your child for as long as both members of the nursing couple enjoy the relationship. We encourage mothers to think of breastfeeding in terms of years and not months. At this point you may ask, "What on earth has this to do with disciplining my child?" Earlier in this chapter you read about the importance of the infant developing a secure attachment and trust in his caregiver as a prerequisite for that caregiver becoming an effective authority figure later on. Breastfeeding makes this easier to accomplish. Breastfeeding mothers spend more time with their babies. Breastfed babies eat more often, and they are in their mothers' arms more often, enjoying more holding and eye-to-eye contact. We are not saying that breastfeeding mothers love their children any more than bottle-feeding mothers, but we do feel that breastfeeding gives the mother a head start in knowing her child better, and the child is given a head start in feeling right. These two elements are basic to the foundation for effective discipline.

The second feeding practice we encourage you to consider is *nibbling*. This may sound like heresy, a blatant attempt to undermine the accepted custom of requiring a young child to sit still, consume three square meals a day, with perhaps one scheduled snack. But consider the child's limitations, especially at two or three years of age. He does not have the attention span to sit still and finish a large meal. He is simply too busy. This often results in mealtimes becoming battles between parents and child instead of positive experiences. Medically speaking, it is better for a young child to nibble on nutritious foods all day long because this prevents blood-sugar swings and the mood changes that often accompany them in an active child. The behavior of young children deteriorates in late morning and mid-afternoon when they are the most hungry and their blood sugar is the lowest. See chapter 12 for tips on feeding your toddler and young child.

The third feeding practice that will improve your child's behavior is *avoiding junk food.* Junk food and its detrimental effects on your child's behavior are also discussed in detail in chapter 12.

Shaping Your Child's Environment

One of your most basic jobs as disciplinarian is to create an environment that does not foster a conflict of wills. Having to fight you constantly will not help your child develop good relationships with authority figures. Having you control him constantly does not allow him to learn or become his own person. Remember that discipline is mainly guidance. If you make your home and your family into a place where it is not too difficult to be a child, the environment itself will help you discipline the child and you will avoid many conflicts.

"Baby Proofing" and "Distract and Divert" are the two main tools you use to shape environment for the young toddler. Respect your toddler's healthy curiosity by moving your valuables and breakable family heirlooms up a few feet. Bring them down in a few years when she is old enough to understand. The out-of-reach and out-of-sight environment is certainly much easier on child and parent than a constant stream of "no-no" and "don't touch." Taking precautions against a toddler on the loose is certainly safer and less exhausting than a system that requires constant policing. It also produces less anger in the parents, so the whole relationship is healthier. Constantly saying no and frustrating the child's drive to explore only serves to produce continual anger in your child or to produce a robotlike compliance that includes shutdown of any growth toward a healthy sense of personhood.

Since it is normal and healthy behavior for a toddler to turn knobs, push buttons, and pull drawers, give your child her own things to turn, push, and pull. A curious toddler deserves at least one eye-level drawer in the kitchen that she can pull out, sort through, and fill with her own belongings. The concept of "me" and "mine" is important at this age.

A child's hands are the tools she uses to explore cause-and-effect relationships. For this reason, childhood development experts recommend that you do not slap a child's hands to discourage her touching things. Hand slapping to a curious toddler just beginning to reach out into the world is just as insulting and confusing and frightening as face slapping is to an adult. Instead, teach your child how to touch things; use phrases such as "hot touch," "gentle touch," and "one-finger touch." The more positive feedback she receives ("Thank you for bringing Mommy the clothes"; "Show me your car."), the less likely she is to want to touch the things that are off limits. Create a positive environment, a get-into-things and a hands-on approach that respects the normal, innate curiosity of a developing toddler and makes negative discipline less necessary.

When your youngster does head for a "no-no," simply distract her from her pursuit by calling her name or initiating an activity. When that's not sufficient, divert her physically away from the "no-no." This should be done calmly and cheerfully. As your toddler gets closer to age two, you may want to read ahead to the sections "Discipline Undesirable Behavior" and "What About Spanking?" on pages 347–355.

Be creative in high-risk situations that make good behavior difficult. It is unrealistic to expect a curious toddler to walk down the aisle in a supermarket and not touch anything. You would be very suspicious of a young child who walked like an obedient soldier with his arms at his sides down the aisle of a supermarket and did not try to grab all those delightful things on the shelves that are screaming "Buy me!" Keep his mind and hands busy with things that he is allowed to do. Let him help you find things, get them off the shelf, and put them in the basket. After all, that is the model he sees—his mother is walking down the aisle grabbing things. A few times we let our toddlers take their own kiddy shopping cart to the store, when we had lots of time to spare. (This is not the fastest way to get through the grocery store, but you'll be having more fun than most of the people there.) Or keep him safely seated in the shopping cart (with a restraint strap) and carry on a conversation with him that lets him feel included in the shopping. When he balks at sitting, have your baby sling handy so he can easily be carried.

When you can, replace "no" with "yes" or simply "stop." One of the first words a baby says is *no* because *no* is one of the first and most frequent words he hears. When an eighteen-month-old is sitting quietly and playing, nobody says anything to him. But let him start exploring and he excites everybody; he gets lots of attention. The child does not know, in most instances, which behavior is most acceptable, but he soon learns which behavior gets the quickest response from adults. He learns how to behave directly from the behavior you use toward him.

Speak politely and gently even when correcting him, even though it is hard not to sound rude when you are irritated. And rather than grabbing a "no-no" from his hands, model asking for it ("Give it to Mama, please.") and show him how to place it in your outstretched hand. Have an equally desirable item to trade with. If the object is dangerous, snatching it away may actually inflict injury. You can guide his hand so that the scissors (or whatever) cannot do any damage while you are teaching him to hand it to you. These are matters of common courtesy—the way you would respect a friend.

Toward the end of the second year the development of language gives the toddler a more precise avenue of communication with the world around him. The combination of language and locomotion gives the toddler power to use the world around him for his own needs or desires. For example, being unable to get the right peg in the right hole, a frustrated toddler runs over and tugs on Mommy's skirt, saying, "Mommy do it." This is not an attempt to control mother. When a child begins to use another person as a resource for a problem he cannot solve by himself, he has learned a vital educational skill. The toddler also will vacillate between "I do it myself" and "Mommy do it." There will be incessant chants of "No! No! No!" and plenty of pleas to "Pick me up." This normal toddler behavior should not be interpreted as manipulation of the parents by the child, but rather healthy communication which calls for an appropriate response. If you respond to a toddler's cues appropriately and provide him with direction, he is motivated to develop his newly discovered powers further. A toddler who is motivated by his parents rather than controlled, feels right; he is further stimulated to continue developing these powers and to learn how he fits in the world. And he learns how to communicate in a healthy way.

Develop Your Role as an Authority Figure

Between eighteen months and two years, a parent adds the role of authority figure to that of environmental designer. The child's level of dependence is still high, and he is still quite ambivalent. However, now he begins to think and calculate. By this time he has learned cause-and-effect and how to manipulate his environment to get what he needs. For example, he begins to think of a stool when he needs to be taller. He also knows that the cookies are in the cupboard. He puts the two together, figuring out that if he pulls the stool in front of the cupboard he can climb up and get the cookies.

Setting Limits, Part 1: The ability to calculate coupled with childish impulses usually leads to some power struggles between parent and child at this age. And this is where parents emerge as authority figures. A child must know who is in charge; just as you took charge of your child as an infant by comforting him and helping him feel right, you must now take charge of your child by helping him fit into his environment. You do this by setting limits. *With attachment parenting you must set limits; parents who fail to do this have real problems.* A child needs security and direction; he becomes confused when he is left on his own, without predictable boundaries. Psalm 23:4 says, "Your rod and your staff, they comfort me."

Setting limits does not mean that at a given age you suddenly decide to clamp down on your child. Your role as an authority figure involves a lot more than shouting, "No," and "Time out!" You must take charge of your child's whole world, encouraging her natural developmental curiosities to flourish while protecting her from harm until she has the wisdom and discernment to do this for herself.

Children need boundaries that take into consideration their capabilities at each stage of development. The very first limit setting, or discipline scenario, you have with your baby is teaching her how to latch on correctly at your breast. Then you teach her she can't bite you while she's nursing. Next she learns your limits when she pulls your hair. The more she develops, the more you set limits, always appropriate to her development. By the second half of her second year, you and your toddler have worked out a healthy system—you set a boundary and she tests it. You make sure the boundary is strong enough to stand up to her testing, and she knows she is secure.

The frustration your limit-setting causes is necessary, so don't try to protect your child from being frustrated. By nine months, babies can handle a small amount of frustration, with your support. By eighteen months, handling frustration has become a familiar part of everyday life for your toddler and she learns to feel right when she handles it. Parents who struggle with handling their own frustration will have trouble watching their child be frustrated and will not be able to teach the child. If you see this happening, you should get some counseling so that both you and your child can move on to the next stage, prepared for its challenges. (See "Know Your Tolerance Levels," p. 238, for how to locate a counselor who understands and supports attachment parenting.)

Discipline depends on setting limits. All humans need limits—and the younger the human, the clearer those limits must be. When children have no boundaries, no fences, they have no security. Their lives are threatened and they are terrified because they know they are powerless to keep themselves safe. Setting limits requires balance—overly strict limits keep a child from learning; loose limits keep a child from feeling secure, and he cannot understand what is expected of him. You need wisdom to have appropriate limits that are individually suited for your child. Here's where knowing your child well pays off.

As your toddler grows, you will continually update the limits you have for him to keep them appropriate to his individual temperament and development. An example of how limits change as your toddler develops is his need to have his hand held in certain situations. As his motor skills improve, he no longer needs your hand for balance. Then the day comes when having his hand held is too restricting, so you shift the limit of hand holding so he can run free, unless the setting is unsafe or inappropriate—crossing the street, crowded malls, parking lots, or herding him to a seat in church. You firmly set the limit: streets, malls, parking lots, church *only* while holding hands. There is no option.

He'll test your limit and you don't dare relax it. The minute you even think about relaxing it, he senses you hesitate. (Save your thinking for later, once the event has passed, so you can evaluate your limit for next time.) When you are inconsistent about your limits, your child will be confused, wondering if you really mean what you say. He'll have to keep testing you from time to time anyway, but not as much if you don't confuse him.

DISCIPLINING THE CHILD TWO TO THREE YEARS OLD

The two- to three-year-old is characterized by three interesting features: (1) mastery of expressive language; (2) increasing awareness of self; and (3) the beginning of social peer relationships. The two-year-old is beginning to verbalize his feelings and demands, which enables him to hold the attention of adults and even of his peers. He will soon be less likely to act out his anxiety because he will be able to express it with words. His developing language skills will enable him to become a truly social person. This ability adds power to his concept of self.

At this stage, stubbornness will begin to rear its head (in some children more than in others), but there is generally less negativism on both sides of the parent-child relationship. Many two-year-olds will become less clingy and obstinate, and at the same time, their parents can become less restraining. And by two years of age, most children have suffered enough bumps and bruises to have learned the limits of their home environments and therefore feel more comfortable and secure and in control of their own bodies.

If you have succeeded in setting appropriate limits for your one- to two-year-old, he will begin to develop some inner controls during his next year. The behavior of the two-year-old starts becoming less impulsive; he considers alternatives before acting. He has become increasingly aware of cause-and-effect relationships. The usual two-year-old is still very egocentric. He sees things entirely from his own point of view, and he tries to figure out how he can use the world around him to suit his own needs. Appreciate this as normal behavior at this age, a behavior that is not to be squelched but directed.

Manipulation?

Consider now what is an appropriate parental response to this God-given two-year-old behavior of using his resources to get what he wants or needs. Is this manipulation, and if it is, what's good and what's bad about it? The term *manipulation,* unfortunately, has fallen into disrepute in Christian parenting circles. It has come to suggest a situation where a child connives to wrap his parents around his little finger and use them to get whatever he wants. Manipulation suggests that the child controls the parents. "I feel like I'm being manipulated," is a common parental complaint at this stage, which often leads parents to overreact.

At this stage of development, a child sees her interaction with her parents mainly as *communication,* not manipulation. A young child with a healthy self-image who feels good using her growing abilities to communicate with her environment will normally try to get everything she can. A two-year-old does not yet have the ability

TWO—TERRIBLE? OR TERRIFIC?

The twos are often presented in very negative terms. Some mothers say, "The terrible twos—I'll be glad when this stage is over." Any self-respecting toddler would disagree with these unfair words and would feel that he is simply misunderstood. The media has done toddlers a disservice. If all children really acted in the way they are portrayed, there would be many families with only one child. For parents, this is one of the most exciting, yet admittedly exhausting, stages of child development. Your toddler is really not a negative little person, he is very positive. He knows absolutely what he wants, and he is determined to get it at all costs. The "no-nos" come from his outside world. Perhaps this should be called the "negative stage of parenting" rather than the negative stage of the child.

Toddlers are not willfully destructive or disobedient; they simply have not yet developed control systems to govern their intense impulses. The late Selma Fraiberg stated beautifully in her book *The Magic Years,* "Toddlers exhibit a declaration of independence, but they have no intentions of unseating the government." Rather than regard this stage as a critical threat to your parental powers, consider it a passing developmental stage. And regard your toddler as "terrific."

to understand what and how much of anything is good for her. She needs direction in order to learn this. Parents, avoid the tendency to overreact to your child's constant efforts to get what she wants. This leads to a power struggle in which your primary communication with your child will be negative, telling her what you are not going to let her do, rather than positive, helping her learn what she needs to know. When you direct her efforts to manipulate (rather than trying to squelch them), she is encouraged to communicate her needs, and she feels right in communicating them.

Put very simply, a child should always feel right in "asking and seeking and knocking." (That invitation from Jesus is recorded twice, in Matthew 7:7 and Luke 11:9.) She should always feel that there is a tuned-in receiver for the signals she sends out. It is up to you to receive all of these signals, interpret the message, and guide your child in the way she should go. Sometimes, this will mean saying yes, sometimes gently saying no. At times you will go along with your child's wishes, even if it's not the most convenient alternative for you. ("Sure, we can visit the fish at the pet store on the way home.") Other times you'll suggest an alternative. ("It's too close to supper for a peanut butter sandwich, how about some carrot sticks?") Your decisions may depend on the time of day, the weather, your child's mood, your mood, and what are the immediate needs of the moment. You will do some talking with your child in the process. All this give-and-take does not mean that your child is controlling you. This is a healthy kind of manipulation, where your child tests out her ideas and abilities on someone she trusts to set her on the right path. It takes some patience to respond to your child in this way, but even if it seems at times that it would be easier to just say no, remember that your child is seeking guidance from you, not just permission.

Unhealthy manipulation occurs when a parent, by being unavailable, unobservant, or uninterested, ignores the child's signals and feeds back nothing to him until he makes a huge fuss that finally compels the parent to give in. Or a parent may react to all of the child's signals without selectively processing them, becoming overindulgent and never giving the child the opportunity to discern what's good for him. Squelching becomes a problem when adults automatically say no to every childish request that is not part of their grown-up agenda. All of these extremes—the child who receives nothing, the child who receives everything, the child forced to make a big scene—are equally unhealthy.

How do you know when to say yes? Follow all the principles: be available; be observant; consider your own needs and those of other family members; know your child and the direction he should go; and, above all, pray, asking God for wisdom. How you deal with your child's wants and needs now will affect your ability to communicate in the years to come.

How to Encourage Good Behavior

Behavior modification principles begin to be useful now and they are especially applicable to two-year-olds who will naturally gravitate toward the behavior that gets the biggest response (positive or negative). If a child likes the response he gets from good behavior, he will be inclined to repeat this behavior. Catch him in the act of being good and tell him what you like about what he is doing. Try to use more affirmative words in talking with your toddler and fewer negative words.

Acknowledge your child's creativity. Two-year-olds are able to scribble, stack, finger paint, and play with clay. By age three, your little artist will be taking great pride in what she does and will be eager to share her work with you. No matter how haphazard it may seem to you, to her the page full of scribble is an artistic accomplishment, and she wants an approving response from her most trusted art critic. A positive response to your child's creativity at this stage is a powerful way to reinforce positive behavior. If a child feels better about the response she gets from putting things together than about the response to tearing them apart, she is likely to continue the constructive behavior.

Give choices. Let your two-year-old feel that there are plenty of things he has a say about. Give him some practice making choices (that are within safe limits) so that he will feel that he has some power in his world. Letting him make some decisions on his own ("The red shirt or the blue one?" "Come with Daddy or stay with Mommy?" "Snack now or when the video is over?") can help him be more accepting of the times when you need to make the decision.

Maintain order in the house. Around two years of age, children show an innate appreciation for order. A young child's developing brain is searching for organization, and this starts with organizing his belongings. Your role as designer of your child's environment now includes organizer of his environment.

Try these suggestions to provide order in your child's environment. This will make it easier for him to be independent and learn to clean up after himself.

1. Instead of piling toys in toy boxes and corners, use low shelves with one-foot-square compartments, each containing one or two valued toys. Too many toys confuse the child who is already trying to sort out the busy world around him. Rotate the toys he uses if there are too many to organize.
2. If you want your child to pick up after herself, let her know that's what you expect, and then model that concept for her. This means you must discipline yourself in supervising and encouraging this to happen, so allow for the extra time it will take. Anticipate which rules you'll need to establish early on, habits you yourself will need to have, such as "Take out only one toy at a time. Put it back before getting out another one."
3. Give your child his own table and chairs. Child-size furniture improves his comfort and his attention span, encouraging task completion and concentration.
4. Use eye-level wooden pegs where he can hang his clothing.
5. Have a special place for keeping shoes so your child can easily find them when it's time to leave the house. Help him remember to put them there as soon as he takes them off.

This orderly environment reinforces the sense of order in the child's mind and also encourages a sense of responsibility. One of the most common difficulties in children of all ages is a lack of an inner sense of responsibility. Developing responsibility for one's actions begins with learning responsibility for one's own belongings, and this can begin around two years of age.

Discipline Undesirable Behavior

Encouraging desirable behavior in your young child should be your primary focus and consume the majority of your discipline energy. However, as Proverbs 22:15 says, "Folly is bound up in the heart of a child." Your child will get off the track at times. There is in every child this bent toward disobedience and undesirable behavior. You don't have to teach him to disobey. After recognizing the folly in a child, the Proverbs passage adds, "But the rod of correction will drive it far from him." In this mandate, God has told parents very simply, but very clearly, "Parents, take charge of your child; pick him up and get him back on the track." (Please see chapter 15 for further explanations of the "rod" verses.)

Some children by their inherent nature have more foolishness than others. Some children take longer to get the point than others. Every child's temperament has its undesirable qualities, a sinful nature that God has allowed to be there from the moment of conception (Ps. 51:5). We cannot reverse it. We can only modify it and channel it. Parents, when your child is naughty, do not feel guilty and wonder where you have gone wrong. This is especially important if you have been blessed with a high-need child who is endowed with a greater than average amount of foolishness. Accept your child as he is and realize that your God-given role is to impart to your child above-average discipline.

For you to correct your child's behavior, she must feel right within herself, and she must be secure in her trust and love for you. Just as those feelings are the foundation for encouraging desirable behavior, they are also necessary for your child to accept correction from you. In every disciplinary correction you want to convey two feelings to your child: (1) "I love you, my son or my daughter. You are very valuable to me and to God. You are a special person." (2) "Because I love you and because I am in charge, I will remain in charge until you are able to take full responsibility for your own actions." Pray and seek counsel if your disciplinary methods do not seem appropriate to you or are not working. If you base your disciplinary actions on the above considerations, you are not likely to go wrong. Here are suggestions for what to do about common undesirable behaviors in two-to three-year-olds.

1. *Whining.* Language is a newly found source of power for a young child, and it is

only normal that he will use his God-given power to try to get what he wants. Whining is what happens to a child's voice when he isn't listened to right away or when he doesn't get what he asks for. A young child soon learns what kind of communication gets the quickest reaction from his parents, and what kind of communication will eventually wear them down. Children whine because it works—they learn that the very first time. It's normal up until about the age of six, when children are able to express the intensity of their feelings with actual words, in a regular tone of voice. When your child whines, learn to read the underlying emotion he's feeling.

Take the example of the usual cookie jar struggle. Your two-year-old has already consumed his allotted number of cookies for the day. He asks for another but you turn him down. If you say no nicely—"I'm sorry I can't give you anymore,"—you may forestall the whining. There is nothing to be gained by being rude in words or tone of voice or gesture. Not getting a cookie may cause him to feel angry—don't provoke him to more anger yourself. "Fathers, do not exasperate your children" (Eph. 6:4). Offer an alternative, if possible.

What if your child decides to test the limits and ask again? His request may be a feeble whine this time, a clue that he expects a negative response. But when the request is denied, his whining may increase in volume, to the level where he knows you may give in just to restore peace and quiet. A child usually doesn't lose it just because you say no, but because the limit you are setting isn't clear. If he got as many cookies as he wanted yesterday, why not today! At this point you may say: "Billy (address your child by name, because this raises his status as a person), Mommy knows that you want a cookie (you understand his position). You already had three cookies today, and I am not going to give you any more (he has been treated fairly, at least according to your rules, or for the older child, according to a mutually agreed upon allotment). My ears will not listen to whining (the undesirable behavior is not rewarded). Now come over and talk nicely to Mommy and help me wash these grapes, and we can have some together after suppertime (desirable behavior is acknowledged and rewarded and delayed gratification is encouraged.)" Offer Billy three or four grapes as an appetizer, or some carrot sticks. He probably sees you nibbling as you work in the kitchen!

If the whining is mild, not too irritating, and diminishing in degree, you simply may ignore it from this point on since you said your ears do not listen to it anyway, and the fire seems to be dying out (undesirable behavior unrewarded will stop). However, suppose Billy's whining grows increasingly irritating. Sit down next to him, put your hand lovingly on his shoulder, look him squarely in the eyes, and say, "I'm sorry, Billy, that I can't give you any more cookies. Now I'm going to set the timer for one minute. When the buzzer goes off, I expect you to start talking nicely with Mommy. Then we will have some fun. And if you do not talk nicely, you will have some time out." You have conveyed the expected behavior, along with the consequences of continuing the undesirable behavior. You have also given him a little time and space to regain control of himself and choose what to do. If at this point Billy stops whining, it is very important to follow through with the reward for desirable behavior and sit down and have some fun with him. He learns that it is more desirable to work with the family government than to overthrow it. Your sitting with him may be what he really needed in the first place.

Suppose the buzzer goes off and Billy is still whining. More than the cookie is on the line: your child's feelings are out of control and your authority is on the line. If you give in to your child simply to get him off your back, you have failed to take charge of his behavior and you have lost an opportunity to help him learn about self-control. You also risk perpetuating this undesirable behavior and you weaken your future position in confrontations where the stakes are much higher than a cookie. It's time for time out, which should be used to further address the underlying cause for Billy's whining. He probably needs you to show him how to stop whining. Have him take some deep breaths and blow them out slowly, like you learned for relaxation in childbirth class. If you have managed to stay peaceful and calm through all this, Billy will be able to do this with you. If you did not keep your peace, now is a good time to get it back. Time out, for peace.

Here's another way to handle whining. A three-year-old should be able to comprehend a little talk like this one: "Billy, God gave you a beautiful voice that Mommy likes to hear. He doesn't want you to whine, and I don't want you to whine. Let's both pray and ask God to help you talk nicely to Mommy and not whine. Come, let's do this together." You turn a potentially negative situation into a positive one. You make your point and clear the air of ill feelings. You also go one step further and help your child realize that there exists a support upon whom you rely and whom you want him to value. He will learn that prayer is a valuable resource in times of need.

One more thing about whining—watch your own speech habits. When your feelings get punched up a few notches, does the pitch and timbre of your voice change? Could it ever sound like whining to your child? A parent's job is to help a child learn. If you can observe whining in yourself, you can understand how to help your child. What would you want someone to do for you? Some empathizing would help ("It's hard to hear no."), or some understanding ("I know you want that toy a lot!"), or some encouragement ("Come and let me give you a hug!"), or even just the chance to start over ("I can't understand your words. Tell me again.").

2. *Temper tantrums.* Tantrums are a part of growing up, just as anger is a part of being human. Neither can be avoided. Our job as parents is to take a young toddler from the stage of being at the complete mercy of his emotions to a time, later in childhood, when he can manage his anger. Being angry is not the problem—Jesus had anger. So many adults never learn to control anger, so when we see it in our children it can trigger anger in us, make us very anxious and unable to help our child. The goal of Christian parents is in Ephesians 4:26, "In your anger, do not sin." Remember, the goal is to help your toddler get through a tantrum.

Two kinds of situations are at the root of most temper tantrums. In the first situation, the young child's desire to do something is greater than her capability. Example: the two-year-old who tries to carry Dad's heavy briefcase. Facing this reality can lead to intense frustration that can only be expressed by a tantrum, since she doesn't know how to use words in that way. This kind of tantrum needs loving support, gentleness, and understanding; guide the child toward successfully achieving her goal or channel her efforts into something he can do.

The second type of temper tantrum is related to a two-year-old's sense of self. The two-year-old's newly found power with language and her desire to be "big" and in control compel her to assert herself. Hearing "no" from a parent is a challenge to her growing independence. This creates a difficult conflict she cannot resolve without a fight. She wants to be big, but her world tells her and shows her how small she is. She is upset, but she does not have the ability to handle conflicting emotions with reason, so her inner emotions erupt into an outward display—a tantrum. Think of your child's tantrums in terms of her newly forming sense of self coming unglued. She needs someone to keep her from falling apart, since she doesn't have enough inner control to do the job.

The most intense temper tantrum is breath-holding spells. During the rage of a tantrum a child may hold his breath, turn blue, become limp, and may even faint. Breath-holding spells cause the tantrum to frighten parents. Fortunately, most children who hold their breath resume normal breathing just as they are on the brink of passing out. Even those children who faint momentarily quickly resume normal breathing before harming themselves. These episodes usually stop when the child is old enough to express his anger verbally.

Temper tantrums can be exhausting and frightening experiences for both child and parent. Discipline mild tantrums just as you would discipline whining. In a more severe temper tantrum the child is out of control and will need help from you to regain control. Even if she wants to, she may not be able to calm down on her own.

How are temper tantrums handled? First, realize that you can't handle tantrums, you can only support your child when he has them. Temper tantrums reflect your child's emotions, which *he* has to handle. Excessive interference deprives the child of a way of releasing his inner tensions, but too little support leaves him to cope all by himself when he doesn't have the ability to do so. What is the issue causing the temper tantrum? If he has chosen an impossible task and it becomes apparent he is not going to achieve it but won't give up, simply be on standby. Temper tantrums bring out the best in intuitive mothering. Keep your arms extended and your attitude accepting. Often a few soothing words or a little help ("I'll untie the knot and you put on your shoe.") will put him on the road to recovery.

If the issue at stake is a conflict of wills (for example, he wants a toy that you have said he should not have), then the temper tantrum should be approached with the usual firm and loving double whammy of effective discipline: "I love you, my child, and I am in charge here." Sometimes, a strong-willed child will lose complete control of himself during a tantrum. When his behavior reaches this stage, simply hold him very firmly but lovingly and explain: "You are angry and you have lost control (you understand his position). I am holding you like this because I love you, I want to help you, and you will be all right (I'm in charge here)." You will discover that after a minute or so of struggling to free himself, the child melts into your arms as if thanking you for rescuing him. You can end the scene on a spiritual note, with an offer to pray with your child. Our little ones welcomed prayers as a way to regroup, as though sensing God's blessing and forgiveness—a sense of having a fresh start.

Temper tantrums in public places are embarrassing, and it is often difficult to consider your child's feelings first. "What will people think of me as a parent?" is likely to be your first thought. In this situation, take your child to another room or outside where he can have his tantrum in private. If the tantrum is based upon an inner frustration, then open arms and an accepting attitude will help defuse the child's explosive behavior. If the issue is one of power, you must lovingly maintain your authority, letting your child know that you are in charge and you will help him regain control. Sometimes a child who is crying uncontrollably can't stop when you ask him to. He may or may not want to stop, but he literally cannot get hold of himself. When he does want to stop, an offer to pray with him for help is all that is needed for both of you. An in-arms prayer time is extremely comforting.

Sometimes tantrums can be so exhausting to parents that giving into the child seems the best solution because this stops the disruptive behavior immediately. However, keep in mind the principle that undesirable behavior, if rewarded, will persist. In addition to weakening your authority, rewarding temper tantrums will plant the seed in the child that aggressive and violent behavior will get him what he wants, just like he learned that whining worked to get his way.

Tantrums often occur when parents impose unrealistic expectations on a child. Expecting a curious toddler to be a model of obedience in a toy store where he is surrounded by a smorgasbord of tempting delights may be asking too much. Children who are overly tired or hungry are especially prone to mood changes and temper tantrums, which may explain why many temper tantrums occur in the late morning or late afternoon when children are most tired and most hungry. Appropriately timed naps and the practice of nibbling (see chapter 12 for tips for nibbling) may lessen the tendency for these tantrums.

Some tantrums occur when the child, during a high-need period, senses that his parents are not tuned in to him. He resorts to a tantrum in order to break through to them.

Most temper tantrums do not have lasting effects on the child. Fortunately, toddlers are magnificently resilient. They usually do not sulk for long periods of time, and a properly supported tantrum usually wears off quickly. Parents, take heart. The temper tantrum stage seldom lasts long, and it is self-limiting. Physical abilities eventually catch up with a child's desire for accomplishment, and as soon as he develops enough language and maturity to express his emotions in words, his tantrum-like actions will mellow. Children do not like how they feel during tantrums; they want them to stop too.

3. *Aggressive behavior against other children* (biting, hitting, scratching, pushing). Aggressive behavior begins between the ages of eighteen months and two and a half years, and lessens when the child can communicate her feelings effectively with words rather than actions. Because a toddler's mouth and hands are her first tools of communication, biting and hitting are forms of communication that do not seem intrinsically bad to her. Frustration (anger) is what sets off the aggression. The parent's goal is to patiently teach better ways to express anger.

A child soon learns that aggression is not socially-acceptable behavior by the responses she gets from her victim or a nearby adult. If Isaac Newton had been a psychologist rather than a physicist, perhaps he would have worded his first law of child behavior: "For every undesirable action there is an equal and opposite reaction." The more quickly a young child can learn that undesirable behavior yields an undesirable response, the more quickly she will stop this behavior.

To stop a child's biting and hitting, consider these points. Determine the circumstances conducive to your child's aggressive behavior, usually something like several children in a small space with a few toys. If your child becomes aggressive in groups in small spaces, your first disciplinary action (design her environment) is to avoid circumstances that entice her to hit or bite.

Beware of falling into the trap of negatively reinforcing hitting and biting. Aggressive behavior attracts attention very quickly. If the child wants to be the instant center of attention, biting especially is sure to bring everybody running and set her apart as a special person. Biting fulfills the craving in some children for attention, and the fuss made over their action reinforces their undesirable behavior. In the small percentage of biters for which this is true, ignoring the biting (or minimizing the fuss over it) may be the best solution.

In general, however, do not ignore undesirable behavior in which one child harms another. Biting and hitting are not only hard on the tender little body parts of unsuspecting victims, but they are also hard on parents. The parent of the biter or hitter is both disturbed and embarrassed, and the parent of the victim is naturally upset that her child has been hurt. Negative feelings between parents can result. You can ease a potentially tense situation by discussing beforehand with the other parent that your child is aggressive at times and that you are aware of her need for supervision. Biters always should be carefully supervised in groups. When a child hurts another, immediately remove her from the play group with appropriate admonitions such as "Biting hurts—you will stay with me until you are ready to play nicely." This isolation will teach the biter a valuable social lesson. Then verbalize your child's feelings: "You are angry because Mary took your toy"; then describe a better way: "Use your words instead of hitting—ask Mary to give it back."

"Should I bite him back?" is certainly a valid question that a parent of a persistent biter may ask. No! Don't bite her back. Biting is an immature act, and you are a mature person. The biter already knows biting hurts by the reaction of the child who was bitten. If she really seems to not understand, or she is a younger biter, you can encourage her to feel the effects of her own sharp teeth on her fleshy forearm. When your child's verbal skills improve and her emotions can be expressed better by language, her biting should subside (by three years of age). Biting in the child more than three years old who has good verbal skills is certainly of greater concern. In such cases, professional guidance should be obtained.

What About Spanking?

Parents have a God-given right to expect obedience from their children. God's order for children is that they obey their parents: "Children, obey your parents in everything, for this pleases the Lord" (Col. 3:20). "Honor your father and your mother," the commandment says. However, the term *honor* implies not only obedience, but also respect for authority. It is honor that you want from your children, not just obedience. Honor is more than just obedient actions. It is an attitude based on feeling and conviction, as suggested in *The American Heritage Dictionary*. This kind of honor must be earned.

Some parents think that the way to get their children to obey is to use the *rod*, which they interpret to mean spanking (more about our interpretation in chapter 15). They think they must force their children to do what they want them to do. However, the biblical meaning for the word *obey* is not simply "to do as I say." The Hebrew root word *shama* means "to hear intelligently." This implies that children need to understand what they are hearing their parents ask or command, and that parents must ask in a way that children will be able to understand. This can be difficult at any age, but especially with toddlers. Their minds don't work like adults' minds. Most toddlers understand much more than they say because receptive language development is more advanced than expressive language. They certainly understand the words for concrete objects they can recognize, such as *doggie, horsey, cat,* and so on. But even older toddlers usually cannot understand abstract concepts or rules. They can easily say no to a parental request, but they cannot understand how and why they are expected to obey. When they say no, they don't mean "No, I *won't;*" they mean "No, I *don't want* to." It is your job as parents to help them *want* to obey. This is also known as motivating your child, and it sets the stage for inner-directed discipline later on.

Spanking toddlers, before they are old enough to understand why they are being spanked, would not be in keeping with the true biblical concept of obedience. Toddlers can be trained that certain actions warrant certain negative responses, but this is neither "intelligent hearing" nor true obedience. The positive steps of attachment parenting and a creatively designed child-considered environment can be used to elicit the same response and start the child on the path to both obeying and honoring his parents. Let's say you want your toddler to come get in the car to go shopping. You see he is busy with his trucks and will hate being interrupted. Instead of just telling him to come (and then making him come), you motivate him by talking about something fun you'll do when you get there (see the doggies, ride the horsie). How much nicer for both of you than for you to have to pick up a kicking, screaming child and force him into his car seat.

Another positive way to handle this situation is helping the child leave his activity. First, try to give him a five-minute warning so he doesn't have to cope with a sudden shift. Then if he is still upset with having to leave his play, help him say, "Bye-bye trucks, see you later." Bringing closure to his play gives him a sense of control and helps him look forward to a reunion. When parents know their child, they will be able to choose an approach that fits with God's design for disciplining that individual child.

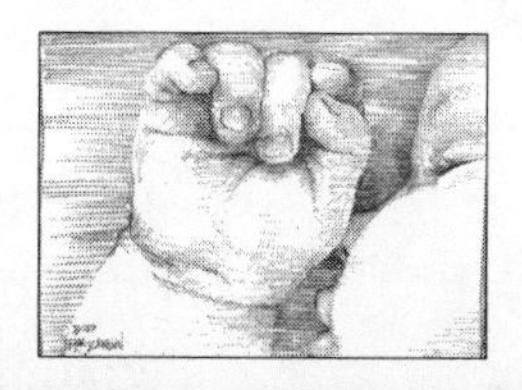

CHAPTER FIFTEEN

Principles of **Discipline**

Discipline is equipping your children with the tools they will need to succeed in life. This begins with being parents who have the tools you need to discipline your children. Realistically, every interaction you have with your child falls into the category of discipline, or teaching. The ultimate goal of discipline is not only getting your children to behave, but getting your children to want to behave. While there is not a one-size-fits-all method of discipline that works for every child in every family situation, there are some general principles of discipline that apply to nearly all children in nearly all family situations. One of these principles you will see is "Spare the Rod." Spanking is one of the more controversial discipline decisions parents will make. A discussion of our understanding of this subject is included in the last half of this chapter.

SOME PRINCIPLES OF DISCIPLINE

Your approach to discipline is even more important than your techniques. Realistically, every interaction you have with your child falls in the category of discipline. The key to discipline is not getting your children to behave; it's getting your children to want to behave.

What Discipline Really Means

Discipline begins with having the right *relationship* with your child more than practicing the right techniques. It is something you do *with* a child, not *to* a child. If your discipline techniques aren't working, first examine your relationship with your child; second, what techniques you are using. If you use discipline as a list of external punishment techniques rather than as an internal guidance system in which you teach your child inner controls, you run the risk of approaching your child as a project and not a person. Discipline begins with a mutual trust between parent and child. The infant trusts the parents to meet her needs; the parents trust themselves to be able to read their infant deeply enough to know what her needs are—they trust the baby to give the cues that will let them know. From the basis of mutual trust and mutual sensitivity grows your role as authority figure. Discipline is basically giving your children the tools to save their souls and succeed in life.

Discipline is not to be equated with punishment, yet an important part of discipline is correction and teaching the child that choices have consequences. One day during her nine-month-old baby's check-up, I (Bill) watched a mother relate with her baby. She gave her baby lots of eye-to-eye contact, nursed her baby on cue, gave her infant a nurturant response when the baby cried, and after the baby's check-up the mother walked around the office carrying her baby in a baby sling. There was a mutual trust and sensitivity between mother and child. They were connected. I couldn't resist complimenting her: "You sure are a good disciplinarian." She looked a bit shocked and exclaimed, "But I don't spank our baby." Like many parents, this mother thought of the word "discipline" as punishment. Although punishment is an important part of the whole discipline picture, it is not the larger part; it's important to have balance. A child who is punished too much or too severely behaves more out of fear of the punishment and the punisher than from an inner feeling and knowledge of right and wrong and how he is supposed to act. In this relationship, a distance develops between the punisher and the child, the parent-child relationship becomes a power struggle, and the parent-child relationship operates on a basis of fear and anger rather than a trust for the authority figure. A child whose behavior is punishment-controlled never has the chance to learn inner controls. The child who is punished too little does not have the tools to succeed in life. This child runs wild with no outer controls or inner controls and does not learn, like a speeder on the highway getting a ticket, that misbehavior has consequences. This child does not respect the authority of his parents and will therefore not respect the authority of teachers and other persons of significance later in life. Punishment, when given appropriately, is part of a balanced discipline package, as long as the external controls are aimed at eventually teaching the child how to control himself. One more point: punishment does not have to be physical.

As parents of eight, we have learned that household discipline is basically doing what you need to do to like living with your child. Children do annoying things; parents need peace. In family living, discipline means showing children what behavior is expected of them and the consequences of misbehavior. The home is like a mini society for a child, the first social group in which they are required to behave. Children are searching for a norm, "How am I supposed to act?" It's up to parents, as disciplinarians, to show and tell them how.

Know Your Child

These three little words are one of the most important starter points for discipline. "Train up your child in the way he should go. . . ." (Prov. 22:6). This master verse for discipline implies we know our child, that we know age-appropriate behavior—what behavior is usual for children at each stage of development—and especially what behavior comes from the temperament of your individual child. Read your child. Become an expert on your child. No one else will. When you know your child, you will know intuitively what situations trigger undesirable behavior and set the conditions that encourage desirable behavior. Knowing your child deeply helps you get behind the eyes of your child and make on-the-spot discipline decisions that are appropriate for the behavior and your child's stage of development.

It took us six children to realize how important it was to get behind the eyes of a child and analyze the child's behavior, and then come up with appropriate disciplinary action. Our sixth child, Matthew, is a very focused child. As a toddler, he would become so engrossed in his play that when we told him it was time to leave he "wouldn't mind." We could have taken the power approach and bodily scooped him up when it was time to go and carried out a protesting tantrum-throwing child, which would leave all of us a wreck. By this time we were experienced enough to have grown in a very important principle in discipline: nurture by nature. We needed to respect Matthew's temperament—that he deeply immersed himself into his play and his agenda was very important to him. We needed to respect that, since a deep attention span is a personality trait that we wanted to channel to later work to his advantage. So instead of using the power approach, we respected Matthew's need to gradually sign off from his agenda and click into ours: "Matthew, say bye-bye to the toys, bye-bye to the trucks, bye-bye to the boys, bye-bye to the girls. . ." Within a few minutes, Matthew would willingly "obey" us because we were able to get behind his eyes and respect his needs, which in the long run made it easier for him to comply to our needs.

One day we were visiting an experienced mother of three whose discipline methods we've always admired and whose kids everyone liked. We asked what her secret was. She told us: "Knowing my children empowers me. This kid knowledge becomes like a sixth sense and enables me to anticipate and control situations to keep our kids out of trouble."

Knowing your child as the basis of discipline is why we have devoted a large part of this book, especially the beginning chapters, to giving you the tools to get connected with your child. In fact, chapter 1 is where discipline really began.

Turn Accidents into Opportunities

Knowing your child allows you to put yourself in your child's shoes and imagine how your child needs you to act. Getting behind the eyes of your child helps you discipline the many kid-created annoyances that happen each day in family living. One evening during our family dinner our two-and-a-half-year-old, Lauren, tried to get the juice out of the refrigerator by herself, spilled it on the floor, and created a splashing mess. I (Bill) was angry and immediately clicked into the mindset: "How inconvenient, what a mess I'm going to have to clean up, etc. . ." Martha, however, had a healthier reaction. Instead of immediately considering her own inconvenience, she turned this misfortune into a teachable moment. Instead of thinking first of her own inconvenience, she thought of Lauren's feelings: *If I were Lauren, what would I want my mother to say in this situation?* She knelt down on the floor, made eye contact with Lauren, and sensed that Lauren was already upset by the mess she made. Sympathetically, Martha handed Lauren a cloth, and they both cleaned up the mess together. As soon as Lauren saw that Martha wasn't angry, her face showed a sparkle of relief, since she didn't have a mess to clean up in her mind along with the juice on the floor.

Lessons like these taught me how to use this discipline technique in our older children.

A week after our son Peter started driving, he stepped on the gas pedal instead of the brake and demolished part of the garage door frame and the car fender. My first reaction was to think of the cost and inconvenience. Peter saw my anger, which further saddened an already dejected child. In order to salvage some of his feelings, I told Peter how happy I was that he wasn't hurt and that he'd had his first accident in the garage rather than on the highway. Three years later Hayden, our next beginning driver, took out the frame on the other side of the garage door, but this time I was a bit wiser and was able to look at a negative situation in a positive light. Instead of focusing on the damage, I focused on her, saying, "I'm glad you weren't hurt." Seeing that her father was more concerned with her than the damage reassured her about what was more important to me. After all, the damage was already done. And I got something priceless in exchange for my $250 insurance deductible: a stronger relationship with my daughter. And both children were helped to appreciate the fine art of maneuvering a vehicle by paying for half the repairs.

Set Limits, Provide Structure

For children to thrive and parents to survive, kids need boundaries. We all know that children need limits. (For instance, they need to know that there are yes-touches and no-touches.) Even Adam and Eve had this lesson. Most parents do a pretty good job of setting limits, but they forget that along with setting limits, they must provide structure. You establish house rules, but at the same time create conditions that make the rules easier to follow. That's what structure is. You say no to an exploring toddler who is headed for breakable objects; that's the limit-setting part. You childproof your home to provide busy minds and bodies a safe place to play and learn; that's the structure part. Structure protects and redirects. You free your child to be a child. Structure means setting the conditions that encourage desirable behavior to happen. Instead of taking a tired and hungry two-year-old shopping at four o'clock in the afternoon, you structure your day to take him with you in the morning. You set limits for your child, so that eventually the child can set limits for himself.

Yeses and No's. Setting limits and providing structure implies knowing when to say yes and when to say no. In their zeal to give children everything they need, some parents risk giving their children everything they want. Your toddler doesn't want to hold your hand as you cross the street. You firmly set a limit: "Street crossing is only done while holding hands. There is no option." Toddlers want someone to set limits. Without limits, the world is too scary for them. Limit setting teaches a child a valuable lesson for life: the world is full of "yeses" and "no's." Try to balance your discipline with more "yeses" than "no's." God even balanced His "shall" and "shall nots" in the commandments. Notice in the Garden that there was only one "no tree." Try to follow a negative with a positive: "You can't play with the knife, but you can play with the garlic crusher," or "You may not have a candy bar, but you may have apple slices with peanut butter."

Distract and divert. Your toddler is getting cranky. You interject: "Billy, let's go play ball." The cue word "ball" is often enough to motivate your toddler's mind and body to change direction. In channeling the behavior of our busy toddlers, we filed away a list of cue words, such as "ball," "cat," "go," which we called "redirectors." Of course, you must carry through and go for a walk, or play ball, or find the cat; otherwise, your child will come to distrust you and you will lose a useful discipline tool.

Shape, Don't Control, Your Child's Behavior

Early in our childrearing career we thought our job as Christian parents was to control our children. Many kids later, we learned that our job was to control situations and teach our children how to control themselves. Throughout Scripture there are clear mandates for parents to take charge of their children. Yet it's easy for parents to confuse discipline with control. You control situations, not people. Think of it as shaping, as if you were a gardener and your child is the plant. You can't control the color of the flower or when it blooms, but you can pick the weeds and prune the plant so that it grows more beautifully. There are flowers and weeds in every child's behavior. Children are born with weeds in their behavior that need to be identified and picked ("Folly is bound up in the heart of a child. . . ." [Prov. 22:15]) and flowers that need to be nurtured ("Train a child in the way he should go. . . ." [Prov. 22:6]). Most of the discipline techniques we mention throughout this book are "shapers" that help you weed out the annoying behaviors in your child that work to your child's disadvantage, and nurture those flowering qualities that will later work to your child's advantage. Here is a list of time-tested behavior shapers:

- *When-then.* "When you put your toys away, then you can play outside." This not only teaches your child house rules, but it teaches him responsibility for his belongings. You convey the behavior you expect. After these repetitions, your child makes his own connection between putting his toys away and playing outside, and learns to shape his own behavior.

- *Praise appropriately.* Acknowledge good behavior so your child makes the connection that good behavior is the norm, the behavior you expect, and not the exception.

- *Give reminders.* Use short, verbal cues that jog the hazy memory of a busy child, a concerning look that prompts the about-to-be-mischievous child that he knows better: "Ahhhhh, where does that plate belong?" We used the piano bench as a time-out place when our children needed to sit and realize they were off track. Sometimes just the warning "piano bench" was enough of a reminder to redirect a child's behavior. Oftentimes, instead of using the negative sounding term "time out," we would personalize the discipline: "Stephen time," or "thinking time." Often we would sit with him, giving him some needed "time in."

- *Give consequences.* An important conclusion that children need to learn about life is that choices have consequences, which means the parents need to tell them exactly what behavior is expected of them and the consequences of misbehaving: the child rides his tricycle out into the street, the tricycle gets put away for a couple of weeks.

A four-year-old developed the annoying habit of banging his bedroom door, despite repeated admonitions from his mother that the annoying sound must stop. Father issued the ultimatum: "If you bang your door again, I'm going to remove the door," and he did. Three days later the door went back up and did not slam again. Consequences lay the foundation for one of the most important principles of discipline that we will discuss below: teaching children to think through what they are about to do; to imagine the consequences of an action before they do it.

Communication Is the Key to Discipline

"Children, obey your parents in everything, for this pleases the Lord" (Col. 3:20). The term "obey" means to intelligently listen to. This implies that parents know how to talk to their children. How you talk to your child often means the difference between compliance and defiance. Here are some discipline tips that keep your role as authority, yet respect your child as a listening person and get results:

- *Constant reminding.* A developmental principle of discipline is called "internalizing," which means the age at which children can remember previous directives and make them part of their usual way of acting. This is why toddlers need to be told a thousand times. But by three, a child can begin to internalize your instructions so that they sink in. For two-year-olds, you may have to repeat, and repeat, and repeat the behavior you expect until it becomes part of them.

- *Connect before you direct.* Engage your child in eye-to-eye contact to get her attention before you issue your directive: "Mary, I need your eyes, I need your ears."

- *KISMIF—Keep it simple; make it fun.* The longer parents ramble, the more likely the child is to become parent-deaf. In giving discipline directives, mothers tend to ramble on, where fathers seem to get right to the point. We have gotten better results using the one-sentence rule, limiting our directions to one sentence: "*When* you get dressed, *then* we'll go out and play." (Using *when* instead of *if* conveys to your child that you expect obedience and there is no other choice.)

- *Give positive alternatives.* Follow a can't-do with a can-do. "In a supermarket we walk; when we get to the park you may run."

- *Rewind and replay.* In this video-watching generation, children understand the terms "rewind" and "replay." When our four-year-old, Stephen, headed for the street, we would redirect him into a safe part of the yard and then play the rewind game. Ten times we would reenact the scene. We'd run toward the curb, stop, look both ways: "Look, no car, look, no car," and then we'd walk across the street holding hands. Playing the rewind game is especially valuable in danger discipline, in which you implant in your child's mind a script that he can later follow if the disciplinarian is not around. When we wanted eight-year-old Matthew to help with the dishes, he was prone to grumble. We would say "replay," take a few steps backward, and reissue the request, giving Matthew a second chance to choose obeying cheerfully.

- *Be sure your child understands* exactly what behavior is expected of him and in what situations, such as how you expect him to behave in a supermarket before you go there. Ask your child to repeat your request back to you. If she can't, it's too complicated or too long. When a child has a clear understanding of expected behavior and still chooses to disobey, the child can perceive that the consequences of disobedience are fair.

- *Let your child draw her own conclusions.* "Matthew, where does the bike belong?" This creates a more lasting lesson than "Put your bike in the garage."

- *Speak respectfully.* Remember, one of the goals of discipline is to give your child tools to succeed in life. How you speak to your child models how they speak to you and to other people. Open your request with the child's name: "Lauren, will you please. . ." Sometimes you have to settle yourself or your child before you issue your discipline directive. If you both are angry, it's not going to sink in. Discipline talk can be therapeutic for the speaker, as well as the listener. A friend told us that when she became a mother she had to work hard not to fly off the handle and yell at her child when he misbehaved. She confided to us:

"I can hear my own mother's voice coming out of my mouth," recalling how much she was yelled at as a child. In disciplining your children, you can give them the start you might not have gotten.

- *Be ever so understanding.* Discussion is fine, as long as you keep your part short and simple, but do not get drawn into an argument. Calmly tell your child that you understand, whatever it is he is wanting. Resist the temptation to add further explanation. You understand, period. You can continue to reiterate that point, calmly, as long as your child does not become annoying. Sometimes a child just needs to be sure he is being heard and understood.

Raise Kids Who Care

As we have repeatedly emphasized, discipline is giving your child the tools to succeed in life. One of the most important tools is empathy—the capacity to care, to consider another person's feelings and rights; to think before he acts, to imagine how his behavior or actions are going to affect the other person—before he does them. Studies on hard-core criminals (the ultimate outcome of undisciplined children) show a common trait—the inability to take responsibility for their behavior, to feel bad when they act bad. They act before they think, not considering how what they do will affect the other person. This capacity to care can be summed up in one word—sensitivity. Raise sensitive children. You plant sensitivity in your child in the early months of parenting by holding your infant a lot and responding in a nurturing way to your baby's cries; you offer an emotional and physical band-aid when your toddler falls; and you are a willing listener to your school-age child's problems. Because you have shown sensitivity to your child, she grows up realizing that sensitivity is the norm. Because you cared for her feelings, she'll care for other people's feelings. Sensitivity then becomes rooted in her inner code of behavior. You plant it in your child in early infancy and you watch it sprout in later childhood. Sensitivity becomes the root of a child's conscience: "I feel good when I act right; I feel bad when I act wrong." Ultimately, the child develops a healthy sense of guilt.

Discipline is planting in your child a security system that constantly reminds her: *think through what you're about to do.* The three-year-old is about to hit his friend (or just *has* hit the friend) and you offer a reminder, "Ahhh. How would you feel if someone hit you?" The five-year-old is about to throw a water balloon at a passing car and you interject, "Imagine how the driver will feel when the water balloon goes splat on the windshield." By repetition of these daily scenarios of "think before you act" the child reaches school equipped with a valuable tool to succeed in life: *the ability to make wise choices.*

Convey to Your Child the Behavior You Expect

Children often misbehave either because they don't understand how they are expected to behave or their parents do not communicate to the child what they expect. For a child to perceive his parents as authority figures in the house, he must have a clear understanding of house rules: "How am I expected to behave?" If previous confrontations have taught you that there are certain situations that trigger unruly behavior, reprogram your child with a clear understanding of how you expect him to act: "We're going shopping in a few minutes and this is what we're going to do. . ." With a hand on his shoulder and a look into his eyes, you convey your expectations calmly and matter-of-factly, not with a tone of voice that says you expect him to misbehave and you want to warn him. This bit of preprogramming is especially valuable if a preschooler is going through one of those negative phases where every parental request is greeted by a "no." Begin your day with some holding time and set your child up: "Today we're going to have a yes-day and see how much fun it is. When I ask you to do something, you give me a yes. When you ask me to do something (providing it's reasonable), I will give you a yes. . ." During a negative phase, you may have to spend a day or two showering your child with frequent reminders—looks of approval and disapproval, an "Ahhh . . . you're getting wild"—emphasizing what he can do rather than what he can't. Eventually, your efforts will sink in, prompting your child to make a self-controlling conclusion: "I am much happier and my life is much smoother when I do what Mom and Dad expect of me." Children need to learn that choices have consequences. Once you achieve this level of discipline, you have taught your child inner controls for life, so that instead of preaching to your children, they preach to themselves.

Spare the Rod

As we will discuss beginning on page 367, you do not have to spank your child to be a godly parent. If you take all the "rod" verses listed on pages 369–70 and substitute the concept of *parental authority* for the meaning of "rod," you are likely to catch the spirit of these verses. The key to discipline is not to consider spanking as the first mode of discipline, but rather to set the conditions in which you do not have to spank your child. Create an attitude in your child and an atmosphere in your home that makes spanking less necessary.

Model Discipline

The eyes and mind of a growing child are like a video camera that records everything she sees and hears. These stored images become part of the child's inner code of behavior and she retrieves these parental impressions as part of how she behaves. A child who grows up with habitually angry parents takes on anger as part of herself, her norm: This is how people act. A child who grows up in an atmosphere of caring arms and happy faces takes on this happy attitude as part of herself. Parents are always on stage in front of their child. Children watch how their parents behave in certain situations and file this as the way to do things. The preschool child does not have a concept of right or wrong, only what she sees and hears. If it's from her parents, it must be right.

You are in the checkout line at the grocery store and the cashier gives you too much change. You can use this as a teachable moment. Discuss this with your five-year-old and let her see that it is right for you to return the excess change to the cashier. Christ used modeling as the best discipline. He not only told His followers what to do, He showed them by His exemplary life.

While modeling is an important determinant of discipline, parents cannot feel guilty about not being perfect. Remember, it's the overall impression a child receives, not an isolated incident. If a child grows up in an atmosphere of calm voices and happy faces, the occasional angry outburst is not going to make a lasting impression. In fact, we have learned to turn our mistakes into opportunities. When we blow it—and we have—we correct it, so that the impression our child gets is "Yes, adults make mistakes, but the right thing to do is to correct them." In fact, we have come to understand that there are no mistakes, only lessons. It's up to you to make sure the lesson is constructive rather than destructive. This is hard to do because it is a new way of being for many of us. Remember Romans 8:1, "Therefore, there is now no condemnation for those who are in Christ Jesus, because through Christ Jesus the law of the Spirit of life set me free from the law of sin and death." God never condemns us as believers—He convicts us. What a difference that makes for us! We need to be sure our children experience conviction from us, never condemnation. From this they learn a valuable discipline lesson: a person takes responsibility for their actions.

CHRISTIAN PARENTS AND SPANKING

To spank or not to spank is the subject of much emotional debate among parents and professionals. The question has produced controversial books, magazine articles, and TV programs, even legislation. Many Chris-

CORRECTIVE VS PUNITIVE CONSEQUENCES

Correction implies a redirection of the child toward future, more desirable behavior; it is only performed out of concern and love (you don't correct someone out of anger). It leaves a child feeling right. Punishment is retribution, a penalty for an offense, which may not of itself focus on a new direction for the future. Punishment is concerned with justice. It can be performed in anger, without regard for the child's feelings, and can leave the child feeling resentful and angry. Correction leads the child back to the path on which he belongs; punishment alone merely penalizes him for taking the wrong path.

There are three goals for discipline: (1) to promote desirable behavior, (2) to stop undesirable behavior, and (3) to restore a child's feeling of being right with himself, his parents, and God. Punishment by itself usually stops undesirable behavior, at least for the moment. It sometimes motivates a child to behave better, though out of fear rather than a desire to do right. Correction carries the process further, to the level that God expects from Christian parents. God's model for corrective discipline involves looking at the whole person. This is how Jesus used corrective discipline during His ministry on earth. God is saying: "Parents, get into your child, find out what is going on inside her, consider why she did what she did, and how she feels as a result of her deed." Give your child the message, "I'm going to help you mend whatever is causing you to act this way. I love you; I want you to feel right inside."

tian childrearing books favor spanking as an effective method of correction. Many child development experts speak out against it. Christian parents are naturally confused about all the mixed messages they receive regarding the subject.

Our opinion of spanking is based upon our experience as a pediatrician and a nurse observing what works and what does not; our joint experience as spanking-, and then nonspanking-, parents of eight; what God says in Scripture regarding correction; and the opinions of other Christian writers with whom we strongly agree. It is also based on the leading of God, as we have prayed for this wisdom. We are sure that the other writers, who favor spanking, have also prayed for and received wisdom and leading from God. It seems that God is saying this is not an either/or decision, and that both "sides" are to stay open to the other.

First, we have to say that it is absolutely wrong and against God's every word to be mean and abusive toward a child or to strike a child out of frustration, hostility, or anger. Everyone with a conscience agrees on that. The only reason some parents dare to do this is that children are small and defenseless. These children will grow up to be angry individuals who will most likely be mean and abusive to their own children. (Unless, of course, God gets a hold of them!)

Second, most everyone agrees that spanking should never be the main strategy in correction. Even parents who believe in spanking ought to strive to create such an attitude within their children and an atmosphere within their homes that spanking is seldom necessary.

Third, if you feel you must spank, it should be reserved for major confrontations, when a parent's authority is on the line, situations in which a child (not a toddler) willfully defies reasonable authority, and other approaches are not getting through.

Here are some basic scriptural and cultural considerations that will help you understand our view that spanking not be used. Ultimately, you must make your own decision based on your beliefs and your family situation. Our position on spanking, one that has evolved over thirty years of parenting eight children, is that we won't do it.

Corporal Punishment in Scripture

In regard to discipline in general, God has given us guidelines in the Bible. We have already discussed the meaning of Proverbs 22:6, "Train up a child in the way he should go." Think of the translation "initiate," instead of the word "train" in connection with giving a child the right start. Discipline begins at birth and involves far more than punishment.

Proverbs 22:15 states, "Folly is bound up in the heart of a child, but the rod of discipline will drive it far from him."

The Book of Proverbs has more to say about the rod. It is here that the Bible appears to take a clear stand on spanking:

Do not withhold discipline from a child;
If you punish him with the rod, he will not die.
Punish him with the rod,
And save his soul from death. (23:13–14)

The rod of correction imparts wisdom,
But a child left to himself disgraces his mother. (29:15)

He who spares the rod hates his son,
But he who loves him is careful to disci pline him. (13:24)

At first reading, it would seem that the Bible takes a clear stand in favor of spanking as an important mode of correction. While these passages seem to support spanking, this is not the only way to interpret them.

While it is clear that the rod does appear to be an object to strike with, the term *rod* is also used in the Bible in connection with the shepherd's staff: "Your rod and your staff, they comfort me" (Ps. 23:4). The shepherd's staff was used to guide the wandering sheep along the right path. The rod was used to beat off predators—not to hit sheep who strayed. This teaching is developed beautifully in the book *A Shepherd Looks at Psalm 23* by Phillip Keller, especially in chapter 8: "Thy Rod and Thy Staff, They Comfort Me."

The original Hebrew word *shebet* means "a stick" for punishing, writing, fighting, ruling, walking. Proverbs 13:24 could be translated: "He who spares his *ruling* [authority] hates his son, but he who loves him disciplines him promptly." Remember, the Book of Proverbs is written in the form of poetry, where words and images usually have symbolic meanings. In other Old Testament books there are uses of the word *shebet* that are obviously symbolic. We feel that what God is saying in these references is simply: "Parents, take charge of your child and bring him into submission to your authority." Since the child can be brought into submission just as well (or better) by other means, we feel that spanking need not be used, or at least only rarely.

References to the rod are found primarily in the Old Testament. The Old Testament's basic approach to justice, and possibly also to discipline, is different from that of the New Testament.

For example, in the New Testament, Christ modified the eye-for-an-eye system of justice (see Matt. 5:38) with His turn-the-other-cheek teaching (see Matt. 5:39–44). In the New Testament, Christ preached gentleness, love, and understanding, as did Paul: "Shall I come to you with a rod, or in love and a spirit of gentleness?" (1 Cor. 4:21). In the New Testament, Christ did not overturn the laws of the Old Testament but simply fulfilled them to a higher level of spirituality and understanding: He stressed discipline and direction from within rather than direction by force from without. Given the context of the total Bible, we feel God makes it clear that you don't have to spank to be a godly parent.

Reasons for the Anti-spanking Movement

There are three reasons why the anti-spanking philosophy has developed over the past thirty years. First, the unwillingness to spank children was a natural spin-off from the general movement toward a greater awareness of the feelings and dignity of the child. Some of this awareness comes from research into child development. Some of it originates with parents. The gentle-childbirth philosophy has indeed enriched people's regard for the dignity of a newborn as a feeling person, and the same feelings that changed childbirthing practices have carried over into childrearing practices. During the 1970s, a growing number of parents began practicing concepts found in attachment parenting. To these parents, spanking became synonymous with hurting and violence. Therefore, spanking was naturally foreign to their whole way of thinking about the parent-child relationship. They became more interested in alternative methods of correction and were willing to put an enormous amount of energy into those methods. They wanted their children's behavior to be directed from conscience and right feelings within rather than by an external force. Parents who have shied away from spanking for these reasons are to be commended. They know they can follow God's command to raise responsible children without spanking them. If you feel a conflict in your feelings toward spanking, pray and ask God to give you the wisdom to decide what is right for your family based upon a careful reading of Scripture.

The second reason behind the anti-spanking movement, and one with which we have no sympathy, is the carryover from the permissive approach to discipline. A child left to himself will find his own way, according to this approach. The Bible is clearly against this doctrine (see Prov. 29:15 and 22:6). A child left to himself will depart from you, will not respect your authority, and disgraces his mother. We feel that parents who do not spank because they follow this general permissive attitude show a lack of concern and lazily shirk their responsibility as authority figures. They will be held accountable here on earth for the outcome of their children and in the hereafter by the judgment of their Lord. Of course, their fault is not that they have failed to spank, but that they have failed to discipline their children at all.

The third reason spanking is generally losing favor as a correction technique is the belief that tolerance for spanking opens the door for child abuse, which has reached epidemic proportions. If a child's behavior is spank-controlled throughout childhood, he is very likely to continue this same parenting practice with his own children. Parents are powerful role models for their children. The model presented by parents who spank can indeed be a concern. When a child sees a parent spank another child, or when he himself is spanked, the concept he picks up is that it's all right for a big person to hit a little person. While most parents would argue that their way of spanking is a far cry from child abuse, accepting spanking as a principal part of correction makes it possible for other parents with less self-control to justify hitting children in anger or using spanking to punish minor misdeeds.

How to Avoid the Use of Spanking

Remember, one of your discipline goals is to create an attitude within your child, and an atmosphere within your home, that makes spanking seldom, if ever, necessary. Being reluctant to spank or refusing to spank at all may actually make you a better disciplinarian. The search for alternatives to spanking forces you to find more positive ways of directing your child's behavior. You end up knowing your child better, and your child actually has more respect for your authority because he knows that you can deliver the help he needs to not only control, but to learn better behavior. Spanking can tend to devalue a child, making him feel weak and powerless. This kind of self-image will not help him fight off temptation in the future.

For the most part, children who are the products of attachment parenting are easier to correct without spanking. Here is how knowing your child and helping him feel right will help you avoid spanking:

1. Children who are the products of attachment parenting can love and trust their parents so deeply that they willingly submit to parental authority. They can handle the concept of submission because they view authority as love and security, not an infringement upon their rights. Consequently, they are less defiant, and defiance is what usually gets children spanked. Or, if they are defiant, their parents understand it in a different light and do not feel their authority is challenged by it.

2. These children know what behavior is expected of them because their parents have taken the time and energy to teach them what they expect as well as the consequences of misbehavior.

3. Because their parents have taken the time and energy to encourage desirable behavior, the children are less likely to deviate into situations that could get them spanked.

4. These children are motivated to please their parents because they have learned that this allows the whole family to feel right and in harmony with one another.

5. Parents depend more on encouragement and discipline rather than on rewards and punishment.

6. Older children who have been reared in this style of parenting are motivated to depend on and please God, their heavenly Father, just as they have learned to trust their parents and to please them.

7. Young children who have received attachment parenting soon learn that their world runs more smoothly and that they actually have more fun when they live

according to the rules set by their parents and by God.

The end result of attachment parenting is an attitude within children and an atmosphere within the home that promote desirable behavior. The children have direction from within themselves. They are motivated toward desirable behavior because they enjoy the right feelings this desirable behavior promotes. They are so accustomed to feeling right that they naturally avoid situations that make them not feel right. They are on their way toward having Christian consciences.

Admittedly, this level of discipline is not easy to achieve in some children, and it takes much more time and energy to create this attitude in your child and this atmosphere in your home than it does to administer a whack on the bottom. However, spanking can be least effective with children who are difficult to discipline (i.e., strong-willed or high-need children).

Correcting the high-need child can be paradoxical; most parents who attempt to spank-control their high-need children usually report, "I'm spanking more and getting less results. Spanking seems to be hurting me more than her." Because their inner will is so strong, high-need children require correction methods that are primarily concerned with their own inner direction.

Today's children are generally spanked less than children were years ago. We feel this is a natural consequence of better informed parents being more aware of what children are thinking and feeling. Less spanking is a step in a positive direction toward a better, more sensitive, society, as long as that society is still strongly committed to discipline and correction.

If You Feel You Must Spank

Suppose you were to ask several parents, "What would you do if your three-year-old were making an unruly nuisance of himself at a family gathering?" Parent A might respond, "That's simple, I would take him in the other room and redden his bottom; I'll bet he would never act that way again, and it didn't hurt the way I turned out." Parent B might respond, "First, I know that she doesn't settle down in crowds. Second, I would have told my child beforehand what behavior is expected of her. For example: 'We are going to Grandma's house where there will be lots of your cousins to play with. I expect you to play outside, to be careful not to pick up any of Grandma's china, and to come in when you are called.' And then I would ask my child to repeat what I had said to him." Parent B might also add the reminder: "I will have to take you into the other room and spank you if you do not do what I ask." This parent would carry through on the spanking if necessary and follow the spanking with a sign of love and an explanation of why the child was spanked. Parent C might say, "If he seemed to be getting into trouble, I would first go through my checklist. Is he tired, hungry, bored, etc.? If he 'forgot' after I reminded him of the rules, I would take him upstairs and help him take a nap, or take him outside for some father-son time together, maybe have a snack. He responds beautifully when I take the time to understand him."

Here's our opinion of the approaches taken by Parent A, Parent B, and Parent C. Parent A went directly to spanking as the first resort. This is lazy parenting; it exhibits power more than authority, and does nothing to strengthen the respect or love relationship between parent and child. Parents B and C, on the other hand, took time and energy to follow a wiser approach to discipline:

1. They conveyed to the child what behavior was expected of him and took the time to be certain that the child understood.

2. They considered the child's needs and feelings and made an effort to channel the child into some play activities that would encourage desirable behavior.

3. If the child showed undesirable behavior, the parents put time and interest into understanding what the feelings and circumstances were that prompted the behavior. They focused on the child rather than on the undesirable actions.

4. Parent B carried out the admonition of spanking if it seemed necessary, but he also followed the spanking with a sign of love. Parent C is programmed not to spank.

Parents B and C conveyed both love and authority to the child. The child knew what behavior was expected of him or her, and the consequences of misbehaving: the result was a greater respect for the authority of his or her parents. Parent B may seem like a last-resort spanker (save your "big guns" till last) which some Christian writers are against (because the child was just waiting for the "big guns" anyway). We don't think so. The big guns won't be needed in most situations. Parent C's approach requires the most investment of time and energy, but he'll likely have the best relationship with his child.

When You Should Not Spank

We've made our feelings about spanking very clear, but we also realize that not all Christian parents are in agreement on this subject. Some approaches to spanking are better than others, and even spanking advocates agree that in some situations spanking is wrong and harmful. There are times when you absolutely should not spank your child.

1. *Do not spank in anger:* "In your anger do not sin" (Eph. 4:26). The emotion of anger in itself is not wrong. God tells people not to allow any of their actions to be motivated solely by anger. He also said that anger should be justified and short-lived. This admonition applies especially to actions toward children. If you are a parent easily provoked to anger, be on guard against the temptation to spank to release your anger or vent your frustration.

Don't wait until you're angry to pray for patience. Ask the Holy Spirit to prepare you ahead of time for these moments. Look for a flashing warning light in your emotions that tells you, "Wait; take time out for a minute, pray, and examine your motives for spanking. Let your hostility settle down." When your thoughts are not clouded by anger, you can usually come up with a more effective response to misbehavior than spanking. If your primary motive is to avenge your anger, then hold off. Pray for guidance to act according to God's will. "If any of you lacks wisdom, he should ask God, who gives generously to all without finding fault, and it will be given to him" (James 1:5).

For example, your three-year-old sits down to eat breakfast—her mind is full of fantasy, her attention span is short, and she is thinking about everything but her food. Oops! There goes her glass of milk all over the clean kitchen floor! You are naturally angry. You just washed that floor. Should you spank? No! This is an example of childish irresponsibility rather than willful defiance. Your child did not spill her milk deliberately. This is an accident. Don't be afraid to show that you are angry; children need to know that parents have feelings too. But keep your anger in line with reality. If you explode, you'll have to apologize. Follow your statement of dismay with, "I understand that this was an accident," then add an admonition, "but I expect you to be more careful when you sit at the table." You may also follow your reaction with logical consequences: she helps you clean up the mess, and if this is a recurrent problem, you fill her cup only half full next time or switch to a "little kid" cup with a lid.

Take that same child and the same glass of milk. Suppose you notice the glass of milk is getting closer and closer to the edge of the table. You ask your child to move the glass away from the edge because it may fall and spill. (A creative mother shared with us, "I put a large circle on the table with red tape and instruct my child that his glass must stay in the circle.") She defies your admonition and deliberately pushes the glass toward the edge of the table; as you predicted, it falls and makes a mess. This is a more serious offense, one that calls for correction. Testing the limits of authority is a classic childhood ploy. Much more is at stake here than milk spilled on the floor; you must reestablish your authority over your child. Your child expects this. What do you want to accomplish by correcting her? (1) You want her to know who is in charge; (2) you want to show that defiance of your authority will always be corrected; and (3) you want to teach her to conform to your authority, and God's, in the future. You also want your authority and God's to be established within her, as her conscience, so that she will eventually follow this inner authority. But be aware that asserting your authority over your child does not mean you must spank or be punitive.

Here are some alternatives to spanking in this situation. A logical first step would be to calmly give her directions for cleaning up the mess. This is a time for both of you to cool down. Then you think about what she was feeling—you want to understand why she acted that way. Was she feeling angry or jealous, left out or resentful (crabby inside)? Why did she feel compelled to get your attention in a negative way? Is this an isolated incident or one of many times your child deliberately disobeys? Once you have analyzed your child's behavior, you decide what to do next. (Repeated behavior like this is a red flag that the child and the family may need professional help.) A further consequence might be that you assume she does not want any more milk since she pushed it away on purpose. A negative reinforcement could also be used here, such as asking her to leave the table and sit in a "time-out place." If you do this without anger, she will be more likely not to resist. If you are both still angry, you will need to cool off so you can help her cool off before proceeding, or whatever you do will be perceived as punitive and no learning will take place. She can come back to the table when she can apologize, and she may need your help doing that. She may need you to pray with her. She may need you to hug or hold her, or spend some time with her.

2. *Do not spank toddlers and young children.* Some biblical scholars who have studied the use of the term *rod* in the Scriptures conclude that Proverbs probably intends the use of the rod for much older children, not toddlers and young children. They believe the rod was reserved for particularly wicked deeds done by a child old enough to fully comprehend the meaning of the spankings, possibly in a public forum. These interpretations may have some validity. Spanking is certainly useless and harmful in young children who have little grasp of the relationship between the misdeed and the punishment. And if you are spanking more and more as your child gets older, this is a sign of a breakdown in your parent-child communication and in your approach to discipline. Professional guidance should be obtained.

3. *Do not spank if you have a weak parent-child relationship.* Knowing what is going on inside your child is necessary before spanking should ever be considered. With-

out mutual understanding between parent and child, there are no lessons to be learned from corporal punishment. If you spank, you are imposing a heavy burden on a fragile foundation which, with continued stress, may eventually crumble, turning both your parent-child relationship and your child's self-image into a pile of rubble. If you have built a solid foundation of love and trust with your child, an occasional swat to clear the air will not damage this relationship, but it will not improve it either.

Spanking should be considered only after you have tried more positive methods of correction. At this point, some Christian parents will choose to spank a child who continues to defy reasonable authority. If this is your choice, be sure of the following points first:

1. You have followed the principles of attachment parenting in order to build up a secure love-and-trust relationship with your child.
2. You have clearly defined for your child what behavior you expect of him, and he understands what you expect.
3. You have tried alternative methods to no avail.
4. Your child willfully defies reasonable authority, and this is a major situation where your authority and your relationship with your child are on the line.
5. You have prayed for guidance about the best method of correction for your child in a given situation, and your conclusion is that a spanking is in the best interest of your child's inner direction and your authority relationship.

Parents sometimes consider spanking to be reasonable in life-threatening situations. For example, your three- to six-year-old is told not to ride his tricycle into the street. If he does, the tricycle will be put in the garage for one week (logical consequence), and he will be spanked. He rides into the street, respecting neither your authority nor the inherent danger of the situation. So you spank him. Will this make him more careful? Failure to carry through on what you said you were going to do will weaken your future authority relationship and lessen your child's respect for you.

But spanking alone will not teach safety lessons. A child must be taught to recognize and respect danger. He must not be left with access to the street until he is old enough to comply. You must be with him, teaching him, until you *know* he will not ride onto the street and he understands why he must not do this. You also want him to be able to stop and look both ways before crossing the street and to understand why he must do this. You will have a rule that until he reaches a certain age he must come and ask you first, so you can watch him. You want him to understand how

FINDING ALTERNATIVES TO SPANKING

There are many helpful books, both Christian and secular, that will guide you as you seek ways to discipline your children. Look for books that explain child development, as well as those with discipline "how-to's." File this information away in your brain and call it up when you need to use it. See the bibliography for recommended reading.

Also, look for ways to nurture yourself as a parent. All of us reach the end of our rope with our children more quickly when we are feeling frazzled or anxious. Be aware that when you run out of alternative methods or just can't muster the patience to recall them, you will revert back to the way you were corrected as a child and will repeat your own parents' worst moments. Learn to recognize your own warning signs so that you can take hold of yourself, calm down, and then handle the situation in a way that leaves you feeling right. If you struggle in this area, you could benefit from counseling. See page 238 for how to locate a counselor who understands and supports attachment parenting.

seriously he could be hurt by a passing car. You don't want him to learn only that he should look back for you when crossing the street to see whether you are around.

Develop a Spanking Wisdom

There are so many variables and so many different parent-child relationships that it is not possible to make hard and fast rules about spanking. Here are some general guidelines to help you develop your own guidelines for spanking:

Pray for wisdom to know whether spanking in general is the proper way to deal with your child's offenses. Disregard all opinions you have heard about spanking, lest they cloud your judgment. Open your ears to God's direction, asking Him for an inner sensitivity to spanking in general and to spanking in specific circumstances.

For our own family, we have concluded, after much prayer and experience, that (1) we will not let unacceptable behavior go uncorrected; (2) we are committed to creating an attitude within our children and an atmosphere within our home where spanking is not necessary; and (3) given all the possible ways to correct a child, spanking is a poor option. In short, we do not spank our children; and we devote a lot of time and energy to utilizing alterna- tives to spanking. This has been a healthy approach for our family. Other parents may choose another viewpoint.

Consider if there are specific risk factors in your family that affect your attitude toward spanking. Parents who are most likely not to abuse spanking:

- have practiced the principles of attachment parenting all along so that they know their children and their children feel right,
- have children whose temperaments are generally easy-going,
- were not spank-controlled as children.

Parents who may spank inappropriately:

- have a shaky relationship with the child being corrected,
- were abused as children,
- have high-need children,
- find that repeated spanking does not work,
- are prone to impulsive anger.

If you have any of the risk factors that might hinder you from spanking appropriately, examine your entire parent-child relationship and examine your relationship with God. Some parents simply cannot handle "the rod" wisely. Accepting this and seeking help in using alternative means of correction (see box on p. 378) will benefit you and your child. The cause of abusive spanking is anger; the product of abusive spanking is also anger. An angry child will grow to be an angry adult, and the cycle of poor parent-child relationships will continue.

Examine your motive for spanking. Your child will certainly pick up on this. Are you spanking him for his own good or for *your* own good? If you are a parent easily provoked to anger, be on guard. A child spanked in anger will retaliate in anger. This is the main reason parents say, "He's so stubborn; the harder I spank him, the worse he gets."

Spank soon after the offense. It is important to cool down, but a spanking should be given as soon as possible after the offense and by the person whose authority is at stake. Don't say, "Wait till your father gets home and then you'll get it."

Help the child accept the spanking. To help avoid a struggle, explain the whole spanking process to your child at a time she is not about to get a spanking. You should not have to drag her kicking and screaming off to her "execution." Then, if she resists her spanking, she is either being defiant or else she feels unjustly treated. In either case, the spanking has not accomplished its goal and you may need to reexamine your decision.

Explain to your child why you are spanking him. Some parents may not agree that a child needs to understand the reason for the punishment. These parents may equate explanations with apologies, which they interpret as weakening their position. But an appropriately administered spanking should not alienate the spanker and the spankee. A wise parent conveys to the child that the spanking is done out of love and out of a God-given duty "because the Lord disciplines those he loves, and he punishes everyone he accepts as a son" (Heb. 12:6). This is a good scriptural reference to support your position. Hebrews 12:11 states, "No discipline seems to be pleasant at the time, but painful. Later on, however, it produces a harvest of righteousness and peace for those who have been trained by it." An excellent discussion of how to use spanking to correct a child's behavior is found in Jack Fennema's book *Nurturing Children in the Lord* (see bibliography).

Encourage a confession (see James 5:16; 1 John 1:9). Confession of wrongdoing is very scriptural and therapeutic. A child is seldom going to welcome a spanking, but understanding and acknowledging he was wrong can help him accept the punishment. When a child sees the fairness of a correction, he usually respects the authority figure administering the spanking. He struggles less, which makes spanking easier. "Johnny, did Dad tell you not to ride your bike out into the street? . . . What did you do? . . . You disobeyed me, right? . . . You were wrong, and you could have been hit by a car. . . . You agree that you deserve a spanking?" Johnny will probably manage a few feeble yeses during this interrogation. This simple dialogue allows Johnny to feel and release guilt and helps to shape his conscience. He learns to recognize his feelings when he has done wrong and accept a very real fact of life that wrong deeds bring consequences.

Choose a proper instrument for the spanking. The nitty-gritty details of how to spank may offend readers who absolutely disdain any form of spanking. Let us repeat that our view of spanking is summed up in one word: DON'T. However, as a pediatrician with twenty-five years' experience, Bill is painfully aware that spanking can lead to child abuse. This section is written primarily for parents who have already made up their minds to spank their child and need guidelines to avoid physical and emotional abuse.

There are two schools of thought on what to spank with—a neutral object (a stick, a wooden spoon, etc.) or the hand. Proponents of the neutral object feel that the hand, as part of the parent, is a tool for loving and learning and not an object to be feared. This concept is a carryover from animal behavior psychology. Pet owners were advised never to use the hand to strike with, because animals shy away from the objects they are struck with. So, if you want your dog to fetch your morning paper, you don't use a rolled-up paper for correction. Interestingly, now dog owners are advised never to strike the animal. Corrections are given using a training collar.

Some parents associate a stick with "beating" and a hand with spanking; they feel better using their hands. By using your hand you will feel the force of your strength. Other parents feel that if they program themselves away from using their hands to spank, they are less likely to hit their children reflexively out of anger. Having to go get the neutral spanking object allows them time and space to cool off. We are more concerned about the attitude behind spanking than the choice of the instrument.

Let us suggest using neither the hand nor a clublike object such as a wooden spoon. A switch is a safer spanking tool—a thin, very flexible stick such as a willow branch that inflicts some stinging pain but no injury to the child's bottom. Most cases of child abuse Bill has seen were inflicted by an angry person behind a heavy hand or a wooden spoon.

Spanking is traditionally administered to the child's buttocks with one or two swats. We feel it is very important to respect the child's sense of modesty and never bare the buttocks. (If a child is still in padded diapering, he or she is way too young to be spanked anyway.) To spank a child anywhere else on his or her anatomy is to risk injury. For example, above the buttocks are located the spine and the kidneys, below are the more bony areas of the legs and knees. The face and head must never be struck due to the delicate structures and the emotional insult and trauma that would be caused. On this same subject, toddler hands never should be smacked because the hands are the tools of exploring. See "Baby Proofing" and "Distract and Divert," page 339.

Follow up after spanking. A spanking should leave both parent and child feeling better. An inappropriately administered spanking will leave an angry child and a parent who feels guilty. To avoid bad feelings all around, follow the spanking with an expression of love. The child may be hesitant to ask for forgiveness or to admit he deserved what he got, and you may not know what to say. Saying "I'm sorry" or "I didn't want to spank you" is confusing to the child. He gets mixed messages: "If you didn't want to spank me, why did you do it?" Or "If you are sorry, then you did something wrong." (Of course, if the spanking was done in error, before you had all the facts, you *must* make a sincere apology to your child. Never be afraid to admit you were wrong. This is the best way to teach a child to say he is sorry.) End a spanking with, "Now let's pray together," after the crying has subsided and you have gathered the repentant child into your arms.

Your prayer should include an expression of love for your child, forgiveness, and thanks to God for forgiveness. During the after-spanking prayer, your child should pick up that you (and God) forgive him. Both you and your child should emerge from a spanking with a clean slate. This is a lot for a child to understand and digest. He would have to be old enough and emotionally mature enough to be able to participate in this process.

Father, we acknowledge You as the author of all discipline. We accept the responsibility You have given us to discipline our child. Your instructions are clear, our spirits are willing, but our flesh is weak. Discipline us that we may discipline our child and by so doing see him and his children and his children's children return to You, our Heavenly Father. Amen.

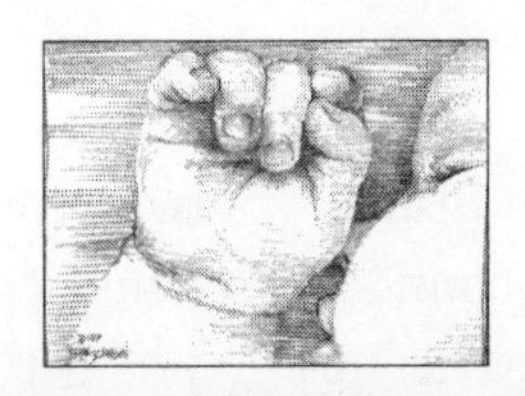

CHAPTER SIXTEEN

Discipline and Spiritual Training
Three to Six Years Old

By three years of age children are very self-aware—they know what they feel, what they are comfortable doing, and what they cannot yet do. They have mastered the art of using their parents as a resource and have defined their place in the family structure. The person you have seen developing over the past three years has arrived. Any further development that takes place falls into the category of refining what has been built. You have your work cut out for you—your little person is ready and willing.

Your three-year-old has come a long way in acquiring considerable motor and adaptive skills. Three-year-olds are aware of how much physical wear and tear their developing muscles and bones can handle comfortably. As they learn to protect themselves from injury, the constant watching of the previous stage gradually lessens. Brain maturation means threes can easily sleep through the night (barring any disturbance in physical systems). They, of course, retain their need for a pleasant bedtime ritual, and many still need the parents' help to relax off to sleep.

By three years of age your child has developed enough language to communicate his desires and feelings effectively. He understands you and feels that you understand him. Since he is more able to express his negative feelings with words rather than actions, his use of tantrums lessens considerably. Three-year-olds have mastered the important lesson of cause and effect. This important milestone makes exploring behavior less impulsive and more calculated and reasoning. This and their mastery of language also make it easier for them to understand what is expected of them and to follow directions.

So we have the coming together of acquired skills, basic temperament, intelligence potential, and parental guidance. Children who have achieved their potential during the first three years enter the three- to six-year-old stage with a solid foundation, ready to refine these skills. Children who have not built this foundation in the first three years must continue to expend energy mastering basic skills and self-awareness; they are always trying to catch up on what they've missed. A child's basic personality (the sum total of her skills and feelings reflected in her behavior) may not be completely determined by this age, but it is certainly well along the way. Changing a behavior trait becomes increasingly difficult with advancing age.

These years are generally smoother for both parents and child because the refinement of acquired skills usually produces less anxiety than the struggles to acquire these skills during the first three years. We see tantrums and other behavioral anxieties of two-year-olds as a manifestation of the struggle to get themselves together. When you get your act together, you feel good about yourself, and we think this is true for three-year-olds. Your child is fun to talk with, to take walks with, and to play word games with. At this stage, your child often experiences you as a companion who is fun to be around. (This is normal and healthy as long as your roles of authority figure and spiritual trainer prevail.) It is much easier to get the concept of discipline across to your child if he or she enjoys being with you.

The child who got good attachment parenting from the start, who by three knows his mother is there for him and tuned into him, is ready—out of the safety of that bonding—to explore the larger world. The larger world consists of his father, his grandfather, his grandmother, the neighbors, his preschool teacher, his Sunday school teacher, and friends his own size. When this child is frightened or overwhelmed, he will rush back to the safety of his mother's arms or come and lean on her knee. However, the well-attached child will head out again on his adventures, exploring the larger world of relationships. Some mothers make a serious mistake trying to keep their three-year-old tightly attached, which suggests to the child that he is in danger exploring the world. These mothers do this seductively by saying such things as, "Stay here, let me read to you. Stay here, and you won't get hurt. Stay here, and let me tell you a story." There is absolutely nothing wrong with reading to a child, and he certainly won't fall off and hurt himself if he's sitting on your lap. However, the child gets the wrong message because his personality and cognitive development depend on his exploring. Youngsters who are crippled by an overly protective mother grow up being afraid.

SPIRITUAL NURTURING OF THE THREE- TO SIX-YEAR-OLD

This is a critical period in a child's spiritual development. This is the stage when he or she is most receptive to learning about God. During this stage, your child unquestioningly accepts the values of his primary role models, his parents. Your values are his values, and what is important to you is important to him. At no other time in a child's life will his mind be so receptive to what you will teach him. In the normal process of maturing spiritually, as a child grows older he becomes more selective and will make more of his own choices. When your child reaches the stage where he is trying to define his own values, you want him to have your spiritual values as part of himself. This is why it is so important to fill him up with spiritual values during the three- to six-year receptive stage. The more he learns about God from his primary spiritual models during this stage, the more he will look to God in the years to come. Appreciate the high level of responsibility you have at this stage to train up your child in the way he or she should go. Perhaps at no other stage of a child's development is the investment/return ratio so high.

Attachment parenting contributes to spiritual nurture. You have already laid the foundation for your child's spiritual growth in the way you have parented your child from infancy on. The early investment of attachment parenting creates an attitude of giving within the parent and an attitude of receiving within the child. The attachment style of parenting in those early formative years builds up a trust relationship between parent and child, based on achieving the two goals of knowing your child and helping your child feel right. This trust-and-authority relationship makes your child more receptive to guidance from you, and so the fourth goal of parenting is made easier: leading your child to Christ.

Attachment parenting will also help you explain God to your child in ways that are meaningful to him. The guidelines for spiritual nurturing in this chapter are only general information. As an attached parent, you can get behind the eyes of your child and understand his simple faith. You will know when your child is ready to learn about respecting God's commandments and when he needs to hear that Jesus loves and forgives him. Your experience as an attached parent will also help you model Christ to your child.

You know your child in the way God knows you, from the inside out.

Be spiritual models for your child. We like to think of leading a child to Christ not as training or the imparting of dogma, but rather as *spiritual giving.* Spiritual giving implies that leading your child to Christ flows naturally from your own walk with Christ rather than proceeding from someone else's list of "shoulds" and "musts." Just as discipline and guidance flow naturally from attachment parenting, the spiritual discipline of your child will flow naturally from your attachment with God.

What about newborn Christians who have not laid this spiritual foundation during their first three years of parenthood? Is it too late? No! Just as early bonding with a newborn gives you a head start in parenting, an early spiritual foundation gives you a head start in spiritual training. But with effort and commitment (and the help of the Holy Spirit) you can make up for missed opportunities. As you yourself are catching up in your spiritual growth, you probably will have to be more conscious of the how-tos before spiritual training naturally flows from you into your child. Remember, children are resilient and adaptable. Children profit from Christian discipline at any age. If Christian parenting is new to you, openly share your newfound love of Jesus with your child, and she will respond with faith and love.

Teaching Your Child about God

During the first three years, your child basically learned that God is an important person. In the three- to six-year-old stage, this concept is carried one step further: God is an important person because . . . At this point many Christian parents need help: What do I teach my child about God? How do I teach him? How much can my child understand about God at this stage?

We want parents to understand a very basic, sobering truth about children. To our children we are "God with skin on." If you were to write down all the things that a mother is—someone to trust, who cares for his every need, who protects him, who holds him securely, who answers his cries—that is the same description a child would have of God. (So would we, if we know Him well enough). When a child grows old enough to understand these things in so many words, it's easier for him to believe those things about God if he has been able to experience these things from his mother. This is another reason why attachment parenting helps lay a foundation for teaching a child about God.

Set some goals for your child's spiritual life. What do you want your child at this age to learn about God? To answer this question, let's consult the Manufacturer's Handbook. God told us how and what to teach our children.

"Love the LORD your God with all your heart and with all your soul and with all your strength" (Deut. 6:5). This verse is so important that Jesus quotes it when talking to the Jewish teachers of the Law in the New Testament. When they asked Jesus which is the most important commandment, He quoted that verse to them. So, the first concept to teach your child is to love the Lord.

But what does it mean to love God? Open the Bible again to Deuteronomy where God said that the next step is to make the love of God part of yourself: "These commandments [to love the Lord] that I give you today are to be upon your hearts" (6:6). The next step is to "impress them on your children" (6:7). How do you teach your child to love God? The more your child knows about Him, the more he will learn to love Him.

Our daughter Hayden at age four told us she loved us more than she loved God because she knew us more than she knew God. The love a child feels for his parents can be explained as a simple feeling: "I want to be near that person who does good things for me, who takes care of me, who makes me feel good, who is so big and strong and powerful that he (she) can drive a car and fix bicycles. I miss him (her) when I am not near him (her)." It is vitally important that a child trust and love his parents whom he can see so that he can understand the feeling of trusting and loving God whom he can't see. Beyond this, a child's parents can help him know and love God by pointing out all the things that God made (including us) and all the ways in which He cares for us.

By hearing Bible stories a three- to six-year-old child can learn about Jesus more easily than he can learn about God. A young child can learn that Jesus loves little children (the song "Jesus Loves the Little Children" is a favorite at this age), that He protects little children (the story of the good shepherd searching for the one lost sheep), and that He is kind and gentle (the story of how He placed His hands on them and prayed for them). Jesus is God's Son, which makes Him God too.

Fear the Lord and walk in His ways. In Deuteronomy 10:12 God said, "What does the LORD your God ask of you but to fear the LORD your God, to walk in all his ways." The biblical term *fear* means an awed respect for the power and greatness of God.

Learning the fear of the Lord along with the concept of sin is a major turning point in the young child's discipline. The child less than six years old can grasp this simple notion of sin: "This big person whom Mom and Dad call 'God' makes rules. I can't see Him, but He sees me. He knows when I don't get things right, but He still loves me anyway just like Mom and Dad do." You may introduce the teachings of the Ten Commandments to the child of four or five, but keep them in simple, everyday terms: worship God in a special way on a special day, obey your parents, be kind to your friends and don't hurt them, tell the truth, don't take other children's toys.

By introducing these concepts to your child, you are laying the foundation for building a conscience in the next stage of development. The child of five or six should be able to feel the beginning of a conscience, "I feel good when I do the right thing; I don't feel good when I do the wrong thing." Both your rules and God's rules should be consistently repeated and presented to the young child when he is most receptive to the concepts of right and wrong. And he is learning those concepts of right and wrong as you live out your life in front of him. This is one reason we are told, "Be joyful always; pray continually!"

Social Discipline

"Love your neighbor as yourself" (Mark 12:31). Jesus said this is the second greatest commandment after loving the Lord. One of the major milestones in a preschooler's development is the beginning of peer relationships. Three-year-olds want to play with other children and show varying degrees of social readiness. Their social interaction evolves from parallel play (playing separately) to a more cooperative play pattern of sharing other children's toys and making up games together. Preschoolers become more comfortable in peer play groups of varying sizes, and it is in these play groups that they learn what is socially acceptable behavior. Demanding, possessive, assertive, and withdrawn behaviors are all realistic expectations at this age. The "law of the jungle" (or "may the most assertive child win") may prevail in these peer groups unless parents, caregivers, or preschool teachers step in and help children learn other ways to get along.

This is the time to introduce the "love your neighbor" rule. Show a child a picture of Jesus with the little children and tell her how Jesus said she should love and be kind to the children she plays with. In the middle of toy squabbles it often helps to take a few minutes out and encourage (but not pressure) children to put their arms around each other, saying something like, "Love each other. Jesus wants us to love each other." Young children need to learn that this is not a give-me-give-me world, but that sharing and giving are the Christian way.

Nevertheless, squabbles over toys are to be expected at this age. Young children are still learning the concepts of ownership, sharing, and respect for another's possessions. When another child plays with your child's favorite toy, your child may feel very anxious; at this stage, holding the toy or playing with it is equivalent to owning it. If sharing is a major problem for your child, ask children to bring a few toys of their own when they come to visit. Capitalize on your child's natural desire to play with another child's toys. As she explores someone else's toy, another child will play with her toy. Have a rule that even though it is her toy when she is alone, in a play group, if a toy is put down, another child is allowed to pick it up and play with it. She will learn to give a toy to get a toy, and eventually, sharing can be the law of the jungle. If your child has a special toy she doesn't wish to share, allow her to put it away when friends come to visit. This will make it easier for her to share other toys.

A parent often states, "I don't want him to always be pushed around." A common discipline problem facing you at this stage occurs when your child is acted upon aggressively and wronged. Should she be encouraged to fight back? In our opinion, it is healthy to teach children to be assertive, but not aggressive. A child is assertive when she protects her own territory and speaks up for herself and her feelings; a child is aggressive when she infringes upon others' territory.

Being assertive is within the realm of Christian interaction, and perhaps assertiveness teaches the aggressor a valuable social lesson. This is the time to remind a child to "use your words" and, if necessary, to seek assistance from an adult in solving play problems. When young children play together, a certain amount of pushing and shoving is inevitable. They have neither the language capacity nor the self control to talk out every problem. But you do want your child to learn better ways of solving problems, solutions that don't depend on one child overpowering the other—physically or verbally.

As your child's self-control improves, you can also teach her to empathize with the other child. Ask your child to imagine how she would feel if . . . . Teach her to "do to others what you would want them to do to you." Remember, though, that your most powerful teaching tool is the way you handle conflicts in your home. How your child treats other children will often reflect how you treat her and others in your family. Finally, help your child forgive or ask for forgiveness after an act of aggression. Children should learn to say "I'm sorry" and "That's OK," or to hug or help each other feel better in some way after a disruption in their relationship.

Expect your child to apologize and forgive, yet realize that around age four or five some will resist. They have a hard time admitting they did wrong. It does no good to force a child to say "I'm sorry" or "That's OK." You can make sure your child sees you sincerely apologize and forgive him and others. Then he knows how it's done and what the result is. For most situations it is enough to simply let your child know you want him to "make peace" with the other person, and

PLAY-ACT SCRIPTURE

Play-acting is a good way to teach Bible stories to children at this age; they can dress up like Bible characters and put on a family skit, or do it with a group of friends. Christmas and Easter are particularly valuable times for play-acting from Scripture, but don't confine it to holidays. Of course, you include lots of props—a doll for baby Jesus, a little wagon or box for a manger, and an assortment of stuffed animals. We've been part of a six-week home worship group that did this every Sunday. The children were directed in acting out stories of Jesus, like the wedding feast at Cana, the healing of the paralytic (complete with a "roof" through which the stretcher was lowered), and Jesus calming the storm. The children took turns being the various characters, so each story was acted out several times. Now when we hear or read those stories from the Bible, they seem so much clearer and more concrete. Hopefully, it had the same effect on the children!

leave it up to him to decide how he'll do that. It doesn't have to be a formal apology, or even done with words. You and the children involved will know if peace has been made. If a child is unwilling to make peace, he should know what the consequence is. A little time on his own will help him appreciate sweet fellowship.

Teaching Your Child to Pray

Teach your child to pray and to praise. This is a wonderful age for a child to learn to talk with God. Use short, simple phrases that you want your child to pick up: "Father . . . we thank You . . . we love you . . . keep us safe . . . we ask . . . we praise You . . . please bless Grandma and Suzy and Mrs. Smith and . . ."

Pray often. Before he goes to sleep and on waking up in the morning are two important times to pray with your child. You want your child to begin each day with God and end each day with God; and in between times he can pray as often as the need or desire arises. Pray spontaneously. Be vigilant for openers: a child is hurt or frightened, or a child's behavior has deteriorated. This teaches your child that he can talk to God at any time.

Teaching Your Child about Scripture

In the beginning when you teach your young child about the Bible, wait for openers. If your child sees you reading the Bible often enough, she will eventually climb up onto your lap and ask you to read to her too. This is especially true if you are reading the Bible as a family. She doesn't want to be left out. Tell her the baby Jesus story, or about the boy who gave Jesus his lunch to feed all the people. Give her her own book about Jesus. There are many picture Bibles and Bible story books written for all levels of child development. You may find that much of your Scripture-reading time is spent reading to your child out of her picture Bible. This is not wasted Scripture time for you; you may be surprised at how much you can learn by getting down to your child's level, seeing God through her eyes, and finding simple answers to her questions. Jesus said, "Unless you change and become like little children, you will never enter the kingdom of heaven" (Matt 18:3).

Encourage Scripture memorization. Give your child short, one-sentence memory verses and include the Scripture reference: "God is love," 1 John 4:8. Young children enjoy the challenge of memorizing. Talk about the verse and see if she can tell you about it.

Young children live from moment to moment, neither thinking about the past nor anticipating the future. (It is interesting that Jesus told us to be like children and not to worry about tomorrow.) Scheduled spiritual teaching doesn't work as well as spiritual moments that occur while you are simply having fun together. For example, a walk through a park or the woods with your child will open up a variety of opportunities to find God in nature. You see a beautiful sunset and stop and say, "Bobby, let's thank God for the pretty red sky." After you have prayed, your child may ask a question like, "Where does the sun go at night?" which gives you the chance to talk more about God's wonderful creation.

Teaching Your Child about Jesus

A child under six blends Jesus and God and is just as likely to say "Jesus made me" as "God made me." If you show him a picture of someone with a beard wearing a robe, he is likely to answer that the person is Jesus. Of course, no one knows what Jesus looked like, and in your child's various picture books, Jesus looks a bit different in each one. Children are not confused by this. They can always pick out which one is Jesus because He is the one the child is drawn to from the story in the text. Some children believe that the pastor at church is Jesus and their faith will survive your setting the record straight at this point. (Actually, discerning Jesus in the pastor is not off base.) Young children tend to think in concrete rather than abstract ways about God. When teaching your child about Jesus, emphasize His humanity because children can relate to this. From hearing stories about Jesus, your child can learn that Jesus is kind, patient, and gentle and that He especially loves little children.

A child this age can grasp the concept that Jesus is the Son of God (or that God is Jesus' Daddy). She understands the concept of a son and that Jesus was a man, but do not confuse her with the concept of the Trinity at this age. It is more important for the child to be comfortable first with the humanity of Christ and the idea that Jesus loves us and cares for us. Basically, you want the young child to be concerned with what Jesus teaches, what He does for us, and what He tells us to do. Without much trouble, your child will grasp the fact

that if Jesus is the Son of God, He must be God too.

When teaching your child about Jesus, relate His life to the real life of the child: Jesus was born as a baby. He grew up in a house, and He helped Joseph work as a carpenter. When Jesus was twelve, He taught people about His Father God in heaven. When Jesus was a grown man, He told us the right things to do and what was wrong to do. Many people listened to what Jesus taught, followed Him, and loved Him, and they were called Christians. Tell them know if Mommy and Daddy are Christians, too, and let them know anyone who wants to can invite Him into his heart. Some children as young as three or four seem to understand and want to do this.

This is a wonderful experience to share with your child. God honors these childlike invitations, and it does indeed make a difference in their young lives. We love hearing from parents the stories of how their little ones express faith in Jesus. Allow us to tell two from our family.

When our daughter Erin was four she told us, "I have Jesus in my heart." We asked her what that meant, and she responded, "I love Him." We asked, "Is Jesus really in your heart?" and she surprised us by her answer, "No, but His Spirit is." We felt comfortable that she had in her "heart" what ought to be there, based on her own level of spiritual development and understanding. She was expressing a sincere and simple love for Jesus, the deep, strong faith of a child.

Three-and-a-half-year-old Lauren was busy in the kitchen making playdough with me (Martha). It was late November. We remembered a special baby Jesus figure that she had first seen in a large creche in a shop window decorated for the holidays, and then carried around in the shop. That lead to a discussion of how we really don't know what Jesus looked like since we can't see Him because He lives in heaven with God, His Father. I then explained how Jesus can also live in our hearts if we ask Him to; she wanted Jesus to live in her heart. Of course, I helped her invite Him in, rejoicing in His wonderful timing.

Teaching about Death and Heaven

Hearing that Jesus died on the cross will help a child grasp how much Jesus loved us—that He would do that to save us, so that we could go to live with Him in heaven when we die; and, of course, there's the glorious happy ending, that He didn't stay dead but came back alive. Children by the age of three can already understand the terror of death. They may think about it, and even realize that their parents could die and they would be left alone. It is crucial for a child to be taught that death is a part of life and is nothing to be afraid of, since Jesus died for us and showed us that we will live again in heaven, all together, with Him.

Giving children a clear, concrete concept of heaven helps them understand and accept the death of a loved one. Tell him Grandma is in heaven with Jesus, and she is very happy because she is with Him and Grandpa. Someday when you are out having ice cream ask your child to think about the kinds of things Grandma might be doing in heaven with Jesus at that moment. This gives them the opportunity to use their own imaginations to explore the concept of heaven. Our four- and five-year-olds would often ponder this thought of enjoying heaven with Jesus. They would come up with things on their own, that they were looking forward to.

Establishing and Improving Family Devotions

Family devotions are an important part of the spiritual life of your child. However, for most families it is difficult to set aside time in the day exclusively for the Lord. There is stiff competition for your time and also for the minds of your children. In our own busy home, we struggle to make the concept of family devotions work. This section will give you some practical suggestions on family devotions.

Tell your children why family devotions are important: God has blessed our family, and we want to come together to thank Him. The Bible says that God is with us when we pray together. We are going to take five or ten minutes each night to pray together as a family. Then rely on the Holy Spirit to make this time come alive. Spirit-filled prayer can be irresistible, so learn how to let the Spirit help you lead these devotions.

For us the best time is after the evening meal. Everyone is already gathered at the table, reducing start-up time. On weekends try having family devotions after breakfast. Occasionally have devotions as part of a special outing. On family trips, devotions can be held during the car ride. The important thing is that your family does pray together, not where you pray together.

Don't feel you have to convince your children that devotions are "fun." Teach them that devotions are "special." Children are already obsessed with the idea that everything has to be fun. Children can learn to delay their need for entertainment. Family devotions are not in the same category as a family TV program.

Keep your devotions brief, according to the attention span and interest level of your children. Holding devotions consistently is more important than how long they last. It is more important to have them often than to wait until there is enough time to have a "real" devotion.

How can you hold your child's interest? Give everyone a part and get the children involved right away. Ask your children to contribute suggestions on how to run the family devotions, and you may be amazed at what they come up with. Our son Peter at the age of seven suggested that we take the phone off the hook during our devotional time, and we all concurred that it was a terrific idea.

Even if your child appears to get nothing out of the devotions, persevere. If your child gets only one message—that family devotions are important because God is important to your family—then your efforts are worthwhile. Even if a young child does not actually understand all the words, he will perceive the attitude of the prayers and praise.

Every family member could have a Bible, a notepad, and a pencil. The Living Bible, a children's edition, or a picture Bible is good for young children. You could maintain a prayer calendar to write down specific prayer requests, and later on, write down when and how they were answered—praise God for answered prayers. A typical devotion time could include an opening prayer, a Scripture lesson, sharing prayer needs, celebrating answers to prayer, and a closing prayer.

DISCIPLINE FOR THE THREE- TO SIX-YEAR-OLD

Discipline of the child between the ages of three and six brings new challenges. Development brings increasing skills and more reaching for independence. Yet, children do not develop in a smooth progression. They often take a step backward after having just taken two steps forward. They go from equilibrium ("She's such an angel.") to disequilibrium ("Is this the same child?"). Growing up is not easy for any child. Be prepared to meet each new stage with renewed prayer for wisdom, understanding, and strength.

Teaching Impulse Control and Delayed Gratification

Children between the ages of three and six are ready to exercise some self-control and to learn that living with others means being considerate of their wants and needs. They need to learn that not everything they want is good for them, and that not everything that is good for everyone else is good for them. Today's children are growing up in a world where they are constantly being told of material things they need to *fulfill* them. Start early helping your child hear "no"—learning to manage frustration is a lifelong task, but you need to start young. The inability to control their impulses and to say no to some of their desires is one of the main weaknesses that gets adults into trouble. Self-control is one of the fruits of the Holy Spirit (see Gal. 5:23).

As your infant matures into a child, you can begin to differentiate between his needs and his wants. This process begins when you gradually extend your reaction time to your baby's complaints of boredom or wanting to be picked up. Where once his needs were paramount, as time passes, you begin to weigh the intensity of his need against your need to complete a task or even enjoy a few moments of peace and quiet. By the time children are three, they are learning self-control in many areas: taking turns, not hitting, sharing toys, letting Mom take care of the baby, not interrupting parental conversations. You can also model delayed gratification for your child: "Instead of getting ice cream cones now, let's buy some ice cream to take home for everyone to share." Or, "We can't buy the toy today, but let's write it down on your birthday list." Or, "If you help me clean the kitchen, I can play a game with you when we're finished."

Assign Chores

While your three-year-old has accomplished most of the basic skills of childhood, she needs some direction about what to do with them. This is the time to build a sense of responsibility in the young child. Channel her skills in the right direction, and she will have fewer opportunities to get into trouble. This is often the last age at which a child will voluntarily want to help Mommy and Daddy around the house. A young child does not often distinguish between work and play, with one exception: doing any task with a parent is play; doing it alone is work. Let him do dishes, sweep the floor, and pick up clothes. Involving your young child in helping helps him experience jobs as a positive thing. In later stages, many children see work as somewhat undesirable, and they often resist. Your main goal is to give your child a sense of competence, rather than you delegating jobs just to get it done faster and better. (You'll be learning to deal with perfectionism!)

As you encourage your child to work with you, gradually require him to do specific jobs on his own and hold him accountable for their completion (for a list of chores appropriate at various ages, see p. 398). At this stage you are building on a principle in child discipline, the privilege/responsibility ratio: increasing privileges means increasing responsibilities. When the privileges are unearned and multiply faster than the responsibilities, children grow up thinking the world owes them a living.

Choose jobs for your three-year-old wisely. Keep the tasks short, simple, and achievable. Be certain he can see immediately the fruits of his labors. An example is having

DISCIPLINING THE HIGH-NEED CHILD

In some respects, all children are strong-willed, but some have stronger wills than others. These are the high-need children. They are a challenge to parents' disciplinary ingenuity, and rearing them calls for extra reserves of patience and stamina. Often the disciplinary techniques that work for more easy-going children don't seem to work for high-need children. These children are so challenging to discipline because the same temperament traits that make them creative and interesting also get them into trouble.

The high-need child is impulsive. He has great difficulty saying no to himself and even more difficulty saying yes to you. He is driven. The high-need child very often has higher than average intelligence. He is not satisfied with average teaching or learning. He requires above-average parenting, above-average teaching at school, and above-average spiritual nurturing in the home. These children need focused attention from their parents, a lot of touching and gentling, a lot of playing with, building with, reading with, and talking with.

On the surface it would seem that the high-need child needs more corrective discipline, and more firmly administered than does the average child. Actually, for most high-need children, the opposite is true. Spanking and frequent punishment can turn a sensitive, high-need child into an angry, resentful child who rebels against complying with his parents' wishes. With a high-need child you need to show even more love (just like you needed to hold them more as babies) and to be very careful about how you correct behavior. They are very good at sensing your emotions. When you are angry, they are quick to notice when your anger starts interfering with your parenting skills. Our high-need children were the ones who taught us the most about recognizing our anger and controlling it. Once Hayden said to Martha, "Stop looking at me like that," and Martha was forced to recognize that her eyes were expressing a rage she was not being careful to manage. The surest way to get a high-need child to balk is to give in to your anger. "A gentle answer turns away wrath" (Prov. 15:1).

For more information on this subject, we recommend the discipline chapter in our book *Parenting the Fussy Baby and High-Need Child* (see bibliography).

AGE-APPROPRIATE CHORES

Each child has his own timetable, so ages are suggested and approximate. Ages given are on the early side; for boys, who mature more slowly, add up to six months to ages given.*

1½ Years
- Getting diaper for self or new baby
- Putting disposable diaper in trash
- Picking up small items from floor
- Shutting cabinet doors
- Turning on dishwasher

2 Years
- Putting away toys
- Unloading dishwasher—putting away plastic dishes and cups

2½ Years
- "Folding" napkins
- Helping set table
- Putting away silverware
- Peeling carrots
- Pouring measured items into mixing bowl
- Putting away broom and dustpan

3 Years
- Dusting lower shelves
- Emptying small trash cans
- Carrying stacks of clothes to rooms

4 Years
- Feeding baby
- Putting away books
- Further dusting
- Sorting recyclables

5 Years
- Making bed
- Setting table
- General straightening of rooms

6 Years
- Pouring milk for family needs
- Clearing table
- General folding
- Polishing silver, brass

7 Years
- Vacuuming
- Loading dishwasher
- Sweeping floor
- Opening cans
- Cleaning windows

8 Years
- Washing pans
- Cleaning bathrooms
- Beginning cooking skills

9—10 Years
- Changing baby's diapers
- Further cooking skills
- At this age, the child should be able to learn any housekeeping skill, as long as you are willing to teach him.

*From *Small Beginnings* by Barbara Curtis (Nashville, TN: Broadman & Holman Publishers, 1996). Used by permission.

him sort a load of laundry. The child gets his specific instructions, the task is short, he starts with a full basket, and he quickly sees his accomplishment.

Acknowledge and Affirm

Praise can be a valuable shaper—children want to please you and keep your approval. But it can backfire if you're not careful. If you say "good girl" she has to wonder if that means she's a "bad girl" when she doesn't get praised. (No child is bad. Let the phrases "bad boy" and "bad girl" never cross your lips.) Direct your remarks to the job well done: "Nice job," "I like the colors you used," "You are being so quiet!" Don't praise every time your child turns around. It's enough to acknowledge what's done and let your child assume you like it. You can pass on acknowledging things he does for his own reasons. If you expect right behavior, you're more likely to get it.

Affirmation, saying positive things, is easy, but only if you have the knack for it. Many parents don't if they were not affirmed as children. If you were not bonded as a child, the world's criticisms were taken way too seriously. One important thing attachment parenting does for a child is that it lets him experience being seen and heard clearly, so that his sense of self is secure. Try this experiment: keep track in one day of how many positive, affirming things you say to your child, and how many negative, critical things. Then you'll have a clear idea of the direction in which you are headed.

Let's Cooperate

Some children will balk at any suggestion, direction, or decision you make. We won't belabor why this might be—the question is how do you encourage right behavior with this child. The concept of cooperation needs to be introduced to this youngster, and it goes like this: When you cooperate with me (I asked you to get dressed . . . or, pick up your toys . . .), I'll cooperate with you (we'll go to the park . . . or, you can watch a video . . .). You always have something your child wants. Does she want to have a "yes day," or a "no day"? Life's a whole lot more fun when everyone says yes.

DISCOURAGING WRONG BEHAVIOR

The other half of the equation in discipline is dealing with wrong actions, words, and attitudes. Children and adults miss the mark on a daily, even hourly, basis. When encouraging right behavior doesn't work, here are some ways to discourage wrong behavior.

Setting Limits, Part Two

Limits, by their nature, have to be continuously updated, since most limits change as the child grows. Your three- to six-year-old will go through many limits, outgrowing them nearly as fast as you can set them. Be wise about setting limits; don't have too many rules. As the spectrum of rules gets wider the older your child gets, be careful to discern the "biggies," as we call them, from the "smallies." Don't sweat the small stuff. Your big limits will mean more and you'll have the energy to enforce them. Leave room for messing up, and be willing to let your child learn from his mistakes. If you have a rule for every possible situation, he won't learn to make choices.

The biggies can be defined as behaviors that result in injury to your child, others, or property. Smallies are nuisances or annoyances that you can live with. (If you can't, it's a biggie. One more measure of a behavior is, does it disturb your peace?) Then program yourself to deal graciously with the smallies. For example, your child spills something: you take a deep breath, walk away, assess the damage, and ask yourself, "How important is this?" Think about what you'd want your mother to say. Probably something like, "Oops, you made a mess. Here's a towel, let's clean it up," or "I really don't like what you did. What can we learn from this?" This may not be the way you were talked with when you were little, so you may have to do some rehearsing.

Consequences of Wrong Choices

After God set the limits in the Garden of Eden, He stated the consequence of a wrong choice—they were free to eat from any tree, but not from the one tree, "for when you eat of it you will surely die" (Gen. 2:17). This was God's method for discouraging wrong behavior, and it's just as perfect today as it was then. One caveat, of course, is that you must stick to the consequences, as God did. Notice also that God said, "When," not "if"—He knew they'd sin;, and you know this about your child, so be prepared with consequences. Experiencing the consequences of their wrong choices is the only way children can learn self-discipline. They learn to think, and when that happens, you've done your job. Be sure the responsibility for the choice remains with your child.

There are two kinds of consequences, natural (you defy gravity, you fall) and logical (you ride your tricycle out of the driveway, it gets put up for a week). Parents decide on the rules (remember, stick to the biggies) and set up the logical consequences to correct the breaking of these rules, with input from the children as they show interest and an appropriate attitude.

Every wrong behavior can be corrected this way. It sounds so simple! The part that makes it hard is having the wisdom and discernment to impose the best consequences. If the consequences are too severe or unjust, the child's spirit will be broken (or he'll eventually rebel). Punitive parenting produces fear and anger in children. Permissive parenting, having consequences that are token gestures with no teaching power, produces insecurity and unruly behavior. Your biggest job in the correction department is choosing your child's consequences in order to provide appropriate guidance to your child. The box on page 368 entitled "Corrective vs Punitive Consequences" will help you choose wisely.

Time Out

One of the most commonly used consequences, time out is probably the most misapplied correction value. When it is done in a punitive way, it loses its correction value. It is seen as a penalty one pays (like benching in hockey) for misconduct without much incentive for long-term changes in behavior. It can cause a child to be angry and set you both up to struggle for power. Properly used, time out should do two things: stop wrong behavior and give the child time and incentive to reflect. An angry child won't do much thinking. To discern whether your time outs are corrective or punitive, listen to how you say the word to your child when you call the time out. Is it angry and threatening, or is it helpful and hopeful? Is its purpose to banish your child, or to benefit your child?

Time out also helps parents. It gives you a tool to stop a misbehavior, and it gives you time to regroup, think, and pray. It prevents parents from impulsively punishing, either physically or verbally. It can be a peacemaking tool, a chance to recapture what little peace you had left and ask God to multiply it, and a chance to make peace with your child, and he with you, when you take time out together.

One of Martha's favorite ways to let our children know they are being annoying is to announce, "That is disturbing my peace." They know that if the disturbing behavior doesn't stop quickly, she will remove herself to a place that is peaceful. Even if you are home alone with a three-year-old, you can safely go into the sanctuary of your own room. This "time out" is a good way to let your child know that to have you available to her, she must not be annoying.

The Right Way to Punish

Consequences, whether natural or logical, fit into the category of punishment. The use of consequences, whether it be a withdrawal of privileges or a simple time out, needs to be loving and kind, wisely handled. Giving a punishment does not have to be punitive in spirit. Adam and Eve were punished, banished from the Garden, but God did it kindly. He gave them animal skins to cover themselves, and directions on how to fend for themselves. He may have been angry (probably was, in fact) but He didn't use His anger to hurt them. He made sure they knew that this consequence was upon them because of what they had done. They couldn't go away pouting and resentful, saying it was all His fault, because He didn't give them a mixed message. The guidelines we have developed for spanking should be applied to all punishments. Read "Develop a Spanking Wisdom," in chapter 15, and consider certain of these sections in regard to any punishment. For example, "Examine your motive for punishing," "Punish soon after the offense," "Help the child accept the punishment," "Explain to your child why you are punishing," "Encourage a confession," and even "Follow up after punishing." This sounds like a lot to have to think of, but it can all be done quite quickly and smoothly once you have thought it through. If these guidelines are applied to any situation involving correction or punishment, you will avoid all potential for abusive behavior, including verbal and emotional abuse (yelling, put-downs, name calling, and so on).

Tantrums and Whining Revisited

We looked at these behaviors at the earlier stage and now we want to update you. Yes, older children do still whine and tantrum, usually until around six, but the approach changes somewhat. For one thing, a child this age has enough language to use it to express feelings accurately. Encourage your child to use his words and teach him how by verbalizing for him what you know he wants to say. Empathetic statements like, "That makes you really angry," help your child put words to his feelings. Give your child alternate forms of physical expression. Instead of throwing himself on the floor and kicking and screaming two-year-old style, he can throw himself on his bed and pound his pillow. Maybe he's seen you do this. Or let him see how when you need to blow off steam you take an "angry walk." Tell him he can sit on his bed and grab a stuffed animal and "squeeze it to death." When in public you can say sternly to your child, "You may not embarrass me," as one friend told us. At home, she becomes so bored by the tantrum that it soon stops. And, of course, never let a child who is having a tantrum get what he wants. Ever.

Whining in a preschooler can be even more exasperating than in a toddler. You think by now she should know how to speak in a regular tone of voice, especially if she knows you are not going to listen. There will be days when you wonder if you'll ever hear a normal, tension-free word from her lips again. Tension has a way of inviting tension. Check yourself on those days and you'll see what we mean. This is another chance to use your empathetic listening skills. Listen for the underlying problem, even if you aren't "listening to the whining." An example from our home again: five-year-old Lauren saw we passed her favorite yogurt shop and went straight to whining speed. So, of course, I

(Martha) couldn't stop. She knows we don't do whining. But I made active listening sounds, "Oh?" and "Hmmm," and suddenly I was hearing the whole story about how her sister Erin had gotten a treat there the other day and wouldn't share it with her. "Oh," I said, "that was not very nice, was it!" End of scene.

The chance to air this ungenerous treatment she had experienced from her sister was what Lauren needed. My empathetic response, simple and straightforward rather than emotional, helped her settle her feelings. "No, it wasn't very nice," she concluded, and then she started chatting away about something else.

Sometimes it's how you say "no" to a child's request that sets off whining and tantrums. Try using phrases that are less negative when the situation allows. Keep the tone of your voice kind and try to think how you would want to be spoken to. If you stick to the facts, keeping your emotions out of it so that your voice does not betray you even if you are feeling exasperated or irritated, you will not be inviting an emotional reaction to your "no."

GRACE AND MERCY

It is very hard for any of us to admit we are wrong, even to ourselves. When confronted with wrong we have done, we have all kinds of excuses, or we look to blame someone else. This started in the Garden when God confronted Adam and Eve. And remember, they were hiding. We also don't like that naked feeling of being wrong. God simply called to Adam, "Where are you?" His presence was convicting, but it was not condemning.

Your child needs help admitting wrongdoing. You can help this process by taking care not to have a condemning attitude when you find wrongdoing. You should expect the best from your children, and be sure they know what you expect. Yet, you should not be crushed, dismayed, or even surprised when they do not measure up. Handle these times with equanimity—remaining calm, even-tempered, composed—and your child will have much less trouble understanding and admitting that he is wrong.

If you were raised by a perfectionist, this will not come naturally. You will need a lot of grace and mercy for yourself, even before you can offer it to your child. If you are too hard on your children, you are probably also being too hard on yourself. God knows we will sin as long as we have breath in our bodies. The apostle Paul said he struggled with doing what he should not do and not doing what he should do (see Rom. 7:15). Brother Lawrence, a seventeenth-century monk, said it this way, "When I fail in my duty, I readily acknowledge it, saying *I am used to doing so; I shall never do otherwise if I am left to myself.* If I fail not, then I give God thanks, acknowledging that the strength comes from Him." * Whether your child's misbehavior is actual wrongdoing or whether the offense is accidental, you must be able not only to forgive, but to give your child the message that you (and therefore God) will be there to help him do better next time.

A FINAL WORD ON DISCIPLINE

Parenting, and disciplining in particular, is not easy, as you can see from these last three chapters. You need all your wits about you and all the energy you can muster. Let us share a final discipline tip that we've had to learn the hard way:

Get the rest you need and the nutrition you need for your body and your mind to function well. Get the emotional and spiritual rest and feeding you need. You want to be able to step out onto your mission field each day ready for the day's work. God bless you!

*From *The Practice of the Presence of God,* edited by Gilbert P. Symons,(Cincinnati, OH: Forward Movement Publication), p. 11.

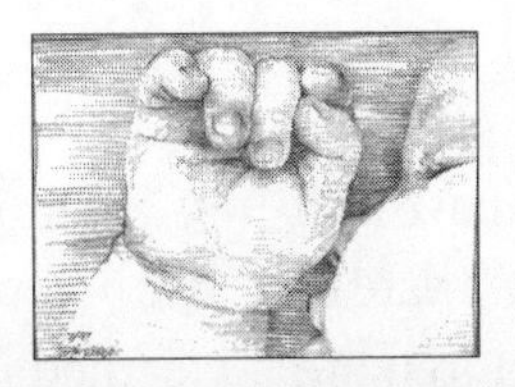

FINAL THOUGHTS

Anchoring Your Child **for the Future**

In the first six years of parenting, we can claim the proverb with a promise: "Train up a child in the way he should go, and when he is old, he will not depart." Between five and six years of age, most children begin to depart from the home. Most children by six or seven will actually spend the majority of their waking hours away from home—in school, even on overnights, or on group trips, such as scouting or church activities. They are exposed to outside values. How firmly they are grounded in the values at home influences whether or not they will "depart."

One of our favorite worship hymns is "The Anchor Holds," which talks about a ship that holds fast in a storm. Christ is the anchor in this hymn, yet the same principles apply to parenting. In the first six years, the family is the anchor. In this relatively short window of a child's life, children unquestionably accept the values of their parents. They learn what's important in life. They learn spiritual and social attitudes. In essence, children in the first six years learn what is the family norm. They become grounded in spiritual values, so their anchor is more likely to hold when they depart into the school-age years and are exposed to many "alternative lifestyles" or different norms.

This book was written on the job. Over our twenty-five years in pediatric practice and our thirty-one years in parenting our own eight children, we have become keen observers of what parenting styles work for most families most of the time. We have also become both joyfully and painfully aware of the relationship between how children are parented in those early, formative years and how they later turn out. While parents should not take all the credit or the blame for the person their child later becomes, the style of parenting your child receives in the preschool years has a great influence on the child's style of living for the rest of his or her life.

Throughout this book, we have shared with you many parenting tips that we have learned in our family and professional lives. Consider these basic tools from which you will fashion your own style of parenting based upon biblical principles, the individual temperament of your child, and your individual family situation. As you develop as a parent, don't forget to enjoy the time you and your child share together, for this child is a wonderful gift from God to your life!

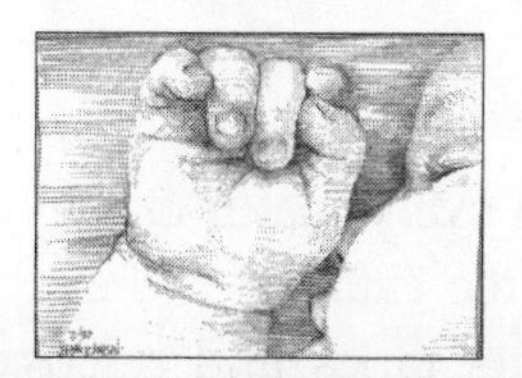

BIBLIOGRAPHY

Suggested Resources **for Parenting**

The following books and resources are arranged according to their major subjects, although many of them cover a wide range of topics on parenting.

Please bear in mind that when recommending a book, we are not necessarily endorsing every statement made in it. We have chosen to recommend those books which, in our opinion, contain important messages that will contribute to your growth as Christian parents or that develop certain topics which are beyond the scope of this book. Not all of the books on the following list are specifically Christian, but they are not non-Christian either.

GENERAL RESOURCES

Organizations

La Leche League International, P. O. Box 4079, Schaumburg, IL 60168-4079, 800-LA LECHE or 847-519-7730.

This organization not only teaches better mothering through breastfeeding but teaches better mothering in all aspects of parenting and child care. There is a local La Leche League in every major city in the United States and throughout the world. Write for a free catalog of their breastfeeding publications, which contains books, pamphlets, tapes, and videos on all aspects of parenting, as well as breast pumps and other breastfeeding products and accessories. Many of the books we have recommended in this bibliography are available in their catalog.

The Nurturing Parent, 303 E. Gurley Street, Suite 260, Prescott, AZ 86301, (800) 810-8401. For e-mail: letters@TheNurturingParent.com or www.TheNurturingParent.com.

The Nurturing Parent is a journal published to "encourage healthy parent-child relationships through attachment parenting practices." Not only are the articles wonderfully supportive to parents, *The Nurturing Parent* also helps families network by having a list of parents available who are interested in meeting one another to support and encourage.

Videos

Breastfeeding Your Baby: A Mother's Guide, produced by Medela, Inc. (the breast pump company) in cooperation with La Leche League.

A one-hour video with William Sears, M. D., Jay Gordon, M. D., celebrities, and breastfeeding experts who instruct and encourage; families speak on breastfeeding benefits. Available through La Leche League.

The Baby Video, Getting to Know Your Baby Through Attachment Parenting, with William Sears, M. D. and Martha Sears, R. N., produced in cooperation with Chariot Family Publishing and Crossroads Producers Group.

Some of the areas covered in this video are birth bonding, breastfeeding, babywearing, responding sensitively to baby's cries, and sleeping with your baby.

BREASTFEEDING

The Womanly Art of Breastfeeding, Judy Torgus, editor: La Leche League International.

La Leche League International's *The Womanly Art of Breastfeeding* includes an expanded section on the history of the world's foremost breastfeeding organization. It reports the latest findings from the most recent breastfeeding research and explains the substantial benefits of human milk for babies. *The Womanly Art* covers breastfeeding information for mothers with a warm, supportive, practical approach. This classic book explains the heart and soul of what La Leche League and is a valuable resource for any mother who wants to give her baby the very best.

Breastfeeding Pure & Simple by Gwen Gotsch: La Leche League International.
Provides new mothers with a basic introduction that will guide them through the early months of their nursing relationship. Clear, straightforward text combined with lots of photos makes this book inviting and easy-to-read.

The Nursing Mother's Companion by Kathleen Huggins: Harvard Common Press.
This comprehensive manual tells how to prevent and solve breastfeeding problems of all sorts. It explains how to position a baby correctly for nursing, how to tell if a baby is getting enough milk, how to increase the milk supply, how to prevent and heal sore nipples, how to choose a breast pump, and how to combine working and nursing. Also covered, special circumstances often thought to preclude nursing—such as prematurity, cleft lip or palate in the baby, diabetes in the mother, and adoption—and common drugs and their safety during breastfeeding.

Nursing Mother, Working Mother: The Essential Guide for Breastfeeding and Staying Close to Your Baby After You Return to Work by Gale Pryor: Harvard Common Press.
Pryor covers everything a working mother needs to know about the basics of breastfeeding, choosing and using a breastpump, ways to store and transport milk safely, how to get support from coworkers and childcare helpers, how to go on a business trip without having to wean, and much more.

The Nursing Mother's Guide to Weaning by Kathleen Huggins and Linda Ziedrich: Harvard Common Press.
By suggesting alternative ways of resolving breastfeeding problems, Huggins and Ziedrich help women avoid weaning prematurely. They describe the safest, least stressful ways to wean at every age, from early infancy through toddlerhood and beyond. They answer questions like these: Must I wean before I return to work? Can I breastfeed part-time? Should I wean to a bottle or a cup?

Do children ever really wean themselves? Does abrupt weaning endanger a child's health or psyche? Will weaning help my child sleep through the night?

Mothering Your Nursing Toddler by Norma Jane Bumgarner: La Leche League International.

Warmth, wisdom, and wit illumine this lively discussion of breastfeeding past the age of one. Besides exploring the "why" of nursing a toddler, the book helps mothers cope with the challenges: getting enough rest, dealing with criticism from family and friends, weaning, and more.

Breastfeeding and Natural Child Spacing by Sheila Kippley: The Couple to Couple League International, P. O. Box 111184, Cincinnati, OH 45211, (513) 471-2000.

This book explores an aspect of breastfeeding which is often misunderstood and underrated—its contraceptive effect. With factual information based on scientific research and personal experience, the author explains the difference between "ecological" and "cultural" breastfeeding and how each method affects fertility.

DISCIPLINE

The Discipline Book: Everything You Need to Know to Have a Better Behaved Child by William, M. D. and Martha Sears, R. N.: Little, Brown, & Company.

Explores a wide variety of parenting options and helps parents decide which type of parenting philosophy will work best for their family. Emphasizes the importance of attachment parenting.

Nurturing Children in the Lord by Jack Fennema: Presbyterian and Reformed Publishing Company.

A study guide on developing a biblical approach to discipline, this is an excellent book for Christian parents who wish to base their discipline on scriptural principles.

Help! I'm a Parent by S. Bruce Narramore: Zondervan Publishing House.

A practical, biblical guide for handling daily discipline problems, such as lying, sibling fights, messy rooms, homework hassles, and power struggles. Offers excellent insight on the difference between punishment and discipline and shows that it is the foundation of everything a parent does in dealing with a child's behavior.

Kids Are Worth It! Giving Your Child the Gift of Inner Discipline by Barbara Coloroso: Avon Books.

With courage, compassion, and commonsense, the author provides a philosophy of loving guidance that is respectful, yet effective. As a result, children are free to accept the gift of inner discipline every parent hopes to instill.

Siblings Without Rivalry by Adele Faber and Elaine Mazlish: Avon Books.

Dialogue and cartoons help parents teach children to express their feelings without doing damage and teaches parents to reduce rage between battling siblings.

How to Talk So Kids Will Listen and Listen So Kids Will Talk by Adele Faber and Elaine Mazlish: Avon Books.

Communication skills for parents: how to listen and deal with feelings; and alternatives to nagging and punishment.

FAMILY PLANNING

The Art of Natural Family Planning by John and Sheila Kippley: The Couple to Couple League International, P. O. Box 111184, Cincinnati, OH 45211, (513) 471-2000.

To be used either on your own or as part of an instructional program, the book teaches the sympto-thermal method of fertility control. Part one explains the "why" of NFP; Part two the "how to." Our favorite chapter is entitled "Marriage Building with NFP."

Breastfeeding and Natural Child Spacing by Sheila Kippley: The Couple to Couple League International, P. O. Box 111184, Cincinnati, OH 45211, (513) 471-2000.

This book discusses the concept of natural mothering and how it can postpone the return of fertility.

Your Fertility Signals: Using Them to Achieve or Avoid Pregnancy Naturally by Merryl Winstein: Smooth Stone Press.

A concise presentation of the sympto-thermal method of natural family planning—richly illustrated, and easy to understand.

The Fertility Awareness Workbook by Barbara Kass-Annese, R. N., N. P. and Hal Danzer, M. D.: Putnam.

A concise, how-to book on natural family planning. Contains good illustrations and diagrams.

MARRIAGE

How to Become One with Your Mate by Lawrence Crabb Jr.: Zondervan Publishing House.

This is a small, very readable excerpt from *The Marriage Builder*, by Lawrence Crabb, on oneness of body and spirit in the marriage relationship. Looking to Christ to fulfill our needs enables us to minister to our mates.

Men and Women: Enjoying the Differences by Lawrence Crabb, Jr.: Zondervan Publishing House.

Explores the concept of becoming other-centered rather than staying in the patterns of self-centeredness.

His Needs, Her Needs: Building an Affair-Proof Marriage by Willard Harley: Fleming H. Revell.

Identifies the ten most important marital needs of husbands and wives and teaches how those needs can be fulfilled.

Love Life for Every Married Couple by Ed Wheat, M.D, and Gloria Okes Perkins: Zondervan Publishing House.

How to fall in love, stay in live, and rekindle your love.

Under the Apple Tree: Marrying, Birthing, Parenting by Helen Wessel: Bookmates International, Inc., Apple Tree Family Ministries, P. O. Box 2083, Artesia, CA 90702-2083, (562) 925-0149.

In this companion work to *The Joy of Natural Childbirth,* Mrs. Wessel explores the biblical perspective on basic concerns young couples face. Here is a wealth of information in one volume about such issues as personhood, sexuality, marriage, family planning, natural childbirth, breastfeeding and weaning, child nurturing, and Christian family lifestyles.

Becoming Soulmates by Drs. Les and Leslie Parrott: Zondervan Publishing House.

A book not just to read but to use to help restore the soul of your marriage.

Love's Unseen Enemy – Overcoming Guilt to Build Healthy Relationships by Drs. Les and Leslie Parrott: Zondervan Publishing House.

Understanding the power of guilt and the power of forgiveness frees couples to move into a deeper relationship.

PARENTING AND CHILD CARE

The Baby Book: Everything You Need to Know About Your Baby From Birth to Age Two by William Sears, M. D. and Martha Sears, R. N.: Little, Brown, & Company.

From bonding and breastfeeding, to temper tantrums, this book emphasizes a baby's basic needs and helps new parents to meet those needs through the loving, nurturing attachment style of parenting. This book might become the "parenting bible of the 90s"; no new parent should be without it.

25 Things Every New Mother Should Know by Martha Sears, R. N., with William Sears, M. D: Harvard Common Press.

A heartwarming book that talks about the process of becoming a mother. Helps a brand-new mother understand her new role by encouraging her to respond intuitively to her baby. From giving birth to breastfeeding to meeting baby's needs, this small, easy-to-read book covers all aspects of new motherhood and reinforces a mother's confidence by assuring her that "You are the expert on your baby."

Growing Together: A Parents' Guide to Baby's First Year by William Sears, M. D.: La Leche League International.

From birth to one year, this book charts the development of a tiny newborn into a curious toddler. Over 150 black and white photos and 16 pages of color photos illustrate the growth of motor, language, social, and cognitive skills. This book teaches parents to enhance their baby's development through their responsiveness.

Small Beginnings: Releasing Your Toddler's God-given Abilities by Barbara Curtis: Broadman & Holman Publishers.

This book explains the keys to a child's learning process, and suggests ways to encourage children to establish good learning habits, concentrate, work independently, and help others.

How to Really Love Your Child by D. Ross Campbell: Victor Books.

This book, written by a Christian psychiatrist, discusses the importance of touching, eye-to-eye contact, and focused attention. It offers practical tips on how to convey your love to your child.

Hide or Seek by James Dobson: Fleming H. Revell.

This book deals with the extremely important issue of how to build self-esteem in your child.

Becoming a Father: How to Nurture and Enjoy Your Family by William Sears, M. D.: La Leche League International.

Addressing the joys and problems of parenthood from the male perspective, Dr. Sears writes from experience about the ways in which a child can help strengthen a marriage and bring about increased love and maturity.

The Fussy Baby by William Sears, M. D.: New American Library.

Fussy or "high-need" babies need extra attention from parents. Dr. Sears explores "back to the womb" techniques to help parents of these children cope. Tips on feeding, fathering, reassurance, and avoiding burnout are included in the book.

Nighttime Parenting by William Sears, M. D.: New American Library.

A great book for expectant or new parents, or parents whose child has a problem sleeping. This book explains the differences in babies' sleeping patterns compared to those of adults. It also introduces a style of nighttime parenting to help put an end to sleep problems.

Parenting the Fussy Baby and High-Need Child by William Sears, M. D. and Martha Sears, R. N.: Little, Brown, & Company.

Discusses the difficulties faced by parents of challenging children and shows how responsive parenting can turn these challenges into advantages for both the parents and the child.

Raising Your Child Not by Force But by Love by Sydney Craig: Westminster Press.

This classic book, written from a biblical perspective, helps parents gain an understanding of discipline as a positive concept. It has great insight into the feelings of children and the effect of discipline (good and bad) upon them. It also gives insight into why parents get angry with their children and provides alternative ways of expressing and managing that anger.

You Can Raise a Well-Mannered Child by June Hines Moore: Broadman & Holman Publishers.

Written by a natiuonally recognized manners expert, this book offers parents contemorary rules of correct behavior, plus detailed instructions on how to teach them effectively, to improve their children's self-confidence.

PREGNANCY AND CHILDBIRTH

The Pregnancy Book: A Month-by-Month Guide by William Sears, M. D. and Martha Sears, R. N., with Linda Hughey Holt, M. D., FACOG: Little, Brown, & Company.

For each stage of pregnancy, the authors deal with the questions and decisions that arise and discuss important issues to keep in mind, such as: creating a healthy womb environment; choosing healthcare providers and childbirth classes; understanding tests and technology; eating right for two; watching baby grow; and understanding physical and emotional changes. Helpful tips on everything from overcoming morning sickness to exercising and keeping fit to traveling while pregnant.

The Birth Book: Everything You Need to Know to Have a Safe and Satisfying Birth by William and Martha Sears: Little, Brown, & Company.

This is a definitive guide to birthing, giving parents-to-be the kind of information they need to plan a happy and safe birth experience. Topics include: physical and emotional preparation; lessening the discomfort of and speeding up the labor process; the father's role; how to select the kind of birthing environment you want; and much more.

Childbirth Without Fear by Grantly Dick-Read (Fifth Edition), edited by Helen Wessel: Harper and Row.

This is the classic book on natural childbirth which demonstrates how laboring women can overcome the fear-tension-pain cycle.

The Joy of Natural Childbirth: Fifth Edition of Natural Childbirth and the Christian Family by Helen Wessel: Bookmates International, Inc., Apple Tree Family Ministries, P. O. Box 2083, Artesia, CA 90702-2083, (562) 925-0149.

A must for all Christian parents, this is a revised and updated edition of the classic book on God's design for birth. Mrs. Wessel, a mother of six, thoroughly explores the scriptures related to childbearing in a very readable style, and adds a Christian perspective to the childbirth-without-fear techniques described by Dr. Grantly Dick-Read.

Under the Apple Tree: Marrying, Birthing, Parenting by Helen Wessel: Bookmates International, Inc., Apple Tree Family Ministries, P .O. Box 2083, Artesia, CA 90702-2083, (562) 925-0149.

In this companion work to *The Joy of Natural Childbirth,* Mrs. Wessel explores the biblical perspective on basic concerns young couples face. Here is a wealth of information in one volume about such issues as personhood, sexuality, marriage, family planning, natural childbirth, breastfeeding and weaning, child nurturing, and Christian family lifestyles.

SEXUALITY

For Adults

The Christian Woman's Guide to Sexuality by Debra Evans: Crossway Books.

A biblical perspective on being a woman; finding the inner beauty of femininity; handling the stress of daily living; fertility and childbearing; sexuality in a healthy marriage; and living with a cyclical nature.

The Gift of Sex: A Christian Guide to Sexual Fulfillment by Clifford and Joyce Penner: Word Publishing.

A comprehensive and upbeat guide to sex for Christians. The Penner's approach their subject tastefully and frankly, from a biblical perspective.

Sex Facts for the Family by Cliff and Joyce Penner: Word Publishing.

Sound, up-to-date information on sexuality issues for newlyweds and long-marrieds, parents and children, singles and seniors. The section on teaching children about sex is especially helpful.

For Children:

How Babies Are Made by Andrew Andry and Stephen Schepp: Little, Brown & Company.

This is a perfect starter book for teaching the reproductive process to children. Illustrated with paper sculpture, figures are realistic yet simple. Begins with plants and animals, and tastefully illustrates humans. For ages 3-10. Ends with the mother breastfeeding her baby.

The Wonderful Way That Babies Are Made by Larry Christenson: Bethany House Publishers.

The miracle of human reproduction from a Christian perspective – a book especially written to "grow" with your child. It has two sets of text, one to be read to a younger child (3-8), and one which is completely explicit and, according to the author, appropriate for the child from 9-14.

YOUR CHILD'S DEVOTIONAL LIFE

The Family Devotions Idea Book by Evelyn Blitchington: Bethany House Publishers.

This book is full of practical ideas on how to conduct meaningful family devotions.

Family Night Tool Chest: An Introduction to Family Nights (Book one) by Jim Weidmann and Kurt Bruner: Focus on the Family Publishers.

The authors suggest fun-filled ways to pass on important Christian values to your children using ordinary objects you have around the house.

Building Your Child's Faith by Alice Chapin: Thomas Nelson.

Simple, fun ideas for teaching children how to pray, worship, and discover the Bible.

Teaching Your Child About God by Wes Haystead: Regal Books.

This is an easy-to-read book with practical advice on the spiritual training of the child at various stages.

It's You and Me, Mom: 25 Cool Devotions for Moms and Kids by Greg Johnson: Broadman & Holman Publishers.

This innovative combination of Bible drill, workbook and Q&A games is a great way for moms to teach their children about the Bible. For moms with children in grades three through six.

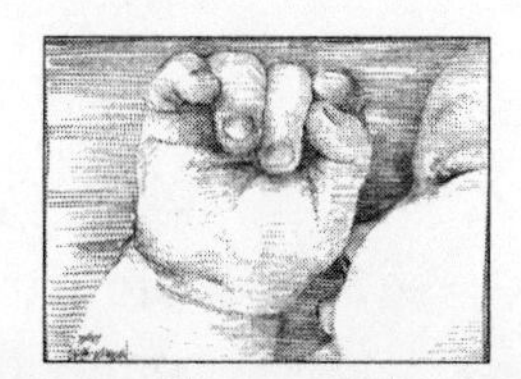

Index

U

V

W

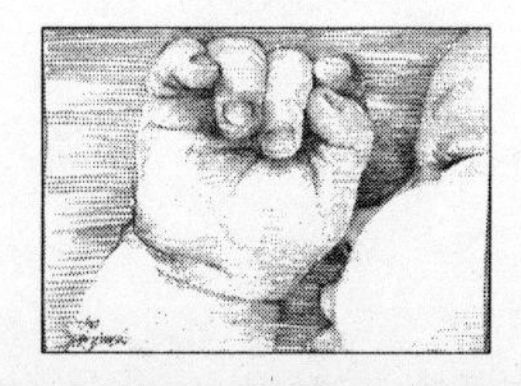

About the **Authors**

William Sears, M.D., one of America's most renowned pedicatricians, trained at Harvard Medical School's Children's Hospital and the University of Toronto's Hospital for Sick Children, the largest children's hospital in the world, where he was Associate Professor of Pediatrics. A pediatrician for twenty-five years, he currently practices pediatrics in San Clemente, California. He is the father of eight children, the author of twenty-two books, a frequent writer for *Parenting* and *Babytalk* magazines, and a frequent guest on national television shows such as: "The Today Show," "Good Morning America," "Dateline," "20/20," "The Oprah Winfrey Show," "Donahue," and "The 700 Club."

Martha Sears, R.N., mother of eight children, is co-author of many of the Sears's books, and a former childbirth educator. She is currently a lactation and parenting consultant and a frequent speaker on parenting issues.

The Sears live in Capistrano Beach, California.